CONTRIBUTIONS TO GENERATIVE PHONOLOGY

*This book is published with the assistance of the
Dan Danciger Publication Fund.*

Contributions to
GENERATIVE PHONOLOGY

edited by MICHAEL K. BRAME

UNIVERSITY OF TEXAS PRESS AUSTIN AND LONDON

Library of Congress Cataloging in Publication Data

Brame, Michael K   1944—
    Contributions to generative phonology.

    Includes bibliographies.
    1. Grammar, Comparative and general-Phonology.
2. Generative grammar. I. Title.
P217.B68   414   73-38921
ISBN 0-292-71001-1

Composition by Beljan, Ann Arbor, Mich.
Printing and binding by Edwards Brothers, Inc., Ann Arbor, Mich.

TO MORRIS HALLE

whose inspiration awakened our interest in phonology

CONTENTS

PREFACE

The papers that comprise this volume entertain questions pertaining to phonology. Practitioners of generative phonology are interested in studying the rules that relate the more abstract systematic phonemes of a language to their superficial realizations. Their goal is to discover the formal mechanisms needed to articulate the phonological component of all natural languages: What properties do phonological rules exhibit, what relationships do the rules bear to one another, what conditions or constraints are to be imposed on the phonology, and so forth. In short, the phonologist seeks to determine how the phonological component is structured. It is in this spirit that the present volume was conceived. Thus, the majority of papers included in this book provide a substantial body of data on the basis of which the theoretical issues are formulated.

It is hoped that these papers will not only be a stimulus to other investigators in the field, but will also serve as a text for students interested in learning about and pursuing phonological issues. In recent years, we have witnessed the appearance of several readers in syntax and semantics. Unfortunately, no adequate collections of readings in phonology have kept this pace. This volume should aid to some extent in remedying this situation. The papers have purposely been solicited in hitherto unpublished form so as to ensure their being current and on the frontiers of research.

I wish to thank Harper and Row for granting permission to publish some extended quotes from *The Sound Pattern of English* that appear in several of the contributions and Luise Brame for valuable criticism.

University of Texas   M.K.B.

INTRODUCTION

Although the study of the principles that underlie phonological processes is still in its infancy, a substantial body of knowledge has already accumulated, and, on the basis of this knowledge, a theory of phonology has emerged. The broad outlines of this theory, which has been termed *generative phonology*, appear to be reasonably well established. That many questions remain unanswered and many issues very much open can best be illustrated by taking a concrete example. In the phonology of English there is a rule that drops the segment *g*, when preceded by ŋ and followed by a word boundary. This rule may be informally stated as (i).

(i) $g \rightarrow \emptyset / \eta$___#

This rule accounts for the absence of phonetic *g* in *long* [lɔŋ]; *singer* [siŋər], from basic *sing#er*; *ringing* [riŋiŋ], from *ring#ing*; but the rule allows for its presence in such words as *longer* [lɔŋgər], from *long+er*; *finger* [fiŋgər]; and so forth. Another rule of English functions in very much the same capacity as (i). This rule may be formulated as follows:

(ii) $b \rightarrow \emptyset / m$___#

Rule (ii) stipulates that all occurrences of *b* between *m* and word boundary elide. Although convincing examples illustrating the operation of this rule are difficult to find, one can point to such alternations as *bomb* [bam] versus *bombard* and *bombardier*, the latter two examples displaying phonetic *b*, whereas the former case does not. The similarity between (i) and (ii) is obvious. In generative phonology an attempt is made to capture such generalizations by reducing the two statements (i) and (ii) to a single statement. The two rules may be collapsed in terms of distinctive features. The result is rule (iii).

(iii) $\begin{bmatrix} +\text{obstruent} \\ +\text{voiced} \\ -\text{continuant} \\ -\text{affricate} \\ -\text{coronal} \end{bmatrix}$ → $\emptyset$ / [+nasal]___#

This rule provides for the elision of voiced obstruents in the relevant environment. It excludes voiceless obstruents, such as *p* and *k*, as well as voiced obstruents that are [+coronal], that is, *d*, thus, correctly allowing for such words as *hemp*, *bank*, and *send*. In addition, (iii) requires that the relevant obstruent be [-continuant] and [-affricate], thereby inhibiting elision of phonetic *z̆* and *ǰ* from such words as *bums* [bəmz], *cringe* [krinǰ], and so on. (If words ending in *ǰ* in phonetic representations, i.e., *cringe*, *range*, etc., are to be represented with final *e* in underlying representations and if the *e*-elision rule follows (iii), then the feature [-affricate] may be omitted from (iii).)

There are some dialects of English that exhibit yet a further change resembling (i) and (ii). For convenience of reference this process may be recorded as (iv).

(iv) d → $\emptyset$ / n___#

At least one such dialect is spoken in Texas, and in this dialect such words as *send, mend, bend, hand,* and *band* are pronounced [sin], [min], [bin], [hæn], and [bæn]. (Notice that *e* becomes *i* before a nasal in this dialect.) Rule (iv) accounts for the loss of *d* from these and similar examples. But this process can be accounted for by a simple extension of rule (iii) in the direction of greater generality.

(v) $\begin{bmatrix} +\text{obstruent} \\ +\text{voiced} \\ -\text{continuant} \\ -\text{affricate} \end{bmatrix}$ → $\emptyset$ / [+nasal]___#

Rule (v) differs from (iii) in that one of the lower-level features has been omitted. Apparently this omission is a common means by which languages change over a period of time: the synchronic rule is simplified. Two dialects continue to exist, one employing the less general rule (iii), and the other, the generalized rule (v).

But we have proceeded too rapidly. In hastening to account

for the generalization, we have failed to take note of the differences between (i), (ii), and (iv). Whereas (i) has no exceptions, (ii) apparently does. For example, the learned word *iamb* is commonly, though not always, pronounced with a final *b,* and most dictionaries give both pronunciations. However, there is no learned word in the language that requires a word-final *g* to be pronounced when preceded by ŋ. Thus, there is at least one factor that distinguishes (i) from (ii). Rule (iv) differs from (i) and (ii) in another way. Both *b* and *g* drop before *-ing*, compare *bombing* and *singing.* However, *d* does not drop when preceded by *n* and followed by *-ing*. Thus, in the relevant dialect, *sending* is never pronounced [siniŋ], even though a word boundary apparently separates the stem from the *-ing* suffix in underlying representations. The correct form is [sindiŋ]. Actually (iv) is an oversimplification. The correct rule should allow for the elision of word-final *d* only before a pause or when followed by a word beginning with a nonsyllabic segment. In other words, word-final *d* does not elide in the dialect under investigation if a word beginning with a vowel follows. Thus, in this dialect one says [hæn miy ðə map] for *Hand me the mop*, but [ðə hænd əv feyt] for *The hand of fate,* and never *[ðə hæn əv feyt]. The elision of *d*, therefore, appears to be a low-level phenomenon, no doubt related to the fact that, in careful or elevated speech, speakers commonly fail to employ (iv). Rule (iv) is optional and serves to differentiate styles of speech. On the other hand, rules (i) and (ii) are not optional, as one does not say [bamb] for *bomb* or [siŋg] for *sing* in any style of speech. Rules (i), (ii), and (iv), it may be concluded, differ in several important respects. Clearly, there is a conflicting set of observations, and it is the task of the linguist to decide the following: If the three rules are to be collapsed, how are the differences to be expressed? If, on the other hand, the three rules are not to be collapsed, how is the generalization to be captured? The problem is not easy to answer. Only by discovering a number of examples similar to the one outlined above will the correct answers become evident. Progress in phonological theory through the discovery of crucial examples is what continues to make the study of phonological processes exciting. There is ample room for contribution to the field. The investigator need only find and elucidate the crucial examples.

The problem touched on above illustrates one of the advantages of having an explicit theory. Once phonological processes are stated explicitly, the real problems become apparent. Many of these problems have only recently crystallized into what may be summarized as major issues of synchronic phonology. The main topics relating to these issues may be listed synoptically as follows:

1. Ordering and Application of Phonological Rules
2. Evaluation Metric
3. Interaction between Phonology and Syntax
4. Abstractness

The questions relating to these topics are not necessarily distinct. More often than not they impinge on one another, sometimes in subtle ways. In the following paragraphs some of the questions associated with each topic will be mentioned.

Concerning the first topic there are several subtopics deserving more deliberation. Few linguists doubt the correctness of the claim that some rules are ordered in synchronic grammars. However, Anderson has recently questioned the validity of imposing a *linear* order on phonological rules. Whether the linear ordering theory is to be replaced by Anderson's theory of local ordering, or some variant, is an important question for linguistic theory. The phonological cycle is another question related to the topic of rule ordering and rule application. It is still unclear what kinds of rules may be cyclic and whether there are differing forms of the phonological cycle. It is also unclear whether a specific rule is to apply simultaneously to all domains meeting its specifications or in a left-to-right or right-to-left fashion.

Point two brings up the important question of collapsing rules. There are thorny problems associated with collapsing some structurally similar phonological rules, for instance, those discussed above. There are also questions to be answered regarding the correct means of evaluating structurally dissimilar, but functionally similar, phonological rules of the type recently discussed by Kisseberth. Output conditions become increasingly relevant. Markedness is also related to this topic. Some work in extending and revising the initial theory proposed by Chomsky and Halle is desired, and some questions about rule markedness, marked versus unmarked orders, and so forth, come to mind.

Another topic of considerable interest is that of the interaction of phonology and syntax. The first significant advance in this area is due to Bresnan, whose paper is included in this volume.

Finally, the issue of abstractness in phonology has generated no little discussion in recent years, although no adequate conditions restricting the use of abstract features and segments have as yet been formulated.

Other topics of interest could be mentioned. The brief overview presented here should, however, provide an adequate introduction to some of the issues that are discussed in the following articles, which, it is hoped, may shed light on their resolution.

The Faroese Vowel System

STEPHEN R. ANDERSON
Harvard University

1. Introduction

Faroese, the West Scandinavian language spoken in the Faroe Islands, is closely related to Icelandic in remaining similar in many ways to Old Norse. One way in which it differs both from Icelandic and from Old Norse, however, is in its surface vowel system, whose description has produced a good deal of discussion among Scandinavianists. Most of the facts concerning the interrelationships among the elements of the phonological system have been well described in the traditional grammars (Hammershaimb, 1891; Krenn, 1940; Lockwood, 1955), in historical accounts (Haegstad, 1917; Rischel, 1968), and in dialect surveys (Werner, 1964 and 1968) as rules for the pronunciation of the standard orthography or as a sequence of historical events (sound changes) that have resulted in the modern language. These two kinds of description are closely interrelated, since the orthography is a consciously archaic one, designed to preserve as much of a resemblance to the other West Scandinavian dialects and to Old Norse as possible. Other orthographies have been proposed, including ones based much more on the surface forms of words than the standard orthography is, but the populace has shown little

NOTE: This work is essentially a chapter of my doctoral dissertation (Anderson, 1969). I would like to thank Harry Roe, Morris Halle, and Arthur Schwartz (among others) for help of various kinds. I would also like to thank the American Scandinavian Foundation for support that enabled me to visit the Faroes in the summer of 1968. My errors, naturally, are not to be attributed to any of the above or to the Faroese themselves.

interest in change. The aptness of the apparent archaism will become clearer below.

Most modern treatments of Faroese take the position that the orthography is too artificial to be taken seriously and have rejected the notion that it might provide a basis for any insightful observations. Such treatments as Bjerrum's (1949; a glossematic approach) and Roe's (1965; a straightforward taxonomic phonemic description) have simply started from the phonetic facts and extracted some minimal regularities from them without attempting to account for the role that the various elements posited play in phonological alternations. O'Neil (1964; and McCawley, 1968, which is simply a reformulation of part of O'Neil's description) has adopted a more abstract approach, admitting some facts concerning the interrelation of the elements of the vowel system and a nonbiunique relation between the phonemic and the phonetic levels. This treatment too, however, seems to have erred in staying too close to the phonetic facts, thereby missing some interesting generalizations.

2. Inventory of Vowels

Let us first consider the vowels that are represented in the orthography as unaccented, simple vowels. Forms containing these vowels show a consistent alternation between two sets of phonetic values, depending on whether the syllable in which they appear is long or short:[1]

2.1				
	a :	*lamin*	[læ̜amIn]	'lame' (nom. masc. sg.)
		lamnir	[lamnIr]	'lame' (nom. masc. pl.)
	e :	*gera*	[ȷe:ra]	'to do'
		gert	[ȷɛrt]	'(thou) doest'
	ø :	*kjøti*	[čö:ti]	'meat' (dat. sg.)
		kjøts	[čöts]	'meat' (gen. sg.)
	o :	*tora*	[to:ra]	'to dare'
		tordi	[tordi]	'dared'
	i/y :	*ymissur*	[i:mIssUr]	'different' (nom. masc. sg.)
		ymsir	[ImsIr]	'different' (nom. masc. pl.)
	u :	*rugur*	[ru:wUr]	'rye' (nom. sg.)
		rugbreyð	[rUbbrej]	'ryebread'

---

[1] A long syllable is one that is stressed and either open (i.e., followed by only one consonant plus a vowel) or followed by one of the clusters *pl, pr, kl, kr,* or *tr* (n.b. not *tl*). All other syllables are short.

Assuming that these vowels have the feature values given in table 2.2, we can then account for the alternations shown in 2.1 with a rule that specifies vowels as lax in short syllables, and tense elsewhere. The phonetic reflexes of tenseness will then include length, in the case of the nonlow vowels; in the case of low *a*, tenseness will be realized as diphthongization to [æa̯]. In at least some dialects, tense *e* and *o* are raised to *i* and *u* before *a* by still another rule. A further dialectal phenomenon is the change of lax *a* to [ɛ] before a velar nasal.

2.2	vowel	back	high	low	round
	a	+	-	+	-
	e	-	-	-	-
	ø	-	-	-	+
	o	+	-	-	+
	i/y	-	+	-	-
	u	+	+	-	+

Turning now to the vowels represented in the orthography with an acute accent, we see that they are phonetically diphthongs that have the following values in long syllables:

2.3   í/ý : [uj]
      ú : [üw]
      ó : [ɛw], [öw], or [ɔw], depending on dialect
      á : [oa̯]

The phonetic value of tense *a* ([æa̯]) has been diphthongized from its underlying value of [a] by the insertion of a segment [æ] *before* the vowel. Let us assume that the diphthongs in table 2.3 are also created by a rule of "regressive diphthongization" from underlying representations as the corresponding simple vowels with some diacritic feature, such as [±long], to differentiate them from the short vowels. If we assume that this rule of regressive diphthongization applies to the marked /í, ú, ó, á/, it might look like 2.4:

2.4[2]

$$\emptyset \rightarrow \begin{bmatrix} +\text{syll} \\ -\text{low} \\ \alpha\text{high} \\ -\beta\text{back} \\ -\beta\text{round} \end{bmatrix} \Big/ \underline{\quad} \begin{bmatrix} +\text{syll} \\ +\text{long} \\ \alpha\text{high} \\ \beta\text{round} \end{bmatrix}$$

[2]Though this rule may seem simply a fudge, its later role will be seen to have an explanatory function. Such a rule is not unheard of, of course; some dialects of English spoken in the southern and southwestern United

This rule will create the diphthongs /ui, iu, ɛo, oa/. Let us now assume that a rounding adjustment rule applies, which rounds a high vowel before a following rounded vowel; such a rule would be restricted to the position before a *high* rounded vowel in those dialects that have the value[ɛw] for ó, rather than [öw] or [ow]. All diphthongs in Faroese are falling (as will be seen later, the segments in question do not represent the only diphthongs in the language), and it is reasonable to assume a process that converts the second element of a vowel sequence into a glide. The effect of these processes will be to convert underlying [+long] /ú, í, ó, á/ into [üw, uj, ɛw or öw, oa̭].

Up to this point, we have been assuming that only the vowels marked with accents in the orthography are affected by 2.4, that is, that the long vowel system is represented by the following:

2.5   /í/   /ú/
                   /ó/
         /á/

This system lacks a tense mid-front vowel /é/. Historically, this absence came about in the following manner: the vowels of 2.5 are etymologically long vowels; long *é* merged with low front *ǣ* (the umlaut product of long *á*), which was then shortened to *æ*, merging then with the back vowel *a*. The result was the loss of long *é* as a distinct vowel. Observe, however, the effect of positing an underlying /é/; rule 2.4 would convert this /é/ to /oe/, which would then become [oj]. Such a phonetic diphthong does exist in Faroese, corresponding to orthographic *oy*. This diphthong could be eliminated from the underlying representation and replaced with the more natural segment /é/, which would complete the long vowel system.

Evidence for or against this solution is extremely difficult to find. There are virtually no alternations in Faroese between underlying long vowels and the corresponding short vowels; it is, therefore, not at all an argument against this proposal that *oy* does not alternate with *e* in any form. On the other hand, there is no structural reason to represent *oy* as underlying /oj/. There are two other diphthongs in the language that have not yet been discussed: *ei* (=[aj]) and

---

States have quite similar processes, whereby the reflex of long *u*, for instance, may be something like [ɪw].

ey (=[ej]). Their role in such alternations as the ablaut system provides compelling evidence (which will not be described here) for their representation as underlying /ai/ and /au/. The diphthong *oy*, however, does not play any comparable role in alternations and is thus an isolated element of the system.

Since there is no reason not to represent *oy* as underlying /é/, we can ask further whether it is plausible for such a representation to have arisen and whether there are any historical facts that it assists in explaining. This historical question is of course completely independent of the synchronic representation, but answers to it can at least be suggestive.

Historically, Faroese *oy* represents an Old Norse diphthong variously represented as *øy*, *ey*, and so on, which originally arose as the *i*-umlaut of the diphthong *au*. In Icelandic, the reflex of this diphthong is [ej], with which the diphthong *ei* (=/ai/) has fallen together. In the Faroese of circa 1500, the diphthong *oy* seems to have been phonetically [ej], with *ei* (= modern [aj]) represented as [æj], if one can rely on the scanty documentary evidence for the period. It would not, therefore, have been implausible for the isolated diphthong [ej] to have been treated as a simple long vowel /é/ at the time that the diphthongization rule 2.4 was added to the language. The other long vowels were apparently similar in nature at the time: *í* = [ij], *ú* = [uw], *ó* = [ow], and so forth. At this stage of the language, it would be natural for children learning the language to have constructed a grammar in which [ej] was represented as /é/, a vowel that had otherwise disappeared from the language as described above. When they then added the diphthongization rule 2.4 to their grammars, this /é/ would be treated in the same way as the other original long vowels and converted to [oj].[3] Thus, the assumption that this diphthong was reanalyzed as underlying /é/ at a very early point provides an explanation of its otherwise inexplicable development. As such, we have sup-

---

[3] One difficulty might arise if the change of *au* to [ej] is accepted as very early, as is traditionally assumed. In this case, the split of the two [ej]'s would be hard to explain. However, the [ej] from *au* is still structurally /au/ and hence distinct from the other [ej]. Furthermore, the only evidence for the early date of *au* → *ej* is the palatalization rule, which is adequately explainable in terms of the surface phonetics. For the argument, cf. Hægstad (1917).

porting evidence for both the representation of *oy* as /é/, and the rule of diphthongization 2.4.

One further rule should be mentioned at this point in order to explain the phonetic shapes of vowels: diphthongs ending in [a̭] (i.e., [æa̭] from /a/ in long syllables, and [oa̭] from /á/) lose this element with compensatory lengthening before an immediately following [a]:

2.6   [+syll]   a̭   a
$$\Longrightarrow \quad \begin{array}{ccc} 1 & \emptyset & 3 \\ [+\text{tense}] & & \end{array}$$
         1   2   3

We have now arrived at the following vowel system for the underlying representations of Faroese forms:

2.7

short vowels			long vowels		diphthongs	
i		u	í	ú	ai	au
e	ø	o	é	ó		
	a			á		

It will be observed that, with the exception of ø, this system is the same as that of Icelandic.

3. The Glide-Epenthesis Rule

There is a rule in Faroese that inserts a glide between two adjacent vowels in forms like those in 3.1:

3.1				
	a.	*siður*	[si:jUr]	'custom'
	b.	*kvæði*	[kvæa̭ji]	'ballad'
	c.	*devður*	[dejjÛr]	'dead'
	d.	*soðin*	[so:jIn]	'boiled'
	e.	*maður*	[mæa̭vUr]	'man'
	f.	*leður*	[le:vUr]	'leather'
	g.	*suður*	[su:wUr]	'south'
	h.	*húðir*	[hüwwIr]	'skins'

We note that the glide inserted is either *j*, *w*, or *v*, depending on the surrounding vowels. All instances of *v* follow a [-high] vowel; furthermore, no instances of *w* appear in this environment. It is a general property of the language that *w* becomes *v* in all positions except after a [+high] vowel. We can assume this rule here and will see other instances of its application below. Thus, the glide-insertion process that we presume to be responsible for the forms in 3.1 need only discriminate between environments in which *j* is inserted and those in which *w* is inserted.

Table 3.2 gives the glides that are inserted to break up any given sequence of vowels V_1V_2. Since V_1 is the only one of the pair that could possibly be stressed, and only the three vowels *a*, *i*, and *u* can appear in unstressed positions, the following are the only values that need be considered for V_1V_2:

3.2

V_1 \ V_2	a	i	u
i	j	j	j
u	w	w	w
e	Ø	j	w
ø	Ø	j	w
o	Ø	j	w
a	Ø	j	w

We see that the glide-insertion process can be described by a pair of rules, one that inserts a "similar" glide after a [+high] vowel and before another vowel, and another that inserts a "similar" glide after any vowel and before a [+high] vowel. Thus, if neither of the two vowels V_1 and V_2 is [+high], no glide is inserted; and the quality of the first vowel, if it is [+high], takes precedence over that of the second. These two rules can be formulated 3.3:

3.3 *a.*

$$\emptyset \rightarrow \begin{bmatrix} +son \\ -cons \\ -syll \\ +high \\ \alpha back \end{bmatrix} \bigg/ \begin{bmatrix} -cons \\ +high \\ \alpha back \end{bmatrix} \underline{\hspace{1cm}} [-cons]$$

b.

$$\emptyset \rightarrow \begin{bmatrix} +son \\ -cons \\ -syll \\ +high \\ \alpha back \end{bmatrix} \bigg/ [-cons] \underline{\hspace{1cm}} \begin{bmatrix} -cons \\ +high \\ \alpha back \end{bmatrix}$$

From forms like *deyður* [dejjUr], from /dej+Ur/, and *húðir* [hüwwIr], from /hüw+Ir/, we see that the second element of a diphthong, as well as a vowel, can condition the application of the rule. Thus, the surrounding segments are specified as [-cons], rather than as [+syll].

The rules do not apply, however, to break up diphthongs or glide-plus-vowel sequences within a morpheme. It is therefore necessary to restrict the operation of 3.3 to the position at a morpheme boundary, which will be obtained if we insert a morpheme boundary + before the blank in 3.3*a*, and after the blank in 3.3*b*. The two rules in 3.3 are obviously related, since they specify the same change in two environments that are related by symmetry. Rules of this sort were first discussed in the generative literature by Bach (1968); further examples were adduced by Langacker (1969) and Anderson (1969). In the latter work it was shown that such rules, when applying to representations in terms of categorial features, must be applied disjunctively (in the sense of Chomsky, 1967). A notation was proposed, according to which 3.3 could be abbreviated as a single schema:

3.4

$$
\emptyset \;\rightarrow\; \begin{bmatrix} +\text{son} \\ -\text{cons} \\ -\text{syll} \\ +\text{high} \\ \alpha\text{back} \end{bmatrix} \quad \% \quad \begin{bmatrix} -\text{cons} \\ +\text{high} \\ \alpha\text{back} \end{bmatrix} \;+\; \underline{\quad}\; [-\text{cons}]
$$

This schema is expanded as the (amended) pair of rules 3.3*a* and 3.3*b*, applying in that order. Observe that if they apply conjunctively (that is, if one part can apply even after the other has applied), a form like /biw+a/, to be discussed below, will be converted first into /biw+wa/, and then into /biww+wa/. This form would be incorrect; only one of the two parts of the schema can be allowed to apply. Thus, we see that the rules expanded from 3.4 must be applied disjunctively.

4. The *Verschärfung*

Let us consider the consonantal alternation known as *Verschärfung*, a name originally given to a sound change in the history of Germanic. This change accounted for correspondences between glides in certain WGmc forms and velar-/palatal-plus-glide clusters in NGmc and EGmc (*ddj* or *ggj* = [j̃] and *ggw* = [gw]). As Roe pointed out in his recent, highly useful study (Roe, 1965), the alternation, which has occasioned as much discussion as virtually any other single topic in Gmc historical phonology except the consonant shifts, has generally been regarded as a peculiarly

Gmc phenomenon, with the result that parallels in other languages have sometimes been neglected. For instance, It *maggiore* 'greater,' from Lat *māior*, shows the same correspondence. In the history of Gujarati the future infix *-iya-* becomes *-iyya-* and then *-ija-*. Other examples include Pr, Cat, Sp, Pg *guardar*, from Gmc *wardon* 'to ward off,' and Sp *guadanar* 'to mow,' from Gmc *waidanjan*, from *waida* 'meadow.' Examples could be multiplied from a variety of languages. In each case, the first step in the change is apparently the development of lengthened glides under some circumstances; although the conditions under which these changes arise remain problematic in some cases, the change itself is of a not uncommon sort and by no means restricted to Gmc.

Such a change is the basis of a productive rule of *Verschärfung* in modern Faroese. For instance, most verbs that have the clusters *ggj* (=[ʃ]) and *gv* (=[gv]) before vocalic endings, such as the *-a* of the infinitive, show simply a (diphthongized) long vowel before consonantal endings, such as the *-r* of the 3 sg. pres. of strong verbs:

4.1   *a. búgva*   [bɪgva]   'to dwell'; 3 sg. *býr*   [bujr]
     b. grógva   [grɛgva]   'to grow'; 3 sg. *grǿr* [grör]
     c. doyggha [doʃa]   'to die'; 3 sg. *doyr*   [dojr]
     d. spýggja [spUʃa]   'to vomit'; 3 sg. *spýr* [spujr]

It will be seen that the vowels in the 3 sg. forms of strong verbs have been affected as well by an umlaut rule, which converts back vowels into front ones—*ú/u* become *ý/y*; *ó* becomes *ǿ*; *o* becomes *e*; and *a* becomes *e*. This alternation is completely independent of *Verschärfung* and will simply be assumed here.

In 4.1, there is, in addition to the alternation between cluster and glide, an alternation between simple vowels (in the infinitives) and complex vowels (in the 3 sg. forms). There is, furthermore, no dialectal variation in the quality of the nucleus of the reflex of *ó* in the infinitival forms, though this vowel normally varies between [o], [ö], and [ɛ]:

4.2   *skógvur*   [skɛgvUr] 'shoe'
     skos   [skɛws, sköws, *or* skows]   'shoe'
                                    (gen. sg.)

Furthermore, the nuclear vowel in *búgva* is [I] rather than [ü], the usual reflex of *ú*. These various facts make it unap-

pealing to deal with the *Verschärfung* alternation purely in
terms of the alternation of consonant with Ø, even with the
loss of the second element of a diphthong before such consonant clusters.

Let us see what happens if we represent these forms in the
underlying system arrived at above, taking the form without
Verschärfung cluster as basic:

4.3   *a* . /bú+a/   /bú+r/
      b . /gró+a/   /gró+r/
      c . /dé+a/   /dé+r/
      d . /spí+a/   /spí+r/
      e . /skó+ur/   /skó+s/

After the umlaut rule referred to above has applied, the 3 sg.
forms with back vowels (i.e., the second column of 4.3*a* and
4.3*b*) will be altered, yielding

4.4   *a* . /bú+a/   /bí+r/
      b . /gró+a/   /grø+r/

Now the diphthongization rule (2.4) will apply to these forms,
yielding the following:

4.5   *a* . /biu+a/   /bui+r/
      b . /greo+a/   /grø+r/
      c . /doe+a/   /doe+r/
      d . /spui+a/   /spui+r/
      e . /skeo+ur/   /skeo+s/

At this point, the first element of each diphthong can receive
stress, and the second can be reduced and turned into a glide:

4.6   *a* . /biw+a/   /buj+r/
      b . /grew+a/   /grø+r/
      c . /doj+a/   /doj+r/
      d . /spuj+a/   /spuj+r/
      e . /skew+ur/   /skew+s/

Now recall the glide-formation rule, which was finally formulated as the schema 3.4 above. This rule will apply to these
representations, inserting glides after the morpheme boundaries in the forms with vowel endings, but leaving unaffected
the forms with consonant endings:

4.7   *a.* /biw+wa/   /buj+r/
      b. /grew+wa/   /grø+r/
      c. /doj+ja/   /doj+r/
      d. /spuj+ja/   /spuj+r/
      e. /skew+wur/   /skew+s/

At this point the vocalic endings in the forms that are to undergo *Verschärfung* are preceded by geminate glides, while the endings that do not cause *Verschärfung* are preceded by simple glides or simple vowels. It was suggested above that this lengthening of glides gave rise to the corresponding processes in other languages; we could now simply state a rule converting long glides into consonant clusters.

It is possible to relate this rule to another rule in Faroese, however, thus giving at least a partial explanation of its presence in the language. Faroese, like the other West Scandinavian languages, has a rule (or rule schema) that dissimilates the continuance of a sequence of consonantal sonorants. In various WScan dialects, these rules may affect some or all of such clusters as *nn, rr, ll, nr, rl,* converting the first element to a stop (*d*), thus yielding, in this case, *dn, dr, dl, dr, dl.* In Faroese, the rule of dissimilation applies without further restriction to *ll,* and with the restriction "after a long vowel or diphthong" to other clusters. This rule produces such alternations as those in 4.8:

4.8   *a. seinur* [sajnUr]   *seinni* [sajdni] 'later'
            'late';
      b. morgun [mɔrgUn]   *morni* [mɔdni] 'morning'
            'morning';   (dat. sg.)

While the exact structural description for this rule is not clear, the structural change carried out by it is stated as follows:

4.9
$$[+\text{son}] \rightarrow \begin{bmatrix} -\text{son} \\ -\text{cont} \end{bmatrix} / \begin{bmatrix} \underline{\hspace{1em}} \\ +\text{cons} \end{bmatrix} \begin{bmatrix} +\text{son} \\ +\text{cons} \end{bmatrix}$$
(with further restrictions)

Let us assume that this process, whatever its precise statement, was generalized at some point in Faroese to apply not simply to sequences of [+cons] sonorants, but also to all sequences of [−syllabic] ones that agree in the feature [±cons]; that is, to glides as well as to liquids and nasals. The effect

of this process on geminate glides will be to turn the first
elements of *jj* and *ww* into the feature complexes below:

4.10   *a.*

$$/j/ \rightarrow \begin{bmatrix} -\text{syll} \\ -\text{son} \\ +\text{cons} \\ -\text{cont} \\ +\text{high} \\ -\text{back} \\ +\text{voi} \\ . \\ . \\ . \end{bmatrix}$$

b.

$$/w/ \rightarrow \begin{bmatrix} -\text{syll} \\ -\text{son} \\ +\text{cons} \\ -\text{cont} \\ +\text{high} \\ +\text{back} \\ +\text{voi} \\ . \\ . \\ . \end{bmatrix}$$

But 4.10*a* is the segment g_1 (palatalized *g*), and 4.10*b* is just
g. Thus, the result of applying the rule 4.9 to the forms
in 4.7 will be to create the forms in 4.11:

4.11   *a.* /big+wa/   /buj+r/
       b. /greg+wa/   /grø+r/
       c. /dog₁+ja/   /doj+r/
       d. /spug₁+ja/   /spuj+r/
       e. /skeg+wur/   /skew+s/

Before a front vowel or glide, velars are palatalized to [ǰ]
and [č] by a rule that is necessary to produce the following:

4.12   *a.* *stingur* [stIŋgUr] 'pain'; *stingi* [stInǰi] 'pain'
                                                         (dat. sg.)
       b. *liggja* [lĨǰa] 'to lie'; underlying /ligg+j+a/;
                                      cf. 3 sg. *liggur* [lIggUr]

This palatalization rule will affect the first columns of 4.11*c*
and 4.11*d*, yielding 4.13:

4.13   *c.* /doǰ+ja/   /doj+r/
       d. /spuǰ+ja/   /spuj+r/

Recall the suggestion that the quality of the first elements
of *ó* and *ú* was produced by a rounding rule applying before
rounded vowels (in some dialects, only before high rounded
ones) or glides. If this rule applies to the forms produced
up to this point, we will have an explanation for the lack of
rounding in forms like *grógva* and *búgva*, since the segment
following the vowel will be a *g*, not a rounded vowel. In
addition, the rule converting *w* into *v* (referred to above)

must apply to the clusters of *g+w* in 4.11*a*, 4.11*b*, and 4.11*e* (this last rule applies anywhere except after a [+high] vowel). After these rules have applied, together with the rules for obtaining the phonetic interpretations of vowels, we will obtain the correct phonetic outputs:

4.14   *a.* [bɪgva]   [bujr]
        b. [grɛgva]   [grö:r]
        c. [dɔȷ̌a]   [dojr]
        d. [spUȷ̌a]   [spujr]
        e. [skɛgvUr]   [skɛws], [sköws], or [skows]

Thus, all the rules that are necessary to account for the *Verschärfung* alternation can be shown to be independently motivated in the language if the most natural assumptions are made about the shapes of the underlying forms. In positions other than before vocalic endings, *Verschärfung*, if it occurs, can also be shown to follow from the rest of the grammar. For instance, in a form like *hoyggj* [hɔȷ̌], where the *Verschärfung* appears in final position, it again results from the dissimilation of a geminate glide by rule 4.9; in this case, the first element of the geminate is from the diphthong *oy*, and the second element represents the effect of a rule that converts final *g* to *j* after a high front vowel or glide (a rule that is independently needed in the grammar). The presence of this underlying *g* is shown by forms like the genitive [hojks], the *g* appearing as *k* before the ending /-s/.

There are other instances in which the *Verschärfung* is apparently unexplained. One instance is the word *brúgv* 'bridge.' In accounting for the second element of the geminate glide that gives rise to the *gv* cluster, we can make use of an explanation that is required to explain another set of apparently unmotivated glides. In certain forms, the glide *v* appears after a nonhigh vowel and before another nonhigh vowel, a position in which it could not have arisen regularly by the operation of the glide-epenthesis rule (3.4):

4.15   *a.* *æða* [æ̯ava] 'eider duck'; *æðu* [æ̯avu] 'eider duck' (oblique cases)
        b. *røða* [rö:va] 'speech'; *røðu* [rövu] 'speech' (oblique cases)

In these cases, the glide that is present in the oblique-case forms has evidently been reanalyzed as part of the root;

the stems in 4.15 are taken to be /aw/ and /rǿw/, respectively. If the same reanalysis affects *brúgv* (in whose other
forms, such as the plural *brúgvar*, a glide is present regularly by 3.4), this stem will then be taken as /brûw/, which
will account for the final *Verschärfung*. Besides the form
classes just discussed, there remain only a few instances of
unexplained *Verschärfung*, mostly in the form of consciously
preserved archaic doublets (cf. Roe, 1965, for details).

5. Some Apparent Exceptions

Let us now turn to a large class of forms in which
Verschärfung does not occur, although we would expect to
find it on the basis of the rules discussed so far, if the underlying form that is apparently motivated by the phonetic form
is taken as basic. In these forms, the conditions apparently
exist for the creation of the geminate glides that give rise
to the *Verschärfung* clusters. The forms contain phonetically
long glides, but for some reason these long glides do not
dissimilate to form the consonant clusters.

5.1	*a. víga*	[vujja]	'dedicate'
	b. júgur	[jüwwUr]	'udder'
	c. síga	[sujja]	'lower'
	d. blíður	[blujjUr]	'friendly'
	e. týða	[tujja]	'translate'

Unless some basis can be found for the lack of dissimilation
of these glides, we will be left with a large class of forms that
must be marked, ad hoc, in the lexicon to indicate that the
rule does not apply. Such an arbitrary subcategorization of
the lexicon is to be avoided if at all possible. One explanation
might be that the long glides have not yet been created at the
point rule 4.9 applies or that some other segment still
separates them at this point, a segment that is (presumably)
deleted later.

From the forms 5.1*a*, 5.1*b*, and 5.1*c*, an immediate explanation of the latter sort is available. These forms have
a *g* between the two vowels in the underlying form. Intervocalic *g* is deleted in all positions in Faroese. Consider
some other forms in which these segments are deleted:

5.2	*a. ǿga*	[ö:a]	'increase'
	b. siga	[sija]	'say'
	c. fagur	[fæ̰avUr]	'beautiful'

The presence of *g* in the underlying forms of 5.1*a–c* and 5.2 is demonstrated by the appearance of this segment in other forms of the words, where the *g* is no longer intervocalic:

5.3 *a. vígdi* [vujgdi] 'dedicated'
   b. júgs [jüwks] 'udder' (gen. sg.)
   c. sígdi [sujgdi] 'lowered'
   d. ǿgdi [ögdi] 'increased'
   e. sagdi [sagdi] 'said'
   f. fagran [fagran] 'beautiful'
      (acc. masc. sg.)

These forms show that we need a rule to delete intervocalic *g*. If this rule is required to apply *after* 4.9, it will follow that the forms in 5.1*a–c* will not show dissimilation, since the segment *g* will still intervene at the point this rule applies.

The other forms in 5.1 in which dissimilation is absent (5.1*d–f*) are ones with an ð in the orthography, in a position separating two vowels. The presence in the orthography of such a segment is, of course, no evidence for much of anything, but the forms in 5.1 had a phonetic [ð] in this position in Old Norse. Historically, [ð] merged with [γ] (the phonetic shape of intervocalic *g*), and both later disappeared. This disappearance is not, however, of demonstrably greater age than the *Verschärfung*. In any case, it is by no means implausible that, even though they have disappeared from the surface forms, these segments left traces in the synchronic grammars of later stages of the language, due to the effect their presence may have had on other phonetic processes. In this case, the effect might remain in the abstract representations of the grammar.

A segment does show up in the position of the orthographic ð in other forms of the same words that fail to show dissimilation. In weak verbs, for example, forms with ð show an intrusive *d* before the *d* of the preterite, while other forms have only a single *d*:

5.4 *a. striða* [strujja] 'struggle'; *stríddi* [strujddi] (pret.)
   b. týða [tujja] 'translate';   *týddi* [tujddi] (pret.)

Similarly, adjectives of the type that fail to show dissimilation before the ending *-ur* of the nom. masc. sg. show an extra *t* before the *t* of the nom. neut. sg.:

5.5[4]   *a. bliður*   [blujjUr]   'friendly' (masc.);
                                  blitt [blujʰt] (neut.)
        b. fróður   [fröwwUr]   'wise' (masc.);
                                  frott [fröwʰt] (neut.)
        c. prúður   [prüwwUr]   'handsome' (masc.);
                                  prútt [prüwʰt] (neut.)

In other similar adjectives, the position of ð is occupied by *d* before a following *n* if syncope applies before a vocalic ending:

5.6   *a. heiðin*   [hajjIn]   'heathen'; *heidnan* [hajdnan] (acc.)
      b. soðin   [so:jin]   'cooked'; *sodnan* [sɔdnan] (acc.)

On the basis of these facts, one might be tempted to set up an underlying dental in the position occupied by ð in the orthography and mark it to be deleted later. Other facts, however, argue that the position of the ð is not always occupied by a dental:

5.7   *a. tráður*   [troạvUr]   'thread'; *traðri* [træạgri] (dat.)
      b. veður   [ve:vUr]   'weather'; *veðri* [vegri] (dat.)
      c. suður   [suwUr]   'south'; *syðri* [sIgri]
                                        'more southerly'

These forms seem to require a velar in the position of the ð. We can now ask whether there are in fact two such disappearing segments, one a dental and one a velar, or whether they should both be represented in the same way.

On the basis of the facts in 5.7, we might say that if one or the other is to be chosen as the underlying representation, it should be the velar. All positions in which the segment in question appears as a dental are before another dental, and it would not be implausible to have an underlying velar assimilated to the position of a following dental. There are, in fact, forms in which an overt velar is manifested in similar positions as a dental:

5.8   *a. draga*   [dræ:a]   'drag'; *drignan* [drIdnan]
                                          (acc. masc. sg. p.p.)
      b. níga   [nujja]   'sink down'; *nignan* [nIdnan]
                                          (acc. masc. sg. p.p.)

---

[4]The geminate *t* is realized as preaspirated in many dialects, thus remaining distinct from single *t*.

Here a *g* is assimilated to a following *n* as *d*, just as would be required for 5.6. Only some *g*'s are assimilated, however, and it would be a mistake to represent all the segments we are concerned with as *g*. We might represent all of the "missing segments" as [γ], the spirant corresponding to *g*.

There are other facts, however, that argue that at least some of the missing segments be represented as dentals. Thus, in the ablaut system, the second class of strong verbs consists of forms showing a stem vowel *ó* or *ú*. These vowels are distributed as follows: *ó* before dentals and before ð, and *ú* elsewhere:

> 5.9   *a. njósa* 'sneeze'; *njóta* 'enjoy'; *bjóða* 'offer'
> *b. krúpa* 'creep'; *fúka* 'rush'; *flúgva* 'fly'

In order to maintain this generalization, we will have to represent at least these ð's as dentals.

In fact, the only forms for which such a representation would be ill advised would be the very rare set in 5.7, where there is no basis for the conversion of an underlying ð into *g* before *r*. But there are few forms in this class, and there do not appear to be any for which it would not be perfectly possible to represent the segment in the position of orthographic ð as *g*. Thus, these forms have no real bearing on the question of the feature composition of the other ð's, and we should follow the most natural course and represent these latter as dentals. Since *t* and *d* already appear in underlying representations, the logical candidate is the corresponding spirant [ð]. We will then require a rule of spirant deletion:

5.10[5] $\begin{bmatrix} +\text{obst} \\ +\text{cont} \\ +\text{voi} \end{bmatrix} \rightarrow \emptyset$

Rule 5.10 will eliminate the segment ð from phonetic representations, after allowing it to influence other processes. One of its effects will be to be converted to *d* or *t* in the environments 5.4, 5.5, and 5.6; another will be to block the

---

[5]Probably, this rule can be used to account for the deletion of intervocalic *g* at the same time; it would be extremely reasonable to have *g* go to γ in this position, in which case the segments to be deleted would be the only voiced spirants in the language. Other apparent voiced spirants (in particular, *v*) are the result of late rules converting *w* into *v*, as described above, and *f* into *v* in intervocalic position.

dissimilation rule in 5.1*d–f*. None of the arguments given above on the feature composition of the segment are in any way relevant to the question of its existence, of course, which is adequately shown by the forms cited.

The forms 5.1*d–f* and other similar forms to which dissimilation does not apply are explained by the presence of intervocalic *g* or *ð* in the representations at the point at which rule 4.9 should apply. In order for this explanation to have any force, however, it is necessary to include the requirement that the dissimilation rule not apply *after* the deletion rule(s). We have already seen that the dissimilation rule must apply after the glide-epenthesis rule (3.4), since this rule provides the long glides that are to be dissimilated. Observe, however, that the rule of glide epenthesis must follow the rule of spirant deletion, since the deletion of the spirant results in the insertion of a glide, as shown in the forms of 5.1. We have thus the following ordering relations:

5.11   *a.* dissimilation precedes spirant deletion (a marked order)
         b. glide epenthesis precedes dissimilation (an unmarked order)
         c. spirant deletion precedes glide epenthesis (an unmarked order)

This situation clearly represents a paradox in terms of generally accepted notions about the character of the ordering relation between rules. In particular, it violates the requirement of transitivity, according to which if A precedes B, and B precedes C, then A must precede C. In Anderson (1969), however, it was argued that this requirement (among others) is not correct and that the notion of linearly ordered phonological rules must be replaced with a theory of *local ordering*. In such a theory, rule orderings are given as statements about pairs of rules (which may or may not be consistent with an arrangement into a single linear list); markedness considerations (in the sense of Kiparsky, 1968) are allowed to play a role in these statements, with only marked orderings (and unpredictable ones) appearing explicitly in the grammar. When an ordering is unmarked, it need not be stated. In this theory, only the statement of 5.11*a* need appear in the grammar of Faroese; the other orderings, being unmarked, follow as a natural consequence of the theory.

It has been suggested[6] that the paradox of 5.11 can be avoided if, instead of claiming as we do here that the glides in 5.1 are the result of the normal glide-insertion rule 3.4 and that this rule can apply after the spirant deletion, we reformulate the spirant-deletion rule so as to convert the spirants into glides, rather than deleting them. There are several points against this proposal. First, it would require rule 3.4 to be completely restated, since it is the entire complex of facts captured by that rule that determines which glide is to be inserted. Thus, exactly parallel to 3.4, we would need another rule

$$
5.12 \qquad \begin{Bmatrix} \eth \\ \gamma \end{Bmatrix} \rightarrow \begin{bmatrix} +son \\ -cons \\ -syll \\ +high \\ \alpha back \end{bmatrix} \quad \% \quad \begin{bmatrix} -cons \\ +high \\ \alpha back \end{bmatrix} \quad + \underline{\quad} [-cons]
$$

whose operation exactly duplicates that of 3.4, without being collapsible with it, because at least dissimilation must intervene between the two. Second, the rules of glide epenthesis and spirant deletion are necessary parts of the grammar in any case. That is, the segment ð must appear in underlying representations, although it does not appear in phonetic representations; in forms like those shown above, where it is not converted into something else and where no glide appears (because both surrounding vowels are [-high]), it must still be deleted. Thus, rule 5.10 must appear anyway; the solution proposed—a rule like 5.12—would implicitly claim that the glides in the forms in 5.1 are a result of the presence of the spirant, not of the juxtaposition of the vowels. That is, under the most natural application of the rules, the spirants in these forms would be deleted anyway, and the resulting juxtapositions of vowels should lead to the insertion of glides. Rule 5.12 claims that this glide insertion is a purely accidental fact. Third, at least some of the segments that rule 5.12 must turn into glides are velars. There are already rules in the grammar that turn velars into glides, but these are unlike 5.12 in that they are only sensitive to a preceding

[6]Independently by Arthur Schwartz and Morris Halle (personal communications). Incidentally, the plausibility of such a solution is not great, since a direct relation between a dental spirant and a glide is rather far-fetched.

front vowel. Thus, the existing evidence shows that in Faroese such a process is not as general as 5.12 would claim. Another rule that affects velars, and that is sensitive to both front and back vowels, is the velar-fronting rule (part of the palatalization process described above); this rule is also sensitive to both preceding and following vowels, but in this case the following vowel takes precedence rather than the preceding vowel, as in 3.4 and its siamese twin 5.12. These last two arguments merely suggest, of course, that such a process as that hypothesized in 5.12 would be counter to the "drift" of Faroese (in something like Sapir's sense), but the other objections, concerning the superfluity and lack of generality of a grammar incorporating 5.12, are sufficient to argue against its existence. In any event, 5.12 has as its only real motivation the avoidance of an ordering condition that, on the assumptions adopted in Anderson (1969), is perfectly natural.

REFERENCES

Anderson, S. R. (1969). "West Scandinavian Vowel Systems and the Ordering of Phonological Rules." Ph.D. dissertation, Massachusetts Institute of Technology.
Bach, E. (1968). "Two Proposals Concerning the Simplicity Metric in Phonology." *Glossa* 2:128–149.
Bjerrum, M. (1949). "An Outline of the Faroe Vowel System." *Travaux du Cercle Linguistique de Copenhague* 5: 235–243.
Chomsky, N. (1967). "Some General Properties of Phonological Rules." *Language* 43:102–128.
Hammershaimb, V. U. (1891). *Færøsk Anthologi.* Copenhagen: S. L. Møllers Bogtrykkeri.
Hægstad, M. (1917). *Vestnorske Maalføre fyre 1350*, vol. 2: *Sudvestlandsk.* Kristiania: Jacob Dybwad.
Kiparsky, P. (1968). "Linguistic Universals and Linguistic Change." In *Universals in Linguistic Theory*, edited by E. Bach and R. Harms. New York: Holt, Rinehart, and Winston.
Krenn, E. (1940). *Föroyische Sprachlehre.* Heidelberg: Carl Winters Universitätsbuchhandlung.
Langacker, R. (1969). "Mirror Image Rules II: Lexicon and Phonology." *Language* 45:844–862.
Lockwood, W. B. (1955). *An Introduction to Modern Faroese.* Copenhagen: Ejnar Munksgaard.

McCawley, J. (1968). "A Note on Faroese Vowels." *Glossa* 2:11–6.

O'Neil, W. A. (1964). "Faroese Vowel Morphophonemics." *Language* 40:366–371.

Rischel, J. (1968). "Diphthongization in Faroese." *Acta Linguistica Hafniensa* 11:89–118.

Roe, H. A. (1965). "Verschärfung in Faroese." Ph.D. dissertation, Harvard University.

Werner, O. (1964). "Die Erforschung der färingischen Sprache. Ein Bericht über Stand und Aufgaben." *Orbis* 13:481–544.

—— (1968). "Welche Stufen phonematischer Reduktion sind für die Dialektgeographie sinnvoll? Das Vokalsystem des Färoischen." *Zeitschrift für Mundartforschung* 4:861–870.

On the Abstractness of Phonology:
Maltese ʕ

MICHAEL K. BRAME

The University of Texas at Austin

1. Introduction

Apart from questions of morpheme structure, the work of the phonologist commences with an attempt to account for phonetic alternations. The postulation of underlying phonological representations, along with rules that relate the underlying representations with their phonetic manifestations, is a result of the concern to account for phonetic alternations in a meaningful and insightful way. Considerations of rationality dictate that, all other things being equal, one of the n alternating phonetic forms will be chosen as the underlying source from which all other alternating phonetic forms are to be derived. Usually, evidence internal to the language in question decides which phonetic form is to be favored as basic. The evidence may involve economy and generalization in the statement of phonological rules, morphological generality, and the like. It sometimes happens, however, that these considerations make it necessary to postulate an underlying representation that

NOTE: I wish to thank Noam Chomsky, Joseph Emonds, Morris Halle, Paul Kiparsky, and John Robert Ross for comments on a preliminary version of this paper written in 1969. Some of the research that went into this paper was carried out in Malta and was made possible by a grant from the National Science Foundation (NSF Grant GS–2468). My greatest debt is to Alfred Cauchi whose dialect is described herein. I would also like to thank Bill and Rose Tabone for first introducing me to the spoken language.

deviates from the *n* phonetic alternations in that this representation does not appear in the superficial representations of the language.

In the past, generative phonologists have not hesitated to set up abstract segments in the underlying representations of natural languages. More recently, however, this step in the direction of abstractness has been criticized. In a recent paper, Kiparsky has illustrated a situation in Sanskrit: he pointed to two possible solutions to the data, one abstract, the other not, and ultimately opted for the less abstract approach. In the Sanskrit case, *k* alternates with *č*, the *č* occurring before phonetic *a*. However, there are instances of *k* that occur before *a* as phonetic *k*. A plausible approach to the problem of accounting for the *k* ~ *č* alternation is as follows: Set up an underlying *e* for all those *a*'s before which phonetic *č* (which alternates with *k*) occurs. The *k* ~ *č* alternation is accounted for by assuming underlying *k* along with a rule turning *k* to *č* before *e*. A later rule will switch all *e*'s to *a* independent of context, since no examples of phonetic *e* exist in the language. Thus, the distribution of phonetic segments is accounted for by such derivations as those listed below.

(1) *a.* ke → če → ča
     b. ka → ka → ka

The rule converting all instances of *e* to *a* regardless of context is a case of what Kiparsky terms "absolute neutralization." He wishes to deny the validity of this type of solution, choosing instead to represent all instances of phonetic *a* relevant to this discussion as underlying *a*. He accounts for the *k* ~ *č* alternation by postulating the following rule of palatalization:

(2) k → č / ___ a

Those *k*'s which do not palatalize are treated as exceptions to rule (2), that is, they are assigned the diacritic feature [-Rule k → č / ___ a].

Kiparsky's is the first serious attempt to constrain the abstractness of phonological systems, and, as such, it must be examined closely. In the following pages I shall present a set of data from Maltese, a dialect of Arabic spoken on the Maltese archipelago, for which the rule-feature approach will lead to a number of undesirable consequences. These data dictate the postulation of a phonological segment that never shows up phonetically, which in turn gives rise to a case of absolute neutralization. For this reason, it seems that the Maltese case will have to be given some deliberation by those wishing to constrain underlying phonological systems.

2. Some Rules of Maltese

Stress in Maltese is in the great majority of cases straightforward and simple. The following examples will serve to introduce the stress system of this language:[1]

(3)	*ḥátaf*	'he grabbed'	*béza'*	'he spit'
	ḥátf+et	'she grabbed'	*béz'+et*	'she spit'
	ḥtáf+t	'I grabbed'	*bzá'+t*	'I spit'

These forms may be generalized by assuming *ḥataf* and *beza'*

---

[1]Phonetic symbols that may not be familiar to the casual reader include the following:

ḥ = voiceless pharyngeal spirant
ʕ = voiced pharyngeal spirant
' = glottal stop

The following distinctive feature abbreviations will be employed:

son = sonorant	str = stress	lo = low
cns = consonant	cor = coronal	vd = voiced
seg = segment	bk = back	

The usual notational conventions of generative phonology are utilized throughout, e.g., C_0 signifies any number of consonants, # stands for word boundary, etc. See Chomsky and Halle (1968) for explication of these and other conventions used in this paper. Some phonetic detail is omitted from the phonetic citations given in this work. One such detail is that brought about by the following rule:

VOICING ASSIMILATION: $[\text{-son}]^* \rightarrow [\alpha \text{vd}]/\underline{\quad}\begin{bmatrix} \text{-son} \\ \alpha \text{vd} \end{bmatrix}$

By this rule, *ni+ktb+u* becomes *ni+gdb+u*, *ni+zfen* becomes *ni+sfen*, etc., cf. (26). Word-final obstruents are also devoiced in Maltese. If the word boundary is specified as [-vd], Voicing Assimilation will also handle this situation. Thus, *kileb* becomes *kitep*, *hadd* becomes *hatt*, etc. In this work, the morpheme boundary is often included in the surface citation, in order to aid the reader in identifying the relevant morphemes. Obviously this boundary has no phonetic reflex whatsoever. Other deviations from strict phonetic citations will be noted as they arise.

to be the underlying stems, followed by the person markers $\emptyset$ 'he,' *et* 'she,' and *t* 'I.' The following rule is needed to account for the actual phonetic distribution of the vowels of these forms:

(4)   APOCOPE: $\begin{bmatrix} V \\ -str \end{bmatrix} \rightarrow \emptyset \; / \; \text{---}CV$

This rule will convert first person *ḥatáf+t* and *bezá'+t* into *ḥtáf+t* and *bzá'+t* as desired. Because examples of the type *séna* 'year,' *ǰóbon* 'cheese,' and *nísa* 'women' are commonly encountered in the language, it is possible to conclude that only unstressed vowels are elided by Apocope. This restriction accounts for the third person masculine forms of (3), *ḥátaf* and *béza'*. Since *ḥátf+et* and *béz'+et* derive from *ḥataf+et* and *beza'+et* and since the assignment of stress precedes the rule of Apocope, it follows that these third person feminine forms should receive stress on the antepenultimate syllable. Thus, it is now possible to state the stress rule.

(5)   STRESS ASSIGNMENT: $V \rightarrow [+str] \; / \; \text{---}C_0((VC)VC_0^1)\#]$

This schema abbreviates the following disjunctively ordered rules:[2]

(6)   (a) $V \rightarrow [+str] \; / \; \text{---}C_0VCVC_0^1\#]$
        (b) $V \rightarrow [+str] \; / \; \text{---}C_0VC_0^1\#]$
        (c) $V \rightarrow [+str] \; / \; \text{---}C_0\#]$

The forms listed in (3) will be generated according to the following derivations:

(7)

ḥataf	*ḥataf+et*	*ḥataf+t*	*beza'*	*beza'+et*	*beza'+t*	
—	*ḥátaf+et*	—	—	*béza'+et*	—	(6a) & STRESS ASSIGNMENT
ḥátaf	—	—	*béza'*	—	—	(6b) & STRESS ASSIGNMENT
—	—	*ḥatáf+t*	—	—	*bezá'+t*	(6c) & STRESS ASSIGNMENT
—	*ḥátf+et*	*ḥtáf+t*	—	*béz'+et*	*bzá'+t*	(4) APOCOPE
ḥátaf	*ḥátf+et*	*ḥtáf+t*	*béza'*	*béz'+et*	*bzá'+t*	

Rule (5) accounts for the stress patterns of these and many other forms in the language. For example, additional mor-

---

[2]See Chomsky (1967) and Chomsky and Halle (1968) for a discussion of disjunctive ordering.

phemes may be suffixed to the first person forms listed in (3),
in which case more c o m p l e x w o r d s result, such as
ma ḫtaf+t+ik+š 'I did not grab you,' and *ma bza'+t+l+ik+š* 'I did
not spit to you,' where *ik* = 'you,' *l* = 'to,' and *š* = 'not.' (The
particle *ma*, also meaning 'not,' is not part of the word.)
Stress is correctly assigned to these more complex words by
the rule of Stress Assignment.

Besides the stress patterns found in (3), the following are
of importance for the correct formulation of the stress rule in
Maltese:

(8) *sultā̃n*   'king'   *'ā̃res*   'sour'
     'attū̃s   'cat'   *ḥdū̃ra*   'greenness'
     ḥayyā̃t   'tailor'   *kmā̃mar*   'rooms'

If the long vowels of these examples are represented as sequences of two identical morae at a more abstract level, and
if a low-level rule operates to distribute stress across such
sequences as well as to lengthen them, then the stress patterns of these examples are also predicted by (5).

(9) *sultaan 'attuus ḥayyaat 'aares ḥduura kmaamar*
     sultáan 'attúus ḥayyaat 'áares ḥdúura kmáamar
                                              STRESS ASSIGNMENT
     sultā̃n 'attū̃s ḥayyā̃t 'ā̃res ḥdū̃ra kmā̃mar
                                              low-level rule(s)

In what follows, this low-level rule(s) will be omitted altogether, since it plays no crucial role in the arguments that
are advanced. Long vowels will simply be entered as vowel
clusters in the phonetic representations of words.

There is more to be said about the third person feminine
singular pronoun suffix *et* found in *ḥátf+et* and *béz'+et*. Under
stress this suffix is *it*, compare *ḥatf+ít+kom* 'she grabbed you
(pl.)' and *bez'+ít+l+ek* 'she spit to you.' The same *e ~ i* alternation can be found in such forms as *kíteb* 'he wrote,' versus
ktíb+t 'I wrote,' where the stem vowel *e* shows up as *i* under
stress. The usual interpretation of this alternation is that *e*
is the underlying vowel, which becomes *i* under stress.[3] It is

---

[3]This possibility is usually adopted in the standard Maltese grammars:
for example, Sutcliffe remarks, "a short unaccented *e* on receiving the
accent generally changes to *i* . . ."; or Aquilina's comment, "Unstressed
vowel *e* in verbs becomes *i* when the accent falls on it."

equally plausible, however, to assume that *i* is the underlying segment and that it becomes *e* by the following rule:

(10)   VOWEL REDUCTION: $i \rightarrow e / \acute{V}C_0$___

There is some evidence that suggests that this approach is correct. First, there are many instances of stressed *e* in the language: *séna* 'year,' *béza'* 'he spit,' cited above, *méss* 'he touched,' *séḥet* 'he cursed,' *t+kéllem* 'he spoke,' and *té+ḥles* 'you free.' If the change were from *e* to *i*, these stressed *e*'s should also be expected to become *i*. Second, there are no examples of the sequence $\acute{V}C_0i$ in the language. This gap in patterning is automatically explained by rule (10). Third, the feminine ending shows up not as *et* but as *it* in such forms as *ma ḥatf+it+kóm+š* 'she did not grab you (pl.),' and *ma ktib+t+úu+š* 'I did not write it,' where the stress actually falls on a syllable following the relevant vowel. The evidence, thus, indicates that the change is from *i* to *e* and not from *e* to *i*. Accordingly, such examples as *ḥátf+et* and *kíteb* will possess the more basic *i*-grade vowel in underlying representations. The derivations are shown below:

(11)
hataf+it	*kitib*	
hátaf+it	*kítib*	STRESS ASSIGNMENT
hátf+it	—	APOCOPE
hátf+et	*kíteb*	VOWEL REDUCTION

The rule of Apocope feeds the rule of Vowel Reduction, that is, it sets up the proper environment for the application of this rule. Hence, from the derivation of *hálf+et*, it is possible to conclude that Vowel Reduction follows Apocope. It is obvious from the statement of Vowel Reduction itself that this rule must follow Stress Assignment.

Feminine *it* alternates with *et*, but it also shows up as phonetic *ot*. Compare the following paradigm with those of (3):

(12)
kórob	'he groaned'
kórb+ot	'she groaned'
krób+t	'I groaned'

These forms may be generated by derivations analogous to those utilized in generating the citations of (3), that is, by steps similar to those of (7). Thus, the underlying stem will be *korob*. The third person masculine form is trivially gen-

erated by the application of a single rule, the rule of Stress
Assignment. First person *krôb+t* derives from *korob+t* by
Stress Assignment and Apocope. However, if *it* is the underlying third person feminine singular subject pronoun, then
'she groaned' is expected to emerge as *kórb+et* instead of the
actually occurring form *kórb+ot*. Apparently an additional
rule of Maltese effects the change required to generate the
latter form. This rule may be stated as (13).

(13)   VOWEL HARMONY: $i \rightarrow o / oC_0$___

By invoking this new rule, *kórb+ot* may be correctly derived
from underlying *korob+it*.

(14)   *korob+it*
       kórob+it   STRESS ASSIGNMENT
       kórob+ot   VOWEL HARMONY
       kórb+ot   APOCOPE

Notice that Vowel Reduction does not figure in this derivation
in any way. In other words, Vowel Harmony must precede
Vowel Reduction if rule (13) is to apply. (Of course (13) could
be restated to allow for the change of *e* to *o*, in which case the
opposite ordering would be possible.) However, no argument
has yet been advanced to prove that Vowel Harmony precedes
Apocope. At present either order will produce the correct
results.

The operation of Vowel Reduction and Vowel Harmony may
be further exemplified by the second person singular object
pronoun suffix. The examples *ma ḥtaf+t+ik+š* 'I did not grab
you' and *ma bza'+t+l+ik+š* 'I did not spit to you,' in which this
suffix shows up as *ik*, have already been cited in the earlier
discussion. This morpheme also shows up as *ek* in such
forms as *ḥtáf+t+ek* 'I grabbed you' and *bzá'+t+l+ek* 'I spit to
you,' as predicted by Vowel Reduction. The suffix appears as phonetic *ok* in such examples as *krób+t+l+ok* 'I
groaned to you,' as predicted by Vowel Harmony.[4]

Rule (13) is an assimilatory process that propagates from
left to right. A similar rule seems to operate in the opposite

---

[4]The idea that *o* is the underlying vowel in the case of second person
singular *ok* is certainly mistaken, as *ok* has a limited distribution compared to *ek* (or *ik*), the latter of which shows up after *i, a,* or *u,* followed
by possible consonants. A rule turning *o* to *i* after *i, a,* or *u* followed
by C_0 would be highly improbable.

direction. The motivation for this rule becomes evident when it is noted that the imperfective stem is typically marked for person by prefixes of the shape *Ci*. For example, the first and second person subject pronoun prefixes *ni* 'I' and *ti* 'you' may be observed in the following citations:

(15)

	I		II
nɨ+msaḥ	'I wipe'	*nɨ+kteb*	'I write'
tɨ+msaḥ	'you wipe'	*tɨ+kteb*	'you write'
nɨ+šbaḥ	'I resemble'	*nɨ+nzel*	'I descend'
tɨ+šbaḥ	'you resemble'	*tɨ+nzel*	'you descend'
nɨ+sḥa'	'I smash'	*nɨ+zfen*	'I dance'
tɨ+sḥa'	'you smash'	*tɨ+zfen*	'you dance'
nɨ+fraḥ	'I rejoice'	*nɨ+freš*	'I spread'
lɨ+ſraḥ	'you rejoice'	*tɨ+freš̌*	'you spread'
nɨ+tla'	'I leave'	*nɨ+tlef*	'I lose'
tɨ+tla'	'you leave'	*tɨ+tlef*	'you lose'
nɨ+sra'	'I steal'	*nɨ+dneb*	'I sin'
tɨ+sra'	'you steal'	*tɨ+dneb*	'you sin'

All the forms listed in (15) are of the shape *tiCCVC*, the stem vowel being *a* in the first column and *e*, from *i* by Vowel Reduction, in the second column. In all examples the first person prefix shows up as *ni*, and the second person prefix, as *ti*. Consider the following sets of imperfective forms:

(16)

	I		II
nô+bzo'	'I spit'	*nɨ+drob*	'I wound'
tô+bzo'	'you spit'	*tɨ+drob*	'you wound'
nô+fto'	'I unstitch'	*nɨ+dḥol*	'I enter'
tô+fto'	'you unstitch'	*tɨ+dḥol*	'you enter'
nô+krob	'I groan'	*nɨ+tloḥ*	'I pray'
tô+krob	'you groan'	*tɨ+tlob*	'you pray'
nô+ḥlom	'I dream'	*nɨ+skot*	'I become silent'
lô+ḥlom	'you dream'	*tɨ+skot*	'you become silent'
nô+'tol	'I kill'	*nɨ+sḥon*	'I become hot'
tô+'tol	'you kill'	*tɨ+sḥon*	'you become hot'
nô+mšot	'I comb'	*nɨ+zlo'*	'I slip'
tô+mšot	'you comb'	*tɨ+zlo'*	'you slip'

nó+rbot	'I tie'	*nɨ+zboḥ*	'I paint'
tó+rbot	'you tie'	*tɨ+zboḥ*	'you paint'
nó+nfoꞌ	'I spend'	*nɨ+zbor*	'I prune'
tó+nfoꞌ	'you spend'	*tɨ+zbor*	'you prune'
nó+lꞌot	'I hit'	*nɨ+ǰbor*	'I pick up'
tó+lꞌot	'you hit'	*tɨ+ǰbor*	'you pick up'
nó+ꞌmos	'I kick'	*nɨ+šrob*	'I drink'
tó+ꞌmos	'you kick'	*tɨ+šrob*	'you drink'

The prefixes show up as *no* and *to* in the examples listed under column I of (16), but remain *ni* and *ti* in the examples of column II. The *o* of prefixal *no* and *to* can be accounted for by a rule that assimilates the *i* of basic *ni* and *ti* to the vowel of the stem, which is also *o* in these examples. However, note carefully that the initial consonant of the stem is relevant to this process, for the quality of the consonants in the examples of column I, where the prefixal vowel is altered, invariably differs from that of the corresponding consonants of the examples of column II. The initial stem consonant of the column I forms is either [-cor] or [+son]. The corresponding consonant of the column II forms is invariably [+cor]. Therefore, the regressive vowel harmony rule may be stated as follows:[5]

$$
(17) \quad i \rightarrow o / \underline{\hspace{1cm}} \begin{bmatrix} +\text{cns} \\ \left\{ \begin{array}{l} +\text{son} \\ -\text{cor} \end{array} \right\} \end{bmatrix} C_0 o
$$

By this rule, *ti+bzoꞌ* will become *to+bzoꞌ*, *ti+ḥlom* will become *to+ḥlom*, *ti+rbot* will become *to+rbot*, and so on. However, *ti+drob*, *ti+skot*, *ti+ǰbor*, etc. will not be affected.

Like rule (13), (17) is a rule of vowel harmony. In both cases the vowel *i* is assimilated to the vowel *o*. Thus, it would be desirable if both cases could be reduced to one. It is in fact possible to collapse the two rules into one.[6]

---

[5]The glottal stop is assumed to be [+cns] contrary to Chomsky and Halle (1968).

[6]It is possible to replace (17) by (i).

(i) $\quad i \rightarrow o / -C_0 o$

This decision entails an additional rule that switches *o* back to *i* before

(18)   VOWEL HARMONY: $i \rightarrow o / \left\{ \begin{array}{l} oC_0 \underline{\quad} \\ \underline{\quad} \left[\begin{array}{l} +cns \\ +son \\ -cor \end{array} \right] C_0 o \end{array} \right.$ (a)

(b)

For facility of reference, in the following discussion (18a) will
be called Progressive Vowel Harmony, and (18b) Regressive
Vowel Harmony. To return to the point raised in conjunction
with derivation (14), that is, the ordering of Vowel Harmony
before Apocope, it is now possible to show that this ordering
is necessary. Suppose the second person object pronoun *ik* is
suffixed to such forms as those of (16)II. This process would
give underlying representations like *ni+zboḥ+ik* and *ni+ĵbor+ik*.
Notice that the stem-vowel *o* is in a position to be elided by
Apocope and that the *i* of the suffix is in a position to be
changed to *o* by Progressive Vowel Harmony. If the stem-
vowel is first elided by Apocope, the vowel of the suffix is no
longer in a position to undergo Vowel Harmony. That is, once
the underlying representations become *ni+zbḥ+ik* and
ni+ĵbr+ik, Vowel Harmony ceases to be applicable. If these
were the actual phonetic representations, the ordering
Apocope–Vowel Harmony would be motivated. However, the
correct superficial representations are *ni+zbḥ+ok* 'I paint you'
and *ni+ĵbr+ok* 'I pick you up,' proving that Vowel Harmony
precedes Apocope. That is, the derivation of these forms
must run as follows:

[+cor] obstruents followed by at least one consonant. This rule is recorded as (ii).

(ii) $o \rightarrow i /\underline{\quad}^+ \left[\begin{array}{l} -son \\ +cor \end{array} \right] C$

The explanation for the morpheme boundary and the extra consonant
in (ii) would take us too far afield. It suffices to point out that (i) and (ii)
give rise to the following derivations:

(iii)   *ti+drob*   *ti+ĵbor*   *ti+bzo'*   *ti+ḥlom*
          to+drob   *to+ĵbor*   *to+bzo'*   *lo+ḥlom*   (i)
          ti+drob   *ti+ĵbor*   —   —   (ii)

If this possibility is adopted, (i) may be then collapsed with (13) by a
further convention of generative phonology, the adjacency convention;
cf. Bach (1968) and Anderson (1969). For a discussion of this possibility
in another context, see Brame (to appear *a*).

(19) *ni+zboḥ+ik*   *ni+ʃbor+ik*
      nî+zboḥ+ik   *nî+ʃbor+ik*   STRESS ASSIGNMENT
      nî+zboḥ+ok   *nî+ʃbor+ok*   PROGRESSIVE VOWEL HARMONY
      nî+zbḥ+ok   *nî+ʃbr+ok*   APOCOPE

By a similar argument, it is possible to show that Regressive Vowel Harmony precedes Apocope as well. This time the masculine singular object pronoun u[7] may be suffixed to the examples of (16)I, which gives such underlying representations as *ni+'tol+u*, *ni+rbot+u*, and *ni+l'ot+u*. If Apocope applies before Regressive Vowel Harmony, basic *ni*, the first person prefix, is expected to surface as *ni*. That is, one expects *ní+'tl+u*, *ní+rbt+u*, and *ní+l't+u* to emerge as the phonetic representations. However, the prefix shows up not as *ni*, but as *no*; *no+'tl+u* 'I kill him,' *no+rbt+u* 'I tie him,' and *no+l't+u* 'I hit him.' These examples prove that Regressive Vowel Harmony precedes Apocope, which is illustrated in (20).

(20)

   ni+'tol+u   *ni+rbot+u*   *ni+l'ot+u*
   nî+'tol+u   *nî+rbot+u*   *nî+l'ot+u*   STRESS ASSIGNMENT
   nô+'tol+u   *nô+rbot+u*   *nô+l'ot+u*   REGRESSIVE VOWEL HARMONY
   nô+'tl+u   *nô+rbt+u*   *nô+l't+u*   APOCOPE

The ordering of the two vowel harmony processes with Apocope is of course consistent with the conflation of these rules into a single rule.

The subject prefixes can again be utilized to motivate a new rule of Maltese. This rule is needed to explain the following examples:

(21)   I   II

    nâ+'sam   'I divide'   *nâ+'bez*   'I jump'
    tâ+'sam   'you divide'   *tâ+'bez*   'you jump'

    nâ+'bad   'I seize'   *nâ+'bel*   'I agree'
    tâ+'bad   'you seize'   *tâ+'bel*   'you agree'

    nâ+'ta   'I cut'   *nâ+'leb*   'I overturn'
    tâ+'ta   'you cut'   *tâ+'leb*   'you overturn'

---

[7]Actually this morpheme may be more abstract in underlying representations, but this possibility has no bearing on the present argument. Cf. Brame (to appear *c*).

nâ+ḥrab	'I flee'	*nâ+ḥdem*	'I work'
tâ+ḥrab	'you flee'	*tâ+ḥdem*	'you work'
nâ+ḥsad	'I reap'	*nâ+ḥseb*	'I think'
tâ+ḥsad	'you reap'	*tâ+ḥseb*	'you think'
nâ+ḥra'	'I burn'	*nâ+ḥleb*	'I milk'
tâ+ḥra'	'you burn'	*tâ+ḥleb*	'you milk'

The examples listed above should be compared with those of (15). As in (15), the stem vowel is either *a* (cf. column I), or *e* (from *i*, cf. column II). However, the prefix of the forms cited in (21) shows up as *Ca*, not as *Ci* as in (15). There is an explanation for the appearance of prefixal *na* and *ta* in these verbs. Unlike the forms listed in (15), these examples all possess a stem beginning with a consonant articulated in the pharyngeal or laryngeal regions of the vocal tract. Since these segments, ' and *ḥ*, are both produced in the posterior reaches of the vocal tract, it is no surprise that they should have an effect on the *i* of basic *ni* and *ti*. The change of *i* to *a* is a backing and lowering process. It is only natural that low back segments should initiate such a change. Consequently, the following rule may be postulated to handle this process:

(22)   GUTTURAL ASSIMILATION: $i \rightarrow a / \_\_\_ \begin{bmatrix} \text{I cns} \\ +bk \\ +lo \end{bmatrix}$

Rule (22) is essentially an assimilatory process. The vowel *i* assimilates to *ḥ* and ' in lowness and backness. By this rule, which I shall term Guttural Assimilation, underlying *ti+'sam*, *ti+'biz*, *ti+ḥrab*, and so on will become *ta+'sam*, *ta+'biz* (ultimately *ta+'bez*), *ta+ḥrab*. In this way, the prefixes of (21) are explained. It should be noted that Guttural Assimilation does not affect *o*, as proven by the fact that *to+ḥlom* 'you dream' and *to+'tol* 'you kill' (cf. (16)I) are not affected. In other words, the rule of Vowel Harmony precedes Guttural Assimilation.

A further rule of Maltese will be relevant to the later discussion. This rule is needed to account for the first person forms of the following citations:

(23)   *lá'at*   'he hit'   *róḥos*   'it (masc.) became cheap'
        lá't+et 'she hit'   *róḥs+ot* 'it (fem.) became cheap'
        il'át+t 'I hit'   *irḥós+t* 'I became cheap'

mášat	'he combed'	*néfa'*	'he spent'
mášt+et	'she combed'	*néf'+et*	'she spent'
imšát+t	'I combed'	*infá'+t*	'I spent'

From the earlier discussion, it is evident that the stems underlying these verbs are *la'at*, *roḥos*, *mašat*, and *nefa'*. The third person masculine and feminine forms may be accounted for in the same way as were the analogous forms of (3) and (12); compare (7) and (14). However, the first person forms present a new twist. One expects underlying *la'at+t*, *roḥos+t*, *mašat+t*, and *nefa'+t* to become *l'át+t*, *rḥós+t*, *mšát+t*, and *nfá'+t* by Stress Assignment and Apocope. But unlike the earlier examples listed in (3) and (12), the first person forms of (23) possess an extra vowel, an initial *i*. This vowel is found preceding all analogous forms beginning with one of the sonorants *r*, *l*, *m*, or *n* followed by a consonant. That is, there is no word beginning with one of these segments followed by a consonant in the phonetic representations of Maltese.[8] This distribution of surface forms suggests that there is an epenthesis rule that inserts *i* in the first person examples of (23), which would give rise to the following derivations:

(24)

la'at+t	*roḥos+t*	*mašat+t*	*nefa'+t*	
la'át+t	*roḥós+t*	*mašát+t*	*nefá'+t*	STRESS ASSIGNMENT
l'át+t	*rḥós+t*	*mšát+t*	*nfá'+t*	APOCOPE
il'át+t	*irḥós+t*	*imšát+t*	*infá'+t*	PROTHESIS

This new rule, which I have called Prothesis, may be formulated as (25), where *R* is an informal abbreviation for the class of segments *r*, *l*, *m*, and *n*.

(25)   PROTHESIS: $\emptyset \rightarrow i \ / \# \_\_\_ RC$

It is obvious that Prothesis must apply after Apocope. The latter rule creates the environment relevant to the former. Moreover, Prothesis must follow Vowel Harmony, since *irḥós+t* does not become *orḥós+t*, a fact that is consistent with

---

[8]The constraint should be stated in terms of the phonological phrase. That is, the more accurate statement is that such sequences do not begin words that are preceded by words ending in consonants or preceded by a phonetic pause. This restriction entails a complication in rule (25). For the purposes of this paper, however, the oversimplified statement will do.

the ordering of Vowel Harmony before Apocope, as established earlier.

The rule of Prothesis applies to a number of divergent formative types. In addition to applying to perfective verbs, as in (24), it applies to imperfective verb classes. One such class are the so-called hollow verbs. These verbs exhibit a high glide, either *w* or *y*, in the medial radical position. Thus, the underlying sequences *ni+swu'* and *ni+zyid* are motivated by the fact that imperfectives are typically of this pattern—compare (15), (16), and (21), which are all of the shape *CV+CCVC*—and by such alternations as *sew'+aan* 'act of driving' and *zeyd+a* 'excessive.' By rules that are not germane to the main discussion, *ni+swu'* and *ni+zyid* become *ni+suu'* and *ni+ziid*. This change occurs before Stress Assignment, since the long vowel is stressed, whence follows Apocope. Apocope applies, yielding the forms *n+súu'* and *n+zíid*, which meet the conditions for Prothesis. The u l t i m a t e representations, *in+súu'* 'I drive' and *in+zíid* 'I add,' indicate that Prothesis has indeed applied. An analogous situation arises in several derived verb classes. One such class is formed by doubling the second root of the stem. Thus, the root *'abez* 'to jump' becomes *'abbez* 'to boost' in this derived conjugation. The underlying form *ni+'abbez*, the result of prefixation of the subject marker *ni* to the stem *'abbez*, undergoes Stress Assignment and Apocope, yielding *n+'abbez*. Now Prothesis is again needed to account for the c o r r e c t surface form *in+'ábbez*. Another class of forms requiring the application of Prothesis is the nonderived verbal noun of the pattern *CCiiC*. (Cf. *'tiil* 'act of killing,' *ḥtiif* 'a grabbing,' *tliib* 'act of praying,' etc.) If *r*, *l*, *m*, or *n* occupies the consonant-initial position of this pattern, then Prothesis must be invoked, as proven by such examples as *irbiit* 'act of tying' and *infii'* 'a paying,' All these examples lend additional confirmation to the rule of Prothesis.

There is another rule of some interest in Maltese. Before presenting the crucial examples, consider what happens when the plural marker *u* is suffixed to imperfective singulars, such as those listed in (15), (16), and (21).

(26)

	singular		plural	
I. = (15)I				
	ní+msaḥ	'I wipe'	*ní+msḥ+u*	'we wipe'
	tí+msaḥ	'you wipe'	*tí+msḥ+u*	'you wipe'

ní+sha'	'I smash'	*ní+sh'+u*	'we smash'
tí+sha'	'you smash'	*tí+sh'+u*	'you smash'

II. = (15)II

ní+kteb	'I write'	*ní+ktb+u*	'we write'
tí+kteb	'you write'	*tí+ktb+u*	'you write'
ní+zfen	'I dance'	*ní+zfn+u*	'we dance'
tí+zfen	'you dance'	*tí+zfn+u*	'you dance'

III. = (16)I

nó+bzo'	'I spit'	*nó+bz'+u*	'we spit'
tó+bzo'	'you spit'	*tó+bz'+u*	'you spit'
nó+'tol	'I kill'	*nó+'tl+u*	'we kill'
tó+'tol	'you kill'	*tó+'tl+u*	'you kill'

IV. = (16)II

ní+dhol	'I enter'	*ní+dhl+u*	'we enter'
tí+dhol	'you enter'	*tí+dhl+u*	'you enter'
ní+zbor	'I prune'	*ní+zbr+u*	'we prune'
tí+zbor	'you prune'	*tí+zbr+u*	'you prune'

V. = (21)I

ná+'sam	'I divide'	*ná+'sm+u*	'we divide'
tá+'sam	'you divide'	*tá+'sm+u*	'you divide'
ná+hsad	'I reap'	*ná+hsd+u*	'we reap'
tá+hsad	'you reap'	*tá+hsd+u*	'you reap'

VI. = (21)II

ná+'bez	'I jump'	*ná+'bz+u*	'we jump'
tá+'bez	'you jump'	*tá+'bz+u*	'you jump'
ná+hdem	'I work'	*ná+hdm+u*	'we work'
tá+hdem	'you work'	*tá+hdm+u*	'you work'

The examples listed in (26) exemplify the method of forming the plural of the imperfective nonderived conjugation. The plurals are formed from the singulars by suffixation of *u*. That is, the more abstract pattern $CV+CCVC+u$ underlies the plurals of (26).[9] The stem-vowel of these plurals is dropped

---

[9]It may be possible to generalize the perfective and imperfective stems at a more abstract level of analysis to the shape $CVCVC$, which would mean that these imperfectives derive from $CV+CVCVC+u$. The rule that drops the first stem-vowel, however, is not Apocope, which a comparison of this more abstract representation with Stress Assignment

by the rule of Apocope. In this way, *ní+msaḥ+u* becomes
ní+msḥ+u, *nó+bzo'+u* becomes *nó+bz'+u*, and so forth. However, there is another plural pattern corresponding to many of
the singulars of (15), (16), and (21). This pattern is illustrated
in the following:

(27)   singular   plural

     I. = (15)II

ní+tlef	'I lose'	*ni+tîlf+u*	'we lose'
tí+tlef	'you lose'	*ti+tîlf+u*	'you lose'
ní+dneb	'I sin'	*ni+dínb+u*	'we sin'
tí+dneb	'you sin'	*ti+dínb+u*	'you sin'

     II. = (16)I

nó+krob	'I groan'	*no+kórb+u*	'we groan'
tó+krob	'you groan'	*to+kórb+u*	'you groan'
nó+'mos	'I kick'	*no+'óms+u*	'we kick'
tó+'mos	'you kick'	*to+'óms+u*	'you kick'

     III. = (16)II

ní+tlob	'I pray'	*ni+tólb+u*	'we pray'
tí+tlob	'you pray'	*ti+tólb+u*	'you pray'
ní+šrob	'I drink'	*ni+šórb+u*	'we drink'
tí+šrob	'you drink'	*ti+šórb+u*	'you drink'

     IV. = (21)I

nâ+ḥrab	'I flee'	*na+ḥárb+u*	'we flee'
tâ+ḥrab	'you flee'	*ta+ḥárb+u*	'you flee'
nâ+ḥra'	'I burn'	*na+ḥár'+u*	'we burn'
tâ+ḥra'	'you burn'	*ta+ḥár'+u*	'you burn'

     V. = (21)II

nâ+'leb	'I overturn'	*na+'ílb+u*	'we overturn'
tâ+'leb	'you overturn'	*ta+'ílb+u*	'you overturn'
nâ+hleb	'I milk'	*na+hílb+u*	'we milk'
tâ+ḥleb	'you milk'	*ta+hílb+u*	'you milk'

---

will show. The two rules are similar but still different. The new rule
might be stated as follows:

(i) $V \rightarrow \phi/V+C \underline{\quad\quad} CV$

It applies before Stress Assignment, whereas Apocope applies after
stress is assigned. In this paper, I shall continue to refer to the imperfective stem *CCVC* as underlying.

The plurals listed in (27) differ from those of (26) in possessing a vowel in the stem itself. The plural pattern of (27) is $CV+CVCC+u$, whereas in (26) it is $CV+CCC+u$. Furthermore, the vowel that does show up in the stem of the plurals of (27) is the same vowel that appears in the singulars between the second and third radicals in underlying representations. (Recall that e derives from i by Vowel Reduction.) Thus, it appears that the stem-vowel and the second root segment of these plurals have metathesized. In the examples of (26), the stem-vowel has simply elided. The plurals of (27) may be distinguished from those of (26) by the following diagnostic: The medial root segment of all the forms listed in (27) is invariably a member of the class R, that is, r, l, m, or n, which is never true of the medial root segment of the forms listed in (26). The basis for formulating a rule of metathesis to account for the plurals of (27) is therefore evident. The following rule will bring about the desired change.

(28)   METATHESIS: CRVCV → CVRCV

By this rule, $ni+tlif+u$ becomes $ni+tilf+u$, $no+krob+u$ becomes $no+korb+u$, $ni+tlob+u$ becomes $ni+tolb+u$, $na+ḥrab+u$ becomes $na+ḥarb+u$, and so on. However, $ni+zfin+u$, $no+bzo'+u$, $ni+dḥol+u$, and so on will not be affected by (28), so that the stem vowel of these examples subsequently elides by Apocope. The final vowel in the environment of (28), it should be noted, is needed to prevent the rule from applying to the singulars corresponding to the plurals cited above that undergo the rule. Further, the initial C of this environment is needed to prevent Metathesis from operating on such sequences as $rabat$ 'he tied' and $nefaḥ$, 'he blew.'

There is one further point to be cleared up concerning the operation of Metathesis. This rule clearly applies before Apocope. If Apocope applied first, the stem vowel of such examples as $ni+tlob+u$ would be lost. If Metathesis applied before Apocope, however, producing, for instance, $ni+tolb+u$, the vowel of the prefix would drop by Apocope, leaving $n+tolb+u$, to which Prothesis would apply. But the prefix-vowel does not drop. It seems inevitable that Stress Assignment will be utilized to ensure the desired result. The following derivations are illustrative of this treatment.

(29)   *ni+tlob+u*   *ni+tlif+u*

        nî+tlob+u   *nî⊦tlif+u*   STRESS ASSIGNMENT

        nî+tolb+u   *nî+tilf+u*   METATHESIS

        nî+tólb+u   *nî+tílf+u*   STRESS ASSIGNMENT[10]

          —   —   APOCOPE

In other words, the prefixes will be stressed by Stress Assignment, just as in the case of the underlying plurals of (26). However, Stress Assignment must reapply after Metathesis, and the remnants of the prefix stress are sufficient to prevent the rule of Apocope from affecting this vowel, since (4) requires that the relevant vowel be [-str]. There may be a quite natural explanation for the reapplication of Stress Assignment. Consider the examples *hatf+ît+kom* 'she grabbed you (pl.)' and *bez'+ît+l+ek* 'she spit to you' mentioned earlier in connection with Vowel Reduction. These sequences derive from the more basic *hataf+it+kom* and *beza'+it+l+ik*. If Stress Assignment applies directly to these strings, however, a situation will arise that will lead to the wrong results. Thus, if Stress Assignment applies to yield *hataf+ît+kom* and *beza'+ît+l+ik*, Apocope will apply and delete both stem vowels, leaving **htf+ît+kom* and **bz'+ ît+l+ik*.[11] One way of overcoming this difficulty is to assume that Stress Assignment applies

---

[10]By convention, all stresses present when Stress Assignment applies are weakened. The grave accent may be taken as secondary accent.

[11]According to Chomsky and Halle (1968), such a rule as (4) would abbreviate the following disjunctively ordered rules (as well as others):

(i) $\begin{bmatrix} V \\ -str \end{bmatrix} \rightarrow \emptyset / \_\_\_ C+V$

(ii) $\begin{bmatrix} V \\ -str \end{bmatrix} \rightarrow \emptyset / \_\_\_ C V$

In *hataf+ît+kom* and *beza'+ît+l+ik*, there are two environments for Apocope for each word—one that (i) would affect and one that (ii) would affect. Notice that these domains for the application of Apocope are overlapping in such a way as to make the disjunctive principle irrelevant. However, on the basis of slim evidence, Chomsky and Halle have proposed that in cases of such overlapping environments as these, the longest expansion of a rule be applied first; cf. pp. 365–366. If this proposal is correct, (i) will apply first in the case of both representations cited above, giving *hatf+ît+kom* and *bez'+ît l+ik*, as desired. Notice that the prior application of (i) serves to block (ii). This proposal constitutes another possible explanation for these data. The correctness of Chomsky and Halle's proposal must await more empirical examples.

in a cyclic fashion. Subject pronouns will be included in the first cycle. Object pronouns and other material will be included in the second cycle.[12] In this way, the correct phonetic representations can be derived.

(30) [[ḥataf+it]kom] [[beza'+it]l+ik]
  ḥátaf+it   *béza'+it*   STRESS ASSIGNMENT

  ḥàtaf+ĭt+kom   *bèza'+ît+l+ĭk*   STRESS ASSIGNMENT
  ḥàtf+ĭt+kom   *bèz'+ît+l+ĭk*   APOCOPE
  —   *bèz'+ĭt+l+ek*   VOWEL REDUCTION

On the first cycle, only the innermost brackets are scanned and Stress Assignment gives *ḥátaf+it* and *béza'+it*. If there were no more cycles, Apocope and Vowel Reduction would yield the third person feminine forms *ḥátf+et* 'she grabbed' and *béz'+et* 'she spit.' However, in the case of these examples there is a second cycle. On this final cycle, Stress Assignment reapplies, weakening the initially stressed vowel. This weakened stress explains why the initial stem vowel of these sequences is not lost due to Apocope. Apocope and Vowel Reduction may be assumed to be final-cycle rules, that is, rules that apply only on the final cycle. Given this quite natural interpretation of these data, it becomes evident that the reapplication of Stress Assignment in (29) may also be due to the cyclic nature of this rule. Indeed, it is the stem and the subject pronoun that are relevant to the first cycle; the extra material, that is, the plural marker, is crucial to the final cycle. If this explanation is correct, (29) may be replaced by (31).

(31) [[ni+tlob]u] [[ni+tlif]u]
  nî+tlob   *nî+tlif*   STRESS ASSIGNMENT

---

  nî+tolb+u   *nî+tilf+u*   METATHESIS
  nì+tólb+u   *nì+tîlf+u*   STRESS ASSIGNMENT
  —   —   APOCOPE

In this instance, Stress Assignment also applies cyclically. However, Metathesis must precede Stress Assignment on the final cycle, for the latter rule creates the new environment

---

[12]An attempt has been made to justify the same kind of cycle for another dialect of Arabic; cf. Brame (in press) and (to appear *b*).

relevant to the reapplication of Stress Assignment. Again, Apocope will have no effect on these derivations.[13]

The careful reader will have noted that, although there are six classes of verbs listed in (26), there are only five listed in (27). Missing from (27) is a class corresponding to (26)I, that is, a class of metathesizing verbs drawn from (15)I. This class may now be illustrated.

(32)   singular   plural
      = (15)I

ní+fraḥ	'I rejoice'	*ni+fírḥ+u*	'we rejoice'
tí+fraḥ	'you rejoice'	*ti+fírḥ+u*	'you rejoice'
ní+tla'	'I leave'	*ni+tíl'+u*	'we leave'
tí+tla'	'you leave'	*ti+tíl'+u*	'you leave'
ní+sra'	'I steal'	*ni+sír'+u*	'we steal'
tí+sra'	'you steal'	*ti+sír'+u*	'you steal'

Here the stem-vowel of the plural forms, that is, the meta-thesizing vowel, appears to differ from that of the singular. However, notice that the segment *ḥ* or *'* occupies the third root position of all these verbs. These are the segments that initiate Guttural Assimilation, the rule that turns *i* to *a* before low back consonants. Thus, if the stem vowel of these verbs is assumed to be *i*, the *a* of the singular is accounted for by Guttural Assimilation. This underlying *i* will account for the vowel of the plurals, if Metathesis is required to apply before Guttural Assimilation. This class of verbs, therefore, is automatically explained by the rules already postulated.

There is much more that could be said about Metathesis.[14]

---

[13]There is a question concerning the precise status of the weakened stress in phonetic representations. One tends to hear a weakened stress, but this delicate question of phonetic detail is best answered by a native speaker. If no weakened stress is actually present in the surface representation, however, we need only propose a further rule that eliminates the nonphonetic material.

[14]For example, the careful reader may have noted a similarity between Metathesis and Prothesis. The latter breaks up clusters of the shape #*RC*; the former prevents clusters of the shape *CRC* from arising. One attempt to reduce these phenomena to a single fact is to forego Metathesis in favor of Apocope along with a generalized version of Prothesis. That is, *CV+CRVC+V* might first become *CV+CRC+V* and then *CV+CVRC+V*. This interesting possibility is met with some difficulties that are discussed in detail in Brame (to appear *a*). For the present, we may assume that there are two rules operative in Maltese phonology.

The preceding discussion will be sufficient for the main arguments that follow below.

Another metathesis rule appears to be operative in Maltese. This rule may be introduced by noting such perfective verbs as *ǰarr* 'he carried,' *ḥább* 'he loved,' *béšš* 'he sprinkled,' and *méss* 'he touched.' This class of verbs is characterized by having identical second and third root segments. For this reason this class is often referred to as the class of "doubled" verbs. In many respects these verbs behave very much like those verbs possessing three distinct root segments, that is, like the verbs that are formed according to the pattern *CVCVC*, for instance, *sera'* 'he stole,' *kîteb* 'he wrote,' and *'átel* 'he killed.' The past participle of the latter verbs is formed according to the pattern *mV+CCuuC*: *mi+sruu'* 'stolen,' *mi+ktuub* 'written,' and *ma+'tuul* 'killed.' This same pattern is found in connection with the doubled forms: *ma+ḥbuub* 'loved,' *mi+bšuuš* 'sprinkled,' and *mi+msuus* 'touched.' Similarly, one of the derived verb classes is formed from the nonderived verb according to the following rule: $C_i VC_j VC_k \rightarrow C_i VC_j C_j VC_k$. That is, this class is formed by doubling the medial radical of the basic root. Thus, *'ábez* 'he jumped,' in this derived class, is *'ábbez* 'he boosted.' Similarly, corresponding to the nonderived doubled verb *béšš* 'he sprinkled,' one finds *beššeš* 'he sprinkled' in the derived formation. These data can be summarized as (33).

(33)   basic verb   past participle   derived verb
       $C_i VC_j VC_k$ $mV+C_i C_j uuC_k$ $C_i VC_j C_j VC_k$
       $C_i VC_j C_j$ $mV+C_i C_j uuC_j$ $C_i VC_j C_j VC_j$

The similarities in derivational patterns that the normal verbs and the doubled verbs exhibit lead one to suspect that the basic verbs of both classes should be reduced to one. If they are reduced, whatever rules are needed to account for the derivational material will be simplified. The doubled verb class may be generalized with the normal class if it is derived from the more abstract pattern $C_i VC_j VC_j$. A rule will then be needed to convert underlying $C_i VC_j VC_j$ into superficial $C_i VC_j C_j$. Two possibilities readily come to mind. First, the second stem-vowel may simply be dropped when it appears between identical segments in underlying representations. Second, $C_i VC_j VC_j$ may be changed to $C_i VVC_j C_j$ by a rule of metathesis, whereupon a second rule of truncation will

be needed to delete one of the two morae. The second alternative appears to be the correct approach; consider the
following imperfective doubled verbs: *t+ḥóbb* 'you love,'
t+bíšš 'you sprinkle,' and *t+míss* 'you touch.' The normal imperfective pattern is *CV+CCVC*, as in *tí+sra'* 'you steal,'
tí+kteb 'you write,' and *tó+'tol* 'you kill.' The doubled forms
are also reducible to this pattern, but the underlying representations would be *ti+ḥbob*, *ti+bšiš*, *ti+msis*, and so on. To
derive the correct phonetic representations, the following
derivations are required:

(34)   *ti+ḥbob* *ti+bšiš* *ti+msis*
        ti+ḥobb *ti+bišš* *ti+miss* new rule
        ti+ḥóbb *ti+bíšš* *ti+míss* STRESS ASSIGNMENT
        t+ḥóbb   *t+bíšš* *t+míss* APOCOPE

Only a metathesis rule will lead to the desired results. This
new rule may be stated as (35).[15]

(35)   IDENTICAL CONSONANT METATHESIS:

$$[+\text{seg}]\ C_j VC_j \rightarrow [+\text{seg}]\ VC_j C_j$$

If this rule is correct, the perfective forms cited above must
derive according to (36).

(36)   *ǰarVr* *habVb* *bešVš* *mesVs*
        ǰaVrr *ḥaVbb* *beVšš* *meVss* I.C. METATHESIS
        ǰarr   *ḥabb*   *bešš*   *mess* TRUNCATION
        ǰárr   *ḥább*   *béšš*   *méss* STRESS ASSIGNMENT

That is, a new rule of Truncation is needed. This rule may be
stated as (37).

(37)   TRUNCATION: $V \rightarrow \emptyset\ /\ V\_\_\_CC$

There is additional evidence proving that Identical Consonant
Metathesis (= I.C. Metathesis) is a rule of Maltese, which
lends credence to derivations (34) and (36). There is a class
of nouns in Maltese referring to instruments. This class of
nouns is formed according to the pattern *mV+CCVC* or
mV+CCC+a. The latter derives from *mV+CCVC+a* by Apocope. Consider such nouns as *mí+nfaḥ* 'bellows' and *ma+tḥn+a*

---

[15]Note that the feature [+seg] is needed to prevent (35) from operating
on such examples as *ti+tla'* 'you leave.'

'mill.' When a doubled stem is involved, however, the pattern differs. One finds *im+'áss* 'scissors,' *im+ḥádd+a* 'pillow,' and *im+ḥákk+a* 'grater.' But these doubled forms are reducible to the normal pattern if I.C. Metathesis is incorporated into the phonology.

(38)
mV+'sas	*mV+ḥdad+a*	*mV+ḥkak+a*	
mV+'ass	*mV+hadd+a*	*mV+ḥakk+a*	I.C. METATHESIS
mV+'áss	*mV+ḥádd+a*	*mV+ḥákk+a*	STRESS ASSIGNMENT
m+'áss	*m+ḥádd+a*	*m+ḥákk+a*	APOCOPE
im+'áss	*im+ḥádd+a*	*im+ḥákk+a*	PROTHESIS

Because the rules of I.C. Metathesis and Truncation allow for so much of the morphology of Maltese to be generalized, it is probably correct to assume that these rules are operative in the phonology.[16]

In the preceding discussion a number of phonological rules of Maltese have been motivated. These rules may now be summarized.

(39)   I.C. METATHESIS: $[+\text{seg}] \ C_j VC_j \rightarrow [+\text{seg}] \ VC_jC_j$

TRUNCATION: $V \rightarrow \emptyset \ / \ V \underline{\quad} CC$

STRESS ASSIGNMENT: $V \rightarrow [+\text{str}] / \underline{\quad} C_0((VC)VC_0^1) \ \#]$

VOWEL HARMONY: $i \rightarrow o \ / \left\{ \begin{array}{l} oC_0 \underline{\quad} \\ \underline{\quad} \left[\begin{array}{l} +\text{cns} \\ \left\{ \begin{array}{l} +\text{son} \\ -\text{cor} \end{array} \right\} \end{array} \right] C_0 o \end{array} \right\}$

METATHESIS: $CRVCV \rightarrow CVRCV$

STRESS ASSIGNMENT: as above

APOCOPE: $\left[\begin{array}{l} V \\ -\text{str} \end{array} \right] \rightarrow \emptyset \ / \underline{\quad} CV$

PROTHESIS: $\emptyset \rightarrow i \ / \underline{\quad} RC$

GUTTURAL ASSIMILATION: $i \rightarrow a \ / \underline{\quad} \left[\begin{array}{l} +\text{cns} \\ +\text{bk} \\ +\text{lo} \end{array} \right]$

VOWEL REDUCTION: $i \rightarrow e \ / \acute{V}C_0 \underline{\quad}$

Recall that Stress Assignment is a cyclic rule. Although it is stated twice in (39), it is a single rule in the grammar. (39) simply illustrates how Stress Assignment is to reapply on

---

[16]There appear to be several classes of exceptions to I.C. Metathesis, one being the plurals of the shape CVC_jVC_j; cf. *sodod* 'beds' and *botˢotˢ* 'light bulbs.'

the final cycle. All other rules, with the exception of I.C. Metathesis and Truncation, are rules that apply on the final cycle. If I.C. Metathesis were post-cyclic, the prefixal vowel of the plurals corresponding to (34) would not be elided. That is, underlying $[[ti+ḥbob]u]$ would receive stress on the prefixal vowel on the first cycle, which would ensure that it did not elide on the final cycle, very much as in (30) and (31). But since we wish to derive *t+ḥóbb+u* 'you (pl.) love,' I.C. Metathesis must be either cyclic or precyclic. The rule of Truncation will also be assumed to be precyclic. Several of the ordering relationships given in (39) were not established above. For example, given what has gone before, it is not clear that Guttural Assimilation follows Prothesis. It could just as well follow Metathesis or Apocope.

3. A Set of Apparent Exceptions

A sizable class of forms of the native vocabulary of Maltese are prima facie exceptions to many of the rules listed in (39). One set of apparent exceptions is listed in (40).

(40)

	singular		plural	
nó+'ood	'I stay'	*no+'óod+u*	'we stay'
tó+'ood	'you stay'	*to+'óod+u*	'you stay'
nó+bood	'I hate'	*no+bóod+u*	'we hate'
tó+bood	'you hate'	*to+bóod+u*	'you hate'
nî+sool	'I cough'[17]	*ni+sóol+u*	'we cough'[17]
tî+sool	'you cough'[17]	*ti+sóol+u*	'you cough'[17]
nî+soob	'I lament'	*ni+sóob+u*	'we lament'
tî+soob	'you lament'	*ti+sóob+u*	'you lament'
nî+laab	'I play'	*ni+láab+u*	'we play'
tî+laab	'you play'	*ti+láab+u*	'you play'
nî+baat	'I send'	*ni+báat+u*	'we send'
tî+baat	'you send'	*ti+báat+u*	'you send'

Although the plurals listed in (40) are correctly stressed by the rule of Stress Assignment, the singulars exhibit a stress pattern quite unlike that predicted by this rule; compare (8) and (9). Moreover, the plurals of (40) are exceptional, but here it is the rule of Apocope that is expected to apply. It is

---

[17]The vowel length of these examples can easily be heard by contrasting them with words possessing short vowels, e.g. *soolt* 'I coughed,' vs. *solt* 'penny,' from *sold* by devoicing of the final obstruent; cf. fn. 2.

not obvious how either of these exceptional classes could be handled by a rule-feature approach of the type mentioned in section 1 in connection with the Sanskrit example. In such a framework, not only would the singulars have to be marked as exceptions to the normal rule that assigns stress, but they would also have to be marked to undergo a new ad hoc rule of stress placement. The plurals, however, would not be marked in any way. But this possibility can be refuted, since the singulars of (40) do undergo the normal rule of Stress Assignment. If the second person singular suffix is appended to these verbs, the resulting forms are stressed according to (5), for example, *no+bóod+ok* 'I hate you' and *ni+báat+ek* 'I send you.' Notice that here, as in the case of the plurals of (40), the prefix vowel is not elided by Apocope as expected. It also seems wrong to mark the prefix vowels of these and the plurals of (40) as exceptions to Apocope, since the same prefix vowel does elide in other examples, for instance, (34), the change of *ti+'áttel* to *t+'áttel*.

Another class of apparent exceptions to a rule listed in (39) is the following set:

(41)   *nó+odos*   'I dive'   *tó+odos*   'you dive'
        nó+oǰob   'I please'   *tó+oǰob*   'you please'
        nó+otoɤ   'I stumble'   *tó+otoɤ*   'you stumble'

Apparently the right-most stem vowel initiates Regressive Vowel Harmony in these forms. But the harmony propagates over the forbidden coronal segments excluded by (17). To account for the examples of (41), either a new rule or a revision of (17) would be needed.

A further set of apparent exceptions is the following set of perfective verbs:

(42)   *'aád+t*   'I stayed'   *'aád+na*   'we stayed'
        baád+t   'I hated'   *baád+na*   'we hated'
        soól+t   'I coughed'   *soól+na*   'we coughed'
        soób+t   'I lamented'   *soób+na*   'we lamented'

We must explain why these forms do not undergo Truncation, rule (37). These examples may now be compared with the following:

(43)   I   II
        imaád+t   'I chewed'   *'aád+t*   'I stayed'
        imaád+na   'we chewed'   *'aád+na*   'we stayed'

máad	'he chewed'	ʕáad	'he stayed'
máad+et	'she chewed'	ʕáad+et	'she stayed'
inaás+t	'I dozed'	baád+t	'I hated'
inaás+na	'we dozed'	baád+na	'we hated'
náas	'he dozed'	báad	'he hated'
náas+et	'she dozed'	báad+et	'she hated'
ilaá'+t	'I licked'	soól+t	'I coughed'
ilaá'+na	'we licked'	soól+na	'we coughed'
láa'	'he licked'	sóol	'he coughed'
láa'+et	'she licked'	sóol+et	'she coughed'
iraáy+t	'I grazed'	daáy+t	'I cursed'
iraáy+na	'we grazed'	daáy+na	'we cursed'
rá	'he grazed'[18]	dá	'he cursed'[18]
ráat	'she grazed'[18]	dáat	'she cursed'[18]

All examples of first and second person forms listed in (43) are exceptions to Truncation. Furthermore, all the third person forms of column I find a corresponding pattern in column II. But there is a difference between the first and second person forms listed under column I and those listed under column II. All the first and second person forms listed under column I possess an initial *i*, which does not show up in any of the forms of column II. Besides explaining why these forms do not undergo Truncation, two additional facts need explaining. First, why is it that the *i* appears in the examples of column I and not in those of column II? And second, why does this *i* not appear in the third person forms as well? Part of the answer is suggested by comparing the forms of (43) with those listed below.

(44)

imrád+t	'I became sick'	brám+t	'I twisted'
imrád+na	'we became sick'	brám+na	'we twisted'
márad	'he became sick'	báram	'he twisted'
márd+et	'she became sick'	bárm+et	'she twisted'
infáh+t	'I blew'	srá'+t	'I stole'
infáh+na	'we blew'	srá'+na	'we stole'
néfah	'he blew'	séra'	'he stole'
néfh+et	'she blew'	sér'+et	'she stole'

---

[18]These forms derive from stems with third radical glides. The rules that eliminate glides will not be discussed here. Cf. Brame (to appear *c*) for a discussion of these processes.

irkíb+t	'I rode'	*knîs+t*	'I swept'
irkíb+na	'we rode'	*knîs+na*	'we swept'
ríkeb	'he rode'	*kínes*	'he swept'
ríkb+et	'she rode'	*kíns+et*	'she swept'
il'át+t	'I hit'	*ḥtâf+t*	'I grabbed'
il'át+na	'we hit'	*ḥtâf+na*	'we grabbed'
lá'at	'he hit'	*ḥátaf*	'he grabbed'
lá't+et	'she hit'	*ḥátf+et*	'she grabbed'

From the earlier discussion, it is clear that all the forms listed in (44) possess underlying stems of the shape *CVCVC*; the first and second person forms undergo the rule of Apocope, as does the third person feminine. Thus, *barám+t* becomes *brâm+t*, *será'+t* becomes *srá'+t*, and so forth. The forms of column I also undergo this rule: for instance, *marád+t* → *mrád+t* and *nefáḥ+t* → *nfáḥ+t*. But all the examples of column I begin with one of the segments *m, n, r,* or *l,* the class of segments that are fundamental in triggering the rule of Prothesis. Thus, *mrád+t* becomes *imrád+t*, and *nfáḥ+t* becomes *infáḥ+t*. None of the examples listed under column II undergoes this rule, since the initial root segment found in these forms is not a member of the class *R*. Since the initial stem vowel of the third person forms of column I is not elided by Apocope, there is no prothetic *i* in these examples. The parallelism between the forms entered in (44) and those listed in (43) is unmistakable. In column I of (43), as in (44), the first root position is occupied by one of the members of *R*. But none of these segments occupies the first root position in column II of (43), again as in (44). It thus appears certain that the initial *i* of the examples of (43)I is inserted by the rule of Prothesis. However, without an abstract analysis, these forms must undergo the rule exceptionally, since no consonant follows the initial liquids in any of the forms of (43)I. Without an abstract approach, only an ad hoc bifurcation of the first-second person forms and the third person forms is required, so that the latter will not exceptionally undergo Prothesis. This approach is certainly the least desired of all possible analyses, for it is unrelated to other phenomena in the grammar.

4. The Abstract Segment

The examples of (43)I offer an important clue to the discovery of how these apparent exceptions are to be treated.

Since initial consonant clusters are essential to the application of Prothesis, the fact that these forms must undergo the rule suggests that an additional consonant was present in these forms at the point in the derivation when Prothesis applied. Suppose that the stems underlying *naas, maad, laaʼ,* and so forth possess three underlying root segments, just as the normal verbs of Maltese, for instance, (44). That is, the stem underlying these forms is of the pattern *CVXVC*, where *X* represents the segment in question. If *X* is a consonant, the distribution of prothetic *i* in (43) is predictable. This situation may be illustrated by taking the verb 'to lick' as representative of the derivation.

(45)

laXaʼ+t	*laXaʼ+na*	*laXaʼ*	*laXaʼ+et*	
—	—	—	—	I.C. METATHESIS AND TRUNCATION
laXáʼ+t	*laXáʼ+na*	*láXaʼ*	*láXaʼ+et*	STRESS ASSIGNMENT
lXáʼ+t	*lXáʼ+na*	—	*láXʼ+et*	APOCOPE
ilXáʼ+t	*ilXáʼ+na*	—	—	PROTHESIS
ilaáʼ+t	*ilaáʼ+na*	*láaʼ*	*láaʼ+et*	later rules

Notice that (45) accounts not only for the distribution of prothetic *i*, but it also accounts for why we find long vowels in the examples of (42) and (43), that is, why these forms are not affected by Truncation.

This approach can also be utilized to account for the stress patterns of the singulars of (40). The usual pattern of the singular imperfect is *CV+CCVC*. Consequently, the troublesome forms of (40) may be assumed to be *CV+CXVC* in underlying representations, where once again *X* stands for some consonant whose identity is yet to be disclosed. This underlying sequence will allow for the correct assignment of stress by the normal stress rule.

(46)

ni+ʼXod	*ni+sXol*	*ni+lXab*	
ni+ʼXod	*nî+sXol*	*ni+lXab*	STRESS ASSIGNMENT
nó+ʼXod	—	—	VOWEL HARMONY
nó+ʼood	*ni+sool*	*ni+laab*	later rules

Consider now the problem of predicting the stress of the plural forms of (40), for instance, *no+ʼóod+u, ni+sóol+u,* and *ni+láab+u.* If there is an additional underlying consonant *X*, then these forms are underlying *ni+ʼXod+u, ni+sXol+u,* and *ni+lXab+u* and should receive stress on the first syllable, not on the second. Thus, whereas the segment X appears to solve the problem of stress in the singulars, it creates new problems in the case of the plurals. However, it is to be recalled that the plurals of (40) are exceptional in another way: it is expected that their prefix vowels should elide by Apocope, which does not happen. In fact, it is this prefix vowel which is stressed if the plurals are assigned the more abstract representations *ni+'Xod+u*, *ni+sXol+u*, and *ni+lXab+u*. In other words, the prior assignment of stress to the prefix vowels of these representations may be utilized to explain the lack of elision of the same vowels by Apocope. This stress assignment explains the lack of Apocope in the case of the plurals of (27); compare (31). Indeed, stress shifts in the plurals of (40) in much the same fashion as it does in (27). This difference in stress assignment may be clarified by the following paradigms:

(47)   I   II

= (27)		= (40)	
nó+'mos	'I kick'	nó+'ood	'I stay'
no+'óms+u	'we kick'	no+'óod+u	'we stay'
tó+'mos	'you kick'	tó+'ood	'you stay'
to+'óms+u	'you (pl.) kick'	to+'óod+u	'you (pl.) stay'
nî+šrob	'I drink'	nî+sool	'I cough'
ni+šórb+u	'we drink'	ni+sóol+u	'we cough'
tî+šrob	'you drink'	tî+sool	'you cough'
ti+šórb+u	'you (pl.) drink'	ti+sóol+u	'you (pl.) cough'
nâ+ḥra'	'I burn'	nî+laab	'I play'
na+ḥár'+u	'we burn'	ni+láab+u	'we play'
tâ+ḥra'	'you burn'	tî+laab	'you play'
ta+ḥár'+u	'you (pl.) burn'	ti+láab+u	'you (pl.) play'

The two classes of examples in (47) are alike in two respects: Both exhibit the same stress patterns, and the plurals of both possess $\breve{V}CV$ sequences, which is contrary to Apocope. The lack of vowel elision in (47)I has already been explained. Paramount to this explanation was the rule of Metathesis. Because of the parallelism that exists between (47)I and (47)II, the same explanation can now be utilized for (47)II. This explanation entails one new assumption—that the segment X is a member of the class R, together with r, l, m, and n. If this assumption is accepted, the plurals of (40) are explained by the following derivations:

(48)

[[ni+'Xod]u]	[[ni+sXol]u]	[[ni+lXab]u]	
nî+'Xod	*nî+sXol*	*nî+lXab*	STRESS ASSIGNMENT
nó+'Xod+u	—	—	VOWEL HARMONY
nó+'oXd+u	*ni+soXl+u*	*ni+laXb+u*	METATHESIS
nò+'óXd+u	*nì+sóXl+u*	*nì+láXb+u*	STRESS ASSIGNMENT
—	—	—	APOCOPE
nò+'óod+u	*nì+sóol+u*	*nì+láab+u*	later rules

In this manner, these plurals are quite naturally explained, as are most of the otherwise exceptional phenomena presented in section 3. Postulating abstract X provides an explanation that is related to other phenomena in the grammar.

5. Pinpointing the Abstract Segment

Although recourse to abstract X provides a solution to a number of complex problems of Maltese phonology, its use will be convincing only if the exact nature of X can be discovered and if X can be shown to exhibit a distribution similar to other root segments. The latter desideratum implies that X must be found to occupy all root positions in one form or another. That is, just as r shows up in the first, second, and third root positions in *rabat* 'he tied,' *baram* 'he twisted,' and *ḥafar* 'he chose,' a similar distribution must be found for X. In this section I shall attempt to determine the features defining the segment X and to show that the distribution of X is like that of the other root consonants. On the first point, a good deal of information about the properties of X has already emerged from the earlier discussion. The segment X is clearly a consonant, since it functions as such in its association with the rules of Truncation, Stress Assignment, Metathesis, and Prothesis. Furthermore, it behaves much like the liquids and nasals r, l, m, and n in participating in Metathesis. Yet X cannot be any of these particular segments, since these do not become vowels, which we know X must become; compare (45), (46), and (48). Thus, X is a consonant, a member of the class R, and later becomes a vowel. The possibility that X is a glide comes to mind. But X cannot be w or y, for, as noted earlier, *ni+swu'* and *ni+zyid* become *in+síu'* 'I drive,' and *in+ziid* 'I add,' quite a different behavior from that of forms with medial radical X, for instance, *nî+laab* 'I play.'

All the examples with abstract X discussed in section 4 were cases in which X occupied the medial root position. Thus, the root underlying *nî+laab* and *ni+láab+u* of (47) in *lXb*. Let us now turn to a possible argument for X as the first root segment, which in turn will help to identify X. Consider again the examples listed in (41). These are repeated below as (49).

(49)   *nó+odos*   'I dive'   *tó+odos*   'you dive'
        nó+ojob   'I please'   *tó+ojob*   'you please'
        nó+otor   'I stumble'   *tó+otor*   'you stumble'

If these forms were derived from underlying $Ci+XCoC$ sequences and if X were a [-cor] segment, Vowel Harmony would apply to yield the desired $Co+XCoC$ sequences. Alternatively, if X were a member of the class R, which is also included in the harmony rule, the correct application of this rule would be ensured.

(50)   *ni+Xdos   ni+Xjob   ni+Xtor*
        nî+Xdos   nî+Xjob   nî+Xtor   STRESS ASSIGNMENT
        nó+Xdos   nó+Xjob   nó+Xtor   VOWEL HARMONY
        nó+odos   nó+ojob   nó+otor   later rules

(Note that whatever rules are needed to change X to *o* are independently needed for derivations such as (48).) These examples indicate that X is either [-cor] or else a member of the class R, or perhaps both. It was argued above that medial radical X is a member of the class R, as in (48). There are cases, therefore, where X fits in nicely as the first radical segment. Only one position in the root remains to be filled, the third root segment. Several facts converge to prove that X is also required in this environment. Consider the following examples:[19]

(51)   I   II
        ni+sîma+u 'we hear'   *nî+tfa+u* 'we throw'
        ti+sîma+u 'you (pl.) hear'   *tî+tfa+u* 'you (pl.) throw'

---

[19]Actually what is represented as final *u* in (51) is *w* in phonetic representations. This *w* is the result of a late rule. Note that, without a more abstract approach, the stress of the examples of (51)I is anomalous if Stress Assignment applies after the *w* is formed, and the stress of the examples of (51)II is anomalous if stress is assigned before the *w* is formed. This difficult problem is cleared up once the abstract solution is adopted.

ni+zîra+u	'we sow'	*nî+bza+u*	'we fear'
ti+zîra+u	'you (pl.) sow'	*tî+bza+u*	'you (pl.) fear'
ni+bîla+u	'we swallow'	*nî+nza+u*	'we undress'
ti+bîla+u	'you (pl.) swallow'	*tî+nza+u*	'you (pl.) undress'
na+'îla+u	'we earn'	*ná+'ta+u*	'we cut'
ta +'îla+u	'you (pl.) earn'	*tá+'ta+u*	'you (pl.) cut'

Here we must ask why the vowel of the subject prefix of (51)I does not elide by Apocope. The absence of stressed *i* in the examples of column II should also be accounted for. Once again, there is an obvious parallelism between the (51)I examples and the plurals of (27) on the one hand and between the (51)II examples and the plurals of (26) on the other. Indeed, all the examples of (51)I exhibit a member of *R* as the second radical segment, but none of the examples of (51)II displays *r, l, m,* or *n* as the second radical segment. This situation again suggests that the forms of column I have undergone Metathesis, but that the forms of column II have not. If *X* is posited as the third radical segment of the examples of (51), we explain why the prefix vowels of the column I examples do not elide.

(52)　[[ni+smiX]u] [[ni+tfiX]u]
　　　　nî+smiX　　*nî+tfiX*　　　STRESS ASSIGNMENT

nî+simX+u	—	METATHESIS
nî+sîmX+u	*nî+tfiX+u*	STRESS ASSIGNMENT
—	*nî ι tfX+u*	APOCOPE
nî+sîma+u	*nî+tfa+u*	later rules

This evidence confirms the need for *X* in the third root position, for without it another large class of forms, like (40) above, remains unexplained. It is now possible to utilize third radical *X* to disclose the remaining features that define this segment. Recall the verbal noun pattern *CCiiC* mentioned earlier in conjunction with Prothesis. There it was noted that such verbs as *'atel* 'he killed' and *ḥataf* 'he grabbed' form their verbal nouns according to this pattern; thus *'tiil* 'act of killing' and *ḥtiif* 'a grabbing.' Some of the verbal nouns corresponding to the verbs listed in (51) are also formed according to this pattern. But notice that in that case the segment *X* shows up as *ḥ*: *bliiḥ* 'act of swallowing,' *tfiiḥ* 'act of throwing,' and *'tiiḥ* 'cutting.'[20] The segment X shows up as $ḥ$ in another pattern. Note that the past participle of nonderived verbs in Maltese is of the pattern *mV+CCuuC*: *ma+'tuul* 'killed,' *mi+nfuuḥ* 'blown,' and *ma+ḥtuuf* 'grabbed.' The past participles corresponding to the verbs of (51) all end in $ḥ$: *mi+smuuḥ* 'heard,' *mi+bluuḥ* 'swallowed,' *ma+'luuḥ* 'earned,' *mi+tfuuḥ* 'thrown,' and *ma+'tuuḥ* 'cut.' Thus, a new phonetic alternation of X has been uncovered. It shows up as $ḥ$ after i and u. However, X cannot be underlying $ḥ$, since underlying $ḥ$ never loses its identity in the course of the phonological derivation; compare *ti+dḥol* 'you enter' of (16)II versus *ti+sool* 'you cough' of (40) for a contrast in the medial radical position; see *to+ḥlom* 'you dream' of (16)I versus *to+odos* 'you dive' of (49) for a contrast in the first root position; and, finally, compare *ti+msḥ+u* 'you (pl.) wipe' of (26)I versus *ti+tfa+u* 'you (pl.) throw' of (51) for a contrast in the third root position. Moreover, consider what happens when past participles corresponding to the verbs of (51) are made feminine, that is, when the vowel a is suffixed to the participle. In the usual case, one finds *ma+'tuul+a* 'killed,' *mi+nfuuḥ+a* 'blown,' and *ma+ḥtuuf+a* 'grabbed.' But, corresponding to the masculine past participles of (51) listed above, we find feminine past participles without phonetic $ḥ$. The data are summarized as (53).

(53)   masculine   feminine
        mi+smuuḥ   *mi+smuuw+a*   'heard'
        mi+bluuḥ   *mi+bluuw+a*   'swallowed'
        ma+'luuḥ   *ma+'luuw+a*   'earned'
        mi+tfuuḥ   *mi+tfuuw+a*   'thrown'
        ma+'tuuḥ   *ma+'tuuw+a*   'cut'

Forms with true underlying $ḥ$ never lose this segment, as stated above. Thus, we find *mi+nfuuḥ* ~ *mi+nfuuḥ+a* 'blown,' *mi+ftuuḥ* ~ *mi+ftuuḥ+a* 'opened,' and *mi+zbuuḥ* ~ *mi+zbuuḥ+a* 'painted,' in which $ḥ$ shows up in both the masculine and feminine past participles. Consequently, X cannot be $ḥ$ at the most abstract level of analysis. Nor is X the glide w or y, even though it shows up as the former in the feminine past participles of (53) and as the latter in the perfective verb forms

[20]A low-level rule inserts $ə$ after a long high vowel and before $ḥ$ and '.

corresponding to the imperfects of (51): compare *smay+t* 'I heard," *smay+na* 'we heard,' *tfay+t* 'I threw,' *tfay+na* 'we threw,' *'lay+t* 'I earned,' *'lay+na* 'we earned,' *'tay+t* 'I cut,' and *'tay+na* 'we cut,' where *y* occupies the third radical position. The segment *X* is not *w* or *y* in underlying representations, since verbs with a genuine glide in underlying representations behave quite differently[21] (as has already been demonstrated for the medial radical position). To prove that *X* is not a glide, consider such examples as *'ʀay+t* 'I read' and *'ʀay+na* 'we read,' which appear to be of the same pattern as the perfectives cited directly above. But here, the third radical *y* is the underlying segment, as shown by the fact that it shows up as *y* in the feminine past participle, for instance, *mo+'ʀiiy+a* 'read (fem.).' This form derives from basic *mo+'ʀuuy+a* by a rule that turns the *u*-grade vowels to *i* before *y*, a rule that finds independent motivation in the grammar. The various verb types may be summarized as (54).[22]

(54)

CCḥ	CCX	CCy	
ftaḥ+t	*'lay+t*	*'ʀay+t*	1st person perfective
mi+ftuuḥ+a	*ma+'luuw+a*	*mo+'ʀiiy+a*	fem. past participle
mi+ftuuḥ	*ma+'luuḥ*	*mo+'ʀi*[23]	

Let us now summarize the evidence bearing on the identification of *X*. First, *X* is a consonant, because it functions as such in a number of rules, including Truncation (cf. (45)),

[21]Further, note that the change from *w* or *y* to *ḥ* is highly suspect.

[22]I have not yet shown that *X* cannot be *w* in the third radical position, although it was demonstrated earlier for the second radical position. To prove that *X* cannot be *w* in the third radical position would require motivation of yet additional rules, as *w* typically becomes *y* in third radical *w* verbs.

[23]The form *mo'ʀi* of the third column will not be accounted for here. This form derives from *mo+'ʀuu y* by rules that are irrelevant to the present discussion. This form further proves that *X* is not a glide, however. Evidence has now been presented that *X* differs from *G*, an abbreviation for [-cns, -voc, +hi], in the second and third radical positions. It is also possible to demonstrate the same for the first radical position. Cf. *wasal* 'he arrived' vs. *oodos* 'he dived,' where *w* remains intact, but where *X* ultimately becomes *o*; or imperfective *ta+sal*, 'you arrive,' which derives from *ta+wsal* by elision of *w*, vs. *ta+ala'* 'you close,' which derives from *ta+Xla'*; see (58) below.

Stress Assignment (cf. (46) and (48)), Metathesis (cf. (48) and
(52)), Vowel Harmony (cf. (50)), and Prothesis (cf. (45)). It is
a member of the class R, since it is crucial to the operation
of Metathesis (cf. (48)). It may be [-cor], because it constitutes the first consonant of the environment of Regressive
Vowel Harmony; compare (50). It must alternate with the
vocalic segments a and o (see (45), (46), (48), (50), and (52)),
with the glides w and y (cf. (54)), and with the laryngeal h (cf.
(53)). What could X conceiveably be? The question may be
answered by considering one additional set of forms—the
singulars corresponding to the plurals listed in (51).

(55)	$ni{+}sma$	'I hear'	$ni{+}tfa$	'I throw'
	$ti{+}sma$	'you hear'	$ti{+}tfa$	'you throw'
	$ni{+}zra$	'I sow'	$ni{+}bza$	'I fear'
	$ti{+}zra$	'you sow'	$ti{+}bza$	'you fear'
	$ni{+}bla$	'I swallow'	$ni{+}nza$	'I undress'
	$ti{+}bla$	'you swallow'	$ti{+}nza$	'you undress'
	$ná{+}'la$	'I earn'	$ná{+}'ta$	'I cut'
	$tá{+}'la$	'you earn'	$tá{+}'ta$	'you cut'

Following the discussion of the plural forms, we would assume
all these forms to derive from underlying $ti{+}CCiX$ sequences.
But there is no natural way of eliminating i, so that X could
become a. It appears, then, that the a of these forms is
actually the stem vowel itself and that X has been dropped.
Further, there is a well-motivated rule that turns i to a
before the low back consonants h and ', that is, before pharyngeal and laryngeal segments. If X were a laryngeal, then i
could be changed to a quite naturally by Guttural Assimilation,
to be followed by elision of X. That is, the following derivations might obtain:

(56)	$ti{+}smiX$	$ti{+}tfiX$	
	$ti{+}smiX$	$ti{+}tfiX$	STRESS ASSIGNMENT
	$ti{+}smaX$	$ti{+}tfaX$	GUTTURAL ASSIMILATION
	$ti{+}sma$	$ti{+}tfa$	later rules

It has already been shown that X cannot be h. But neither can
X be ', since ' remains throughout the phonological derivation,
just as does h, as in $ta{+}hra'$ 'you burn' and $to{+}l'ot$ 'you hit.'
Hence X must be some other pharyngeal or laryngeal seg-

ment. Let us quickly observe the system of phonetic obstruents of Maltese, which are underlying segments as well.[24]

(57)   voiceless: p   f   t   t   t^s s   š   č   k   ḥ   '
           voiced: b   v   d   z   j   g

There are several gaps in this system.[25] There is no d^z corresponding to t^s, no $ž$ corresponding to $š$, and no voiced
counterpart to $ḥ$, that is, no voiced pharyngeal spirant, the
segment usually represented by the symbol ʕ. This latter is
precisely the segment that will account for the change of i to a
in (56). That is, like $ḥ$ and ', ʕ is a low back consonant
and, as a consequence, will trigger Guttural Assimilation. If
X is represented as underlying ʕ, a gap in the underlying sys-

---

[24]Some of the gaps are filled at the phonetic level. For example,
$ž$ derives from $š$ by Voicing Assimilation; cf. fn. 1. Thus, $li+žbah$ 'you
resemble' derives from $ti+šbah$; cf. $šebḥ$ 'resemblance.'

[25]The segments p, v, t^s, $č$, and g are typically associated with the
foreign vocabulary, which is extensive in Maltese. There is a question
about the underlying status of j. It may derive from the more abstract
g. Consider the following native vocabulary:

I		II	
$il+bieb$	'the door'	$it+tifel$	'the boy'
$il+fomm$	'the mouth'	$id+deeb$	'the gold'
$il+melḥ$	'the salt'	$in+nisa$	'the women'
$il+kelb$	'the dog'	$ir+raḥal$	'the village'
$il+ḥaliib$	'the milk'	$il+laḥam$	'the meat'
$il+'attuus$	'the cat'	$is+sena$	'the year'
$il+jebel$	'the stones'	$iz+ziemel$	'the horse'
		$iš+šewka$	'the thorn'

The initial i of these examples is epenthetic. The prefixal l of column I
is the definite article. Note that this l assimilates to a following [+cor]
segment, as illustrated in column II. The one exception to this generalization is the j of column I, to which l does not assimilate. If j derived
from underlying g, this anomaly could be explained. The assimilation
of l would apply before the change of g to j. In support of deriving j from
g, we might note that $č$ fits in with the column II examples. That is, l
does assimilate to $č$, which would not be expected if the assimilation
rule were stated so that it excluded j; cf. $ič+čiraasa$ 'the cherry,' $ič+čayta$
'the joke,' etc. However, if this abstract approach is taken, a diacritic
feature is needed to distinguish those g's which become j from those
which remain g. The choice, then, is between a rule taking g to j
employing a diacritic, along with a generalized version of l-Assimilation,
and a more complicated rule of l-Assimilation without the rule of g to j
and the diacritic it entails. In the absence of any clear-cut evidence,
it is not easy to make a choice between the two possibilities.

tem of Maltese is filled. Also important is that ʕ is the most
phonetically plausible segment imaginable to represent *X*. It
is well known that ʕ possesses many of the acoustic properties of vowels. Thus, it is not surprising that ʕ should become
a vowel or a glide by a phonological rule. Further, it is not
unusual for the segment ʕ to function together with the liquids and nasals as a natural class. Many Aramaic handbooks
group ʕ together with the segments *r, l , m, n, y, w*, and ' with
respect to the *ʕamlai nuhrai*, or the *nuhrai ʕalmai*, which is
assumed to be a rule of metathesis involving these segments.
Finally, the fact that ʕ shows up as phonetic *ḥ* is again quite
natural, for this change appears to be part of the general tendency to devoice final obstruents. (See fn. 2.) But there is
still more evidence corroborating the identification of *X* as ʕ.
Consider the following examples:

(58)   *ná+ala'*   'I close'
       tá+ala'   'you close'
       ná+asar   'I squeeze'
       tá+asar   'you squeeze'
       ná+araš   'I tickle'
       tá+araš   'you tickle'

Why the underlying prefixes *ni* and *ti* show up in (58) as *na* and
ta must be explained. Their appearance is accounted for if
the first root segment of these words is assumed to be ʕ.

(59)

ni+ʕla'   *ti+ʕla'*   *ni+ʕsar*   *ti+ʕsar*
ní+ʕla'   *tí+ʕla'*   *ní+ʕsar*   *tí+ʕsar*   STRESS ASSIGNMENT
ná+ʕla'   *tá+ʕla'*   *ná+ʕsar*   *tá+ʕsar*   GUTTURAL ASSIMILATION
ná+ala'   *tá+ala'*   *ná+asar*   *tá+asar*   later rules

Finally, as a clinching argument that *X* is the pharyngeal ʕ,
we may note the following facts about morpheme structure:
Although every underlying consonant may occupy any root
position—first, second, or third—in some root or another,
there are constraints on the cooccurrence of two or more
consonants within a single root. Just what these restrictions
are in detail will not be discussed here. It will suffice to
point out one constraint on the cooccurrence of root consonants. No two segments may occupy the second and third root
positions of a single root if they differ only in the feature of
voicing. Thus, we find no roots of the shape *Cdt, Ctd, Csz*,

Czs, and so on. Also, there are no roots for which we would have to postulate ʕ in the second radical position and ḥ in the third radical position of a single root, or ʕ in the third radical position, along with ḥ in the second position. This distribution follows quite naturally from the general constraint on voicing of root consonants in the second and third radical positions. But it follows only if the abstract segment ʕ is postulated in underlying representations.

The segment ʕ, thus, meets every test. It is a consonant, a quite natural extension of the class R, a [-cor] segment, and, as a low back consonant, will trigger Guttural Assimilation. It is not unnatural for ʕ to alternate with vowels, glides, and ḥ. Indeed, it is one of the few segments that do. Further, ʕ fills a gap in the phonological system and squares nicely with independently motivated morpheme structure constraints. The quest for X may now be abandoned. It has been pinpointed as ʕ.[26]

6. Conclusion

In the preceding discussion, a number of apparent exceptional forms were brought to light. The examples of the first column of (40) display stress patterns totally at variance with that predicted by Stress Assignment, while the plurals of (40) and (51)I appear to be exceptions of Apocope. The examples of (42) and (43) are exceptions to Truncation. The examples of (41) appear to violate the rule of Vowel Harmony, and the examples of (58), Guttural Assimilation. The examples of (43)I appear to undergo Prothesis exceptionally. Thus, a rule-feature approach of the type discussed in section 1 in connection with the Sanskrit example fails to offer any insight into these apparent exceptions. In fact, this approach cannot even generate the stress patterns of (40) without postulating a totally new ad hoc rule of stress placement. On the other hand, the abstract approach, again of the same general type as that discussed in connection with the Sanskrit example, ex-

---

[26]It is to be noted that some dialects of Maltese exhibit x (not to be confused with the X used above) where the dialect discussed here possesses ḥ. I have not investigated these dialects in any detail. However, if no reason can be given for deriving x from ḥ in these dialects, it does not seem implausible that the abstract segment is to be identified as γ for such dialects, i.e., the voiced counterpart of x. The literature on this and other interesting dialectal features is nonexistent.

plains the apparent exceptional phenomena. By this approach,
adopted in sections 4 and 5, all exceptions turn out to be perfectly regular—in fact, to be expected. In summary, the
postulation of an abstract segment ʕ, which never appears
phonetically, permits a revealing solution to the problem of
Maltese stress, vowel elision, prothesis, truncation, and so
on. Furthermore, it allows us to retain the generalization that
all roots are made up of three consonants as well as to predict why there are no roots of the shape *CXḥ*, where *X* is what
I have argued is ʕ.

Any student of Semitics knows that the majority of instances of Maltese ʕ derive from the historically prior ʕ of
proto-Arabic.[27] However, the discussion in section 5 was not
an exercise in historical reconstruction. Instead, great pains
were taken to demonstrate that the evidence for underlying ʕ
is in the phonetic data. That is, the child coming to the
language-learning situation is capable of inducing ʕ on the
basis of Maltese phonetics alone. It would be absurd to ascribe
historical knowledge to the language learner.[28] The fact that
abstract ʕ must be postulated in the phonological component of
Maltese is of consequence for the ultimate formulation of a
naturalness principle of the type some have recently been
interested in developing. First, any such condition will have
to allow for phonological segments that never show up on the
phonetic surface. Second, the condition will have to allow for
rules of absolute neutralization, since apparently one of the
rules needed to account for the phonetics of Maltese is of this
type. This rule is stated as (60).

(60)   ʕ → a

Among others, this rule will account for the phonetic reflex of
ʕ observed in the derivations listed in (52). The fact that
abstract segments and absolute neutralization must be countenanced in linguistic theory should lead one to seriously
reconsider Sanskrit-like cases. Although evidence internal to
Sanskrit must ultimately decide the issue of the $k \sim \check{c}$ alternation in that language, the fact that such situations as the Mal-

---

[27]Some, however, derive from earlier γ.

[28]In view of fn. 27, it is clear that the synchronic situation does not
overlap with the historical situation, since there is no evidence for underlying γ in the dialect under investigation.

tese case do arise in a language gives the abstract solution of Sanskrit the edge, *mutatis mutandis.* Considerations of naturalness and rule plausibility will of course be decisive in determining such cases as that of Sanskrit, and the possibility that the putative *k* ~ *č* alternations of Sanskrit are lexical will have to be investigated. Assuming that these alternations in Sanskrit are to be related by a phonological rule, as in Maltese, the natural solution is the abstract solution, for *k* typically becomes *č* before front vowels, but rarely before *a*.[29]

REFERENCES

Anderson, S. R. (1969). "West Scandinavian Vowel Systems and the Ordering of Phonological Rules." Ph.D. dissertation, Massachusetts Institute of Technology.

Aquilina, J. (1965). *Maltese.* London, English Universities Press.

Bach, E. (1968). "Two Proposals Concerning the Simplicity Metric in Phonology." *Glossa* 2:128–149.

Brame, M. K. (in press). "Stress in Arabic and Generative Phonology," *Foundations of Language.*

——(to appear *a*). "Metathesis and Anaptyxis in Maltese."

——(to appear *b*). "Stress Assignment in Two Arabic Dialects." In *Festschrift for Morris Halle,* edited by S. Anderson and P. Kiparsky.

——(to appear *c*). *Topics in the Phonology of Maltese.*

Chomsky, N. (1967). "Some General Properties of Phonological Rules." *Language* 43:102–128.

——, and M. Halle (1968). *The Sound Pattern of English.* New York: Harper and Row.

Hale, K. (1970). "On Papago Laryngeals." In *Languages and Cultures of Western North America,* edited by E. H. Swanson, Jr. Pocatello: Idaho State University Press.

Kiparsky, P. (1968). "How Abstract is Phonology?" Mimeographed. Cambridge, Mass., Massachusetts Institute of Technology.

Sutcliffe, E. (1936). *A Grammar of the Maltese Language.* Oxford University Press, London. (Reprinted by Progress Press, Valetta, Malta, 1960.)

[29]For another discussion of abstract segments, again guttural segments, see Hale (1970), which contains a particularly interesting series of synchronic arguments.

The Segmental Cycle

MICHAEL K. BRAME

The University of Texas at Austin

That certain rules of English apply in a cyclical fashion remains one of the principal results of *The Sound Pattern of English* (hereafter SPE).[1] These rules include stress-assigning rules, such as the Main Stress Rule (hereafter MSR) and the Alternating Stress Rule (hereafter ASR). The following hypothesis may well reflect the true nature of cyclic rules in natural language:

[1]One of the many arguments that Chomsky and Halle provide in support of the phonological cycle is the need to explain such pairs as [kåndếnsÅšən], which is a nominalized verb, meaning 'act of condensing,' and [kåndənsÅšən], which is a noun, meaning 'a condensed state or form.' The former example must have an underlying verb cycle, which explains the weakened stress preceding primary stress. The latter, like *information,* does not derive from an underlying representation with a verb cycle, which accounts for the reduced vowel preceding the syllable with [1stress]. To these examples cited in SPE may be added the following, which exist in my own speech: [pròhíbíšən] vs. [pròəbíšən]. The former shows up in such expressions as *the prohibition of X by Y* and is more closely associated with the underlying verb *prohibit.* The latter occurs in such expressions as *the days of Prohibition* and is less closely associated with the verb. In the first example, there is an extra verb cycle, which again explains the weakened stress preceding primary stress, as well as the presence of *h*. In the latter example, there is no extra cycle, which accounts for the reduced vowel as well as for the absence of phonetic *h*. The segment *h* is commonly elided before unstressed vowels in English; cf. the two pronunciations of *Amherst.* [ámhèrst] vs. [ámərst], the latter being the pronunciation of the city's residents; or [nihílity] vs. [níyəlism], for *nihility* and *nihilism.* Such pairs as those cited above constitute strong evidence for the phonological cycle.

Hypothesis I: Any kind of phonological rule may be cyclic.

Although this hypothesis is logically possible, the appearance of more and more phonologies provides evidence that the most convincing candidates for the cycle are rules that assign stress. Moreover, many putative cases of the segmental cycle have been shown to be treatable as noncyclic. For these reasons, many investigators have adopted the following principle:

Hypothesis II: Only stress-assigning rules may be cyclic.

Chomsky and Halle have themselves expressed some displeasure with Hypothesis I, as evidenced by their comment, "examples of cyclical application of rules seem to be restricted to prosodic features and segmental modifications associated closely with prosodic features."

The phonological cycle is an interesting theoretical construct, but, at the same time, a very powerful one, for it permits the generation of a great many phonological systems. Hypothesis II represents a serious effort to constrain this power. It is obvious, therefore, that we must look for more empirical examples that decide between the two hypotheses presented above or among the many others readily conceivable. In this article, some examples that may bear on the correct formulation of the cyclic principle are examined. A new hypothesis that lies between Hypothesis I and Hypothesis II in expressive power is advanced, but it should be noted that the one counterexample to our hypothesis, the SPE rule taking y to i and i to y, is overlooked. It is my feeling that this rule should be reexamined. If this rule turns out to be correct, then Hypothesis III will have to be further relaxed as hinted at by Chomsky and Halle.

The first case to be discussed will relate to a class of adjectives in English, those ending in *-ative* and *-atory*. More specifically, the relevant examples include adjectives bearing these suffixes preceded by a single consonant, that is, forms of the shape schematized in (1).

(1) ... VC $\begin{Bmatrix} \text{ative} \\ \text{atory} \end{Bmatrix}$

These cases may be illustrated by the examples found in (2), listed under columns I and II.

(2)   I   II

    divínatory   *assímilatory*
    inflámmatory   *congrátulatory*
    oblígatory   *antícipatory*
    derívative   *íterative*
    impérative   *génerative*
    dispútative   *ejáculative*

These examples exhibit two stress patterns. Those listed
under column I display stress on the syllable immediately
preceding the endings *-ative* and *-atory*. This pattern may
be designated *presuffixal stress*. Under column II a second
stress pattern is encountered: stress falls on the second
syllable before the relevant suffixes. This stress pattern may
be termed *pre-presuffixal stress*. The question immediately
arises as to how stress should be predicted for these two
classes of words. There is no overt clue in (2) as to how
stress assignment might be accomplished. Indeed, the oppos-
ing examples of I and II constitute near minimal pairs, and
in taxonomic phonemics these stress patterns must be considered phonemic and unpredictable. That is, both *divínatory*
and *assímilatory* possess the ending *-atory*, preceded by the
lax vowel *i* plus a single consonant. But the former example
displays presuffixal stress, while the latter exhibits pre-presuffixal stress.

    It is possible to predict the stress difference of these
examples by the normal stress rules found in SPE if the presuffixal vowels of the column I examples are represented in
abstract representations as tense, namely, *divInatory*, *in-
flAmmatory*, *oblIgatory*, *derIvative*, *impErative*, and *dispUta-
tive*. (Capital letters indicate that the vowels in question are
[+tense].) The forms with pre-presuffixal stress, that is,
those listed under column II, will be specified with presuffixal
lax vowels in underlying representations. Thus, the difference in stress will be predictable, since there will be a
difference in underlying representations, namely a difference
in the feature of tenseness. There are alternations related
to these forms in which the relevant tense vowels actually
show up phonetically as tense, which gives empirical confirmation for postulating the underlying tense vowel for the
column I examples. Thus, we find *divIne*, *inflAme*, *oblIge*,
derIve, *impEre*, and *dispUte*, all with phonetically tense

vowels. We also know from other alternations that the *a* and
o of the suffixes *-atory* and *-ative* arc underlying tense,
so that more correctly we have underlying *divIn+At+Or+y*,
inflAm+At+Or+y, *derIv+At+iv*, and so forth. Notice that the
phonetic laxness of the presuffixal vowels of column I is
automatically predicted by the rule of Tri-Syllabic Laxing
(cf. SPE, pp. 180–181), which has the effect of laxing vowels
followed by two or more syllables. This rule, along with the
stress rulcs of SPE and the underlying lenseness distinction,
allows us to satisfactorily predict the stress patterns of the
forms listed in (2). If we take *divinatory* and *assimilatory*
as paradigm cases of the two classes, the derivations according to SPE are as follows:

(3)$[[\text{divIn}]_V At + Or + y]_A$ $[[\text{assimil}+At]_V Or + y]_A$

cycle₁	1			1		MSR, case (e)
			1	2		ASR
cycle₂	2	1	2	3	1	MSR, case (a)
	1	2	1	4	2	MSR, case (c)
post- cycle	a		a [-stress]			AUX. RED. I
	i					TRI-SYLLABIC LAXING
		3		3		STRESS ADJUSTMENT

On the first cycle the innermost labeled bracketing is
scanned, and stress is placed on the last strong cluster
by case (e) of the MSR. In the case of *assimilate,* which is
at this point *assimilÀt*, the ASR is now applicable, yielding
assímilÀt. If no other cycles existed, *assímilÀt* would be
correctly derived. On the second cycle, the tense *o* is
stressed in both examples by case (a) of the MSR. Next,
case (c) of this rule applies to both examples, giving *assimilAtÒry* and *divInAtÒry*, which by further rules become
assimilatÒry and *divinatÒry*, as desired.

Given the rules of SPE, one would expect to find cases
exhibiting the alternation ...*V̆CVCate* ~ ...*VCV́Cative*, where

Michael K. Brame

the stressed vowel of the second alternation must have been underlying tense for stress to have been correctly assigned. More concretely, we expect to find some example, such as hypothetical *génerãte ~ genérative*, where the second *e* would have to be underlying tense to predict stress, but where *e* never shows up as phonetically tense because of the rule of Tri-Syllabic Laxing.[2] This pair is of course nonexistent. However, crucial examples do exist for which this presuffixal stress is predicted by SPE, but for which pre-presuffixal stress actually obtains. Consider in this regard *sálivatÒry* and its corresponding verb *sálivÀte*. Given the rules of SPE, we would expect this adjective to be stressed *salívatÒry*, since the *i* of this example is underlying tense, as shown by the alternation *salíva*, where the *i* does show up as phonetically tense. The derivation, according to SPE, is as follows:

(4) $[[\text{salIv} + \text{At}]_V \text{ Or} + \text{y}]_A$

cycle₁		1		MSR , case (e)
	1	2		ASR
cycle₂	2	3	1	MSR , case (a)
	3 1	4	2	MSR , case (c)
post-cycle		a		AUX. RED. I
		[-stress]		
		i		TRI-SYLLABIC LAXING
	4		3	STRESS ADJUSTMENT
	4 1	3		
		salivatOry		

Case (c) of MSR should apply on the second cycle very much as it did in the derivation of *divinatory* in (3). But we do not find *salívatÒry*, as (4) predicts. Rather, the correct stress pattern is *sálivatÒry* with pre-presuffixal stress, not with presuffixal stress. The underlying distinction between *sálivatÒry* with pre-presuffixal stress and *divínatÒry* with pre-suffixal stress becomes evident upon a cursory examination

---

[2]This was first pointed out in Kiparsky (1968), in which forms bearing the suffixes *-ative* and *-atory* are also discussed. Kiparsky's explanation for the gap is invalid. Counterexamples to his explanation include *carmínative, pejórative, interrógative, derógatory,* and *impérative* for those who do not possess the verb *impere*.

of (4) and (3). The former example derives from a verb ending in *-ate*. The latter does not. Instead the *-ate* appears to be part of the adjective-forming suffix, which becomes clear when we compare the examples of (2) once again. Thus, the verbs corresponding to the adjectives listed under column II all end in *-ate*, for instance, *assimilate*, *iterate*, and *generate*. These adjectives have primary stress in just the position where primary stress is found in the corresponding verbs. On the other hand, the adjectives listed under column I of (2) have verbs without *-ate*, for instance, *divine* and *derive*, although *obligatory* corresponds to both *oblige* and *obligate*, to which I will return directly. Once again, note that the adjectives take primary stress in accord with the stress or their corresponding verbs. These facts may now be summarized as (5).

(5) I II

adjectives	verbs	adjectives	verbs
divínatory	*divíne* *divinate*	*assímilatory*	*assimil(e)* *assímilate*
inflámmatory	*infláme* *inflammate*	*congrátulatory*	*congratul(e)* *congrátulate*
oblígatory	*oblíge* *óbligate*	*antícipatory*	*anticip(e)* *antícipate*
derívative	*deríve* *derivate*	*íterative*	*iter(e)* *íterate*
impérative	*impére* *imperate*	*génerative*	*gener(e)* *génerate*
dispútative	*dispúte* *disputate*	*ejáculative*	*ejacul(e)* *ejáculate*

As this paradigm illustrates, adjectives with pre-presuffixal stress, that is, those of column II, correspond invariably to verbs ending in *-ate* and receive primary stress on the same syllable as the corresponding verbs. Similarly, adjectives with presuffixal stress, that is, those of column I, correspond to verbs without *-ate* and also receive primary stress on the same syllable as the corresponding verbs. Returning now to the example *oblígatory*, which corresponds to both *oblige* and *obligate*, we may be certain that this adjective derives from *oblige*. Further, there are some speakers who pronounce the adjective *óbligatory*, proving that they derive their adjective from *obligate*. However, as with *sálivatory*, the latter case is not derivable by the rules of SPE.

Following up these observations, let us determine how *sálivate* and *óbligate* derive from underlying *salIv+At* and *oblIg+At*.

(6) $[salIv+At]_V$ $[oblIg+At]_V$

	1		1	MSR , case (e)
1	2	1	2	ASR
i		i		AUX. RED. I
	3		3	STRESS ADJUSTMENT

Notice that tense *i* is laxed by Aux. Red. I in the derivation of these verbs. But this laxing is exactly what is needed to correctly derive *sálivatory* (and *óbligatory*). We must allow Aux. Red. I to apply on the first cycle.[3]

(7) $[[salIv+At]_V Or + y]_A$

cycle₁		1		MSR , case (e)
	1	2		ASR
	i			AUX. RED. I

cycle₂	2	3	1	MSR , case (a)
	1	4	2	MSR , case (c)
		a		AUX. RED. I
	[-stress]			

		3	STRESS ADJUSTMENT
1	3		
salivatOry			

In other words, Aux. Red. I applies on the first cycle, just as it does in (6), and also on the second cycle, analogous to the derivation in (3). However, in (3), as in SPE, this rule was considered to be noncyclic. The derivation given in (7),

---

[3]If the *-voc-* of *advocate* and *-voke* of *evoke* are to be related, a similar explanation is required to derive *ádvocàtive* vs. *evócative*.

which is apparently unavoidable if these forms are to be correctly generated, proves that Aux. Red. I is a cyclic rule. Let us state the relevant rule according to the statement given in SPE.

(8)

AUX. RED. I:

$$V \rightarrow \begin{bmatrix} -stress \\ -tense \end{bmatrix} \Big/ \left\{ \begin{matrix} \left[\overline{\underline{\gamma stress}} \right] \\ [\,1stress\,]\ C_0\underline{\quad\quad} C_0\ [-cons] \end{matrix} \right\} [-stress]_0 \#$$

Condition: γ is weaker than 2

I now turn to a case that is similar to, but nevertheless different from, the English example. The paradox that will be illustrated below is taken from Harris (1969). However, the conclusion I draw is quite different from that drawn by Harris. The problem is one of predicting high glides in the superficial representations of Spanish. Consider the following examples:

(9) (a) *láudano, náufrago, farmacéutico, terpéutico*
     (b) *alícuota, cónyuge, cuadríyugo, pléyade*

Orthographic *u* of the examples of (9a) and of the first example of (9b) is pronounced as the glide *w*. The orthographic *y* of the remaining (9b) examples is pronounced as phonetic *y*. It is possible to derive these glides from underlying vowels by means of the following rule:

(10) GLIDE FORMATION: $\begin{bmatrix} V \\ +high \end{bmatrix} \rightarrow G \Big/ \left\{ \begin{matrix} \underline{\quad} V \\ V\underline{\quad} \end{matrix} \right\}$

The symbol *G* is an informal abbreviation for *w* or *y*, depending on the quality of the underlying vowel. By this rule, underlying *laudano* would become *lawdano, coniuge* would become *conyuge,* and so forth. Nouns and adjectives in Spanish normally receive stress on their antepenultimate syllable. Thus, if stress were assigned before Glide Formation applied, *laudano* and *coniuge* would be stressed *laúdano* and *coniúge,* which would be incorrect. Stress must be assigned to the syllable preceding the phonetic glides. Thus, stress is assigned not before, but after, the glides are formed by rule (10). In other words, the derivations listed in (11) are required.

Michael K. Brame

(11) *laudano*   *coniuge*
      lawdano   *conyuge*   GLIDE FORMATION
      láwdano   *cónyuge*   STRESS ASSIGNMENT

Another set of examples exemplifying the change of high vowels to high glides is illustrated by the following:

(12) *amplío*   'I enlarge'   *insinúo*   'I insinuate'
      amplyámos   'we enlarge'   *insinwámos*   'we insinuate'

The stems of these verbs appear to be *ampli* and *insinu*, and these are the actual phonetic representations associated with the singulars of (12). In the plurals, however, the stems show up as *amply* and *insinw*, that is, with glides. According to Harris, verbs are typically stressed on the penultimate syllable, and it is rather obvious that stress plays a crucial role in determining which stems of (12) will bear high glides, and which will bear high vowels. To account for the difference, the following rule of Glide Formation is proposed:

$$(13)\ \text{GLIDE FORMATION:}\quad \begin{bmatrix} V \\ +\text{high} \\ -\text{stress} \end{bmatrix} \rightarrow G \Big/ \left\{ \frac{}{V}V \right\}$$

This rule may be ordered after the rule that assigns stress, giving rise to the following derivations:

(14)

ampli+o	*insinu+o*	*ampli+a+mos*	*insinu+a+mos*	
amplí+o	*insinú+o*	*ampli+á+mos*	*insinu+á+mos*	STRESS ASSIGNMENT
—	—	*amply+á+mos*	*insinw+á+mos*	GLIDE FORMATION (13)
amplío	*insinúo*	*amplyámos*	*insinwámos*	

But we are now faced with an apparent contradiction. The two instances of Glide Formation are sufficiently similar to indicate that they are the same rule. Yet in one case, Glide Formation must precede Stress Assignment, as in (11), and, in another it must follow Stress Assignment, as in (14). Harris concludes from this ordering contradiction that such examples as those listed in (9) should possess glides in underlying representations, which of course makes rule (10) unnecessary. However, there is another alternative. Notice that the first application of Glide Formation applies to stems, whereas the second application applies to material associated with morpheme boundaries. This state of affairs is indicative of a cyclic rule. Let us assume that rule (13) is the correct formulation of Glide Formation and that it applies in a cyclical fashion: Glide Formation will apply on the stem cycle and later on the word cycle after stress has been assigned.[4] This possibility, if adopted, clears up the ordering contradiction noted above.

There is a similarity between the two cyclic rules discussed above. In the English example, the feature [-stress] is mentioned in the structural change of the relevant rule (cf. (9)). In the Spanish example, the feature [-stress] is again mentioned in the relevant rule (cf. (13)), but this time in the structural analysis. However, both cases are similar in that the feature [-stress] is mentioned in the matrix of the affected segment, that is, it is specified in the matrix of the segment that does not serve as the left or right environment of the appropriate rule. This property may be a characteristic of cyclic rules. Accordingly, I advance the following hypothesis:

Hypothesis III: Only rules that specify the feature *stress* in the matrix of the affected segment may be cyclic.

This hypothesis makes all cyclic rules dependent on stress. Rules that mention the feature *stress* only in the left or right environment are precluded from being cyclic. It is immediately obvious, however, that stress-assigning rules, such as MSR and ASR, qualify under Hypothesis III. Thus, Hypothesis III falls between Hypothesis I and Hypothesis II in expressive power.[5]

---

[4]Stress placement is itself a cyclic process, cf. Foley (1965) and Harris (1969), but apparently does not apply on the stem cycle. One might distinguish two kinds of cyclic rules, those that are stem-cyclic and those that are word-cyclic, where *word* does not correspond to the use of this term in word-level phonology.

[5]The cyclic principle adopted here may have to be revised in the light of new examples or new evidence bearing on the treatment of the cases presented above. For example, if the rule of Glide Formation in Spanish could be proven to be noncyclic, the principle might be tightened up so as to require *stress* to be mentioned only in the structural change, which would include rule (9) along with all stress-assigning rules but would rule out (13).

REFERENCES

Chomsky, N., and M. Halle (1968). *The Sound Pattern of English*. New York: Harper and Row.
Foley, J. A. (1965). "Spanish Morphology." Ph.D. dissertation, Massachusetts Institute of Technology.
Harris, J. W. (1969). *Spanish Phonology*. Cambridge: M. I. T. Press.
Kiparsky, P. (1968). "How Abstract is Phonology?" Mimeographed. Massachusetts Institute of Technology.

On Sentence Stress and
Syntactic Transformations

JOAN W. BRESNAN

Massachusetts Institute of Technology

Perhaps the fundamental insight of generative phonology is that phonological phenomena are predictable from grammatical representations by a system of ordered rules. These grammatical representations are themselves "predictable" — that is, generable—given the base and transformational components. In this paper I wish to advance a proposal concerning the interaction of certain phonological and syntactic rules that extends the predictive power of the phonology and at the same time provides a new source of information about syntactic representations. If this proposal is correct it has interesting and far-reaching consequences for linguistic theory. The phonological rule to be discussed is the Nuclear Stress Rule (NSR).

The NSR is a cyclic rule applying after all rules that affect the stress of individual lexical items have applied; it is formulated as follows:[1]

NOTE: For suggestions for improving several earlier versions of this paper I am very grateful to Noam Chomsky, Morris Halle, and James D. McCawley, who of course are not responsible for the remaining defects. This work was supported in part by the National Institutes of Mental Health (Grant MH-13390) and by the National Institutes of Health (Grant 5 T01 HD00111). A slightly different version of this paper appears in *Language* 47:257–281. For criticism and further development of the ideas here, see *Language* (June 1972), which includes my "Stress and Syntax: A Reply."

[1]This is the preliminary formulation given by Chomsky and Halle (1968:17), though they later collapse the NSR with another rule. If the proposal of the present paper is correct, the NSR should remain as it was

NSR $\quad \overset{1}{V} \rightarrow 1 / [_A X \overset{1}{V} Y \underline{\quad} Z]$

where Z may contain no $\frac{1}{V}$ and where A ranges over major categories such as NP, VP, S. Given the convention that any application of 1-stress within a cycle reduces all other stress values by 1, the NSR has the effect shown in (1).

(1)

$[_S$ [Mary]	$[_{VP}$ [teaches]	[engineering] $_{VP}]$ $_S]$	
1	1	1	(word stress)
	2	1	1st cycle: NSR
2	3	1	2nd cycle: NSR

There is a question of whether the NSR should be allowed to cycle on VP. Note that if it does not cycle on VP, the stress contour [221] will result in (1). But there is another rule that alters [221] to [231].[2] Thus, instead of the derivation shown in (1), the type of derivation shown in (2) may be correct:

(2)

$[_S$ [Mary]	[teaches]	[engineering] $_S]$	
1	1	1	(word stress)
2	2	1	NSR
	3		$[221] \rightarrow [231]$

For the moment I shall ignore this detail in the application of NSR. It is clear that this rule results in primary stress falling on the rightmost constituent in a sentence, which is, in general, the "normal" intonation for an English sentence. There are, however, well-known classes of exceptions to this pattern. Final anaphoric pronouns do not normally receive primary stress:

Helen tĕaches it.
*Helen teaches it.

---

first formulated. The statement of the rule in Chomsky and Halle (1968) omits the condition on Z that guarantees that only the rightmost primary-stressed vowel receives 1-stress by the NSR.

[2]This rule is tentatively stated in Chomsky and Halle (1968: 115–117) as a word-stress rule; they note that it could be generalized to such cases as I am considering here. I am assuming that the NSR may apply to any phrase node, including VP, in isolation.

("Normally" means "excluding emphatic or contrastive stress.") Nor do final indefinite pronouns receive primary stress normally:

The boy b$\overset{1}{\text{o}}$ught some.

*The boy bought s$\overset{1}{\text{o}}$me.

Other anaphoric items, even when grammatically definite, receive no 1-stress:

John knows a woman who excels at karate, and he av$\overset{1}{\text{o}}$ids the woman.

In what follows I will assume that by some means anaphoric and indefinite elements are not assigned primary stress, and generally I will ignore the stressing of items that are not relevant to the point at issue.

The stress patterns of certain syntactically complex constructions appear to violate the general prediction made by the NSR. There are four cases that I will be concerned with here. The first is the type of contrast observed by Newman (1946):

(Ia) George has pl$\overset{1}{\text{a}}$ns to leave.

(Ib) George has plans to l$\overset{1}{\text{e}}$ave.

Roughly, the meaning of (Ia) is that George has plans, which he intends to leave, while (Ib) means that George is planning to leave. The next pair of examples belongs to the same category:

(Ic) Helen left dir$\overset{1}{\text{e}}$ctions for George to follow.

(Id) Helen left directions for George to f$\overset{1}{\text{o}}$llow.

(Ic) means that Helen left directions, which George is supposed to follow, while (Id) means that Helen left directions to the effect that George should follow.

The second case I will consider is quite similar:

(IIa) Mary liked the pr$\overset{1}{\text{o}}$posal that George left.

(IIb) Mary liked the proposal that George l$\overset{1}{\text{e}}$ave.

As in case I there is a syntactic difference corresponding to a difference in stress.

A third case involves questions, direct and indirect:

(IIIa) John asked what Helen had wr$\overset{1}{\text{i}}$tten.

(IIIb) John asked what b$\overset{1}{\text{o}}$oks Helen had written.

(IIIc) What has Helen wr$\overset{1}{\text{i}}$tten?

(IIId) What bóoks has Helen written?
(IIIe) You can't help noticing how he is.
(IIIf) You can't help noticing how seréne he is.
(IIIg) Whose have I táken?
(IIIh) Whose umbrélla have I taken?

It should be noted here that the interrogative *which* is inherently contrastive; in the sentence

Whích books has John réad?

"reading" is implicitly contrasted with some other notion:

He has *read some* books but only *skimmed others*.

That such sentences with *which* do not have the intonation characteristic of case III is therefore of no concern here.

The fourth case involves relative clauses again:

(IVa) George found someone he'd like you to méet.
(IVb) George found some friends he'd like you to meet.
(IVc) Let me tell you about something I sáw.
(IVd) Let me tell you about something stránge I saw.

The interesting fact about the above apparent exceptions to the NSR is that they are all predictable without any special modifications in that rule, given one assumption: the *Nuclear Stress Rule is ordered after all the syntactic transformations on each transformational cycle.*

Note, first, that if transformations cycle on the nodes NP and S (Chomsky, 1970) but not VP, the above assumption entails that the NSR apply not on VP within S, but only on NP and S (and on any other transformationally cycled nodes). Second, the above assumption entails that the NSR be cyclic. I will now verify the above claim.

First, I will derive (Ic) and (Id); (Ia) and (Ib) are similar, but involve an additional deletion. The following grammatical representations are only approximate.

(3)

$[_S$ Helen left $[_{NP}$ directions $[_S$ for George to follow directions $_S]_{NP}]_S]$

1	1	1	1	1	1	(word stress)
			2	2	1	1st cycle: NSR
					Ø	2nd cycle: syntax
2	2	1	3	3		3rd cycle: NSR

Derivation of (Ic)

[$_S$ Helen left [$_{NP}$ directions [$_S$ for George to follow $_S$] $_{NP}$] $_S$]

1	1	1		1	1	(word stress)
			2	1	1st cycle: NSR
		2	3	1	2nd cycle: NSR
2	2	3	4	1	3rd cycle: NSR

Derivation of (Id)

As shown in (3), the stress difference in (Ic) and (Id) is predictable, because in the deep structure of (Ic) *follow* has a direct object, while in (Id) *follow* has no direct object and hence receives primary stress as the rightmost constituent. Case II is parallel.

(4)

[$_S$ Mary liked [$_{NP}$ the proposal [$_S$ that George left the proposal $_S$] $_{NP}$] $_S$]

1	1	1	1	1	1	(word stress)
			2	2	1	1st cycle: NSR
					∅	2nd cycle: syntax
2	2	1	3	3		3rd cycle: NSR

Derivation of (IIa)

[$_S$ Mary liked [$_{NP}$ the proposal [$_S$ that George leave $_S$] $_{NP}$] $_S$]

1	1	1	1	1	(word stress)
			2	1	1st cycle: NSR
		2	3	1	2nd cycle: NSR
2	2	3	4	1	3rd cycle: NSR

Derivation of (IIb)

In the derivation of case III, I have bracketed the examples to reflect the phrase structure rule

$$\overline{S} \rightarrow \text{COMP} \ S$$

where $\underset{+WH}{\text{COMP}}$ is Q, the interrogative morpheme. This rule is justified in Bresnan (1970b). I have omitted the corresponding bracketing from the preceding cases because it plays no role there. I shall derive (IIIa) through (IIId).

Joan W. Bresnan

(5)

[$_S$ John asked [$_{\bar{S}}$ COMP$_{+WH}$ [$_S$ Helen had written something$_{+wh}$ $_S$] $_{\bar{S}}$] $_S$]

1 1		1	1	(word stress)
		2	1	1st cycle: NSR·
	something +wh			
			Ø	2nd cycle: syntax
2 2		3	1	3rd cycle: NSR

Derivation of (IIIa)

In (5) the object of *written* is the interrogative pronoun *what* (which I am assuming to be derived from *something*, though this assumption is not necessary for the point at issue); pronouns, it should be recalled, do not receive primary stress. Thus, the verb retains primary stress.

(6)

[$_S$ John asked [$_{\bar{S}}$ COMP$_{+WH}$ [$_S$ Helen had written some books$_{+wh}$ $_S$] $_{\bar{S}}$] $_S$]

1 1		1	1	1	(word stress)
		2	2	1	1st cycle: NSR
	some books +wh 1				
				Ø	2nd cycle: syntax
2 2	1	3	3		3rd cycle: NSR

Derivation of (IIIb)

As shown in (6), the full NP object of *written* receives primary stress, causing the stress on *written* to be lowered. The difference in stress between (IIIa) and (IIIb) reflects the stress difference between the simple sentences embedded in them:

> Helen had wr$\overset{1}{i}$tten something.
> Helen had written some b$\overset{1}{o}$oks.

The same is true of (IIIc) and (IIId):

(7)

[$_{\bar{S}}$ COMP$_{+WH}$ [$_S$ Helen has written something$_{+wh}$ $_S$] $_{\bar{S}}$]

	1	1	(word stress)
	2	1	1st cycle: NSR
something +wh		Ø	2nd cycle: syntax:
			QUESTION FORMATION
	has	Ø	SUBJECT-VERB INVERSION

What has H$\overset{2}{e}$len wr$\overset{1}{i}$tten?

Derivation of (IIIc)

$[_{\bar{S}}\ \underset{+WH}{COMP}\ [_{S}\ \text{Helen has written some books}\ _{S}]\ _{\bar{S}}]$

			(word stress)
1	1	1	(word stress)
2	2	1	1st cycle: NSR

some books   2nd cycle: syntax:
+wh   1   Ø   QUESTION FORMATION
        has   Ø   SUBJECT-VERB INVERSION

What bóoks has Hélen wrítten?

Derivation of (IIId)

The analysis given in case III correctly predicts the existence of a stress difference associated with the two readings of sentences like

The parable shows what suffering men can create.

The readings may be indicated as follows:

The parable shows what (suffering men) can créate.
The parable shows (what suffering) men can create.

These examples are exactly analogous to those of case III: the pronominal object *what* permits the verb to retain primary stress; the full object *what suffering* causes the verbal stress to be lowered. There are many similar examples, for instance, *I forgot how good bread smells*.

In cases I and II, the stress difference depended on whether the verb had an underlying object: if it did, the verbal stress was lowered; if it did not, the verb retained primary stress throughout the derivation. In case III, the crucial factor was what kind of object the verb had: if pronominal, the verb kept primary stress; if a full object, the verbal stress was lowered. In case IV, it appears that the kind of object—pronominal or full—affects the stress contours of relatives just as it does of questions:

(8)

$[_{S}\ \text{George found}\ [_{NP}\ \text{someone}\ [_{S}\ \text{he would like you to meet someone}\ _{S}]\ _{NP}]\ _{S}]$

1	1		1	1	(word stress)
			2	1	1st cycle: NSR
				Ø	2nd cycle: syntax
2	2		3	1	3rd cycle: NSR

Derivation of (VIa)

[ₛ George found[_NP_ some friends[ₛ he would
  1   1   1
                                like you to meet some friends ₛ]_NP_]ₛ]
                                  1   1   1 (word stress)
                                    2   2   1 1st cycle: NSR
                                                                $\emptyset$ 2nd cycle: syntax
  2   2   1   3   3   3rd cycle: NSR

Derivation of (VIb)

This fact would lead one to predict that the difference between *plăns to leave* and *plans to lĕave* is neutralized when the head is pronominal. In other words, there should be a stress contrast between the relative clause construction of case I— *George has plăns to leave*—and the same type of construction with a pronominal head. This prediction is borne out: *George has something to lĕave.*

In general, where the simple sentence embedded in a relative would receive verbal primary stress by itself—

    I lĭke a man (like that).

—the corresponding relative has verbal primary stress:

    He's a man I lĭke.

In these two examples *a man* is predicative. If *a man* is specific, it can receive primary stress in the simple sentence:

    I like a (certain) măn.

And correspondingly we find

    A (certain) măn I like . . .

There are sentences in which just this stress difference decides the reading.

    A man I like believes in women's liberation.

When *man* has greater stress than *like*, the sentence is understood as being about a certain man; when *like* carries greater stress than *man*, the sentence is, in a sense, about the speaker.[3]

All the cases discussed involve the movement or deletion of verbal objects rather than subjects. The reason is that,

---

[3]Under the latter reading the sentence is generic and may be paraphrased (approximately) as

since the NSR assigns primary stress to the rightmost element, only cases in which the underlying rightmost element has been affected by transformations can provide crucial evidence. Thus, both the ordering hypothesis advanced here and the previously proposed ordering can account for the stress in

I asked whose children bit Fído.

the man whose children bit my dóg

a desire to éat

But only the new ordering hypothesis accounts for the stress in

I asked whose chíldren Fido bit.

the man whose chíldren my dog bit

fóod to eat

In the latter examples the underlying objects have moved from their original rightmost position, where they had caused the verbal stress to be lowered during cyclic application of the NSR.

The ordering hypothesis explains the fact that the stress patterns of certain syntactically complex constructions reflect those of the simple sentences embedded within them in deep structure. This preservation of basic stress pattern through the syntactic derivation provides a new method for determining underlying grammatical representations and for deciding questions of syntax. To illustrate this method, I will consider the following question. It has been proposed (most recently by Emonds (1970) but earlier by Lees (1960)) that certain infinitival complements should be derived from deep structure VP's rather than S's. Suppose that this proposal is applied to the analysis of certain adjective + complement constructions. The question is whether in a construction like

It is tough for students to solve this problem.

A [=any] man I like $\begin{Bmatrix} \text{must} \\ \text{would} \end{Bmatrix}$ believe . . .

Some examples of the general types I have been discussing are given in Bolinger (1968) as counterexamples to the observations in Newman (1946). As I have shown, they are only apparent counterexamples to the theory of generative phonology. A very few of Bolinger's examples—mostly idiomatic, e.g., *money to búrn*—remain unexplained.

there is an underlying S = [for students to solve this problem]
or an underlying PP + VP = [for students] [to solve this
problem].[4]

There are several facts that argue against the sentential
analysis. First, if there were an underlying sentence, one
would normally expect such a sentence-cyclic transformation
as *There* Insertion to take place.[5] But, though one can say

[4]This alternative is not exhaustive since, if VP and S are both available
as underlying complements, one would expect a full range of possible
subcategorizations for adjectives: VP, S, PP + VP, PP + S, etc. These
possibilities are compactly expressed in the rule

$$VP \rightarrow \ldots (PP) \left(\begin{Bmatrix} VP \\ S \end{Bmatrix} \right)$$

In fact, as will become clear, all these possibilities are realized with
various adjectives. But there do exist predicates that clearly resist S
complements, including PP + S complements:

*For John to accept this view would be tough (for him).
*It would be tough for John for him to accept this view.
*For us to solve that problem was a bear (for us).
*It was a bear for us for us to solve that problem.
Cf. That problem was a bear for us to solve.

In Appendix I the possibility of "preserving" an S analysis for *tough*,
a bear, and other predicates by deriving their PP + VP complements from
PP + S is discussed.

Note that it is immaterial here whether the complement is conceived
as originating in subject position or at the rightmost position in VP.
See Emonds (1970) for a general argument in favor of the latter view.

[5]*There* Insertion places the expletive *there* in subject position before
certain indefinites:

There will be a son of the nobility present.

There Insertion is cyclic, since it may both follow and precede Passive
in a derivation. It follows Passive in the following derivation:

While you watch, a pig will be roasted. →
While you watch, there will be a pig roasted.

(The latter sentence must be carefully distinguished from

?While you watch, there will be a roasted pig.
?While you watch, there will be a pig that is roasted.

In these examples, Passive has not applied to the main sentence.)
There Insertion precedes Passive in this derivation:

△ proved that mercury was in the bottle. →
△ proved that there was mercury in the bottle. →
There was proved to be mercury in the bottle.

> It will be tough for at least some students to be in class on time.

one cannot say

> *It will be tough for there to be at least some students in class on time.

Compare cases that are truly sentential:

> The administration is eager for there to be at least some students in class on time.
> The commander left directions for there to be a soldier on duty at all times.
> It wouldn't surprise me for there to be countless revolutionaries among the secretaries.

Second, the *for* complementizer of a true sentential complement allows many types of objects that the preposition *for* after *hard* does not:

> Emmy was eager for that theorem on modules to become known.
> *It was tough for that theorem on modules to become known.
> It would surprise me for a book on Hittite to please John.
> *It would be tough for a book on Hittite to please John.

Third, the complement of *hard*, *tough*, *a bear*, *a breeze*, and similar predicates does not behave as a sentential constituent under S Movement: compare a true sentential complement—

> It is surprising [for a woman to act that way$_S$]
> [For a woman to act that way$_S$] is surprising

—with the complement of *hard* or *tough*:

> It is hard for a woman to act that way.
> *For a woman to act that way is hard.
> It's tough for students to grasp this concept.
> *For students to grasp this concept is tough.

It is a difficult syntactic problem to determine the correct analyses of *for* constructions.[6] The above ordering hypothesis

[6]The problem lies in determining the correct criteria for distinguishing among the many possible analyses. The S-Movement criterion is probably the best type for determining simple sentencehood.

provides new evidence bearing on this problem, for *tough*, *hard*, and the other adjectives of this construction are subject to a transformation that affects the object of the complement to produce such sentences as

> This theorem was a breeze for Emmy to prove.

Given that transformations do not cycle on VP, the hypothesis advanced above results in exactly the right stress contours for these sentences if the complement is represented as PP + VP. To illustrate, suppose that (9) shows a permissible deep structure for *That theorem was tough to prove*, ignoring details.

(9)

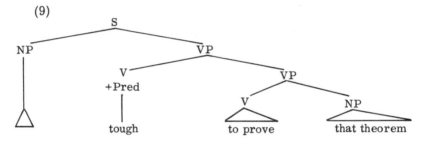

As noted, there is no cycle on VP, so that no rules will apply until S. At that point, the object of *prove* is shifted, yielding the derived structure shown in (10).

(10)

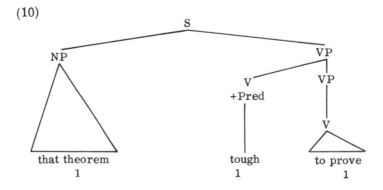

Then NSR will apply, giving the contour [221], which will eventually become [231] by the rule referred to in footnote 2.

On the other hand, suppose that this example came from

a deep structure having a sentential complement to *tough*, for example that shown in (11).

(11)

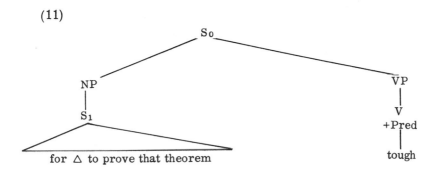

Again, the exact details of the representation are immaterial. The NSR would apply on the S_1 cycle, producing *próve that théorem*; on the S_0 cycle *that théorem* would be moved into subject position and S_1 extraposed as seen in (12).

(12)

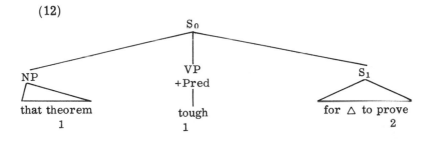

Again NSR would apply, yielding the incorrect contour *[213].[7]

Thus, one is led to conclude from both stress and syntax that VP as well as S must be a possible adjectival complement in deep structure. (See Appendix I for further discussion.) A given adjective may therefore be subcategorized for VP or S (or both). If the Object Shift transformation applies only to adjectives with VP complements, there will be no need to resort to rule features in order to describe this phenomenon;

---

[7]The connection between this type of construction and the ordering hypothesis advanced here was brought to my attention by Joan Maling.

that is, arbitrariness in the grammar may be reduced by stating Object Shift in such a way that it will apply only to VP complements.[8]

There is in fact a class of adjectives permitting both S and PP + VP complements, namely, the class including *good, bad, sweet, pleasant,* and *appropriate.* The ambiguity in such cases was noticed by Lees (1960). The sentence

It is good for John to leave.

may mean either

For John to leave is good.
= It is good (for John to leave)

or

To leave is good for John.
= It is good for John (to leave)

---

[8]Object Shift may be (tentatively) stated as follows:

$$[_S \; \triangle \; \text{Pred (PP)} \; [_{VP} \; V^* \; \text{(P) NP}]]$$

where V^* represents an arbitrarily long string of Verbs. This formulation would permit derivation of

John is easy for Bill to please.
John is hard for Bill to even try to please.
John is hard for Bill to even begin to try to please.

but not

*You are tough for me to believe that Harry hates.
(Postal, 1968:103)
*Harriet is tough for me to stop Bill's looking at.
(Postal, 1968:109)

Postal (1968:102) states that Object Shift (his "*Tough* Movement") transports an NP into subject position only from an "immediately lower clause." This statement leads him both to awkward complications of the rule and to ad hoc theoretical elaborations. While Postal's version states that Object Shift may not occur across more than one S-bracket, the version of the rule given here states, in effect, that Object Shift may not occur across any S-bracket. There is, therefore, an empirical difference between these two versions, and the crucial evidence is presented in paradigm (X) of this paper. The evidence there, as the reader will note, crucially favors an "intrasentence" version of the rule over any "cross-sentence" version; that is, any version like Postal's will incorrectly predict that (Xa) is a grammatical sentence.

Lees maintains a clear distinction between the ambiguous class (*good*; his type 7) and the unambiguous class (*hard, tough*; his type 8), but some speakers may class certain of the latter with the former, permitting sentences like[9]

$$\text{For John to please Mary is} \begin{Bmatrix} \text{hard} \\ \text{easy} \\ \text{difficult} \end{Bmatrix}.$$

The possibility of both VP and S complements for these adjectives accounts for the following paradigm:

(Xa) *Such things are not $\begin{Bmatrix} \text{good} \\ \text{appropriate} \end{Bmatrix}$ for there to be children involved in.

(Xb) It is not $\begin{Bmatrix} \text{good} \\ \text{appropriate} \end{Bmatrix}$ for there to be children involved in such things.

(Xc) Such things are not $\begin{Bmatrix} \text{good} \\ \text{appropriate} \end{Bmatrix}$ for children to be involved in.

(Xd) It is not $\begin{Bmatrix} \text{good} \\ \text{appropriate} \end{Bmatrix}$ for children to be involved in such things.

The ungrammaticality of (Xa) is precisely what is predicted from the analysis given here, because *good* and *appropriate* may take both S and VP complements. Object Shift can apply only to VP complements, as shown in footnote 8, and *There* Insertion can apply only to S complements. The presence of *there* in (Xa) and (Xb) forces the "S interpretation" of the

---

[9]One such speaker is Postal (1968:25), who writes: "One must observe that the whole construction involves a subtle structural ambiguity of a not understood type. A string like:

3.(8) It was difficult for Tony to rob the store

has two different Surface Structures:

3.(9) *a* it was difficult for Tony (to rob the store)
      b it was difficult (for Tony to rob the store)

The difference in meaning is real though subtle. The first seems to associate the difficulty directly with Tony personally. The second allows for a more generic attribution of difficulty. The difference shows up clearly in two variant pronunciations."

complement in both (Xa) and (Xb), and hence the shifted object in (Xa) is ungrammatical.[10]

I have discussed adjectives, like *tough*, that take only (PP) + VP complements as well as adjectives, like *good*, that take both (PP) + VP and S. It should not be surprising to discover adjectives taking (PP) + S, which is what we would expect if VP is, with S, a possible complement generated in phrase structure. The phrase structure rules will specify VP as an alternative choice wherever S is specified, as in the following rule:

$$VP \rightarrow \ldots (PP) \left(\begin{Bmatrix} VP \\ S \end{Bmatrix} \right)$$

One adjective that displays the possibility PP + S is *good*:

[10]The sentence *John was good to leave* is itself ambiguous: John may be understood as the one leaving (*It was good of John to leave*) or the one left (*It was good to leave John*). Corresponding to these readings is a difference in stress:

John was good to leave (*John* is subject of *leave*) — stress: John³ good² leave¹
John was good to leave (*John* is object of *leave*) — stress: John² good³ leave¹

The former is probably transformationally derived from

It was good of John to leave. — stress: good² John³ leave¹

Of John is probably a PP complement to *good*: the stress on *good¹ of John³* in isolation suggests that it is the Compound Rule that is applying. The Compound Rule (Chomsky and Halle, 1968:17) results in the characteristic initial stress of English compounds: *blackbird¹ ₃* is produced by the Compound Rule, while *black² bird¹* is produced by the NSR. Thus, we would have a derivation like the following:

```
[It was [good [ of John] ] [to leave] ]

              1    1  1          1        (word stress)
                 2  1                     1st cycle: NSR
            1    3  2                      2nd cycle: Compound Rule
    2                                      3rd cycle:
   John        ∅  ∅                          syntax
    3    2                      1          NSR
```

Notice that to avoid deriving **Mary was good of John to leave* by Object Shift from *It was good of John to leave Mary*, either the prepositional phrase *for NP* must be distinguishable by the rule from *of NP*, or the infinitive must in these cases be an unreduced sentence at the point at which Object Shift would apply.

> For Mary to learn karate would be good for her.
> It would be good for Mary for her to learn karate.

In fact, one would predict that Object Shift cannot apply to these examples, since a full S follows *for Mary,* and this prediction is borne out:

> *Karate would be good [for Mary$_{PP}$] [for her to learn$_S$]
> Karate would be good [for Mary$_{PP}$] [to learn$_{VP}$]

The ungrammaticality of *Karate would be good for Mary for her to learn* is another crucial example in favor of the formulation of Object Shift given here.

To conclude, because both the *tough to prove* and the passive construction have rightward primary stress, I have ordered the NSR after all transformations on each cycle. This ordering guarantees that on a given cycle Object Shift or Passive may apply before the NSR:

> John was seen by $\overset{1}{\text{Mary}}$.
> John was hard to $\overset{1}{\text{see}}$.

Note that the same ordering applies to noun phrases: the passivization of nominals (Chomsky, 1970) also precedes the NSR:

> the enemy's destruction of the $\overset{1}{\text{city}}$
> the city's destruction by the $\overset{1}{\text{enemy}}$

On the other hand, within a derivation Question Formation and Relative Clause Formation must apply after the NSR has affected the simple S's embedded in interrogative and relative structures:

> What $\overset{1}{\text{books}}$ has Helen written?
> I wonder what $\overset{1}{\text{books}}$ Helen has written.
> Here's a $\overset{1}{\text{book}}$ for you to read.

This ordering follows automatically from the principle of the transformational cycle and from the analysis of syntactic structures given, in which there is a simple S embedded within interrogatives as well as within relatives (Bresnan, 1970b). That Question Formation and Relative Clause Formation actually do apply on the transformational cycle is shown by independent syntactic arguments in Appendix II.

Some Consequences

The ordering of the NSR proposed here has interesting consequences for linguistic theory. The most immediate consequence is, of course, the inadequacy of a basic assumption of generative phonology (Chomsky and Halle:15): "It is well known that English has complex prosodic contours involving many levels of stress . . . It is clear even from a superficial examination that these contours are determined in some manner by the surface structure of the utterance." Instead, it appears that the stress contours of English sentences are determined in a simple and regular way by their underlying syntactic structures. Further, because prosodic stress rules, like the NSR, require prior assignment of word stress, the latter must occur either on deep structure or in the lexicon.[11] However, if word stress is assigned prior to the syntactic transformations, it follows automatically that transformationally attached affixes are stress-neutral.[12] For example, the primary stress on the verb *derive* is unchanged by the affix *-ing* but shifts when *-ation* is affixed:

    deríving
    derivátion

This difference in stress would follow if *-ing*, but not *-ation*, were attached to *derive* by a syntactic transformation, which

[11]Since the ordering hypothesis entails that some phonological rules apply in deep structure or in the lexicon, it is natural to ask whether all phonological rules so apply. It is clear that the rules of "external sandhi" in some languages, affecting segments across word boundaries, must apply on surface structure, because two words that have separate locations in deep structure may be contiguous in surface structure and undergo sandhi. Such rules of "external" phonological phenomena are analogous to the post-cyclic or last-cyclic syntactic rules, in that both apply after the cyclic rules. Prosodic rules, such as the NSR, are analogous to cyclic transformations in a way that the ordering hypothesis makes clear. Word-internal rules affecting stress or segmental phonology (see Chomsky and Halle, 1968) are analogous to rules of derivational morphology and doubtless interact with them. Further research pursuing the parallel articulation of phonological and syntactic rules and their interactions may prove interesting.

[12]Arlene Berman first pointed out this consequence to me, and Noam Chomsky called the further consequence for the lexicalist hypothesis to my attention.

Needless to say, it does not follow that stress-neutral affixes are transformationally attached, but only that a non-stress-neutral affix is

is exactly what Chomsky (1970) argues on independent syntactic and semantic grounds. His lexicalist hypothesis states that such gerundive nominals as

Wanda's deriving the answer

—which are productive and sentence-like—are created by a syntactic transformation, while derived nominals like

Wanda's derivation of the answer

—which are restricted and noun-like—are created by lexical rules. Because the NSR may apply on the first syntactic cycle, and because word-stress assignment precedes prosodic stress assignment, all lexical insertion must occur on or before the first transformational cycle. If there is some level in derivations at which all lexical insertion converges, then deep structure, in the sense of Chomsky (1965), exists. The assignment of word stress prior to prosodic stress simply follows from the principle of the phonological cycle (Chomsky and Halle, 1968): in other words, the stress of the whole is a function of the stress of the parts. Therefore, *it is a consequence of the ordering hypothesis presented here, together with the principle of the phonological cycle, that the lexical hypothesis* (Chomsky to appear) *is correct and that deep structure exists.*[13]

---

not transformationally attached. This consequence raises a number of problems for further research. For example, inflectional morphology often involves radical phonological changes, yet the context for a passive vs. active verb or a nominative vs. accusative noun is determined transformationally. Since it is still an open question whether passive and active deep structures differ in some way (see Hasegawa, 1968), it is possible that passive verbs are lexically inserted as such. Case-marking and number/gender agreement rules operate on derived structures. It is possible that these rules apply to already inflected items, that is, that they are "feature-checking" rather than "feature-changing," in an obvious sense.

[13]Deep structure is definable as the phrase marker P_i of a derivation $\Sigma = (P_1, \ldots, P_n)$ s.t. (a) for $j < i$ P_j is formed from P_{j-1} by a lexical transformation and (b) for $j > i$ P_j is formed from P_{j-1} by a nonlexical, or syntactic, transformation. A lexical transformation inserts a lexical item into a phrase marker. (See Chomsky (to appear) for further exposition.)

Strictly speaking, the phonological cycle and the ordering hypothesis imply that all lexical insertion *within the domain of cycle C* must occur on or before any transformation on C. But in this case, all lexical-insertion

Those grammarians who accept the transformational hypothesis (see Chomsky (1970) for references) must reject either the stress ordering hypothesis presented here or the principle of the phonological cycle. Let us see what is entailed in giving up the latter. One concrete way of rejecting the phonological cycle is to claim that the NSR assigns stress to nonterminal symbols only and that word stress occurs subsequently.[14] This proposal implies that prosodic stress does not depend in any way on lexical information, but only on syntactic configurations. Yet, as we have seen, the NSR must "know" whether it is applying to a pronoun or to a fully specified lexical noun phrase in order for the systematic difference between such pairs of examples as the following to be explained:

Helen detests misógynists.
Helen detèsts them.
The parable shows (what sùffering) men can create.
The parable shows what (suffering men) can creàte.

(Because the ordering hypothesis entails that pronouns are in deep structure, it is interesting to observe that recent work has shown independently that they are present in deep struc-

---

transformations can be reordered before all cyclic and postcyclic syntactic transformations without loss of any linguistically significant generality. To see this, consider a hypothetical cyclic syntactic transformation that precedes a lexical-insertion transformation L. Our hypotheses imply that on a cycle C at which T applies, all lexical insertion into the domain of C had taken place prior to T's application. Therefore, L must occur on the "next higher" cycle C'. However, on C', L cannot insert into the domain of the previous cycle C without inserting a lexical item *for other lexical items*, which is impossible. Therefore, L must insert into some sub-phrase-marker of the domain of C' not in the domain of C. Thus, L is independent of the output of T and can be reordered prior to any application of T.

Concerning L, I am making the generally accepted assumptions (i) that lexical items are not strictly subcategorized for syntactically transformed structures and (ii) that lexical items are not in general substitutable for lexical items. (i) is necessary since, otherwise, any L that inserted into C'-C a lexical item subcategorized for a derived structure in C that is the output of T obviously could not be reordered before T.

If one could display a well-motivated precyclic syntactic transformation that preceded an L, then the above definition of deep structure would have to be given up. However, a slightly weaker notion of deep structure would still be definable by omitting (a) from the definition.

[14]This formulation was suggested to me by James D. McCawley.

ture and not created transformationally: see, for example, Jackendoff (1969), Dougherty (1969), and Bresnan (1970a).) The same is true of semipronouns, like *people* and *things*:

> I líke people.
> There are many people I líke.

Similarly, the derived stress contours of sentences containing anaphoric and nonanaphoric noun phrases differ:

> Jóhn knóws a wóman. (2 3 1)
> Jóhn avóids the wóman. (2 1 3)

Different stress contours are produced by the NSR because of the difference in stress between anaphoric and nonanaphoric lexical items. It is hard to see how this dependency of stress contour on the stress level of individual lexical items can be explained if the phonological cycle is given up.

There is another interesting consequence of the ordering hypothesis. English is not a VSO (Verb Subject Object) language in the sense of McCawley (1970)[15] for the following reason: McCawley proposes that English has underlying VSO word order throughout the transformational cycle and converts to SVO (Subject Verb Object) only by a postcyclic verb-second rule. In McCawley's system, intransitive verbs precede their subjects throughout the cycle and thus get reduced stress by the cyclic application of the NSR. Instead of

> Jésus wépt. (2 1)

the incorrect contour

> *Jésus wépt. (1 2)

would result as the normal English intonation. On the other hand, if McCawley's verb-second rule were cyclic, his arguments for underlying VSO order in English would disappear.

We see that the stress ordering hypothesis provides a kind of "naturalness condition" on syntactic derivations: the formal properties of surface structures cannot diverge too greatly from those of deep structures without destroying the relation between syntax and prosodic stress. In a sense, it is natural that a close relation should exist between sound and syntactic structure; after all, languages, unlike the countless

[15]This consequence was called to my attention by James D. McCawley.

logics and "logical languages" invented by philosophers, are spoken. It is not surprising that McCawley's system, explicitly modelled on one kind of notation used in symbolic logic, is an inadequate syntactic basis for a description of English stress contours.

Having sketched these consequences for linguistic theory, I would like to mention three problems for further research.

The first problem concerns such sentences as

> This theory was believed by George to have been thought by Paul to have been refuted by Jim.

It is possible that such sentences derive from an underlying form close to

$$[_S \text{ George believed } [_S \text{ that Paul thought}$$
$$[_S \text{ that Jim refuted this theory } _S] _S] _S]$$

by a sequence of operations indicated in (13); note the derived stress contour.

(13)

```
[ George believed [ Paul thought [ Jim refuted this theory ] ] ]
      1         1         1        1        1        1            1              (word stress)

                          this theory was refuted by J.        PASSIVE
                                  1              1       1
                                  2              2       1      NSR

        Paul thought this theory[Ø to have been refuted by J.]
          1       1          2                       2      1    SUBJECT RAISING

        this theory was thought by P. to have been refuted by J.
              2            1        1                   2      1    PASSIVE
              3            2        2                   3      1    NSR

George believed this theory [Ø to have
  1        1                3     been thought by P. to have
                                    2        2     been refuted by J.]  SUBJECT
                                                        3       1    RAISING

this theory was believed by G. to have
      3              1        1  been thought by P. to have
      4              2        2        2       2  been refuted by J. PASSIVE
                                       3       3        3      1
                                                        4      1 NSR
```

Evidently, these syntactic processes can be repeated indefinitely:

> This theory was expected by Dave to have been believed

by George to have been thought by Paul to have been
refuted by Jim.

This theory was said by John to have been expected by
Dave to have been believed by George to have been
thought by Paul to have been refuted by Jim.

In such a way the derived subject *this theory* may receive
stress indefinitely weak compared to the verb. This result
is clearly wrong. Therefore, if the syntactic derivation of
such sentences is correct, it appears that some convention
limiting repeated stress reduction is needed. Just this conclusion is argued independently in Bierwisch (1968). Further
research on the form and scope of the stress-reduction
convention is necessary; if stress reduction is limited, the
observed variation can be effected by "rhythm" rules, for
instance, [2221] → [2321].

A second problem may lie in the formulation of the Nuclear
Stress Rule itself. The problem is seen when there is more
material than one noun phrase to the right of the verb. Compare the following examples:

Peter used a knífe.
Whose knífe did Peter use?

with the following ones:

Peter sliced the salami with a knífe.
Whose knife did Peter slice the salámi with?

The first pair, but not the second, is explicable from what I
have proposed so far. Following are further examples like
the second pair:

Mary found a car on Thursday évening.
On what evening did Mary find a cár?
Mary gave a book to Peter's chíldren.
Whose children did Mary give a bóok to?
What book did Mary give Peter's chíldren?[16]

Recall that the NSR lowers stress on every element to the
left of the rightmost primary stress within the appropriate
contexts. The above examples suggest that perhaps all
primary-stressed items to the right of the verb—and not

---

[16]The problem posed by the dative was pointed out to me by Frank
Heny.

just the rightmost—should retain primary stress until the late application of a rhythm rule. This conjecture is illustrated in (14).

(14)   [$_S$ Peter sliced the salami with a knife]

1	1	1	1	(word stress)
2	2	1	1	revised NSR
2	3	2	1	rhythm rule

[$_S$ $\underset{+WH}{COMP}$ [$_S$ Peter sliced the salami with $\underset{+wh}{someone's}$ knife]]

1	1	1		1	(word stress)
2	2	1		1	revised NSR

someone's knife   Ø   Ø   QUESTION FORMATION
+wh

              did Peter slice   SUBJECT-VERB INVERSION
    whose knife did Peter slice the salami with

1	2	2	1
2	3	3	1	revised NSR

The third problem[17] is to account for the following contrast:

(A) Peter had pláns for dínner.
(B) Peter had cláms for dinner.

As it stands, *plans for dínner* is the predicted stress contour; the problem lies with (B). Note that when a pronoun is used for *clams*, the stress shifts rightward:

Peter had them for dínner.

Further, *plans for dinner*, but not *clams for dinner*, is a constituent:

Plans for dinner were suggested by Peter.
*Clams for dinner were suggested by Peter.

It appears that the formulation of the NSR may have to take into account certain kinds of prepositional phrases.

Although the problem posed by (B) is still unsolved, the basic principle of preserving stress patterns throughout syntactic derivation still holds: compare (A) and (B) with (C) and (D):

(C) The pláns Peter had for dínner didn't come óff.
(D) The cláms Peter had for dinner didn't come óff.

---

[17]This problem was pointed out to me by Peter Culicover.

Therefore, as in the preceding cases, this problem concerns the proper formulation of the NSR rather than the ordering hypothesis: once the principle for applying stress to (B) is found, the ordering hypothesis will predict (D).

APPENDIX I

The existence of VP complements in deep structure is not a *necessary* consequence of the ordering hypothesis presented here. It is possible to "preserve sentences," so to speak, by deriving *John is tough to please* from

John$_i$ is tough [$_S$ . . . to please him$_i$]

The presence of the pronominal object of *please* will allow the verb to retain primary stress on the innermost S-cycle, and the presence of a specified subject *John* would prohibit a sentential subject: **For Mary to please John is tough.* However, this solution leaves unexplained several of the other nonsentential properties of such constructions:

(i) the absence of *There* Insertion
(ii) the selectional properties of *for*
(iii) the generalization that Object Shift does not cross S-brackets

Furthermore, it would require a special constraint to guarantee the presence of a pronominal object in the complement having the subject of *tough* as its antecedent.

It is possible to amend the above solution to take account of (i)–(iii), though the proposed amendment is ad hoc. Suppose that *Mary is tough for John to please* were derived from

(Y) Mary$_i$ is tough [$_{PP}$ for John$_j$][$_S$ he$_j$ please her$_i$]

by two obligatory deletions—Object Deletion, affecting *her$_i$*, and Equi–NP Deletion, affecting *he$_j$*. See Postal (1968a) on the latter transformation. Object Deletion will be written almost exactly as Object Shift is in footnote 8:

$$[_S \text{ NP Pred (PP) } [\text{V* NP}_{VP}] \;] \rightarrow 1\,2\,3\,4\,\emptyset$$
$$\;\; 1 \quad 2 \quad 3 \quad\;\; 4 \quad 5$$

The PP in (Y) would account for (2); a new constraint requiring the subject of the complement to take the object of the preposition as antecedent will take care of (1), since *there* cannot be an underlying subject and cannot replace anaphoric pronouns; and (3) will follow from the pruning of the embedded S after Equi–NP Deletion. This solution requires, of course, that Equi–NP Deletion be cyclic (contra Postal, 1968a): in order to derive *Mary is believed by everyone to be tough for John to please*, Object Deletion must take place before the cyclic Passive rule; and Equi–NP Deletion must precede Object Deletion, so that S will prune to VP.

It is quite striking that this method of preserving a sentential complement for adjectives like *tough* uses only the bare verbal skeleton of the sentence: subject and object are obligatorily deleted pronouns, so that there is no trace of the postulated underlying S in any surface form derived from the proposed deep structure (Y).

APPENDIX II

I have shown that it is possible for the NSR to be ordered within the transformational cycle, but I have not actually demonstrated that it is necessary. I have assumed without explicit justification that Relative Clause Formation and Question Formation are cyclic transformations. If these transformations were not cyclic one might think of ordering the NSR after the entire transformational cycle but before the postcyclic transformations, the latter including Relative Clause Formation and Question Formation.[18] There are two kinds of evidence against this alternative. First, all the stress evidence indicates that the NSR does not precede known postcyclic transformations; for example, we do not have

*Awáy ran Fído.

but rather

Awáy ran Fído.

The former would result if the NSR preceded the postcyclic transformation that preposes *away*. Likewise, we do not have

*Séldom does Jóhn síng.

but rather

Séldom does Jóhn síng.

[18]This alternative was suggested to me by James McCawley.

Yet the former would result if the NSR preceded the post-cyclic transformation that fronts *seldom*.[19] (See Emonds (1970) on both these transformations, Directional Adverb Preposing and Negative Adverb Preposing.)

Second, there is syntactic evidence that Relative Clause Formation and Question Formation are indeed cyclic transformations. Because of the consequences of the cyclicity of the NSR for linguistic theory, I will demonstrate here that Question Formation (QF) and Relative Clause Formation (RCF) are cyclic transformations. The matter is of some intrinsic interest as well.[20] The cyclicity of these transformations and the fact that the NSR precedes these transforma-

---

[19]I have excluded the transformation Topicalization from discussion, because topicalized sentences seem inherently emphatic or contrastive: *Jóhn I like; John I líke*. It is likely that many postcyclic transformations, because they create so-called stylistic inversions, are closely connected with contrast and emphasis.

[20]Because relative and interrogative clauses have special properties that prevent certain kinds of interactions with many of the better-known cyclic transformations, it is difficult to prove that RCF and QF are cyclic from rule-ordering arguments. (See Ross (1967) for an exposition of some of these properties and a proposed explanation.) In Postal (1968a:26–27), an argument is presented that "WH Q Movement" is not cyclic. Postal's argument is actually addressed to a version of QF unlike that assumed here. In this paper, QF is a Complementizer–Substitution Transformation in the sense of Bresnan (1970b): QF scans an S on every S-cycle, but only applies when its structural description is met—that is, when the S is complementized by WH [=Q]—and then QF substitutes the first eligible question word for WH. (See Bresnan (in preparation).) For example, the structural description of QF is met only at S_2 in the following example, and so QF actually applies only on that cycle:

$$[_{S_3} \text{John asked me } [_{S_2} \text{WH } [_{S_1} \text{you thought } [_{S_0} \text{he liked what}]]]]$$

The derived sentence is *John asked me what you thought he liked*. Now the version of QF that Postal assumes permits the following kind of derivations:

John asked me WH you thought he liked what. →
John asked me WH you thought what he liked. →
John asked me what you thought he liked.

The question word (in this case, *what*) is brought to the front of every S until it reaches WH, or "Q." Postal notes that since QF optionally preposes prepositional phrases—

Who did you speak to?
To whom did you speak?

tions while following other cyclic transformations show that
it is indeed cyclic, applying after all the transformations
applying to each cycle.

As preparation, observe that there is a transformation
that performs operations like the following:

> Mary has studied little and yet Mary has accomplished
> a great deal. →
> Mary has studied little and yet accomplished a great
> deal.

This transformation, which I will refer to as Right Conjunct
Reduction, may be thought of as deleting material in the right
conjunct that repeats material from the left.[21] The conjuncts
may be full sentences, as above, or noun phrases:

> The trees in Northern California and the trees in
> Oregon are similar. →

—this version of QF would allow prepositions to be "stranded," producing
ungrammatical strings; for example, in addition to the grammatical sentences

> Who did she think you spoke to?
> To whom did she think you spoke?

an ungrammatical string like the following would result optionally:

> *Who did she think to you spoke?

by fronting the entire phrase *to whom* on the first cycle, but fronting
only *who* on the next cycle. Because QF, under the version I am
assuming, moves question words only into (and never from) WH complementizers, Postal's "stranding" argument does not apply. But even the
version of QF Postal assumes is not refuted by his argument, since the
feature [+wh] could be assigned either to NP or to PP (Prepositional
Phrase), and whichever node carried the feature would be shifted by QF
throughout the derivation. (This possibility was mentioned to me by
Noam Chomsky.)

[21]If Right Conjunct Reduction merely deleted material, the derived
constituent structure would be wrong, for when *the news from France
and the news from Italy* is reduced, *from France and from Italy* behaves
as a prepositional phrase constituent under the Postposing rule, which
will be discussed:

> The news is similar from France and from Italy.
> *The news from France is similar and from Italy.

For a discussion distinguishing various kinds of conjunct reduction rules,
see Kuno (to appear) and the references cited there.

> The trees in Northern California and (in) Oregon are
> similar.

My argument consists in showing that there are derivations in which Right Conjunct Reduction may follow an
application of QF and derivations in which it may precede an
application of QF. To show the latter it will be necessary to
use a transformation that I shall call Postposing. This is
an optional rule which postposes certain complements to
noun phrases, relating pairs like the following:

> The news from Italy was the same. →
> The news was the same from Italy.
> The results on the virus were parallel. →
> The results were parallel on the virus.
> The stories about her are similar. →
> The stories are similar about her.

Such a transformation is needed to explain certain peculiar-
ities about the distribution of prepositional phrases. For
example, the impossibility of

> *That was the same from Italy.

is explained by the ungrammaticality of its source under
Postposing:

> *That from Italy was the same.

Prepositional phrases that can be generated to the right of
predicates are not excluded by such pronominal subjects:

> That is the same in France.
> They were similar during the occupation.

Postposing preserves structure (Emonds, 1970), so that if a
prepositional phrase already occupies immediate post-predicate position, the rule does not apply (i.e., since a node is
moved by a structure-preserving rule only into a place where
the same node can be generated by the base, the transformation does not apply if the place is already filled):

> Some things about France are quite similar to those
> you mention about England.
> *Some things are quite similar to those you mention
> about England about France.

> *Some things are quite similar about France to those
> you mention about England.
> Cf. Some things are quite similar about France.

(The last sentence should be imagined in a conversational
context; e.g., *Concerning what you have just observed about
England, I can add that some things are quite similar about
France.*)

> Their results on that virus were parallel to ours on the
> phage.
> *Their results were parallel to ours on the phage on
> that virus.
> *Their results were parallel on that virus to ours on the
> phage.

A second useful fact about Postposing may be inferred
from the fact that it is structure preserving. We have seen
that the sentence

> Their results on that virus are similar to our results
> on the phage.

cannot undergo Postposing, because there is already a prepositional phrase in immediate post-predicate position:

> *Their results are similar to our results on the phage
> on that virus.

Now suppose that the post-predicate phrase is removed by
QF:

> To whose results on the phage are their results on that
> virus similar?

If it were in general possible for Postposing to follow QF,
then the following ungrammatical strings would result:

> *To whose results are their results on that virus
> similar on the phage?
> *To whose results on the phage are their results simi-
> lar on that virus?

The conclusion is that Postposing precedes QF on any cycle.
Finally, it is necessary for the ensuing argument that
Right Conjunct Reduction precede Postposing on any cycle.
Consider the following derivations, in which Right Conjunct
Reduction precedes Postposing:

> The facts about him and the facts about her were
> virtually identical, but he got the job. →
> The facts about him and (about) her were virtually
> identical, but he got the job. →
> The facts were virtually identical about him and (about)
> her, but he got the job.
> The wines from the eastern regions of France and the
> wines from the western regions of Germany are quite
> similar. →
> The wines from the eastern regions of France and
> (from) the western regions of Germany are quite
> similar. →
> The wines are quite similar from the eastern regions
> of France and (from) the western regions of Ger-
> many.

For Postposing to precede Right Conjunct Reduction in such
cases, there would have to be a step like the following in the
derivation:

> The facts about him and the facts about her were
> virtually identical, but he got the job. →
> *The facts and the facts were virtually identical about
> him and (about) her, but he got the job.

As shown, Postposing would have to separate the prepositional
phrases from their conjoined subjects; but this operation
is in general impossible:

> The rumors about Adele and the gossip concerning
> Jean were similar. →
> *The rumors and the gossip were similar about Adele
> and concerning Jean.

Therefore, taking the second and third facts together, we have
the following ordering on any cycle:

> Right Conjunct Reduction
> Postposing
> Question Formation (QF)

But note that there are two relevant situations that may
arise in deep structure: there may be a single interrogative
S containing conjoined nodes embedded within it, or there
may be two interrogative S's contained within a conjoined

structure. In the latter case we would expect Right Conjunct Reduction to follow QF, if QF were cyclic, which is what happens. To proceed with the argument, note that Right Conjunct Reduction must apply after QF in the following derivation:

> (a) I wonder what strange sights yòu'll see in mý coun-
>   try and what strange sights Ì'll see in yóur country. →
> (b) I wonder what strange sights yòu'll see in mý coun-
>   try and Ì'll see in yóur country.

QF has already applied to (a). If Right Conjunct Reduction only preceded QF in derivations, (b) would not be generable. To apply prior to QF, Right Conjunct Reduction would have to delete the material between the verb and the prepositional phrase that has not yet been fronted by QF: but this operation is in general impossible, producing ungrammatical strings:

> *You'll hit some great spots in my country and I'll hit
>   in your country.

Conjunct Reduction may only delete repeated material at the extreme of the conjunct, which establishes that Right Conjunct Reduction must follow QF to derive (b).

On the other hand, Conjunct Reduction must also be able to precede QF within a derivation. Consider the following assertion and question:

> (y) He said that some things about France and some
>   things about Italy were similar.
> (z) What things did he say were similar about France
>   and (about) Italy?

(z) cannot be taken as a base form for the same reasons that show Postposing to be a transformation. For example, the following sentence certainly has no reading like (y)'s:

> *He said that they are similar about France and (about)
>   Italy.

Therefore, (z) must have an application of Postposing in its derivation. We already know that Postposing cannot follow QF, so it must precede QF in the derivation of (z). Right Conjunct Reduction must in turn precede Postposing in the derivation of (z); otherwise Postposing would have to detach prepositional phrases from conjoined subjects, an operation that has been shown to be impossible:

> He said that what things about France and what things about Italy were similar? →
> *He said that what things and what things were similar about France and about Italy?

But this means that Right Conjunct Reduction must precede QF in the derivation of (z):

> He said that what things about France and what things about Italy were similar? →
> He said that what things about France and (about) Italy were similar? →
> He said that what things were similar about France and (about) Italy? →
> What things did he say were similar about France and (about) Italy?

We see that both sentence (z) and the sentence

> What things about France and (about) Italy did he say were similar?

are derived by applying Right Conjunct Reduction and then QF; the only difference is that in (z) the optional Postposing rule intervenes after Right Conjunct Reduction and before QF. We used Postposing merely as a means of "forcing" Right Conjunct Reduction to apply before QF in this derivation.

Having demonstrated that there is a derivation in which Right Conjunct Reduction must precede and a derivation in which it must follow QF, I conclude that both are cyclic transformations.

Let us turn now to Relative Clause Formation (RCF). We see at once that an argument exactly parallel to the last can be formulated, using a sentence analogous to (z) to show that Conjunct Reduction can precede RCF—

> The things that he said were quite similar about France and (about) Italy were these.

—and a sentence analogous to (b) to show that Conjunct Reduction may follow RCF—

> There are many strange sights that yòu'll see in mý country and (that) Í'll see in yoúr country.

Observe that RCF is not only cyclic, it is NP–cyclic. That is, its domain of application is NP rather than S, just as I have assumed in the stress derivation. This formulation is syntactically necessary to derive "double relatives," such as

> The men she has met that she likes are all artists.
> The only solution I've found that satisfies me is this.

Each example contains two relatives but only one head. For the first, there would be an underlying representation (roughly) like that shown in (15). (I take no stand here on whether relatives come from the Determiner in deep structure; if they do, then the transformation that shifts them to the right of the head must be NP–cyclic to produce the configuration in (15).) If RCF applies to NP, the derivation is easily accomplished by first applying RCF to NP_1 and then NP. Otherwise the sentence cannot be derived without letting cyclic transformations reapply on the same cycle.

(15)

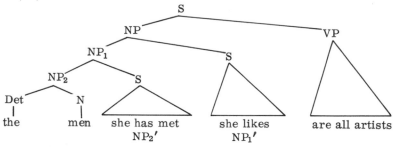

REFERENCES

Berman, A. (1970). "Abstract and Agentive Sentences." Manuscript. Cambridge: Harvard University.

Bierwisch, M. (1968). "Two Critical Problems in Accent Rules." *Journal of Linguistics* 4:173–178.

Bolinger, D. (1958). "Stress and Information." In *Forms of English*, edited by Isamu Abe and Tetsuya Kanekiyo. Cambridge: Harvard University Press.

Bresnan, J. (1970a). "An Argument against Pronominalization." *Linguistic Inquiry* 1:122–123.

—— (1970b). "On Complementizers: Toward a Syntactic Theory of Complement Types." *Foundations of Language* 6:297–321.

—— (in preparation). *The Theory of Complementation in English Syntax.*

Chomsky, N. (1965). *Aspects of the Theory of Syntax.* Cambridge: MIT Press.

—— (1970). "Remarks on Nominalization." In *Readings in English Transformational Grammar*, edited by Roderick A. Jacobs and Peter S. Rosenbaum. New York: Ginn.

—— (to appear). "Some Empirical Issues in the Theory of Transformational Grammar."

——, and M. Halle (1968). *The Sound Pattern of English.* New York: Harper and Row.

Dougherty, R. (1969). "An Interpretive Theory of Pronominal Reference." *Foundations of Language* 5:488–519.

Emonds, J. (1970). "Root and Structure Preserving Transformations." Ph.D. dissertation, Massachusetts Institute of Technology.

Hasegawa, Kinsuke (1968). "The Passive Construction in English." *Language* 44:230–243.

Jackendoff, R. (1969). "Some Rules of Semantic Interpretation for English." Ph.D. dissertation, Massachusetts Institute of Technology.

Kuno, Susumu (to appear). "Some Properties of Non-Referential Noun Phrases." In *Studies in Oriental and General Linguistics*, edited by Roman Jakobson. Tokyo: TEC Co.

Lees, R. (1960). "A Multiply Ambiguous Adjectival Construction in English." *Language* 36:207–221.

McCawley, J. (1970). "English as a VSO Language." *Language* 46:286–299.

Newman, S. (1946). "On the Stress System of English." *Word* 2:171–187.

Postal, P. (1968). *Crossover Phenomena.* Yorktown Heights, N. Y.: I. B. M.

—— (1968a). "On Coreferential Complement Subject Deletion." Yorktown Heights, N. Y.: I. B. M.

Ross, J. (1967). "Constraints on Variables in Syntax." Ph.D. dissertation, Massachusetts Institute of Technology.

A Reformulation of Grimm's Law

JOSEPH EMONDS

University of Illinois, Center for Advanced Study

Grimm's Law expresses the principal sound changes in the Indo-European (IE) stop consonant system that differentiated Germanic from other branches of the IE language family.

IE is generally considered to have possessed three series of stop consonants: voiceless, lax voiced, and tense voiced:

p	b	bh
t	d	dh
k	g	gh
k^w	g^w	gh^w

The Germanic counterparts to the *p*-series are voiceless continuants;[1] the counterparts to the *b*-series are voiceless stops; and the counterparts to the *bh*-series are voiced continuants between vowels and voiced stops initially. Thus, Grimm's Law is usually written in three parts:

G1.	p → ph
G2.	b → p
G3.	ph → f and bh → v

The change of initial *v* to *b* in Germanic I assume to be a subsequent development. For brevity, the changes have been written only for the labials. In terms of distinctive features, G1, G2, and G3 are written as follows:

---

[1] By Verner's Law, these became voiced in certain contexts, but this change is of no concern here.

G1.   [-sonorant, -voice] → [+tense]
G2.   [-sonorant, -tense] → [-voice]
G3.   [-sonorant, +tense] → [+continuant]

We will not be concerned with G3 in this paper or with any of the details of its formulation. In the history of Germanic, G3 may have preceded G2, but this possibility has no bearing on the topics in this paper.

There has been much controversy among linguists about whether G1 and G2 were in some sense "one" linguistic event, or whether they were completely separate historical changes. The former claim, for example, is argued in J. Fourquet's *Les mutations consonantiques du germanique*. Any of the arguments in the present paper are valid, whatever the truth of Fourquet's claim. For purposes of explicitness, I will regard the separate statements of G1 and G2 above as the correct, accepted formulation of Grimm's Law. If I were to start from a basis that incorporated the two rules into one, some of my arguments would require more complicated formulation, which would only render them harder to understand without any compensation in insight or accuracy.

G1 and G2 represent events in our reconstruction of IE history that are not parts of other known events in this history; even if G1 and G2 are one event, it is a complex one, and to isolate it from other IE phenomena is not a desirable analysis.

Therefore, let us consider G1 and G2 to have operated historically in the "reverse" direction. That is, assume that the traditional output to G1 and G2 is actually the original system of the IE obstruents. Thus, Proto-Germanic (minus the effect of G3) would actually represent the most ancient, "pure" form of Indo-European. Let us call this "New Indo-European" (NIE) as opposed to "Traditional Indo-European" (TIE).

TIE:	p	b	bh	NIE:	ph	p	bh
	t	d	dh		th	t	dh
	k	g	gh		kh	k	gh
	k^w	g^w	gh^w		kh^w	k^w	gh^w

It goes without saying that no specific claim about the phonetic nature of the "tense" feature of the IE stops can be made.

The reverses of G1 and G2 (call them Z1 and Z2) would then operate in all those dialects or branches of IE in which Grimm's Law has been said not to operate.

Z1.   p → b
Z2.   ph → p

We will see in this paper how at least Z2 can be related to other known historical processes in IE, in a way that G1 and G2 are not in the traditional analysis of the history of IE. Hence, the total number of historical "events" in my reconstruction of language history can be reduced. (One cannot, however, characterize what constitutes a historical linguistic event in any complete way; for example, one cannot claim that the only historical phonological events are the additions of single rules to grammars; the addition of several related rules at successive intervals may be causally connected and be part of one "event.")

It has often been remarked that the TIE analysis is weak because the reconstructed stop system is intrinsically of doubtful validity. Any quick inventory of stop systems in existing natural languages throws doubt on whether the TIE stop system is even possible in natural language. As Jakobson has observed: "To my knowledge, no language adds to the pair /t/ – /d/ a voiced aspirate /dh/ without having its voiceless counterpart /th/ . . . ; therefore theories operating with the three phonemes /t/ – /d/ – /dh/ in Proto-Indo-European must reconsider the question of their phonemic essence."[2]

This remark cannot be taken as support for the NIE stop system, since the unmarked system that Jakobson and many others would consider more credible than TIE would be *p*, *b*, and *ph*. Although NIE avoids having two series of voiced stops with only one voiceless, it has two tense series and only one lax. The heart of the dilemma is that as long as one considers the *bh*-series to be motivated in IE (because of Indic *bh*, Greek *ph*, Iranian *b*, Germanic *v* and *b*, and Armenian *b*), one must postulate a three-series stop system with voiced aspirates. Such a system would be a rare phenomenon, no matter what the other two series are. Given that two of the

[2]Roman Jakobson, "Typological Studies and Their Contribution to Historical Comparative Linguistics," in *Selected Writings*, vol. I, p. 532.

series are *p* and *bh*, the only relevant question for the analysis presented in this paper is the following: Is a language with *ph* or a language with *b* more natural? Without struggling with this rather abstract question, let us turn to some other arguments that support the NIE rather than the TIE analysis.

(1) The Iranian, Slavic, Baltic, Celtic, and Latin branches of IE exhibit the following development. For convenience, these branches will be referred to as the "central group" (CG).

TIE	p	b	bh
NIE	ph	p	bh
CG	p	b	b

(Actually, in Latin, *bh*, *dh*, *gh*, and *gh^w* became *b*, *d*, *h*, and *w*, and only between vowels was the development this simple.) In the TIE analysis, the two processes G1 and G2 are formally equivalent to the two processes Z1 and Z2 in the NIE analysis. Despite this equivalence, the traditional analysis must postulate a separate historical event to differentiate the central group from Greek and Indic:

$$\text{CG} \quad [-\text{sonorant}] \to [-\text{tense}]$$

But compare CG to the formulation of Z1 and Z2 in distinctive features:

$$\text{Z1.} \quad [-\text{sonorant}, -\text{tense}] \to [+\text{voice}]$$
$$\text{Z2.} \quad [-\text{sonorant}, -\text{voice}] \to [-\text{tense}]$$

In the new analysis, the historical change CG is clearly not isolated from Z2, as it is in the traditional analysis, where the counterpart of Z2 (G1) and CG operate in different language groups. Rather, CG is a *generalization* of Z2 in an obvious sense (dropping a feature in the rule widens its applicability) and is part of the same historical event. Thus, Greek, Indic, and the central group all underwent Z1 and Z2, but Z2 was simplified in the central group and generalized to rule CG. Since the NIE analysis allows us to relate Z2 to another process in IE, namely CG, in a way that G1 could not, we have an important reason for preferring it to the TIE analysis.

(2) The unique reflexes of the IE stop system in Hittite provide further evidence for the NIE analysis.[3]

TIE	t	d	dh
NIE	th	t	dh
Hittite	t	t	d

It is fairly obvious that two rules are needed to derive the Hittite stops from TIE, the second of which is CG, as in section (1).

H.   [-sonorant, -tense] → [-voice]
CG.   [-sonorant] → [-tense]

The operation of CG in Hittite and the central group was probably one event.

However, if we take NIE as the primitive stop system, H can be dispensed with entirely. CG explains the developments perfectly and, incidentally, applies now to two series of IE stops rather than, in somewhat ad hoc fashion, just to one. Thus, in the general picture furnished by NIE, Hittite differed from the central group only in that it did not undergo Z1.

(3) Compare the Germanic and Armenian obstruents that result from IE stops to the TIE and NIE systems. (Dentals will be used in this chart, since *ph* subsequently became *h* in Armenian.)

TIE	t	d	dh
NIE	th	t	dh
Germanic	θ	t	ð–d
Armenian	th	t	d

In the first place, although Armenian is similar to Germanic, it clearly did not undergo G3. Rather, the tense, voiced stops were simply laxed:

A.   [-sonorant, +voice] → [-tense]

This rule must apply, whether one accepts the NIE or the TIE analysis. In either case, it can be related to the rule CG; one could imagine that, when CG was operative in the Iranian branch of IE, a restricted version of it was borrowed into

---

[3]Antoine Meillet, *Introduction à l'étude comparative des langues indo-européenes*, p. 84. The details are in the third paragraph.

Armenian. But this possibility has no bearing on choosing between NIE and TIE.

More important, the TIE analysis must suppose that Armenian also underwent G1 and G2. In particular, it must suppose that G1 and G2 applied independently to Germanic and to Armenian, because the Germanic and Armenian areas are geographically distant and because the two languages do not regularly share the same linguistic characteristics. For example, Armenian is in the *satem* group and Germanic is not; the development of *s* differs in the two, as does the development of the vowels; the accent is fronted in Germanic but not in Armenian; and so forth. If there is a verified principle of dialect geography, it is that, when faced with dialect maps containing isolated relic areas, one assumes that these areas exhibit the older situation in the language.[4] An exception might occur if there was evidence that the speakers in the two areas had at one time been in one linguistic community vis-à-vis the larger group; such evidence would be the sharing of several independent language characteristics.

Since this condition is not fulfilled for the isolated Armenian-Germanic areas, the TIE analysis grossly and arbitrarily violates this dialect geography principle by treating the A area as primitive and the B area as innovative, as is shown in the diagram below.

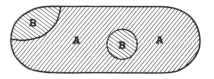

With the same reasoning, the two rules in the TIE analysis, H, necessary for Hittite, and G2, necessary for Germanic and Armenian, are identical, and no explanation other than accident can be given for this fact. Thus, the principle of dialect geography gives us further reasons for preferring the NIE analysis, in which Z1 and Z2 operate on almost all of Indo-European.

(4) Consider next the development of Greek and Indic from

[4]See, for example, the diagrams in Leonard Bloomfield's *Language*, pp. 333, 334, 336.

NIE. As is well known, Greek also requires a rule devoicing the voiced aspirates that appear in Sanskrit.

DV. $[$-sonorant, +tense$] \rightarrow [$-voice$]$

DV yields three stages of development from NIE to Greek:

NIE		ph	p	bh	
Z1:	p → b	ph	b	bh	(This rule applies in Indic, Greek, and the central group.)
Z2:	ph → p	p	b	bh	(This is the Indic system; the central group goes further by means of CG, as discussed above.)
DV:	bh → ph	p	b	ph	(This is the Greek system; both NIE and TIE analyses need DV.)

Another well-known development in Greek and Indic was the laxing of stops directly before other obstruents or before another tense obstruent in the root (but not in a suffix). Examples follow:[5]

Greek:
thi – thē – mi → tithēmi   the – throph – a → tetropha
Sanskrit:
dha – dhā – mi → dadhāmi   bho – bhudh – ye → bobudhye

Greek:
gluph – s – ō → glupsō   e – threph – thēn → ethrepthēn
Sanskrit:
labh – sya – te → labsyate   dhugh – dhve → dhugdhve
                (lapsyate)

Kiparsky, referring to the first of these as cluster reduction (CR) and to the second as Grassmann's Law (GL), has formulated this rule as follows: (I am substituting $[$-*sonorant*$]$ for $[$-*vocalic*$]$.)

$$\begin{matrix} \text{CR.} \\ \text{GL.} \end{matrix} \quad [\text{-sonorant}] \rightarrow [\text{-tense}] \, / \left\{ \begin{matrix} \underline{\quad}\ \text{s, dh, \#} & \begin{bmatrix} \text{-sonorant} \\ \text{+tense} \\ \text{+root} \end{bmatrix} \\ \underline{\quad}[\text{+cont}]_0 \end{matrix} \right\}$$

---

[5]The examples and the basis of the discussion are taken from the third chapter of Paul Kiparsky's "Phonological Change."

The final conclusion reached in Kiparsky's thesis[6] is that certain relic forms in Greek indicate that DV operated historically *after* CR and GL. If this conclusion is true, we can say that CR and GL operated right after Z2 (i.e., that no important historical changes affected tense stops between the operation of Z2 and of CR–GL). In any case CR and GL operated right after Z2 in Indic, since DV is a Greek rule.

But CR–GL is of the same form as Z2, which can be rewritten as follows:

Z2. $[-\text{sonorant}] \rightarrow [-\text{tense}] \, / \, [-\overline{\text{voice}}]$

Thus, Z2 can be formally related not only to general laxing (CG) in the history of the central group, but also to more restricted laxing (CR–GL) in the history of Greek and Indic. Cluster reduction and Grassmann's Law simply represent two more environments in which the laxing tendency, first expressed by Z2, appeared in Greek and Indic.

Even if Kiparsky is incorrect in saying that DV did not intervene between Indo-European Z2 and CR–GL in Greek, it seems plausible that an accurate theory of linguistic change could formally capture the similarity of CR–GL and Z2 as part of the same historical event; however, if Kiparsky is correct, the formalism needed in this case is the very simple bracket notation used for ordering rules in synchronic generative phonology.

Since the possibility outlined above is another way to tie in Z2, but not G1, to a known historical event, namely, the laxing laws in Greek and Indic, we have another reason to prefer the NIE analysis.

(5) IE suffixes begin only with the tense stops of NIE. (Note that even this generalization cannot be stated in the TIE system.) Thus, the following possible stop combinations occur at a suffix boundary:

TIE:			NIE:		
g	+	t	k	+	th
gh	+	t**	gh	+	th**
k	+	t	kh	+	th
g	+	dh	k	+	dh
gh	+	dh	gh	+	dh
k	+	dh	kh	+	dh

[6]Ibid., p. 3–25.

(For simplicity, only the combinations of velars followed by dentals have been listed.) In IE, the first element of obstruent clusters assimilates in voicing to the second element, with the first element losing its tenseness, even in Greek and Indic, by the cluster reduction rule.

In Iranian and Indic, however, the output of the underlying double-starred combination is $g + dh$ ($g + d$ in Iranian, because of CG). Given this irregularity, usually known as Bartholomae's Law, we can state two things using the NIE analysis that are not statable in the traditional analysis. First, the Indic-Iranian rule of voicing assimilation states that *if one of the elements is voiced, the cluster is voiced.* Under the TIE analysis, however, $g + t$ becomes $k + t$. Second, TIE cannot explain how tenseness "crosses" onto the second element in $gh + t$ without an ad hoc rule. But if the tenseness is already there, as in NIE, there is no problem, once the voicing assimilation takes place. The nonvoiced aspirates of NIE that remain such (the unstarred *th*'s in the above chart) are deaspirated by Z2 without the use of an ad hoc rule. Thus, NIE is again preferable over TIE.

It might be well at this point to summarize the development of the various branches of IE from NIE by means of a chart, since the final sections, which deal with the exact form of Z1 and Z2 rather than with the systems of individual language groups, will demand a clear grasp of what has been proposed so far.

Indo-European:	ph	bh	p			
Voicing of p (Z1) in all branches except Germanic, Armenian, Hittite:	ph	bh	b	Relic areas:		
				ph	bh	p
Laxing of voiceless stops (Z2) in all areas having undergone Z1:	p	bh	b			
Generalized laxing in the central group and in Hittite (except for non-intervocalic voiced Latin aspirates)	p	b	b	(Hittite:		
				p	b	p)
Devoicing (DV) in Greek and in the remaining Latin aspirates:	p	ph(f)	b			

Greek *ph* and Indic *bh* further laxed by cluster reduction and Grassmann's Law:	p ph–p b	b	
	p bh–b b		
Operation of G3 in Germanic:			f v–b p
Laxing of voiced stops in Armenian, probably related to CG:			ph(h) b p

(6) One might suggest, as an argument against the NIE analysis and in favor of the TIE analysis, the alternation in Proto-Germanic between the infinitive and the past participle in a verb like "to save": *skapjan* versus *skaftas*. Traditionally, this alternation in Germanic between a stop and a continuant has been thought to be due to the independently motivated rule of voicing assimilation in IE. That is, the IE *skabjan* versus *skaptas* was due to the devoicing of an original *b* before *t*, and the normal operation of Grimm's Law gave the Proto-Germanic forms. (The *t* and *k* in *skaftas* are not aspirated because of a condition on G1 that will be discussed in the next section.)

The Germanic alternation seems to be a valid point in defense of TIE, yet an explanation is not lacking in the NIE framework either. On the one hand, the Modern English *kt* cluster is often pronounced *xt*, and we know that the Latin *k* was eventually weakened to *y* before *t* (*octo* → *ocho*, *huit*; *lactum* → *leche*, *lait*), most certainly by passing through the stage of *x*. On the other hand, the similar behavior of labials and velars is attested in many languages; this behavior is evidence for the feature *noncoronal* in consonants. For example, in Modern English, the only permissible final stop clusters are *pt* and *kt*; in many dialects, *y* in the triphthong *yuw* is retained just after labials and velars; and labials and velars do not occur after the diphthongs *au* and *oi* in final position.

Thus, it is not improbable that the original forms in IE were NIE *skapjan* and *skaptas* and that at least noncoronal stops became fricatives in Germanic before a following stop. Thus, in Germanic, *p* would have first become a voiceless bilabial fricative (phonetically) in *skaptas*; subsequently, when G3 operated to change *ph* to *f*, this bilabial fricative "fell together" with the new *f*.

The above is not meant as a refutation of the usefulness of the TIE analysis to explain this alternation, but rather as a demonstration that the facts of the argument are not incompatible with the NIE position. They can be accounted for by postulating an extra but natural sound change in the history of Germanic.

(7) Consider next the four forms of Proto-Germanic given below:

skapjan (infinitive) — skaphtas (participle)
nasjan (infinitive) — nasithas (participle)

In the traditional analysis, this alternation has been explained by the fact that G1 was not completely general, but operated only after sonorants. In an NIE analysis, one must postulate a rule *within Germanic* to account for the *th*–*t* alternation, since the rules expressing Grimm's Law (Z1 and Z2) operate outside Germanic. This rule is of the form:

LAX.   [-sonorant, -voice] → [-tense] / [-sonorant]___

At first, the necessity of incorporating this rule into a total NIE analysis might seem to be evidence for TIE, but closer examination does not bear this out. First, the context of the rule is nothing more than the complement of the context of G1 in the TIE analysis. Second, there is no reason why LAX cannot be regarded as a rule that applied to all of IE as a synchronic rule, before Z2 began the fragmentation into dialects. Indeed, a quick look at the formulation of Z2 shows that Z2 is a generalization of LAX, just as we have previously argued that CG is a generalization of Z2. Third, there is precedent for postulating a rule like LAX, since this same rule applies to voiceless stops in Modern English. Thus, LAX is a completely natural phonological rule whose presence *within* IE gives a basis for the operation of Z2, the rule that differentiates Germanic from the rest of IE. Also, although TIE describes the alternations given above, its explanation of them is no more convincing than that of NIE, and, inasmuch as NIE gives a synchronic IE basis for a diachronic rule, one might even consider the NIE analysis superior.

(8) In TIE, the only series of stops that occurs after an initial *s* is the *t*-(voiceless) series (I will refer to a series of stops in this section by its dental member), because initial *s* (or *z*) plus a voiced consonant is extremely rare in language.

In NIE, the correspondent to an initial TIE *st* combination is NIE *sth*. But if NIE is the correct view, should it not be possible for an initial NIE *st* (corresponding to TIE *sd*) to occur? Indeed, it should be, but in any such combination Z1 must not have operated to yield *sd* (*zd* by voicing assimilation), since no initial *zd* clusters are attested in the non-Germanic branches of IE. Thus, we must assume that Z1 did not operate after word-initial *s*. After word-internal *s*, however, it did operate, because *zd* clusters are found in non-Germanic IE (*nizdos, ozdos*, etc.).

Let us suppose then that early IE had both initial *st* and *slh*, as well as internal *st* and *sth*. Operation of Z1 internally would give *zd* versus *sth*. Operation of LAX would give *zd* versus *st* internally, but would cause initial *st* and *sth* to fall together as *st*. Thus, the original IE root for the following cognates could begin with either NIE *sth* or NIE *st*.

> Sanskrit: *stighnute*; Slavic: *stignǫ*; Greek: *steíkhō*; Gothic: *steiga*.
> Vedic: *str̥bhíḥ*; Greek: *astēr*; Cornish: *steren*; Latin: *stella*; Gothic: *stairno*; Armenian: *astł*.

These forms now allow us to explain an important irregularity in the TIE analysis. Recall the well-known constraints on morpheme structure in IE, by which root syllables cannot have the following three TIE forms:

$$t \, (+cont)_0 \, dh \; ; \quad dh \, (+cont)_0 \, t \; ; \quad d \, (+cont)_0 \, d$$

(The notation $(X)_0$ means zero or more elements X.) An exception to this constraint in the TIE analysis is the combination $st(+cont)_0 dh$, which can appear as a root. The first example given above is such a root, with final *gh* instead of *dh*. But, in the NIE analysis, we can derive this root from an original NIE $st(+cont)_0 gh$, rather than from NIE $sth(+cont)_0 gh$. The following constraints on morpheme structure exist in NIE terms:

$$th \, (+cont)_0 \, dh \; ; \quad dh \, (+cont)_0 \, th \; ; \quad t \, (+cont)_0 \, t$$

Therefore, no exception for roots with initial *st* need be made. Thus, the NIE analysis eliminates an asymmetry in the TIE analysis. There seems to be no similar natural extension of TIE that can account for this asymmetry in the way a careful statement of the NIE framework can.

(9) Finally, NIE allows us to view the development of the tense, voiceless aspirates in Indic and Greek in a new light. I am not denying, however, that credible theories about their origin have been advanced in terms of TIE (by the introduction of laryngeals, etc.). However, the presence of voiceless aspirates in NIE (the *ph*-series) suggests, as one possibility, an imperfect operation of LAX or Z2 in just those languages where some laxing took place, but in which all aspirated stops were not eliminated by CG. (By "imperfect operation," I mean the existence of a dialect in which the rule failed to operate, the dialect later dying out after contributing a number of "exceptions" to the previously completed historical change.)

If such imperfect operation of Z2 took place, it would account for Indic and Greek *ph*'s that corresponded to *p*'s in the central group and *ph*'s in Germanic. Meillet gives some examples of this type:[7]

> Sanskrit: *phūt-karah*; Armenian: *phukh*; Greek: *phūsa*;
> Lithuanian: *pūsti*.
> Sanskrit: *kakhati* (from *khakhati*, by GL); Greek: *kakházo*
> (from *khakhazo*, again by GL); Armenian: *xaxankh*;
> Slavic: *xoxotŭ*; Germanic: *huoh*; Latin: *cachinnus*
> (*kakinus*).
> Sanskrit: *skhálāmi*; Armenian: *sxalim*; Latin: *scelus*.

The fact that the *ph*'s and *x*'s that occur in the Armenian (and the Slavic) examples do not correspond to the regular development of NIE *ph* and *kh* in those languages supports the notion that "imperfect operation" of Z2 should be interpreted as reintroduction of words from a dialect that did not undergo Z2 (or the other rules that affected Armenian and Slavic development of *ph* and *kh*).

Hypothesizing a similar imperfect operation of LAX—the forerunner of Z2 in the NIE framework—has even more interesting implications. According to this hypothesis, an *Indic* or *Greek ph* should correspond to a *p* in the central group, as before, but to a *p*, not a *ph*, in Germanic. Of course, such a correspondence should only occur after obstruents, which is the context for LAX. The reason for the predicted presence

---

[7]Meillet, *Introduction*, p. 90. Cf. also p. 84, second paragraph.

of *p* in Germanic is that the original NIE *ph*, which is supposedly left intact in the dialect exempt from LAX and rein-
troduced as *ph* later in Indic and Greek, is changed to *p* in all
"regular" IE by LAX, and not just in the central group. In
fact, there seem to be such correspondences of Indic *ph* with
Germanic *p* (just the opposite of the usual correspondence of
Germanic *ph* and Indic *p*). One common example is given by
Meillet:[8]

Sanskrit: *sphuráti*; Armenian: *spiřkh*; Icelandic: *spori*.

Thus, if alternative theories on the origin of voiceless
aspirates in Indic are unconvincing or incomplete, we have
reason to look to the NIE formulation as an improvement over
TIE.

(10) In this paper I have examined numerous arguments
that favor reinterpreting Grimm's Law as having worked
partly in reverse. That is, I have hypothesized that the
original IE stop series were tense voiced (*bh*), tense voiceless
(*ph*), and lax voiceless (*p*), rather than the traditional *bh*, *p*,
and *b*, respectively. It has been shown how this view accords
better with later developments of stops in the various Indo-
European languages. I have also examined, in sections (6) and
(7), some observations that might be taken as objections to the
principal hypothesis and have shown that they do not seriously
undermine it.

It is certainly possible that each of the arguments in this
paper can be refuted or balanced with a counterargument in
favor of the traditional view of the Indo-European stop system.
Nonetheless, it is inadmissible to take this traditional view as
the null hypothesis in discussing Indo-European, since it can
be challenged by many arguments supporting a consistent
alternative position. Any argument about more general questions of sound structure or sound change cannot unquestion-
ingly be based on traditional assumptions about Indo-European
consonant phonology. Rather, a new effort is needed to see
whether Germanic or non-Germanic branches of Indo-European are representative of the most ancient state of that
language.

[8]Ibid., p. 90.

REFERENCES

Bloomfield, L. (1933). *Language.* New York, H. Holt and Co.
Fourquet, J. (1948). *Les mutations consonantiques du germanique.*
   Paris, Les Belles Lettres.
Jakobson, R. (1962). *Selected Writings* vol. 1. The Hague, Mouton.
Kiparsky, P. (1965). "Phonological Change." Ph.D. Dissertation,
   Massachusetts Institute of Technology.
Meillet, A. (1964). *Introduction à l'étude comparative de langues*
   indo-européens. University, University of Alabama Press.

Naturalness Conditions in Phonology, with Particular Reference to English Vowels

JAMES E. HOARD
University of British Columbia

This paper sketches briefly an analysis of the English vowel system in accord with what seem to be necessary constraints on underlying phonological systems. In §1 the problem of determining the segment underlying the diphthong *oi* is taken up.[1] §2 deals with constraints on underlying phonological systems and on phonological descriptions. §3 offers an analysis of the English vowel system that differs in a number of respects from the description in *The Sound Pattern of English* (hereafter cited as SPE). In §3 the feature system of SPE is employed. §4 offers an alternate approach to the analysis of the English vowels using a different feature system and a markedness approach to rule application.

1. What Underlies *oi*?

Chomsky and Halle (1968:191–192) argue that the diphthong *oi* of *coin, boy,* and *point* is derived from an underlying /ȫ/.

Observe that we do have the Diphthongization Rule (21) which inserts a glide after a tense vowel. To account for the glide of [ɔy], we must, therefore, take V* to be some tense vowel to which the y-glide can be attached by rule (21). Since a y-glide is inserted by this rule only after a nonback vowel, we must take V* to be nonback,

---

[1] In this paper the terms *underlying segment* and *phoneme* are used interchangeably.

which means it cannot be [ɔ]. The vowel of phonetic [ɔ̄y] is low and
round; therefore, if we are to avoid adding new rules to the
grammar, we must take the underlying vowel V* to be low and round
as well. We are thus led to the conclusion that V* should be the
tense, nonback, low, round vowel, that is, [ǣ]. In further support of
this conclusion is the observation that [ǣ] in fact constitutes an
otherwise unexplained gap in the phonological pattern, since the
other three tense low vowels (namely, [ǣ], [ā], [ɔ̄],) do appear in
lexical matrices. (p. 192)

There are a number of observations to be made about their
argument. First, the diphthongization rule is not necessarily
formulated correctly. As given by Chomsky and Halle
(1968:183), the rule inserts a *w* after tense, back vowels and a
y after tense, front vowels. In §3, below, diphthongization is
reformulated to insert a *w* after tense, rounded vowels and a *y*
after tense, unrounded vowels. All we need to note here is
that their argument that a front vowel underlies *oi* is consistent with their formulation of the diphthongization rule, but
that their formulation of the diphthongization rule forces the
choice of a front vowel as the segment underlying *oi*.

Second, if by [ɔ] we mean a low, rounded vowel like the
vowel of *caught*, then *oi* should not be transcribed [ɔ̄y] in
General American English. The vowel of *coin* is no lower
than the vowel of *cut*. If *cut* has a mid vowel, so does *coin*. If
we were to use the four-height IPA transcription scheme
u, o, ɔ, ɒ for rounded back vowels, then *oi* would have [ɔ]
(lower-mid), but *caught* would be transcribed with [ɒ]. If we
use only a three-height scheme, *u, o, ɔ*; then *oi* should be
transcribed [ō̜y].[2]

Third, Chomsky and Halle note that *oi* is not subject to
laxing if suffixes are added (1968:122); thus, *exploit-exploita-
tive*. However, there are alternations involving *oi*.

(I)   [oy] ~ [ʌ]   *joint*   *junction*
                   destroy   *destruction*
                   point   *punctual, puncture*
                   counterpoint   *contrapuntal*
                   poignant   *pungent*

[2]For the most part, the practice of transcribing diphthongs as [Vy] and
[Vw] is followed here, even though the transcription of diphthongs using
y and *w* is phonetically inaccurate.

The laxing of the vowel in the words in the second column of (I) is due to the following nondental cluster (SPE rule (20)-(III)). For the word *contrapuntal* the vowel is lax even though it does have a dental cluster. The easiest course is apparently to mark *contrapuntal* exceptionally as [+laxing rule] in the lexicon.

There are other alternations involving *oi*.

(II) [ōy] ~ [ōw]   *spoil*   *spoliation*
                    despoil   *despoliation*
                    voice   *vocal*
      [ōy] ~ [ūw]   *choice*   *choose*
           ~ [ōw]   *chose*

The alternations given in (I) suggest that the phoneme underlying *oi* is a nonlow back vowel; those of (II) only that it is a back vowel. The pronunciation [ōy] suggests that it is a mid vowel. If the diphthongization rule is reformulated to add *y* to unrounded vowels, the obvious solution is to choose /ā̄/ as the phoneme underlying [ōy]. /ā̄/ will undergo diphthongization and rounding adjustment to yield the appropriate segment. Integrating this suggestion into the system of rules proposed in SPE for English vowels is taken up in §3.

As a fourth observation about the argument for *oi* advanced in SPE, I will argue in the next section that /ǣ/ does not fill any "gap" in the English vowel system and thus could not possibly underlie *oi*.

2. Constraints on Underlying Phonemic Systems

There has been much discussion about the formulation of appropriate substantive constraints on the choice of phonemic segments for a language. One possibility is to stipulate that the phonemic system of a language is a subset of the occurring set of phones.[3] However, Brame (this volume) has given a convincing argument that phonemic /ʕ/ is needed for Maltese Arabic, even though it never occurs phonetically.

If the subset hypothesis is too strong, as it seems to be, what is available to the language learner for coding the phonetic data he is presented with? If the linguist is to

---

[3]According to McCawley (1966), Edward Sapir held this view. See also Kiparsky (1968).

describe the competence of speakers of L, presumably the description of L must reflect whatever constraints are imposed on the ideal learner-speaker.[4]

One possibility for a constraint on phonemic systems is that, if a distinctive feature is not used contrastively in a language (i.e., the feature is totally redundant), it is unavailable as a phonemically distinct feature.[5] Thus, for English, such features as secondary closure, suction and pharyngealization will be unavailable for lexical coding.

Assuming the eventual development of a full markedness theory along the lines presented by Chomsky and Halle (in SPE) and Postal (1968), this constraint can be stated as follows:

> Condition 1. Only features that are contrastive in a language can be given marked values in the lexical coding of the language.

This condition immediately narrows the choice of underlying phonemes considerably. For English, it limits the range of possible consonants in particular, but still leaves most theoretically possible vowels as potential phonemes.

In SPE, condition 1 is explicitly denied:

> We do not take this step here, however, [i.e., advocate condition 1—JEH], since we are unable to formulate such a condition in a way which will still permit a wide class of familiar cases in which a distinctive feature is lost phonetically though it remains functional in phonological rules. Thus, to take just one of innumerable examples, in Modern Hebrew the feature of pharyngealization (which in Arabic distinguishes the class of "emphatic" consonants) is phonetically lost in stops, but it (or some other non-phonetic feature) must still be marked in lexical matrices, to prevent postvocalic spirantization in what is historically an emphatic [k], for example. (p. 170, fn. 7).

I have no idea what the "innumerable examples" referred to might reveal, but for Modern Hebrew a nonphonetic feature

---

[4] It should be clear that it is necessary to place constraints on phonological descriptions if the latter are not to be merely mathematical exercises. If we are serious about describing what the speaker "knows," then the model must in some significant areas be psychologically "real."

[5] Segments in contrast are by definition unpredictable, given only phonetic information.

can certainly be employed to distinguish the morphemes that show spirantization from those which do not.[6] By the same token a speaker of English must keep separate the *k*'s that spirantize (*electric-electricity*) from those which do not (*monarch-monarchy*) by a nonphonetic feature.[7]

Condition 1 is, however, far from sufficient as a constraint for deciding what can qualify as a possible phoneme in a language. The theory of markedness now being developed implies what is needed, in addition to condition 1, to adequately constrain the choice of a phonemic system.

> Condition 2. Phonological systems are optimal with respect to markedness theory.

Condition 2 asserts that the language learner (or the linguist) must select one of the optimal phonological systems permitted by markedness theory as the system for the language he is learning (or describing).[8] Condition 2 is given here in its strongest form; that is, the claim is made that all language systems are phonologically o p t i m a l (have no phonemic "gaps") and that the phonological system of a particular language is one of a limited number of universally possible systems.

A somewhat weaker version of condition 2 would stipulate that the system chosen be as nearly optimal as is consistent with the data and with the constraints imposed on phonological rules. This version means that some phonological systems might have real "gaps." To support this version of condition 2, it would be necessary to show that there is a language that

---

[6]Larry Selinker (private conversation) has pointed out to me that neither pharyngealization nor the *k*/*q* distinction is maintained by Israelis of European extraction. There is, however, an orthographic distinction, and pharyngealization is heard from announcers on radio broadcasts. This brings up interesting questions about the possibility of a passive knowledge of pharyngealization for speakers who do not produce pharyngeals.

[7]English, of course, marks *k*'s that spirantize as orthographic *c*.

[8]The theory of markedness presented by Chomsky and Halle in chapter 9 of SPE and by Postal (1968) is not nearly explicit enough. As is well recognized, conditions on symmetry are needed to prevent such "systems" as *p*, *t*, *k*, *b*, *t^h*, *k'*. The term *optimal* is used here in essentially the same sense as in SPE (pp. 409ff.).

lacked phonemic /a/ or one with nasals but no phonemic /n/.[9]
However, I do not know of any such language and would assert
condition 2 in its strong form as a working hypothesis.

In its strong form the condition means that, given an adequate theory of markedness, to be an optimal phonological
system is equivalent to being a possible phonological system.
Thus, the language learner is faced with the task of deciding
which of the optimal phonological systems consistent with
condition 1 can be mapped by a set of phonological rules onto
the phonetic data of the language he is learning. Schematically, the task can be represented as:

X_1 X_2 X_3 X_4 X_i X_n Universal phonological
systems compatible
with condition 1

R_2 R_3 R_i Sets of phonological
rules

L Phonetic data of L

It is obviously not possible to map all optimal phonological
systems onto the phonetic data of a language. For English,
certainly, one of the optimal three-vowel systems, say /a i u/,
is not the system that underlies English, since it has far more
contrasts than /a i u/ can account for.[10]

Assume, however, that a number of optimal systems are
compatible with a language, that is, that some mapping (set of
rules) can be found for each of $X_2, X_3, \ldots X_i$ as in the diagram above. Assume further that the complexity of each of
these systems is such that the lower the subscript of X, the
lower the intrinsic complexity.[11] If $R_2, R_3, \ldots R_i$ are equally
valued, then we pick the least complex underlying system, that
is, X_2 in the diagram. If, however, $R_2, R_3, \ldots R_i$ vary in
complexity, as we might expect, how are we to choose from
$X_2, X_3, \ldots X_i$? One possibility is to assume that the language

---

[9]I have stated the hypothesis in the stronger form for the reasons
discussed in Bach (1968:133ff.).

[10]One could represent the language with only two "phonemes," of
course, if there were no constraints on phonological descriptions. The
naturalness condition discussed by Postal (1968) is relevant here.

[11]How to evaluate the complexity of systems also needs elaboration.
See SPE (pp. 409ff.).

learner selects the phonemic system that entails the minimum number of processes (rules) linking it to the phonetic data: R is minimized. A second possibility is that the least complex underlying system is chosen: X is minimized. Third, one might assume that there is some measure that weighs rule complexity versus phonemic-system complexity and permits the selection of a phonological description. As far as I am aware, there is no way to compare the complexity of an underlying system to the complexity of a set of phonological rules. Furthermore, it would seem unprofitable at the present time to pursue the development of such a comparative measure.

The hypothetical problem just discussed may not be a real problem. The learner-linguist has to choose some system X that is rich enough to account for the basic contrasts of the language (the contrasts that are not predictable in terms of phonetic, morphological, or syntactic considerations). Furthermore, the learner-linguist must provide a rule set R that accounts for the alternations in the language, that maps X onto the phonetic data, and that states the processes of the language in the most general fashion. For the learner-linguist this means that finding a "generalized" R—the R that makes all the appropriate generalizations about the phonological processes in a language—should uniquely determine the choice of X.

Without claiming to have answered the questions of exactly *how* (X,R) is to be minimized, that is, how (X,R) is to be chosen (I have no discovery procedures to offer), I should like to assert a third condition on phonological descriptions.

Condition 3. R is "generalized."

Conditions 1, 2, and 3 taken together determine what can qualify as an underlying segment filling a real gap in the phonological system.[12] Condition 1 excludes setting up in a language underlying segments that use totally redundant features of the language. Condition 2 rules out setting up underlying segments merely on the basis of the cross-

---

[12]At this point in the development of phonological theory one cannot be sure that one knows (1) what qualifies as a possible phonological rule or set of rules; (2) what the "best" choice of distinctive features is; or, (3) what qualifies as an optimal phonemic system.

classificational possibilities of the nonredundant features. It claims instead that the phonemes must form an optimal set. Condition 3 specifies that the phonological system (X,R) be as minimal as possible—where "minimal" means apparently that X is minimized, since R is as general as possible. It should be clear that conditions 1, 2, and 3 in no way preclude the establishment of underlying segments that do not occur phonetically in a language.

As mentioned above, Brame (this volume) has shown the necessity of postulating for Maltese Arabic an underlying segment $/ʕ/$, the voiced pharyngeal, which never occurs phonetically. The arguments Brame advances are based on certain forms, for instance, *óʔood* 'stay,' *oʔóodu* 'stay (pl.),' *óbood* 'hate,' and *obóodu* 'hate (pl.),' which would be quite irregular with respect to a number of phonological rules unless they have the underlying root shapes $Cʕd$. For the examples, the root shapes are $ʔʕd$ 'stay' and $bʕd$ 'hate.'

Brame summarizes his arguments as follows:

. . . postulation of an abstract segment ʕ, which never appears as such phonetically, permits a revealing solution to the problem of Maltese stress, vowel elision, prothesis, truncation, and so on. Furthermore, it allows us to retain the generalization that all roots are made up of three consonants as well as to predict why there are no roots of the shape $CXh̬$, where X is what I have argued is ʕ.

The restriction on root shape is that "no two segments may occupy the second and third root positions of a single root if they differ only in the feature of voicing. Thus, we find no roots of the shape Cdt, Ctd, Csz, Czs, and so on." Since $h̬$ is the voiceless counterpart of ʕ it follows that there are no roots of the shape $*Cʕh̬$.

It is easy to see that $/ʕ/$ "fills a gap" in Maltese Arabic. As far as the occurrence of pharyngeals is concerned, a language has them, apparently, only if it has a $k-q$ distinction (but obviously, not vice versa).[13] Maltese Arabic has $[h̬]$, and voicing is distinctive. Thus, conditions 1 and 2 are satisfied. Actually, to have $/h̬/$ may imply that a language has $/ʕ/$.[14] In

[13]See Kinkade (1967).

[14]This is the case for several Northwest Indian languages: Nitinat, Okanagan, and Coeur d'Alene. See Jacobsen (1969), Kinkade (1967), and Sloat (1966).

any event, adding /ʕ/ to the system means that the system is optimal, that is, a possible phonological system. Further-more, condition 3 is satisfied as well, since adding /ʕ/ tends to generalize *R*. Without /ʕ/ a number of special rules would be needed to account for apparent morphological irregular-ities. Generalizing *R* provides Maltese Arabic with the minimum *X* that works. Conditions 1, 2, and 3 assert that one cannot set up underlying segments in any fashion one pleases merely to account for some otherwise irregular forms or to explain some contrast that is difficult to account for. It is obvious that establishing phonemic /ʕ/ in Maltese Arabic not only fills a gap but also leads to an optimal and coherent phonology.

For English, Chomsky and Halle (1968:233–235) set up /x/ both as the phoneme underlying initial [h] and as the non-phonetically occurring segment that determines stress place-ment and vowel tenseness in such words as *right-righteous*. Thus, *right* in phonemic /rixt/, and /ix/ → [ay] by two rules: V → [+tense] /___ x, and x → ∅ /___ C. The same rules explain such alternations as *paradigm-paradigmatic* if *g* → γ /___ [+nasal]#, and [x, γ] → ∅ /___ C.

It is clear that in some sense /x/ might be said to fill a gap in English. If a language has /x/, it necessarily has /k/ and /s/.[15] English satisfies both typological requirements, so that establishing phonemic /x/ is consistent with condition 2. *R* is to some extent generalized, since we would need rules to account for *paradigm-paradigmatic* and the like in any event and would need other additional rules to account for such pairs as *right-righteous*. In fact, since we must have rules that have the effect /ig/ → [āy], adding /ix/ → [āy] is a gen-eralization of rules otherwise needed.

One should point out that /x/ does not exactly fill a gap in English but is rather an extension of the English fricatives in a symmetric fashion to the velar position. From the point of view taken here, English is optimal with respect to fricatives, and condition 2 would be satisfied, whether we have /x/ or not. However, *R* is not generalized if /x/ is established, since it must be changed to [h] in all other positions. Chomsky and Halle give the rules (234–235) as follows:

---

[15]So it seems, at any rate, from the information given in Hockett (1955).

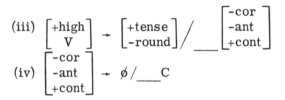

$$\text{(i)} \quad \begin{bmatrix} +\text{high} \\ V \end{bmatrix} \rightarrow \begin{bmatrix} +\text{tense} \\ -\text{round} \end{bmatrix} / \underline{\quad} [x, \gamma]$$

$$\text{(ii)} \quad \begin{bmatrix} -\text{cor} \\ -\text{ant} \\ +\text{cont} \end{bmatrix} \rightarrow \left\{ \begin{matrix} \emptyset / \underline{\quad} C \\ [-\text{cons}] \end{matrix} \right\}$$

Rule (i) can also provide for /h/ by including in the environment [-cor, -ant, +cont], and (ii) can be simplified by dropping the change of /x/ to [-cons], that is, to [h]. The rules can be restated as:

$$\text{(iii)} \quad \begin{bmatrix} +\text{high} \\ V \end{bmatrix} \rightarrow \begin{bmatrix} +\text{tense} \\ -\text{round} \end{bmatrix} / \underline{\quad} \begin{bmatrix} -\text{cor} \\ -\text{ant} \\ +\text{cont} \end{bmatrix}$$

$$\text{(iv)} \quad \begin{bmatrix} -\text{cor} \\ -\text{ant} \\ +\text{cont} \end{bmatrix} \rightarrow \emptyset / \underline{\quad} C$$

The statement of the environment of (iii) is presumably the same as the feature specification of the class $[x, \gamma]$ in rule (i), since there would be no reason to add [+cons] to exclude /h/ in their formulation.

As far as intrinsic complexity is concerned, /x/, according to Chomsky and Halle, is marked for *anterior* and *continuant* (p. 412), and /h/ for *consonantal* (p. 408) and *low* (p. 407, convention XXVI). Since the features *consonantal* and *low* are apparently higher in the feature hierarchy than the features *anterior* and *continuant*, /h/ would seem to be preferable to /x/ for lexical coding, at least as far as markedness is concerned. By condition 3, /h/ is also preferable to /x/.[16]

The postulation in SPE of /œ̄/ as the segment underlying *oi* is unsatisfactory. Postulating phonemic /œ̄/ does satisfy condition 1, since /œ̄/ is among the segments possible by the cross-classification of the features that are contrastive in English. However, /œ̄/ fills no gap in the English vowel system, since English does not have *ü* and *ö*, phonetically or phonemically. As far as I am aware, there is no language that has [œ̄] without having [ü] and [ö].[17] Thus, on typological grounds, hence by condition 2, /œ̄/ is to be rejected as the source of English *oi*. In other words, a language with /œ̄/,

[16]The situation is different for Scottish dialects that retain [x].

[17]This observation is based on an examination of Hockett (1955) and Trubetskoy (1949).

but not /ö/ and /ü/, is simply not possible and not optimal in the strongest sense. There is no evidence at all, as far as I have been able to determine, that Modern English has /ö/ and /ü/.[18]

3. A Description of the English Vowel System.

In SPE, Chomsky and Halle (p. 236) claim that English has a system of eight tense vowels and six lax vowels, which is represented in (III).

(III)	ī		ū	i		u
	ē		ō	e		o
	ǣ	ǣ ā ɔ̄		æ		ɔ
		Tense Vowels			Lax Vowels	

In order to map this vowel "system" onto appropriate phonetic elements, Chomsky and Halle present a set of readjustment rules and a set of phonological rules (pp. 238–245). There are six readjustment rules that affect vowels (pp. 238–239).

SPE (1)

$$V \rightarrow \begin{bmatrix} -\alpha\text{back} \\ -\alpha\text{round} \end{bmatrix} \Big/ \begin{bmatrix} \underline{\quad} \\ \alpha\text{back} \end{bmatrix},$$ in a number of irregular verbs, nouns, and adjectives in certain contexts

SPE (4)

$$V \rightarrow [-\text{rule (20III)}] \Big/ \underline{\quad} \begin{bmatrix} +\text{cons} \\ +\text{ant} \\ +\text{cor} \end{bmatrix} \begin{bmatrix} +\text{cons} \\ +\text{cor} \end{bmatrix} \begin{Bmatrix} [-\text{cons}] \\ [-\text{seg}] \end{Bmatrix}$$

SPE (5) $\quad u \rightarrow [-\text{rule (32)}] \Big/ \underline{\quad} \begin{Bmatrix} C_0\# \\ [+\text{nasal}]\,C \\ V \end{Bmatrix}$

SPE (6) $\quad \bar{a} \rightarrow [-\text{rule (34)}]$ in polysyllables

SPE (7) $\quad V \rightarrow \begin{bmatrix} -\text{rule (30)} \\ -\text{rule (32)} \end{bmatrix} \Big/ \underline{\quad} 1$

SPE (8) $\quad u \rightarrow [-\text{round}] \Big/ \begin{bmatrix} -\text{nasal} \\ +\text{ant} \\ -\text{cor} \end{bmatrix} \underline{\quad} \begin{Bmatrix} 1\begin{Bmatrix}1\\\#\end{Bmatrix} \\ \begin{bmatrix} -\text{ant} \\ +\text{cor} \\ -\text{voc} \end{bmatrix} \end{Bmatrix}$

[18]Old English did, of course, have front rounded vowels; they seem to have been unconditionally lost.

Readjustment rules that apply in phonological environments must be disallowed. Each such rule is simply an ad hoc device to prevent the segment(s) in question from undergoing changes by one or more phonological rules. For example, rule SPE (6) states that ā → [-rule (34)] in polysyllables. Resorting to such rules is a clear indication that something is awry. Basically, if such rules as SPE (6) are permitted, then anything can be derived from anything, and the phonemic "system" can be whatever is appealing since it can always be made to "work" by using readjustment rules. In short, such rules violate the naturalness condition (Postal, 1968) in an extreme way. One is forced to conclude that rule (6) can only mean that /ā/ is the wrong representation in these polysyllabic words or that rule (34) is incorrect, or both.

Rule SPE (4), on the other hand, is simply a negative constraint on the rule laxing vowels before consonant clusters and should be incorporated into laxing rule (20)-(III) directly.

Without using readjustment rules, a different phonological description from the one advanced in SPE results.

In fact, the English vowel system *does* seem to be consonant with the optimality conditions put forth in §2. The system required by the processes in the language is one that has nine tense vowels and five lax vowels. The vowel system is as given in (IV):

(IV)   ī   ɨ̄   ū   i   u
       ē   ʌ̄   ō   e   o
       ǣ   ā   ɔ̄   a
       Tense Vowels   Lax Vowels

The usual phonetic development of the tense vowels is given in (V). In these environments, laxing does not apply.

phoneme   phonetic development   example

(V)   /ī/   [āy]   *divide*
         /ē/   [īy]   *serene*
         /ǣ/   [ēy]   *sane*
         /ū/   [āw]   *pronounce*
         /ō/   [ūw]   *moon*
         /ɔ̄/   [ʌ̄w]   *cone*
         /ɨ̄/   [yɨw]   *music*
         /ʌ̄/   [ōy]   *exploit*
         /ā/   [ɔə̯]   *auditory*

The usual developments of the lax vowels are as in (VI):

(VI)

phoneme	phonetic development			
	medial	final	medial	final
/i/	[ɪ]	[īy]	*sit, division*	*city*
/e/	[ɛ]	Ø	*set, serenity*	*clothe*
/u/	[ʌ]	[ūw]	*pronunciation*	*do, Hindu*
	[ʊ]		*put*	
/o/	[ā]	[ʌ̄w]	*cot*	*echo*
	[ʌ̄w], [ɔ̄ə̯]		*port, song*	
/a/	[æ], [ā̯ə̯]	[āə̯]	*man, bar*	*spa*
		[ə]		*algebra*

Apparently, final /e/ occurs only in the verbalizing suffix {e}. The lax vowels /ɨ/, /ʌ/, /ɔ/, and /æ/ do not seem to be needed at all. Their absence is in accord with markedness theory; /ʌ/, if it were required, would be the most highly marked vowel in the system; /æ/ would be the most highly marked front vowel; /ɨ/ would be more highly marked than any of the five lax vowels that are needed. Thus, the lax vowel system is an optimal system, just as the tense vowel system is.

3.1   In any reasonably complete description of English a number of morphological rules will be required. The morphological rules must specify the underlying phonological shape(s) of inflectional and derivational morphemes. Let us assume that the entire set of morphological rules precedes the entire set of phonological rules.[19] For example, one morphological rule will specify that the morpheme {possessive} is (sometimes) the external suffix #/s/. Another morphological rule will specify that the regular,(i.e., unmarked) {preterite} is #/t/. Other morphological rules will specify that for certain verbs the {preterite} morpheme is to be represented by ablauting the root vowel. English verb morphology requires at least two ablaut rules, one that produces the underlying vowels of *sang, ran, drank, drove, froze,* and

---

[19]Let us assume also that the stress rules, whatever they may be, apply before all the phonological rules that affect segments, i.e., stress is assigned on the basis of the underlying representations provided by the lexicon and by the morphological rules. See Ross (this volume) for a reanalysis of the SPE stress rules.

the like, and another that gives the underlying vowels of *sung*, *run*, *drunk*, *stung*, and *dug*.[20]

A morphological rule will specify that the preterites of *fall*, *hold*, and *do* require the umlaut rule. (The participle of *hold* also undergoes umlauting.) The umlaut rule merely fronts a vowel without changing vowel height. In addition to the three verbs just mentioned, [+umlaut rule] is also specified for some nominalized adjectives that suffix +/Ө/ (*length*, *breadth*, *strength*) and is specified as the morphological rule that accounts for the plural of *man*, *mouse*, *goose*, *woman*, and so forth.

The ablaut rules and the umlaut rule are examples of marked phonological rules; that is, a form must be specifically marked to undergo them. In contrast to such marked phonological rules, there are also unmarked phonological rules, which are applicable to all phonological strings provided that the specified phonological conditions are satisfied. All phonological rules given in §§3.3 to 3.22 are unmarked. The ablaut and umlaut rules replace SPE (1) given in §3.

3.2   Many of the phonological rules required to map the proposed system of English vowels onto appropriate phonetic segments are similar to those given in SPE, but there are fewer rules needed.

The rules are presented below in the order in which they apply. The rules of SPE referred to without page references are from the summary (pp. 238–245).

3.3   The first rule required is the Cluster Laxing rule, which is given as three rules in SPE: (4); (20)-(I); and (20)-(III). The basic rule, (20)-(III), is modified here to include + in the environment.[21]

(1) $V \rightarrow [\text{-tense}]/\_\_\_ [\text{+cons}] + \begin{bmatrix} \text{+cons} \\ \text{-voc} \end{bmatrix}$

Rule (1) laxes the phonemic tense vowel /ā/ of *join* and *point* to [ʌ] in *junction* and *punctual*. The rule accounts for the laxing of /ǣ/ to [æ] (at this point in the derivation) in such

---

[20]For details see Hoard and Sloat (to appear) and §4.4 below.

[21]Constraints on the Cluster Laxing rule are unnecessary, as is clear from a large number of weak preterites that take the preterite suffix /t/ with internal sandhi; for example, *feel-felt*, *mean-meant*, *speed-sped*, and *hide-hid*. See the reference given in fn. 27 for details.

pairs as *contain-content* and *detain-detent.*[22] /ɨ/ of *produce* is laxed in *production* (to [ɨ] at this point).

    3.4   The second rule fronts /a/ in the environment *rri*.

(2)   a → æ /___ rri .

Rule (2) fronts the vowel of *bar* (/barr/), when *-ier* is added, as in *barrier*. Similar are *car-carry, carriage, carrier* and *barbarous-barbaric*.

    3.5   Rule (3) raises æ to ε.

(3)   æ → ε.

Rule (3) produces ε in *men, content, detent, breadth*. In General American, rule (3) yields *barrier, carrier*, and *carriage*, all with [ε]. Rule (3) changes all the æ's produced by rules (1), (2), and the umlaut rule to [ε]. There are no other æ's at this point in the grammar, since æ is not phonemic.[23] In some eastern dialects rule (3) must be restricted:

(3a)   æ → ε/except before *r*.[24]

    3.6   Rule (4) fronts most *a*'s to *æ*. ~ indicates a negative constraint.

$$(4)\quad a \to æ / \sim \begin{bmatrix} 1\text{stress} \\ \underline{} \end{bmatrix} \left\{ \begin{matrix} \#, = \\ r\ C \\ [\text{liquid}][\text{resonant}] \end{matrix} \right\} \begin{matrix} (a) \\ (b) \\ (c) \end{matrix}$$

This rule fronts /a/ to [æ] in *man, bad, sad, Alabama, Alaska, pat, bare* (/bar/), pal (/pal/), *Dalmation, altimeter*, and so forth.

    Constraint (a) specifies that /a/ remain in *spa, la, tra*, and *pa*. /a/ will also remain in *father*, from /fa=Θr/. The morpheme /Θr/, meaning "family relationship," occurs also in *mother, brother, sister*, and *daughter*. Θ → t after fricatives,

---

[22]The final *t* of *constraint* and *complaint* is apparently externally suffixed, and cluster laxing, therefore, does not apply.

[23]For words such as *bare*, General American has /bεr/, dialects with /æ/ have /bar/.

[24]The situation is similar in Swedish and Norwegian where [æ] is found only before *r*. For the necessity of using negative constraints in phonological rules, see Hoard and Sloat (in preparation).

as in /sis+Θr/ and /dah+Θr/.²⁵ Θ → ð in *father*, *mother*, and *brother* by the intervocalic voicing rule (§3.8). If the /a/ is unstressed it shifts to æ, as in *algebra* and *sofa*, and ultimately to [ə].

Constraint (b) specifies that /a/ remain in *harp, art, lark, larch, barb, bard, cargo,* and *large.*

Constraint (c) specifies that /a/ remain in *snarl, bar* (/barr/), *arm, barn, call, calm,* and *walnut.*

Notice that a → æ in *ballot* (/balVt/), *barrel* (/barVl/), and *malnutrition* (/mal/=).

The number of exceptions to rule (4) varies with the dialect. *Restaurant* has [ā̧t] for some speakers, but is [rέstrənt] for others. *Chicago* has [āə̧] for some speakers, [ɔ̃ə̧] for others. Some British dialects have a fairly extensive list of exceptions, including *rather, dance,* and *aunt.*

3.7   Tensing rule (5) operates to lengthen vowels before the verbalizing suffix /e/.²⁶

$$(5)\quad V \rightarrow [\text{+tense}] / \underline{\quad} [\text{-syllabic}] + \begin{bmatrix} V \\ \text{-high} \\ \text{-low} \\ \text{-back} \\ \text{-tense} \end{bmatrix}$$

When this suffix is added to a noun stem with a lax vowel, such as *breath*, the stem vowel is lengthened: /breΘ+e/ → [brē̄Θ+e]. Other examples are *loss-lose, brass-braze, grass-graze, bath-bathe,* and *glass-glaze.* Rule (5) applies vacuously to such examples as *mouthe, use, house,* and *believe,* where the stem vowel of the noun is phonemically tense.

3.8   The *Intervocalic Voicing* rule voices fricatives next to certain formative boundaries.

$$(6)\quad f, \Theta, s \rightarrow [\text{+voice}] \begin{cases} V \underline{\quad} + \begin{bmatrix} \text{-high} \\ \text{+voice} \end{bmatrix} \begin{Bmatrix} + \\ \# \end{Bmatrix} & \text{(a)} \\ V = \underline{\quad} \quad [\text{+voice}] & \text{(b)} \end{cases}$$

²⁵This is, of course, a remnant of a well-known sound change. Another remnant is the [t]/[θ] alternation of the nominalizer +θ; [t] occurs after [+cont -syll] segments, [θ] elsewhere. Thus, *frost, heft, theft, flight* (/flih+t/), *sight* (/sih+t/), *gift,* but *length, width, death, stealth, depth,* and *truth,* etc.

²⁶There is some discussion of the need for such a rule as (5) in SPE (p. 213, fn. 46; p. 232).

Part (a) voices, for example, the /s/ of *use* (v.), /ɪ̄s+e/; the /θ/ of *mouthe*, /mūθ+e/, and *breathe*; and the /f/ of *lives*, /līf+z/.[27] Because the environment of rule (6) is severely restricted, such words as *basic* and *usage* do not show voicing. The specification [-high] in part (a) excludes voicing in *Firthian*, from *Firth+i+an*.

Part (b) voices /s/ of *resemble* and /θ/ of *father*, /fa=θr/, for example.

As given in SPE, rule (25), the environment of voicing given here as part (a) is stated as $\begin{bmatrix} +\text{tense} \\ V \end{bmatrix}$ ___ [-cons].

Chomsky and Halle's formulation has a rather large number of exceptions (many of which they note: pp. 149, 228). Many of the words they set up with /ss/ can be taken to have only /s/; many of the words they set up as /s/, /se/, or /ce/ can be taken to have /z/. Thus, *faze*, /fæz/; *face*, /fæs/; *mace*, /mæs/; *maze*, /mæz/; *mass*, /mas/; *mason*, /mæson/; *iso-*, /īso/; *bosun*, /bōsVn/.

3.9   Rule (6) must precede the Augment rule, (7):

(7)   [+syllabic] → ∅ / + ___ #.

Rule (7) deletes, for example, the verbalizer +e of *use* (v.), *breathe*, and *mouthe* and the lexical augments /i/ of *president* and /f̵/ of *habit*. The last two augments are overt in *presidential* and *habitual*, respectively.

3.10   Rule (8) corresponds to SPE (29) and inserts *y* before *ɨ*.

(8)   ∅ → y / ___ ɨ.

Rule (8) gives [myɨz+ic] from /mɨz+ic/. In General American a late rule drops *y* after liquids and alveolars (some medial *t* + *y* and *d* + *y* sequences become *č*, *ǰ*, respectively).

3.11   SPE (20)-(I) gives a set of rules for laxing vowels. The environments need not be repeated here.

(9)   V → $\begin{bmatrix} -\text{stress} \\ -\text{tense} \end{bmatrix}$ / in a number of contexts.

SPE (20)-(IV) laxes vowels that agree in the features round and back. The rule is altered slightly from that given in SPE:

---

[27] *z* is the regular plural marker. Although normally an external suffix, # → + for some 29 words and causes voicing of preceding voiceless *s*, *f*, *θ*. See Sloat and Hoard (1971).

(10)

$$\begin{bmatrix} V \\ \alpha\text{round} \\ \alpha\text{back} \end{bmatrix} \rightarrow [-\text{tense}]/\underline{\quad} C \left\{ \begin{matrix} C_0 + \text{ic}, + \text{id} \\ (C_1+) \begin{bmatrix} -\text{stress} \\ V \end{bmatrix} C_0 [-\text{cons}] \end{matrix} \right\}$$

The lower environment given in braces laxes the vowels given in boldface in *division, serenity, sanity, pronunciation,* and *conic* from the underlying tense vowels /ī ē ǣ ū ō/, respectively. But the underlying tense vowels of *musician, exploitative,* and *audience,* from /ɨ ʌ̄ ā/, will remain.

In SPE (20)-(IV), rule (10) is given with *+ish* as one of the items in the first environment. The restriction to vowels that agree in backing and rounding is unnecessary here as is apparent from the set *punitive, Punic, punish.*

(11) $V \rightarrow [-\text{tense}]/\underline{\quad} C_1 + ish$

Thus, /pɨn/ remains in *punitive* and *Punic,* since rule (10) does not apply; but /ɨ/ → *i* in *punish,* just as /ǣ/ → /æ/ in *establish* (if it is related to *stable*).[28]

3.12   Rule (12) shifts $o \rightarrow \bar{a}$ before *s, f, θ,* and *ng*. It is similar to the second half of SPE (23)-(III).

(12) $$\begin{bmatrix} -\text{low} \\ -\text{tense} \\ +\text{round} \end{bmatrix} \rightarrow \begin{bmatrix} +\text{low} \\ +\text{tense} \\ -\text{round} \end{bmatrix} / \left\{ \begin{bmatrix} V \\ +\text{back} \\ -\text{high} \\ \underline{\quad} \end{bmatrix} \left\{ \begin{matrix} \begin{bmatrix} -\text{voice} \\ +\text{cont} \\ +\text{ant} \end{bmatrix} \\ ng \end{matrix} \right\} \right.$$

Henceforth, the /o/'s in these environments share the fate of phonemic /ā/. Examples are *loss, office, cloth, long,* and *song.*[29]

Rule (13) shifts $o \rightarrow ɔ$ before *t, d, n, p, b, m, č, ǰ, k, g, v, z,* and ð and shifts $o \rightarrow ɔ$ before liquid clusters.

---

[28]*e-* seems to be a variant of *en-* of *enable, enjoin, enlighten,* etc. Another variant of *en-* is *em-* of *empower.*

[29]Some speakers have a few exceptions before *-ng*. Examples include *tong, thong, bong, bongo, Congo.* All but the last two have [ɔ̰ə] in my speech.

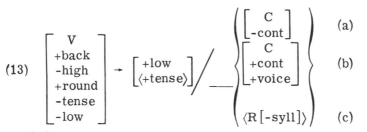

(13)

Thus, /o/ → ɔ at this point in the grammar in *cot, cod, John, hop, bob, Tom, botch, lodge, lock, cog, bother, Oz,* and *Slav.*[30] Examples in nonfinal syllables are *dominant, omelette, oblong, optimal, optometrist, body, bonnet, motto, cogitate, octopus, hibachi,* and *cognate.* Notice also that rule (13) applies to *harmony, harmonic,* and *harmonious* and shifts /o/ → ɔ. Part (c) shifts /o/ → ɔ̄ before liquid-plus-consonant/liquid sequences, as in *old, bolt, folk, Olson, Olga, toll, or* (/or/), *ford, fork, short, forge, porch, torpedo, force,* and so forth. The ɔ̄'s produced by (13c) go through the vowel shift rule along with phonemic /ɔ̄/.

3.13   In SPE, rule (23)-(IV) tenses vowels in a number of environments. Rule (14) is identical to SPE (23)-(IV).

(14)

$$V \rightarrow [+\text{tense}] \Big/ \left\{ \begin{array}{l} \underline{\hspace{1em}} \begin{bmatrix} \alpha \text{low} \\ \beta \text{stress} \end{bmatrix} \left\{ \begin{bmatrix} V \\ -\text{seg} \\ -\text{FB} \end{bmatrix} \begin{array}{l} \text{where } \beta = + \\ \text{if } \alpha = + \end{array} \right\} \\ \left(\begin{bmatrix} \underline{\hspace{1em}} \\ -\text{high} \end{bmatrix} C_1^1 \left(\begin{bmatrix} \alpha \text{voc} \\ \alpha \text{cons} \\ -\text{ant} \end{bmatrix} \right) \right) \begin{bmatrix} -\text{low} \\ -\text{back} \\ -\text{cons} \\ -\text{stress} \end{bmatrix} V \end{array} \right.$$

(a)
(b)
(c)

Environments (a) and (b) tense low stressed vowels and low nonstressed vowels before V, =, and #. Thus, the final vowel of *algebra* will be tensed to ǣ before +*ic* (it was shifted from /a/ to æ by rule (4)); the /i/ of *society* will be tensed to ī before +*ely*; the /a/ of *spa* will be tensed since it is low, stressed, and final; and the /a/ of *father* will be tensed since it precedes =.

Part (c) tenses both nonhigh vowels followed by a single

---

[30]The underlying vowel of *log, fog, dog, hog, bog, jog,* and *noggin* is variously /ā/ or /o/, depending on dialect. There is also a good deal of dialect mixture. Some speakers do not have [av] in *Labov, Slav, Slavic, slovenly.* The last often has [ʌ].

consonant and an optional *y*, *w*, or *r* followed by the vowels *i* or *e* plus another vowel. Hence, the vowel /o/ of *harmonious* will become ɔ̄ before *-ous* (it was shifted from /o/ to ɔ by rule (13)). Rule (14c) also gives *managerial* (/e/ → ē), *repatriate* (/a/ → æ → ǣ), *appropriate*, *colloquial*, *Newtonian*, and *custodian* (/o/ → ɔ → ɔ̄).

3.14   Rule (15) is the same as rule (iii), §2, above.

3.15   Rule (16) is the Vowel Shift rule. It is given in SPE as (33). Only the first environment of the SPE rule is needed.

$$(16) \quad \begin{bmatrix} \gamma\text{back} \\ \gamma\text{round} \\ V \end{bmatrix} \rightarrow \left\{ \begin{matrix} [-\alpha\text{high}]/\begin{bmatrix} \overline{}\alpha\text{high} \\ -\text{low} \end{bmatrix} \\ [-\beta\text{low}]/\begin{bmatrix} \overline{}\beta\text{low} \\ -\text{high} \end{bmatrix} \end{matrix} \right\} \Bigg/ \begin{bmatrix} \overline{} \\ +\text{tense} \\ +\text{stress} \end{bmatrix}$$

As in SPE, rule (16) changes the following:

/ī/ → ē → ǣ
/ē/ → ī
/ǣ/ → ē
/ū/ → ō → ɔ̄
/ō/ → ū
/ɔ̄/ → ō

Notice that /ā/ in *lawn*, *maudlin*, and *audience* is not shifted, and /ʌ̄/ in *point*, *boy*, and *exploit* is not shifted, and that /ɨ̄/ in *musician*, *few*, *feud*, and *fuselage* is not shifted.

Notice also that /o/ in *harmonious*, which was tensed to ɔ̄ by rule (14), undergoes vowel shift and becomes ō by rule (16).

3.16   Rule (17) shifts *ɨ* and *u* to *a* in certain environments.

$$(17) \quad \begin{bmatrix} V \\ -\text{tense} \\ +\text{back} \\ +\text{high} \end{bmatrix} \rightarrow \begin{bmatrix} -\text{round} \\ -\text{high} \end{bmatrix} \Bigg/ \sim \left\{ \begin{matrix} \underline{}C_1C_1 \\ \begin{bmatrix} -\text{nasal} \\ +\text{ant} \\ -\text{cor} \end{bmatrix} \underline{} \begin{bmatrix} -\text{ant} \\ +\text{cor} \\ -\text{voc} \\ -\text{voice} \end{bmatrix} \end{matrix} \right\}$$

Rule (17) shifts *ɨ* to *a* in *punish* and *u* to *a* in *pronunciation*, *hut*, *cut*, *bud*, *mud*, *son* (/sun/), *sun*, *tongue* (/tung/), and *sponge* (/spunǰ/). Because of tensing rule (14), /u/ remains before # in *Hindu* and *do*; /o/ remains before # in *echo*, *motto*, and *isobar* (/īso#barr/); and /o/ remains in *echoic*. /u/ shifts in *brother* (/bru=Ər/) and *mother* (/mu=Ər/), but remains (exceptionally?) before = in *woman*.[31]

/u/ does not become /ʌ/ before two identical consonants. Hence, *pudding, puss, put* (/putt/), *bullet, cushion,* (/kuššVn/), *good* (/gudd/), *look* (/lukk/), and *hood* (/hudd/).[32] /u/ → *a* in *pull, full, purr,* and *dull,* and the *a* drops by a late rule in favor of a syllabic liquid, [pl̩], [fl̩], or [pr̩], if the preceding consonant is [-cor]. Thus, *dull* remains [dʌl].

/u/ does not shift if it is between *p, b, f,* or *v* and *š* or *č*. This environment is given in SPE as part of rule (8). Examples include *bush, push,* and *butch* (/buč/).

3.17   Rule (18) drops one of two identical consonants. This is the Cluster Simplification rule given in SPE as (28).

(18) $C_i → \emptyset / C_i$ ____

3.18   The Diphthongization rule adds appropriate glides. Part (d) corresponds to SPE (31).

(19)

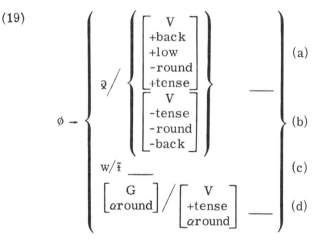

Part (a) adds [ə̯] to /a/ in *father* and *spa,* adds [ə̯] to /ā/ in *lawn, maudlin,* and *audience,* and adds [ə̯] to *ā* from /o/ in *long* and *office.* Part (b) adds [ə̯] to the lax unrounded front vowels (whatever their source), as in *hit, division, set,*

---

[31]*Other* is apparently /u+Ər/. {Ər} is the morpheme in *whether, either, hither* and so on.

[32]There is much variation in such words as *hoof* and *roof*. Some speakers have /huff/ and /ruff/, others have /hōf/ and /rōf/.

serenity, *man*, and *sanity*.[33] Part (c) adds *w* after *ī̵*. Thus, /ī̵/
is now [yᵻw]. Part (d) adds a *w* after the tense rounded
vowels *ɔ̄, ō, ū* and a *y* to the tense unrounded vowels *ī, ē, ǣ, ā*.

3.19   The Rounding Adjustment rule switches the rounding
for a number of back vowels (cf. SPE (34)).

$$(20) \quad [\alpha\text{round}] \rightarrow [-\alpha\text{round}] \Big/ \begin{bmatrix} V \\ -\text{high} \\ +\text{back} \\ \beta\text{tense} \\ \underline{\hphantom{xx}} \end{bmatrix}, \text{ where } \alpha = + \text{ if } \beta = -$$

Rule (20) unrounds *ɔw* to *āw* in *pronounce*, *ōw* to *āw* in *cone*
and in *old*, and *ɔ* to *a* in *hot*. The rule rounds *āy* to *ōy* in *point*
and *āǫ* to *ɔ̄ǫ* in *lawn*, *song*, and *office*. In some dialects the
rule is not restricted to [-high] vowels, and *yᵻw* → *yūw*,
ūw → *ᵻ̄w*, and *u* → *ᵻ*, (the last two rounding adjustments do
not occur after labials).

3.20   Rule (21) tenses *a*.

$$(21) \quad [-\text{tense}] \rightarrow [+\text{tense}] \Big/ \begin{bmatrix} \overline{\hphantom{xx}} \\ V \\ +\text{low} \\ -\text{round} \\ +\text{back} \end{bmatrix}$$

Thus, *a* → *ā* in *hot* and *conic*, and *aǫ* → *āǫ* in *father*.

3.21   Rule (22), Backness Adjustment, is the same as SPE
(35).

$$(22) \quad \begin{bmatrix} +\text{low} \\ V \end{bmatrix} \rightarrow [+\text{back}] / \underline{\hphantom{xx}} [-\text{cons}]$$

Thus, [ǣy] → [āy], as in *divide*. For [āw], some dialects
have [ǣw] everywhere. In this case the rule is as follows:

$$(22a) \quad \begin{bmatrix} +\text{low} \\ V \end{bmatrix} \rightarrow [\alpha\text{back}] / \underline{\hphantom{xx}} \begin{bmatrix} -\text{cons} \\ -\alpha\text{back} \end{bmatrix}.$$

For other dialects [āw] → [ǣw] only after alveolars (and in
others only after [-cont] alveolars).

---

[33]The usual *y* glide before *g*, as in *bag*, and many other details concerning diphthongization are ignored here. The [ə] glide after front lax
vowels is more pronounced before voiced consonants.

(22b) $\begin{bmatrix} +\text{low} \\ V \end{bmatrix} \rightarrow [\alpha\text{back}] / \begin{bmatrix} C \\ +\text{cor} \\ +\text{ant} \end{bmatrix} \underline{\quad\quad} \begin{bmatrix} -\text{cons} \\ -\alpha\text{back} \end{bmatrix}$,

$\quad\quad\quad\quad\quad\quad\quad\quad\quad\quad \beta \quad\quad \beta$

where $\beta = +$ if $-\alpha = +$.

The β index is to be interpreted to mean that the left environment is obligatory if $-\alpha = +$. For the dialect(s) that require it, [-cont] must be added to the left environment.

3.22 The rule for Vowel Reduction is the same as SPE (43).

(23) $\begin{bmatrix} -\text{stress} \\ -\text{tense} \\ V \end{bmatrix} \rightarrow \vartheta$

This rule gives *sofa, algebra,* and *harmony.*

3.23 The vowel system and rules proposed above offer several advantages over Chomsky and Halle's formulation.

First, the vowel system proposed in §3 seems unexceptional vis-à-vis vowel systems commonly found among the world's languages.[34]

Second, no readjustment rules are required. SPE (1) is really the umlaut and ablaut rules. SPE (4) and (8) are negative constraints on other rules. SPE (5), (6), and (7) are unnecessary. As a further observation, note that in SPE rule (8) the feature "round" is used as a diacritic. Chomsky and Halle change $u \rightarrow \dot{i}$ to avoid the shift of $u \rightarrow o$, then change $\dot{i}$ back to u by the rounding adjustment rule.[35]

Third, many of the ad hoc rules of SPE are not required.[36] For example, Chomsky and Halle add w to (their) underlying /æ/ of *spa, art,* and *park.* Later, a "glide-vocalization" rule is required to change $w \rightarrow u$ (SPE 32). Furthermore, a special restriction ([β rule 32]) in the diphthongization rule is needed to prevent vocalization of w after $ɔ$ (from /u/).[37]

Fourth, the use of "silent" e as a diacritic is unnecessary

---

[34]The hypotheses put forth in §2 are obviously not proved. At best, I have shown that English is a white swan, not that all swans are white.

[35]"Round" is also used as a diacritic in SPE rule (23)-(III). The rule shifts u to $\bar{i}$ (to avoid the vowel shift rule), not just to $\bar{u}$.

[36]The term is not being used pejoratively. See SPE (pp. 208ff.).

[37]Rule (19c) above is also an example of adhocracy, w is added to $\bar{i}$ to avoid adding y by part (d).

in the rules I have proposed. In SPE, Chomsky and Halle add /e/ or a low glide (which they symbolize as /ɛ/), freely to make their rules work. Thus, they have "silent" *e*'s in the underlying representations of *few*, *fuel*, *feud*, *Neptune*, *ellipse*, and so on. The morpheme {e} is apparent in the second member of such pairs as *cloth-clothe*, *use*(n.)-*use* (v.), *house*(n.)-*house* (v.), *loss-lose*, *choice-choose*, and *grief-grieve*. The use of {e} when semantically justified, as in the examples just given, is not at issue. However, when there is no semantic reason for the presence of {e}, I do not see how a silent *e* can be employed as a part of the phonological representation of a word. One should also note that in SPE a special rule of *e*-Elision is required, whereas in the proposal above +*e* is simply part of the augment rule.[38]

Fifth, the addition of rule (6), æ → ɛ, avoids the ad hoc [+F] marker Chomsky and Halle use for "exceptional" vowel shift in words like *content* and *biennial*.[39]

4. The Vowel Shift

The vowel system for Modern English proposed in §3 is very much like that of Middle English (less the ME diphthongs). Many of the underlying forms I have suggested look like Middle English, for instance, /putt/ for *put*, /man/ for *man*, and /tung/ for *tongue*. These forms should not be very surprising since the phonological system of a language at any particular time is of necessity the product of historical events, whether these are due to sound changes or to borrowings. Each generation has an opportunity to recode the language, of course, but since sound changes are so frequently conditional, changes in the phonemic representations (and in the phonemic system) must proceed rather slowly. The pro-

---

[38]The situation of underlying forms with double consonants is quite different, as Chomsky and Halle point out (p. 150).

[39]I am unable to follow the argument for an [ãy]-[æ] alternation in *satisfy–satisfaction* (SPE, pp. 201–202). From such forms as *syllabicate*, *syllabificate*, *syllabification*, and *syllabify*, one would think that the suffixes involved are *if*, *ic*, *æt*, *ion* and that the underlying form for *satisfaction* is /satis+if+ik+æt+iVn/, while that for *satisfy* is /satis+if+ī/. In all the examples I have examined, the *i* of *if* is deleted before roots with *i* such as *satis-*. It would seem that a rule *ikǣ* → *æk* gives the surface result.

posal made in §3 is not, however, justified by, or based on, anything that Middle English is supposed to have possessed, but is based entirely on synchronic considerations.[40]

In brief, I think I have shown in §3 that English can be considered to have an optimal vowel system in the sense of the hypotheses advanced in §2. The phoneme /ǣ/ of *sane* is, incidentally, an abstract underlyer, since there is no tense ǣ in General American English.

4.1   The proposal made in §3 (and the proposal of Chomsky and Halle in SPE) has at least one glaring inadequacy. In particular, the vowel shift rule is hard to believe. As formulated above (and in SPE), the vowel shift rule has the following effects:

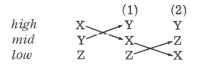

The vowel shift rule is, then, really two processes. Furthermore, the order of application of the processes is crucial. The order must be (1), then (2), or we get:

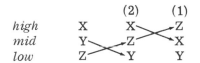

However, there appears to be no evidence that the vowel shift rule really is two processes. If it were, one would expect some dialect of English to have (1) only one part of the rule, (2) the parts in reverse order, or (3) some other process intervening synchronically between the parts of the vowel shift rule. Although it is quite possible in the present formulation, there is no indication that any of the possibilities just mentioned has occurred or could occur.

The fact that the Great Vowel Shift came into the language within a very short time span also argues against a two-process account.

4.2   The vowel shift rule cannot be stated as a single process because the features *high* and *low* permit only three-height vowel systems (since [+high, +low] is impossible).

---

[40]See SPE (p. 54).

What is needed is a feature system that permits vowel systems of four heights. Four-height vowel systems have, of course, been permitted traditionally by the IPA transcription system.

The feature system I propose that would permit four-height vowel systems employs the features *high* and *polar*.

The polar vowels are the vowels in the corners of the vowel quadrilateral. Thus, *a, æ, i,* and *u* are polar vowels, and *e, ε, o,* and *ɔ* are nonpolar vowels.

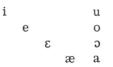

The feature high simply divides the vowel triangle at the midpoint, so that *i, e, o, u* are [+high] and *a, æ, ε, ɔ* are [-high].

The features *polar* and *high* cross-classify, so that we have the following:

+polar	+high	i	u
-polar	+high	e	o
-polar	-high	ε	ɔ
+polar	-high	æ	a

If, as before, we take the lax vowels *i, ε,* and *æ* of *division, cleanliness,* and *sanity* as indicative of the height of the underlying tense vowels of *divide, clean,* and *sane,* then the front vowel system of English is as follows:

/ɪ/   *divide*   /i/   *division, sit*
/ɛ̄/   *clean*   /ε/   *cleanliness, set*
/ǣ/   *sane*   /æ/   *sanity*

The vowel shift rule is now easily stated:

$$
\begin{bmatrix} \alpha\text{polar} \\ \beta\text{high} \end{bmatrix} \rightarrow \begin{bmatrix} -\alpha\text{polar} \\ -\beta\text{high} \end{bmatrix} \Bigg/ \begin{bmatrix} V \\ +\text{stress} \\ +\text{tense} \\ \underline{} \end{bmatrix}
$$

The rule has the following effect:

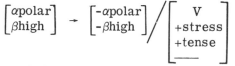
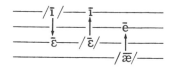

This result is exactly what is desired, for, with diphthong-ization, the resulting phonetic segments will be [ī], *clean*; [eⁱ], *sane*; [ɐⁱ], *divide*.[41] The first element of the diphthongs of *sane* and *divide* has a lax vowel; there do not seem to be any dialects in which it is tense.[42]

The complete lax vowel set for English is as follows:

/u/ is the vowel of *put* (/putt/) and *cut* (/kut/), /ɔ/ is the vowel of *hot*, and /a/ is the vowel of *man*.

4.3   There is another inadequacy of the rules of §3 that is less apparent than that involving the vowel shift rule but that quickly becomes apparent if one tries to state explicitly the ablaut (and umlaut) rules mentioned in §3.1. What becomes clear is that phonological rules ought to be written in terms of marked and unmarked values rather than plus and minus values. In chapter 9 of SPE, Chomsky and Halle propose that the lexicon be coded with *m* and *u* values for features and that these be interpreted as + and - values before being subjected to phonological rules. The phonological rules are to be aug-mented with marking conventions functioning as "linking" rules. The linking rules make the outputs of phonological rules into less marked segments. If, however, the application of phonological rules is in terms of *m* and *u* values, with phonetic interpretation in terms of + and - values following the phonological rules, the need for linking disappears.

As a first example of a rule that lends some support to the above claim, consider the well-known development of Indo-European *e* and *o* to *a* in Sanskrit. If this rule is given in +, - terms we will need to mention (either via linking or in the rule itself), that *o* unrounds. If the rule is stated in terms of

---

[41][ɐ] is used for a lower mid, i.e., [-polar -high], central vowel. [ī] is used for the vowel of *clean*, since speakers of General American, especially the northern dialect(s), typically have a monophthongal pro-nunciation. The vowel with strong diphthongization is lax /i/, typically [iə].

[42]According to John Hart, it was not tense in his speech either. This is noted in SPE (pp. 259ff.).

m, u values, however, the unrounding of o is automatic; assume [u polar] → [+polar] and [u high] → [-high].

$$[m \text{ polar}] \rightarrow [u \text{ polar}]/\begin{bmatrix} V \\ u \text{ high} \\ \underline{\hspace{1cm}} \end{bmatrix}$$

Since e, o, and a are [u round], there is no change in the value of round, and, this feature is not mentioned in the rule.

The development of Old English $\bar{a}$ to Middle English $\bar{\partial}$ also reflects the regular maintenance of unmarked rounding values under changes in vowel height. (This shift is still synchronically valid, as will be seen below in §4.4.)

Turning now to the umlaut rule for English, we note that vowels are fronted, but that rounding remains unmarked. The rule can be stated as follows:

$$\begin{bmatrix} V \\ u \text{ back} \end{bmatrix} \rightarrow [m \text{ back}]$$

if we assume that [u back] → [+back]. If an umlaut rule maintains lip rounding, that is, if the rule is

$$\begin{bmatrix} V \\ u \text{ back} \\ u \text{ round} \end{bmatrix} \rightarrow \begin{bmatrix} m \text{ back} \\ m \text{ round} \end{bmatrix}$$

then only by a more complex rule, in markedness terms, can this fact be stated. Indeed, the more complex rule statement ought to be the case, for umlauting that maintains lip rounding produces (new) vowels of higher markedness than does umlauting of the English type. The loss of front rounded vowels in the Old English period is now statable only as a case of rule simplification—a consequence that seems entirely reasonable.

4.4 If rules operate in terms of m and u, the underlying vowel of English *cone*, *stone*, and *drove* must be /$\bar{a}$/, while that of *auditory* and *lawn* must be /$\bar{\partial}$/, as the pronunciation of the latter suggests. This situation is the reverse of what was given in §3. The effect of the vowel shift rule (as given in §4.2) on the back vowels is as follows:

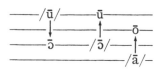

To restrict the vowel shift rule, so that /ō̄/, /ā̄/, /ī̄/ are not affected, the specification [*u* round] (omitted in 4.2) must be added to the environment. Back vowel alternations are exemplified by *cone-conic* for *ā*; *shoot-shot* and *lose-lost* for *ɔ̄*; and *pronounce-pronunciation* for *ū*.

Of greater interest, perhaps, is that, given rules in terms of *m*, *u* and the above treatment of vowel shifts, the ablaut rules for English strong verbs can be stated with some generality. The first ablaut rule accounts for the shift of root vowels to tense and lax *a* (and sometimes to *ɔ*). The variation in tenseness depends upon the tenseness of the underlying vowel of the root.

$$
\text{ABLAUT 1:} \quad
\begin{bmatrix} V \\ \alpha\text{tense} \end{bmatrix}
\rightarrow
\begin{bmatrix} u \text{ back} \\ \alpha\text{tense} \\ u \text{ F} \end{bmatrix}
\quad
\begin{array}{l}
\text{(a) if } \varepsilon C, \text{ then} \\
\quad [m \text{ polar}]
\end{array}
$$

Ablaut 1 accounts for the preterites of *drive, shine, freeze, choose, begin, run, sing,* and *drink*. By vowel shift, *ā → ō̄*; by fronting, *a → æ* (rule (4), §3.6). These changes account for *drove, shone, froze, chose,* but *began, ran, drank*. Special case (a) specifies *ɔ* (which later becomes [a]) for the ablaut vowel of *get, tred,* and so on.

The second ablaut rule generally changes a root vowel to *u*.

$$
\text{Ablaut 2: } [V] \rightarrow
\begin{bmatrix} m \text{ high} \\ m \text{ tense} \\ u \text{ F} \end{bmatrix}
\quad
\begin{array}{l}
\text{(a) if \_\_\_\_ \# , then } [u \text{ tense, } m \text{ round}] \\
\text{(b) if \_\_\_\_nd, then } [u \text{ tense}]
\end{array}
$$

Case (a) specifies *ī̄* for final vowels, as in the preterites of *blow, slay, fly, know, grow, throw,* and *draw*. Case (b) specifies *ū* for *find, grind, bind,* and *wind*. The general case, *u* (which becomes [ʌ]), is exemplified by *dug, clung, hung, drunk, begun,* and *run*.[43]

4.5 A markedness approach simplifies some of the rules given in §3.3–§3.23.

Rule (10) was formulated in §3.11 as follows:

$$
\begin{bmatrix} V \\ \alpha\text{round} \\ \alpha\text{back} \end{bmatrix}
\rightarrow [\text{-tense}]/\text{Env.}
$$

---

[43]A more complete account of ablauting verbs is given in Hoard and Sloat (to appear).

This rule can now be restated (assuming that [u tense] becomes [+ tense]):

$$\begin{bmatrix} V \\ u \text{ round} \end{bmatrix} \rightarrow [m \text{ tense}]/\text{Env.}$$

The vowels that become lax are merely those with unmarked rounding, not those which agree in the features [round] and [back].

Rules (12) and (13) of §3.12 will also be somewhat simplified. The specification of changes of rounding involved in ɔ → a or ā will not be needed. The change of ɔ → ō before s, θ, f, ng will still be complicated, reflecting the fact that it involves a change to a rather marked segment.

Backness adjustment rule (22), §3.21, and rounding adjustment rule (20), §3.19, will have to be reordered. Under natural marking interpretations, by backing adjustment ɛ → ɔ/ ___ y.[44] Rounding adjustment will have the following effects:

(a) ɔy → ʌy
(b) ʌy → ɔy
(c) ɔw → ʌw

(a) gives [ʌy] from /ī/ → ē̄ → ɛy → ɔy → ʌy; (b) gives [ɔy] from /ā/ → ʌy → ɔy; (c) gives [ʌw] from /ū/ → ō → ɔw → ʌw.[45]

4.6   It would be premature to present a complete reformulation of the rules for English vowels in terms of marked and unmarked features, given the present state of knowledge of marking conventions. I was unable to be very specific about condition 3 (§2), because recognizing a particular formulization of rules to be to some extent "generalized" is largely intuitive at present.[46] A more specific account of how to

[44]Vowels of diphthongs with *w* and *y* glides should be laxed by a prior rule. This laxing is probably a part of the diphthongization process itself.

[45]Low-level adjustments to give [ʌ] → [ɐ]/——[glide] can be made as desired. There are several interesting dialect variations that are easily accounted for. I have heard ɛy for /ī/ from Irish speakers (no backness adjustment); ɔy for /ī/ from Cockney speakers (no rounding adjustment); and *a* for /ā/ in *poison, boil, join*, etc. from Irish speakers and as an "old-fashioned" pronunciation in the United States (no rounding adjustment).

[46]The problem of choosing suitable rule schemata also has an obvious bearing on this problem.

formulate a generalized set of rules lies, I think, along the lines sketched in §4 of this paper and will require that more suitable distinctive features be used, that marking conventions be sharpened, and that many phonological rules be stated in terms of markedness.

If condition 3 can be made explicit in this way, then condition 3 together with conditions 1 and 2 will give a phonological theory of far greater explanatory power. Much of the arbitrariness of current phonological practice should be largely removed since the range of possible solutions will be greatly restricted.

REFERENCES

Bach, E. (1968). "Nouns and Noun Phrases." In *Universals in Linguistic Theory*, edited by E. Bach and R. Harms. New York: Holt, Rinehart, and Winston.

Brame, M. K. (this volume). "On the Abstractness of Phonology; Maltese ʕ."

Chomsky, N., and M. Halle (1968). *The Sound Pattern of English.* New York: Harper and Row.

Hoard, J. E., and C. Sloat (to appear). "English 'Irregular' Verbs."

____(in preparation). "Negative Constraints in Phonological Descriptions."

Hockett, C. F. (1955). *A Manual of Phonology.* Indiana University Publications in Anthropology and Linguistics. Baltimore: Waverly Press.

Jacobsen, W. H., Jr. (1969). "Origin of the Nootka Pharyngeals." *IJAL* 35:125–153.

Kinkade, M. D. (1967). "Uvular-pharyngeal Resonants in Interior Salish." *IJAL* 33:228–234.

Kiparsky, P. (1968). "How abstract is phonology?" Mimeographed. Cambridge: Massachusetts Institute of Technology.

McCawley, J. (1967). "Sapir's Phonological Representation." *IJAL* 33:106–111.

Postal, P. (1968). *Aspects of Phonological Theory.* New York: Harper and Row.

Ross, J. R. (this volume). "A Reanalysis of English Word Stress (I)."

Sloat, C. (1966). "Phonological Redundancy Rules in Coeur d'Alene." Ph.D. dissertation, University of Washington.

——, and J. E. Hoard (1971). "The Inflectional Morphology of English." *Glossa* 5:47–56.

Trubetskoy, N. S. (1949). *Principes de phonologie*. Paris: Klincksieck.

Two Phonological Notes:
A-sharp and B-flat

CHIN-WU KIM

University of Illinois

In musical scale (on the piano keyboard, for instance) the two notes A♯ and B♭ represent the same pitch, about 466 Hz (the tenth key above middle C). Yet the two notations A♯ and B♭ differ and reflect their structural dissimilarity despite their sameness in physical pitch. For example, in E-flat major chord, B♭ will never be represented as A♯. The moral of this musical note is that one finds analogous phenomena in linguistics, that is, there are cases in which the physically (or superficially) same phenomenon is represented in two or more structurally different forms. In this paper, I will consider two such cases in phonology.[1]

A. The first case to be considered is that of neutralization. Neutralization refers to the phenomenon whereby two or more phonemes merge together into one and the same phonetic entity in a certain environment. Examples are not hard to come by: for instance, in German, final voiced stops are devoiced, and both *Bund* 'bundle' and *bunt* 'colorful' are pronounced [bunt]; in English, intervocalic *t* is voiced to *d*, creating homonyms in such pairs as *writer* and *rider*; in French, different oral vowels merge into one when nasalized; thus, *en* and *an* into [ã] as in *genre* [žãr], *paysan* [peyzã] 'peasant' (m.), and *in* and *ain* into [ɛ̃] as in *fin* [fɛ̃] 'fine' (m.),

[1]The second part of this paper was presented at the 44th Annual Meeting of the Linguistic Society of America, December 1969, San Francisco, under the title "Language-Specific Metarules in Phonology" (Paper #52, Meeting Handbook, p. 79). I thank C-J N. Bailey, F. Heny, F. W. Householder, C. W. Kisseberth, S-C. Song, and W. S-Y. Wang, all of whom read an earlier version of this paper and gave me valuable comments.

américain [amerikɛ̃] (m.); in Korean, final obstruents are neutralized, as in *nat* [nat] 'a grain,' *nath* [nat] 'piece,' *nas* [nat] 'sickle,' *nac* [nat] 'day,' and *nach* [nat] 'face.' In such cases, it nevertheless is well motivated to represent the phonetically same sound by two or more different phonemes on a higher level of description, since the original nonneutralized forms appear in other contexts. Thus, in German the voice distinction remains before endings beginning with a vowel, for instance, *Bundes* [bundes] vs. *buntes* [buntes] (m./n., sg., gen.); in English the voice distinction between *writer* and *rider* appears in the respective past tense forms *wrote* and *rode*; in French, distinctive oral vowels appear in other contexts, for instance, in feminine forms such as in *générique* [ženerik], *paysanne* [peyzan], *fine* [fin], *américaine* [amerikɛn]; and Korean obstruents retain their distinction in prevocalic position: *nat-ɨl* [nadɨl], *nath-ɨl* [natʰɨl], *nas-ɨl* [nasɨl], *nac-ɨl* [najɨl], *nach-ɨl* [nacʰɨl] (*-ɨl* is an object marker).

A question about the arbitrariness or appropriateness of motivation arises, however, when two supposedly different forms always (i.e., freely in all environments) appear in the one and the same phonetic shape. Borrowing a term from Kiparsky (1968), I will call this phenomenon "absolute neutralization." One may ask why such a concept is necessary at all. The reason is that, phonological processes not always being regular, there are cases where an environment in which a phonetic change takes place needs to be marked for an exceptional case. That is, in the rule of the form

(1) $X \rightarrow Y / \_\_\_ Z$

there may be a subcase of Z before which the change of X to Y does not take place. Rather than mark every lexical item containing this exceptional Z, one can postulate that the exceptional Z is a different phoneme W, in which case the above rule applies without an exception. One then needs a later rule changing W back to Z.

In generative phonology, it has been assumed that a certain behavioral anomaly of a segment at the phonetic level, such as the one just discussed, warrants its representation as two systematic phonemes in the underlying level. Thus, Halle (1962:71) argued that when a phoneme resulting from the merger of two phonemes still behaves like its historical antecedents in the phonological system of the language, one should postulate two underlying phonemes even though the distinction is not phonetically present in any utterance.[2]

The motivation for this sort of practice is of course to give the phonological description a maximum generality, for without such a measure the phenomenon has to be dealt with as an exception. In any case, this practice was followed by many without much argument, until Kiparsky (1968)[3] put forward a serious objection to the uncritical use of such a practice. Kiparsky argued, like Postal (1968:53ff.), that there should be a natural relationship between the two levels, phonemic and phonetic, of phonological representations and that this relationship is in nature not as abstract as some might claim (cf. Fudge, 1967). Kiparsky argues that, if a segment appears in a constant shape throughout the derivation, its underlying representation should be that shape. That is, if a neutralized segment is to be justifiably represented as two underlying phonemes, then the two phonemes must manifest themselves in two different phonetic shapes in at least one context ("the alternation condition" in Kiparsky's term). This condition should rule out the case of absolute neutralization.[4]

[2]Halle's example had to do with the merger of *æ* and *a* to *æ*; a later rule coalesces the original *æ* with *e* while the original *a* remains *æ*. In such a case, "we postulate that . . . /a/ and /æ/ remained distinct entities even though every /a/ was actualized phonetically as /æ/" (Halle 1962:71).

[3]This paper, though not yet in print, generated a series of discussions in phonological circles. Among those of which I am aware are: Brame (this volume), Crothers (1971), Hyman (1970), and Kisseberth (1969).

[4]As Kiparsky examines in detail, two devices have been used in generative phonology to handle the case of absolute neutralization: (a) the diacritic use of phonological features, — for example, postulating abstract underlying /ɨ/, the [+back] counterpart of /i/, to account in a general way for an irregular vowel harmony phenomenon with respect to [i], say, in the phonology of Finnish or Mongolian; (b) the phonological use of diacritic features, e.g., assigning entirely abstract lexical features like +GRAVE or -GRAVE to lexical items that are now phonologically identical with no vowel harmony distinction, then later having the vowel harmony rule change all vowels in the +GRAVE word to [+back] vowels, whether high or low, and all vowels in the -GRAVE word to [-back] vowels, à la Lightner (1965). Kiparsky argues that these devices are more or less ad hoc ways to handle exceptions and proposes to handle them by rule features, i.e., by marking an item that is an exception to a rule, e.g., the vowel harmony rule, as [-Rule x].

I, as a trained phonetician, would like the phonological component to be more empirically motivated and to be closer to phonetic facts, but it appears that phonology is more abstract than Kiparsky wants it to be, or at least that his alternation condition is too strong. I will illustrate this point with examples from Korean.

In Kim (1968a), it was noted that dental consonants in Korean behave differently with respect to palatalization in front of surface [i], that is, some dentals are palatalized before [i], but some are not before the phonetically identical [i]:

(2) *haytoti* [hɛtoji] 'sunrise'   *titita* [tidida] 'step on'
    kathi [kacʰi] 'together'   *thikkɨl* [tʰikkɨl] 'dust particle'

Since palatalization of dentals also occurs in Korean before every /y/, I phonemicized the nonpalatalizing [i] as /i/ and the palatalizing [i] as /yi/, later deleting [y] of /yi/.[5] Thus, it appears that superficially it is a case of Kiparsky's absolute neutralization. But a deeper look into the matter will show that there is more to it.

[5]Actually, the nonpalatalizing [i] is phonemicized as /ɨy/, and the palatalizing [i] as /yɨy/. The fronting rule will give [i] from /ɨy/, and [yi] from /yɨy/, then the glide-deletion rule will delete [y] from [yi]. See below and Kim (1968a) for details.

One might argue that Kiparsky's absolute neutralization has to do with single segments only, not with neutralization of sequences. This point seems to me trivial, since instead of postulating *yi* for the palatalizing *i* and *i* for the nonpalatalizing *i* (later deleting *y* of *yi*), one could have posited *i* for the palatalizing *i* and *ɨ* for the nonpalatalizing *i* (later fronting *ɨ* to *i*); or one could have assigned a distinctive feature [+sharp] (or [+high] = palatalized) to the former and [-sharp] to the latter, thus segmentalizing the sequence *yi*. The difference is in representation, not in concept, and is not crucial for the present argument.

Some Korean grammarians may also point out that palatalization of dental stops generally occurs only across a morpheme boundary, but not within a morpheme, thus voiding the *i–yi* distinction. This analysis, however, necessitates an otherwise unnecessary distinction between oral stops and affricates on the one hand, and nasals, fricatives, and liquids on the other, since palatalization occurs intramorphemically as well as intermorphemically in the latter case, e.g., *si* [ši] 'poem,' *tamnyo* [tamɲo] 'blanket,' *hullyuŋ* [huλλuŋ] 'excellence,' etc.; furthermore, it cannot explain palatalization of oral stops in such loan words as *tube* [cu:bɨ], *radio* [najio], *tulip* [cʰu:ripɨ], etc. Surely, one would not posit a morpheme boundary after the phonetic palatals in the above examples.

When one examines the vowel system of Korean, one notes that vowels take two on-glides, *y* and *w*, rather freely, except that [yi], [wu], [yɨ], and [wɨ] do not occur, although [i], [u], [ɨ], [yu], and [wi] occur. Details aside, what this means is that glides do not generally occur before high vowels of homorganic articulation. Kim (1968a) examined this and other vocalic phenomena of Korean and argued that all Korean vowels are derivable from three basic vowels, /ɨ, ə, a/, in combination with two glides, /w/ and /y/. In particular, it was shown, with examples, that surface front vowels are derivatives of the form /Vy/ by a fronting rule—[i] < /ɨy/, [e] < /əy/, and [ε] < /ay/—and that [u] is of /wɨ/. Table (3) shows a relevant part of the Korean vowel system in which phonetically simple front vowels are viewed as phonemically complex vowels derived via off-glide -*y*, and shows vowel complexes with on-glides as well:

(3)

	basic	__y	y__y	y__	w__
high	ɨ [ɨ]	ɨy [i]	yɨy [yi]	yɨ [yu]	wɨ [u]
mid	ə [ə]	əy [e]	yəy [ye]	yə [yə]	wə [wə]
low	a [a]	ay [ε]	yay [yε]	ya [ya]	wa [wa]

Note that the system generates [i] (from /ɨy/) *and* [yi] (from /yɨy/). That is, the *yi* that I postulated for the palatalizing [i] is not a consequence of an ad hoc trick but is a part of the total system. The system is more general (and symmetric) with it than without. One still has to delete *y* from *yi*, but, again, this initial glide deletion is not a "patch-up" rule but is part of an independently motivated rule already existent in Korean that deletes *w* from *wu*. That is, an initial glide is deleted just in case the glide and the following high vowel agree in gravity (or coronality): thus, *y* is deleted from *yi* and *w* is deleted from *wu*. This is a rather natural phenomenon and is found in other languages. On the other hand, if *y* is not deleted from *yi*, but only *w* from *wu*, which is independently needed, the glide-deletion rule will become less general and more costly. Thus, we see that the postulation of *i* and *yi* at the deep level and their subsequent neutralization at the surface level are a consequence of the system process, not an analyzer's trick adopted as an ad hoc device for handling an exception. One might even say that the system prefers (dictates) neutralization in this case, because with it the system is generalized, while without it, the system becomes less general.

The preceding discussion suggests that one examine the whole phonological component before branding a particular rule as costly or undesirable on some isolated grounds. After all, the phonological component is a tightly woven network in which each rule is an integrated part, not an isolated process. This interrelationship among rules of the phonological component can be seen more clearly in the next note to be examined.

B. The second case has to do with what is now often called a "conspiracy"[6] among rules, that is, the case where two or more rules that are quite overtly different in structural form nevertheless "conspire" and describe the same or similar phonological phenomena. Kisseberth (1970a) referred to this phenomenon as a functional unity of phonological rules. His case had to do with certain surface constraints in Yawelmani; specifically, that there be no consonant cluster word-initially or -finally and no three-consonant cluster word-medially. Kisseberth noted that, in order not to violate these constraints, the language had rules like vowel epenthesis and consonant deletion and showed that these rules, although structurally quite different, are functionally the same.

In support of Kisseberth, I will draw additional evidence from Korean, although what I discuss here is slightly different.

In Kim (1968c) it was noted that several phonological phenomena in Korean pointed toward the same direction under a general condition that I called "the principle of implosion."[7] I noted that this principle overrode several rules of the following type:

a. Fricatives and affricates become stops, that is, obstruents with a narrow closure come to have a complete closure in preconsonantal and word-final position:

---

[6]Cf. Kiparsky (1969), Kisseberth (to appear), Ross (1969).

[7]For lack of a better term. In this paper, I will call it "the principle of close articulation," by which I mean the tendency to minimize the aperture between the upper articulator and the lower articulator in producing speech sounds.

(4) $\{s, ss, c, ch\} \rightarrow t / \_\_ \left\{ {C \atop \#} \right\}$

e.g., *nas* 'sickle' ⎫
　　　　　　　　　 ⎬ → [nat]
　　 nac 'day' ⎬
　　 nach 'face' ⎭

cf. *nas-il* [nasɨl]
　　　(*-il* - object case)
nac-il [najɨl]
nach-il [nacʰɨl]

nas-kwa homi [natkwa homi] 'a sickle and a hoe'
nac-kwa pam [natkwa pam] 'day and night'
nach-kwa son [natkwa son] 'face and hands'
kass-ta [katta] 'went'

b. Glide *w* and liquid *r* become homorganic stops:

(5) $\begin{bmatrix} w \\ r \end{bmatrix} \rightarrow \begin{bmatrix} p \\ t \end{bmatrix} / \_\_ C$

təw-ətta 'it was warm'
təw-i 'warm weather'
təw-im 'warmth'

təp-ta 'to be warm'
təp-ko 'warm and'
təp-so 'it is warm'

kər-ətta 'walked'
kər-i 'walking distance'
kər-im 'walking pace'

kət-ta 'to walk'
kət-ko 'walk and'
kət-so 'is walking'

ithir-nar → *ithit-nar* → [itʰinnal] 'the next day'
hor-nipur → *hot-nipur* → [honnibul] 'single-sheet quilt'
sur-karak [sutkarak] 'spoon (with a long handle)'

c. Stops are unreleased word-finally and before a consonant:[8]

(6) [-continuant] → [-release] / __ $\left\{ {C \atop \#} \right\}$

E.g., [nat°], [nat°kwa], [kat°ta], etc. ([°] = unreleased)

d. Vowels are raised, especially in the Seoul dialect:

---

[8]Languages may be typologically classified into three groups in terms of the release of stops:
　　a. the release is optional, e.g., English *cat* [kʰætʰ] or [kʰæt°].
　　b. the release is obligatory, e.g., French *petite* 'small' (f.) [ptitʰ], *[ptit°].
　　c. the *un*release is obligatory, e.g., Korean *path* 'field' [pat°], *[patʰ].

$$(7) \quad \begin{bmatrix} e \\ \varepsilon \\ \vartheta \\ a \\ o \end{bmatrix} \rightarrow \begin{bmatrix} i \\ e \\ \dot{\imath} \\ \vartheta \\ u \end{bmatrix} \qquad \begin{array}{l} peta \rightarrow [\text{pida}] \text{ 'to cut'} \\ \vartheta pta \rightarrow [\dot{\imath}\text{p}^\circ\text{ta}] \text{ 'there is no'} \\ hako \rightarrow [\text{h}\vartheta\text{gu}] \text{ 'do and'} \\ molla \rightarrow [\text{mull}\vartheta] \text{ 'do not know'} \end{array}$$

e. A portion of the Korean vocabulary ends in two-consonant clusters. When the following affix begins with a vowel, both consonants remain, but when the affix begins with a consonant, one of the two stem consonants is deleted, since medial three-consonant clusters are not permitted in Korean. For example:

(8)   *ps → p, ∂ps-ta* [əp°ta] 'there is no';
              cf. *∂ps-i* [əp°si] 'without'
       ks → k, n∂ks-to [nək°to] 'the soul also';
              cf. *n∂ks-i* [nək°si] 'the soul is'
       nc → n, anc-k∂ra [ankəra] 'sit!'
              cf. *anc-∂tta* [anjət°ta] 'sat'
       lp → p, ccalp-ciman [ccap°ciman] 'although short';
              cf. *ccalp-∂to* [ccalbədo] 'even if short'
       lk → k, ilk-ca [ik°ca] 'let's read';
              cf. *ilk-∂tta* [ilgət°ta] '(he) read'
       lm → m, c∂lm-ta [cəmta] 'is young';
              cf. *c∂lm-ɨn* [cəlmɨn] 'young'

It is not easy to write a rule that captures neatly all the above changes. One can write two rules like the following to describe the phenomenon:

$$(9\text{i}) \quad \begin{bmatrix} -\text{grave} \\ C \end{bmatrix} \rightarrow \emptyset \ / C\underline{\quad\quad} C$$

$$(9\text{ii}) \quad C \rightarrow \emptyset \ / \underline{\quad\quad} CC$$

The middle consonant deletes, if it is a [-grave] (or [+coronal]) segment; otherwise the first consonant deletes. These two rules, though observationally adequate, are hardly explanatory or insightful. They do not show the real process that is taking place, for it is hardly phonologically plausible or natural to say that the cluster simplification is contingent upon the gravity of the middle segment of the cluster. It appears that what is really governing the deletion is the principle of close articulation; that is, of the two stem-final consonants, the more open member is deleted, and the more closed one survives.

As the above examples have shown, the articulatory basis, or phonetic mode, of Korean seems to be a tendency to "close" the articulation, hence the term *the principle of close articulation*. It is clear that Korean phonology falls under this general condition. It is as if this metacondition sits on top of the phonological component, projects itself onto every phonological rule in the language, influences the output of rules in any way it can, and, furthermore, creates rules just to serve its own purpose. It may be likened to a general tendency of Mexican food to be hot, although toward that general end various kinds of spices, for instance, cayenne, black pepper, chili pepper, curry powder, and so forth may be used in different dishes. This analogy is relevant in that the phenomenon I am considering seems to be a language-specific one, just as hotness or sweetness of a national food is an ethnically definable taste. Thus, the tendency toward close articulation seems to be Korean-specific, although there is no reason why some other languages may not show the same tendency.

Although examples from other languages are not readily found, Delattre (1953) noted that French is phonetically characterized by three "modes" of articulation:

(i) Tense ("tendu"), as opposed to English, which is lax ("relâché"). Thus, in French, voiceless stops do not become voiced even intervocalically, stops are not affricated, vowels are sharper and do not diphthongize, and there is no gliding in intonation, while English shows the opposite characteristics.

(ii) Front ("antérieur"), as opposed to English, which prefers back ("postérieur") articulation. This tendency seems to be particularly characteristic, and was also noted by Malmberg (1963:71), who called this kind of phenomenon "articulatory basis,"[9] that is, a certain predilection that a language has for articulation. This predilection would explain such facts as pure dentals, front rounded vowels, no palatali-

---

[9]For earlier mentions of the notion, see Sievers (1901:114) and Jespersen (1904:242). The term "basis of articulation" should not be regarded as implying "un facteur inné, don héréditaire et biologique" (Ginneken, 1933:266), but simply as a term referring to the pattern of native phonetic habits.

zation of dentals, and so on in French, while English is characterized by a tendency to move articulation back in the oral
cavity, thus, alveolar dentals, retroflexion of r, velarization
of l, and the tendency to palatalize alveolar consonants.

(iii) Growing ("croissant"), as opposed to waning ("de-
croissant"), contour in English; for instance, final accent in
French as compared to initial stress in English and ascending
intonational contour in French as opposed to descending
contour in English (particularly in British English).

One may also say that French has "convex" articulation
as opposed to English "concave" articulation, which would,
together with the favored fronting, explain the mysterious
palatalization of velar consonants in French (e.g., *chanter* 'to
sing' from Latin *cantare*; cf. Parisian pronunciation of *quatre*
[kyatr] 'four') and nasalization in French (convex and front
articulation allows ample room in the back of the oral cavity
for the velum to drop down). It might also explain the two
different r's in the two languages, French uvular r being
convex, while English retroflex r is concave.

To return to the analogy I cited earlier, just as there may
be different kinds of hot spices or sweeteners that achieve
the general goal of hot or sweet taste, the language-specific
phonological m e t a r u l e may appear in different shapes
throughout the phonological component. This last point is
particularly relevant, for the currently available device that
allows one to express this kind of related generality is in the
form of collapsing two or more consecutively ordered rules,
using such notations as parentheses and braces just in case
there are extractable common denominators among those
rules. Thus, in the following, rules (a) and (b) may be collapsed into the form of rule (c):

(10i) $A \rightarrow B / X \_\_\_ YZ$ (a)
        $A \rightarrow B / X \_\_\_ Y$ (b)
        $A \rightarrow B / X \_\_\_ Y(Z)$ (c)

or

(10ii) $A \rightarrow B / X \_\_\_ YZ$ (a)
        $A \rightarrow B / X \_\_\_ YW$ (b)
        $A \rightarrow B / X \_\_\_ Y \begin{Bmatrix} Z \\ W \end{Bmatrix}$ (c)

In the current theory of phonology, common denominators
are structurally defined, and therein lies the problem, for a

functional relation or similarity of the kind that I have been discussing is not expressible in a "collapsed" form (or in a "schema"), because of the structural dissimilarity of rules.

It is not at all clear, nor is it easy to see, how one might revise the current theory of phonology to incorporate in a natural and intuitively correct way this kind of phenomenon. The strongest claim would be to say that the current way of formulating rules is grossly wrong. That is, since a functional equivalence is not expressible with the presently available device, the current theory is wholly wrong. I do not wish to make this claim. On the other hand, one may wish to make the weakest claim and say that the phenomenon of "conspiracy" is a spurious one. That is, one might claim that "conspiracy" is not a property of language, and, therefore, the theory of language need not account for it. Even with the small amount of evidence we now have at hand, we know that this is an incorrect claim.

A compromise proposal would be to claim that, while the current theory is in the main adequate, some minor areas, such as notational conventions, constraints on rule application, and so forth, must be revised. There are some indications that this might be the right approach. Kisseberth (1970a, 1970b) proposed to handle his Yawelmani and Tunica cases with a constraint on rule derivation so that the rule application may be either absolutely or relatively obligatory. I will illustrate another kind of proposal on rule application with a hypothetical, but plausible, case.

Suppose that a language does not allow two consecutively stressed syllables. In such a case, it is easy to imagine several rules that would achieve this constraint, for instance, stress deletion, stress shift, and stress reduction, etc. (Cf. English and Tunica stress adjustment rules.) Thus, given a string of the form

(11) $VC_1\text{-}\acute{V}C_2\text{-}\acute{V}C_3\text{-}\acute{V}C_4\text{-}VC_5\text{-}\acute{V}C_6 \ldots$

it is likely that the final output would be something like

(12i) $\acute{V}C_1\text{-}VC_2\text{-}\acute{V}C_3\text{-}VC_4\text{-}\acute{V}C_5\text{-}VC_6 \ldots$
or (12ii) $VC_1\text{-}\acute{V}C_2\text{-}VC_3\text{-}\acute{V}C_4\text{-}VC_5\text{-}\acute{V}C_6 \ldots$

But given the current convention on rule application, that is, simultaneous scanning and simultaneous application of rules (cf. Chomsky and Halle, 1968:344), there is no elegant and

simple way to formulate a rule that would give the correct
output of iambic pattern, for a rule like the following

(13) $\acute{V} \rightarrow V / \acute{V}C$___

would give an incorrect output (14) when applied to (11):

(14) $VC_1\text{-}\acute{V}C_2\text{-}VC_3\text{-}VC_4\text{-}VC_5\text{-}VC_6 \ldots$

If, however, one allows the rule to apply from left to right
iteratively,[10] (and perhaps in both directions with "mirror
image" environment),[11] the correct output can be achieved.
Thus, revising (13) as (15),

(15)   ⓘ $\acute{V} \rightarrow V /$ ⓜ ___ $C\acute{V}$

where ⓘ means "applies iteratively," ⓜ "mirror image
environment," and boldface the most important constituent
in the string from which the iteration starts. Applying (15)
to (16) and (17), one gets the desirable output (12i) and (12ii)
respectively:

(16) $VC_1\text{-}\acute{V}C_2\text{-}\mathbf{\acute{V}C_3}\text{-}\acute{V}C_4\text{-}VC_5\text{-}\acute{V}C_6 \ldots$
(17) $VC_1\text{-}\acute{V}C_2\text{-}\acute{V}C_3\text{-}\mathbf{\acute{V}C_4}\text{-}VC_5\text{-}\acute{V}C_6 \ldots$

I will adopt this middle approach. Yet it is difficult to
propose an algorithm that would adequately formalize the
equivalence relation. The case of Korean, furthermore, is
in a way different from that of Yawelmani or Tunica which
Kisseberth discusses. In Yawelmani, there were well-defined
surface constraints that every rule in the language was not
to violate. In Korean, there is no such well-defined surface
constraint, but an overriding principle. The same can be said
of French. Note that the predominantly front articulation in
French does not allow palatalization of dentals, that is, there
is no rule of dental palatalization in French. In the absence
of such a rule, how does one talk about a rule violating or not
violating a constraint? Earlier, it was also mentioned that
the convex and front articulation probably prompted the
nasalization of vowels in French. But the resulting nasalized
vowels are neither front nor back exclusively. If anything,
nasalization involves a back (velic) articulation.

[10]Cf. Anderson (1967), McCawley (1969).
[11]Cf. Langacker (1969). Langacker uses an asterisk (*) as a notation
marking a mirror-image rule.

To return to the Korean case, I am going to assume for the moment that there is a metacondition sitting on top of the phonological component of Korean stating that no phonological rule should create an output that has a more open articulation than the input to the rule. One might state this condition in the following way:

(18)   (d) $A_i \geq$ (d) A_0

which should read: "When a phonological rule applies, the degree of aperture of the input segment(s) affected by the rule should be at least equal to or larger than the degree of aperture of the output segment(s)."[12] This metacondition would monitor all the phonological rules, and all rules that meet this condition would be grouped as functionally equivalent rules. As to the degrees of aperture, I refer to (19):

(19)

Degree of Aperture[13]	Segments	Examples	
0	unreleased stops	t°	d°
1	released stops	t	d
2	affricates	c	j
3	fricatives	s	z
4	liquids	l	r
5	glides	y	w
6	high vowels	i	u
7	mid vowels	e	o
8	low vowels	æ	a

[12]This is not always true in Korean, for there is a case where *t* becomes *s* before another *s*, e.g., *tat-so* [tasso] 'to close.' Note, however, that this phenomenon is a rather universal phonological process, i.e., it is a very natural case of assimilation. The language-specific nature of close articulation is well borne out by this example, for even though the *t → s* rule violates the Korean-specific output condition, it is overruled by a higher-order universal convention. Therefore, the *t → s* rule is not an exception to the principle of close articulation in Korean, nor does it serve as a "leak" in the conspiracy.

[13]For earlier discussions on lip aperture as a classificatory parameter, see Jespersen (1904:14–25) and Saussure (1916:70–76). Scales of

The rule of consonant reduction in Korean (9) can now be rewritten as follows:

(20) $C \rightarrow \emptyset \, / \, \text{(m)} \, [C \underline{\quad}] \, C$

With condition (18), this rule will delete the more open consonant of the first two. This rule not only dispenses with the necessity to express the phenomenon in two rules, as in (9), but also states the actual phonological process involved.

To summarize, two phonological processes, neutralization and "conspiracy," both of which share the property of having the superficially same phenomenon represented in several different forms, have been examined. In neutralization, it was noted that not all cases of absolute neutralization are consequences of trick manipulation, since there may be a case in which absolute neutralization is dictated by the overall generality of the system. Second, it was noted that there seem to be cases where a certain general tendency of articulation is preferred by and is characteristic of a speech community and that this general condition may be manifest in different shapes throughout the language, so that the current convention of rule formulation does not express this interrelationship (or "conspiracy") among rules. Although one may choose to disregard this phenomenon as spurious, there is enough evidence to suggest an alteration in the current framework of phonology; however, I have merely pointed out such a necessity rather than proposed an adequate solution to the problem.

---

aperture do not represent quantum changes but a continuum. For example, *kipɨm → kibɨm → kiβɨm → kiwɨm → kium* 'mending' in Korean illustrates a change from aperture 1 to aperture 6. Viewed in this way, what is called "rhotacism" would be a change from aperture 3 to aperture 4 (e.g., German *Verlust* 'loss' vs. *verlieren* 'to lose'). Interchanges among stops, affricates, and fricatives need no illustration here. A change from *l* to *y* or *w*, which is not rare, exemplifies the change from aperture 4 to 5, e.g., French *fille* [fi:y] from Latin *filia* 'girl,' Italian *pieno* [pyeno] from Latin *plenu* 'full,' Polish *biw* from Slavic *bil* 'be,' etc. Some changes in reverse direction: from *y* to *j* (from aperture 5 to 2), e.g., German *Jesu* [yezu] → English *Jesus* [ǰizes]; from *l* to *z* (from aperture 4 to 3), e.g., Portuguese *fizo* from Latin *filius* 'son.' Vowel shifts in both directions (vowel raising, vowel lowering) also need no illustration here. For details, see Kim (1968b).

REFERENCES

Anderson, L. (1967). "A Left-to-Right Syllabic Cycle." *Chicago Journal of Linguistics* 1.

Brame, M. (this volume). "On the Abstractness of Phonology: Maltese ʕ."

Chomsky, N., and M. Halle (1968). *The Sound Pattern of English.* New York: Harper and Row.

Crothers, J. (1971). "On the Abstractness Controversy." Project on Linguistic Analysis Report, second series, no. 12. University of California, Berkeley.

Delattre, P. (1953). "Les modes phonétiques du français." *The French Review* 27:59–63.

Fudge, E. C. (1967). "The Nature of Phonological Primes." *Journal of Linguistics* 3:1–36.

Ginneken, J. van (1933). "La biologie de la base d'articulation." *Psychologie du langage* 30:266–282.

Halle, M. (1962). "Phonology in Generative Grammar." *Word* 18:54–72.

Hyman, L. (1970). "How Concrete is Phonology?" *Language* 46:58–76.

Jespersen, O. (1913). *Lehrbuch der Phonetik.* 2nd ed. Leipzig and Berlin: Teubner.

Kim, Chin-Wu (1968a). "The Vowel System of Korean." *Language* 44:516–527.

——(1968b). "When Liquids Become Glides." *Chicago Journal of Linguistics* 2:45–50.

——(1968c). "Regularity of Irregular Verbs in Korean." 43rd Annual Meeting of the Linguistic Society of America, New York (Paper #86, Meeting Handbook, p. 52).

Kiparsky, P. (1968). "How Abstract is Phonology?" Mimeographed. Cambridge: Massachusetts Institute of Technology.

——(1969). "Where do conspiracies come from?" 44th Annual Meeting of the Linguistic Society of America, San Francisco (Paper #50, Meeting Handbook, p. 77).

Kisseberth, C. W. (1969). "On the Abstractness of Phonology: The Evidence from Yawelmani." *Papers in Linguistics* 1:248–282.

—— (1970). "On the Functional Unity in Phonological Rules." *Linguistic Inquiry* 1:291–306.

—— (to appear). "The Tunica Stress Conspiracy." *Linguistic Inquiry.*

Langacker, R. (1969). "Mirror Image Rules II: Lexicon and Phonology." *Language* 45:844–862.

Lightner, T. (1965). "On the Description of Vowel and Consonant Harmony." *Word* 21:244–250.

Malmberg, B. (1963). *Phonetics.* New York: Dover.

McCawley, J. (1969). "Length and Voicing in Tübatulabal." Papers from 5th Regional Meeting of the Chicago Linguistic Society, pp. 407–415.

Postal, P. M. (1968). *Aspects of Phonological Theory*. New York: Harper and Row.

Ross, J. R. (1969). "A Stress Conspiracy in English." 44th Annual Meeting of the Linguistic Society of America, San Francisco (Paper #58, Meeting Handbook, pp. 98–99).

Saussure, F. de (1916). *Cours de linguistique générale*. Paris: Payot.

Sievers, G. E. (1901). *Grundzüge der Phonetik*. 5th ed. Leipzig: Beitkopt und Härtel.

Metrics and Morphophonemics
in the Rigveda

PAUL KIPARSKY

Massachusetts Institute of Technology

1. Introduction: Metrics and Morphophonemics

The questions that generative grammar seeks to answer are fundamentally psychological questions about which earlier linguistics had few concrete things to say. So far, however, the answers to these newly raised questions have still been sought for the most part by the old methods, inherited from structuralism, of formally analyzing the regularities within the closed linguistic system. It is questionable how far this method can take us. Under the structuralist conception of grammar as an "immanent" system existing above and beyond any individual speaker, it was enough to search for the most "elegant" statement of the formal combinatorial regularities of the language. For most linguists, the question of whether a particular analysis was right or wrong did not really arise. However, if we accept as one of our goals the investigation of the system of rules learned in childhood by each speaker that allows him to communicate effectively, the question of right and wrong has a clear meaning and cannot be ignored. In that case, we cannot stay "within" the language, unless we beg the question by saying that the neatest solution (assuming that we even can reach agreement on what that is) must always be also the right one, that is, the one actually reached in the language-learning situation.

To worry about securing other criteria for truth than

NOTE: This work was supported in part by the National Institute of Mental Health (Grant No. MH-13390-05). I would like to thank Warren Cowgill for his stimulating criticism.

theoretical elegance would probably be a waste of time in a
field like physics. However, the situation in linguistics is
unique because of the performance/competence and syn-
chrony/diachrony distinctions. The sort of facts that linguistic theory (especially phonology) intends to explain can, in a
great many instances, be interpreted in terms of a quite different explanatory paradigm, which has a long and extremely
successful tradition in linguistics: that of historical and comparative grammar.

Consider, for example, the claim of generative phonology
that phonological rules in a synchronic grammar apply in
order rather than simultaneously. It takes more to prove
this claim than to make the observation (in itself of course
perfectly correct) that the ordering hypothesis allows one to
account elegantly for the phonological alternations of all
languages that have been investigated so far. If the argument
for ordered rules were that simple, linguists would have come
around to synchronic grammars with ordered rules a hundred
years ago, and the strenuous effort of structuralists to rid
themselves of all vestiges of ordered rules, which marked
American linguistics in the forties and fifties, and, much
earlier, Saussure's development from the *Mémoire* to the
Cours, would be completely incomprehensible. A large portion of the regularities that are explained by assuming that
synchronic grammars have ordered rules can a priori also be
explained by the fact (which has to be recognized whatever we
decide about synchronic grammars) that languages are subject
to sound changes that take place one after the other. The explanatory burden of synchronic rules and their ordering can
therefore be partly carried by sound changes and their relative chronology.

What is wrong with the traditional assumption that the
synchronic structure of language consists simply of paradigms
memorized by the speaker and that the combinatorial regularities in the phonology of a language are all synchronically
accidental, having only historical explanations? That question
has by now been satisfactorily answered in several ways. For
example, it has become clear that the process of sound change
itself cannot be fully understood without the notion of a
synchronic linguistic structure with ordered rules (Halle,
1962; Postal, 1968). Also, synchronic order is by no means
an automatic reflection of chronology. In many cases the two

differ, and both notions are necessary elements in a linguistic explanation (Kiparsky, 1968a). Furthermore, rules that do not correspond to any "sound changes," such as the rule converting English to Pig Latin or the rules spontaneously added by young children, also have to be ordered with respect to other phonological processes (Chomsky and Halle, 1968; Applegate, 1962; Stampe, 1969). Obviously there could not be any historical explanation based on sound change in such cases. All this shows that there is synchronic phonological structure involving ordered rules that cannot be accounted for in purely historical terms.

Nevertheless, it still remains a problem where the relative domains of historical and synchronic explanation end. To solve this problem we must know the nature of the speaker's internalized system of rules much better than we do at present. It docs not seem likely that we can get as far in this quest as we need to through the traditional sort of immanent study of the combinatorial regularities of languages. Thus, it becomes an important task for generative phonology to investigate whatever extrasystemic consequences of its hypotheses can be tested against available or obtainable empirical data.

There are quite a few sources of empirical data that at present promise to be able to test the psychological claims implicit in the theory of generative phonology. Although most of them remain regrettably underexploited, a few have been intensively investigated with good results in recent years. I will mention here only those which can already be said to have yielded real linguistic insights.

(1) Child language. This is a classic field of investigation and needs no comment.

(2) Language disturbances. Compare Jakobson (1942), Weigl and Bierwisch (1970).

(3) Direct psychological experimentation. Psycholinguistic research has so far concentrated on syntactic problems. Examples of what can be done on the phonological side are Zimmer (1969) and Bever (1970).

(4) Borrowing. Hyman (1970a, 1970b) has argued that foreign sounds can be perceived in terms of underlying forms and utilized this fact to investigate the possible existence of constraints on the abstractness of phonological analyses.

(5) Orthography. The question of the ideal orthography of

a language is obviously of great practical as well as theoretical interest. Most linguists would probably agree that a good orthography should be at least partly morphophonemic (Voorhoeve, 1959, 1961; Chomsky and Halle, 1968), although the evidence for this belief is mostly anecdotal (e.g., Sapir, 1933). However, it is very doubtful that the underlying forms that appear in most generative phonologies would prove adequate as the basis for an orthography. One would wish for more information to be made available by field workers and missionaries about their actual experiences with teaching various types of writing systems to speakers of unwritten languages.

(6) Historical linguistics. Some ways in which historical evidence is relevant to phonological theory have been suggested in Kiparsky (1968a).

(7) Metrics. Metrical constraints involve such linguistic entities as sentence or word boundaries, syllables, quantity, and stress. Especially in oral poetic traditions, where the metrics is transmitted by example from one generation of poets to the next, without becoming known to them as a conscious set of rules, one can often find interesting clues about the nature of these linguistic entities. The present paper is a contribution to this topic.

It was long an unquestioned axiom of metrical theory that the metrically relevant features of a line are phonetic, that is, audible in the recitation intended by the poet (although they might be omitted when recited at a later stage of the language, when a linguistic change had taken place eliminating this feature). As Sturtevant put it, "we may take it for granted that an obligatory feature of versification must be in some way audible" (1924:337). A hundred years ago this conception was actually not so much an axiom as a theorem. In the then prevailing view of phonology there was no more to the phonological structure of a language than the distribution of its phonetic elements. No other position than Sturtevant's was really conceivable. As linguists came to recognize the existence of more abstract forms of phonological structure, represented by morphophonemes, it could be asked for the first time whether these more abstract forms of phonological structure have any metrical function. That they should have one is a possibility—though not of course a necessity—which can only be settled as a factual question.

One of the first discussions of the problem was given by

Jakobson (1963). He pointed out that such features of versification as caesurae are not phonetically audible as physical
pauses of any sort in recitation of the South Slavic oral
epics, and this observation surely holds for other poetic
traditions as well. What Jakobson proposed instead of the
audibility requirement was that the features of versification be
potentially audible, that is, that there exist in the language the
possibility of physically manifesting it—as a pause in the case
of a caesura—even though the style of recitation may be such
that this linguistic option is not utilized in poetry. That even
this very natural modification of the classical view of the
relation between phonology and metrics is still not sufficient
was shown by Zeps' (1963) discussion of the metrics of
Latvian folksongs. Zeps showed that a rule of vowel apocope,
obligatory in the spoken language, is optionally disregarded
in the scanning of a line, so that a word reduced by the
apocope from n to n-1 syllables can be metrically counted as
either n or n-1 syllables. Still, Jakobson's suggestion might
be regarded as compatible with Zeps' observations, since
Zeps notes that the syllable deleted by apocope can be rein-
stated in singing (though interestingly enough not necessarily
with the original vowel).

The metrics of the Finnish epic *Kalevala* as recorded in
Ingermanland and described in Sadeniemi (1951) indicates
that versification may be based on even abstracter forms of
phonological representation and that potential audibility is not
always necessary (Kiparsky, 1968b). The phonological representations to which the metrical constraints apply are neither
phonetic nor morphophonemic, but are intermediate representations reached after the application of at least three
rules but before the application of at least four others, only
one of them optional. For example, the scanning of *pojjain*
'my son' (two syllables, initial long), whose morphophonemic
representation must be /poika+ni/ (three syllables, initial
long), is **pojaini* (three syllables, initial short). This form
results from the following derivation:

underlying form	/poika+ni/	(- x x)
epenthesis	poikaini	(- x x)
consonant gradation	*pojaini*	(ˇ x x)
medially		
in closed syllables		

lengthening of consonants between short and long vowel or diphthong	pojjaini	(- x x)
vowel dropping	pojjain	(- x)

The metrical cutoff point, as in all derivations, is reached immediately after the application of the consonant gradation rule. What is especially interesting is that there is no reason to assume that such forms as *pojaini* ever existed phonetically at any historical stage in this dialect. The historical development was most likely *poikani → poikaini → pojjaini → pojjain*, ruling out a priori any attempt to explain these scannings as historical relics.

The findings of Anderson (1969) on Old Icelandic rhyme likewise indicate that prosodic constraints may involve stages in the derivation that are not (even optionally) realized on the phonetic level. Lasnik (personal communication) has found evidence that Old English alliteration works in a similar manner.

Given such a metrical system we can reverse our perspective and look at the morphophonemics in the light of what the metrics shows about it. In cases where the decision between two alternative analyses is moot, as far as purely immanent, structural considerations go, the metrical behavior of the linguistic elements in question may give us a clue as to what synchronic analysis linguistic theory should be required to provide for it. Armed with enough of these clues, we can tentatively try to sharpen the theory itself, so that it is compatible with these new findings, and ultimately check the revision against resulting analyses in other languages by means of metrical, historical, or other kinds of evidence.

2. The Problem of Rigvedic Metrics

I will try to show in this paper that the metrics of the Rigveda also applies to nonphonetic representations and to follow up a few consequences of this circumstance from the viewpoint of phonological and morphological theory. I will concentrate on those aspects of Rigvedic metrics which have the greatest linguistic interest, putting aside both a large portion of the philological documentation that I need to complete my case and almost all discussion of the consequences that the findings have for the history and prehistory of Sanskrit. These topics will be taken up in Kiparsky (forth-coming).

In many thousands of instances, segments represented in the traditional text of the Rigveda as *y* and *v* must be scanned as syllabic *i* and *u* in order for the otherwise very regular syllable count to work out correctly. For example, in a hymn whose meter (*Triṣṭubh*) requires lines of eleven syllables with a caesura after the fourth or fifth syllable, we find the line conventionally written and chanted as follows:

ā ṣaṣtyā́ saptatyā́ somapéyan '[come] here with sixty,
seventy to drink Soma'   (2.18.5)

The only way this line can fulfill the metrical requirements is by reading the first word ('sixty') as trisyllabic *ṣaṣṭiā́*,[1] whereas the second, a morphologically parallel form meaning 'seventy,' has to be read with nonsyllabic *y* (*saptatyā́*). The necessity for this kind of syllabic restoration in the RV has long been known. It was also noticed early that the syllabic *i*, *u* scannings of *y, v* are especially frequent after a heavy syllable, that is, when the vowel of the preceding syllable is either long or followed by two or more consonants. The contrast *ṣaṣṭiā́* (*CCi V̆*) : *saptatyā́* (*V̆Cy V̆*) in the line just cited is, therefore, quite typical of the general distribution.

The first systematic attempt to explain the necessity for frequent syllabic restoration of *i*, *u* for *y*, *v* in the text and the general observation that preceding heavy syllables favor it was made by Sievers (1878). In line with the axiom that metrics reflects pronunciation, Sievers assumed that the traditional text of the Rigveda does not reflect the actual pronunciation at the time of composition, but reflects an importation of the rules of classical Sanskrit into the tradi-tional text of the Rigveda. In classical Sanskrit, *i* and *u* generally become *y* and *v* before vowels, except under certain special conditions, and the extant text of the Rigveda follows these rules quite closely. The original pronunciation, Sievers assumed, was that indicated by the scansion. Sievers pro-posed a sound law according to which, prevocalically, *i* was in complementary distribution with *y* and *u* with *v* (=[w]), with

---

[1]I will write *ia* to indicate a metrical restoration, without prejudging what the pronunciation may have been. The actual pronunciation would not have been *ia*, but must have been either *ya* or *iya*, the latter by a rule that I assume inserts a glide between high and low vowels.

the syllabic variants appearing after $\frac{\bar{V}C_1}{\breve{V}C_2}$ ___ and the non-syllabic variants elsewhere before a vowel.

Sievers' idea was elaborated in several articles by Edgerton (1934, 1943), who collected evidence indicating beyond any doubt that heavy syllables favor syllabic scansion of a following semivowel. (I will use *semivowel* as a cover term for *i*, *y*, *u*, *v*.) Nevertheless, there are many exceptions to this rule. To account for them, Edgerton supposed on the one hand that analogy had already begun to interfere with the operation of Sievers' Law, and on the other hand that the Rigvedic poets composed in a partly artificial dialect that they did not fully control.

Edgerton's appeal to the alleged "imperfect linguistic control by the poets" as an explanation for the many apparent exceptions to Sievers' Law is very weak. The poets otherwise handle the involved morphology of Vedic perfectly well and have no difficulty with an accent system that modern grammarians are hardly able to untangle. Why should the "linguistic incompetence" of the bards have been so concentrated in a persistent inability to observe Sievers' Law, a superficial phonetic rule that depends moreover on the very distinction that underlies the whole Rigvedic metrical system—that between heavy and light syllables? Furthermore, if the apparent exceptions to Sievers' Law are due to linguistic incompetence, then one would expect them to grow more frequent in those portions of the Rigveda which, according to the usual linguistic and metrical criteria, are later, derivative compositions. On the whole, however, they are about equally common in all chronological layers of the Rigveda, as Arnold (1905:105) has shown statistically.

Another circumstance that indicates that the answer is not to be sought in the bards' linguistic incompetence but rather within the linguistic and metrical system in which the Rigveda was composed is that the option of syllabic and nonsyllabic scansion, when it is regularly available, plays a conspicuous role in the design of the verse. The option can serve to fit formulae into different metrical slots, sometimes in such a way that the same word in the same phrase is scanned two different ways in two successive lines. The Rigvedic meters are so constituted that the occasion for lengthening or shortening a verse or colon by one syllable arises easily.

For example, the twelve-syllable *Jagatī* is simply the eleven-
syllable *Triṣṭubh* with an extra syllable in the second colon.
At stanza five of 1.85 the hymn switches from *Jagatī* to
Triṣṭubh, and the transition is made by echoing the last line
of stanza four, with twelve syllables,

> vṛ̣savrātāsaḥ / pṛ̣satīr áyugdhuam (5+7)
>
> '(when) you have harnessed the dappled mares
> with your strong hosts'

in the first line of stanza five, with eleven syllables,

> prá yád rathéṣu / pṛ̣satīr áyugdhvam (5+6)
> 'when you have harnessed the dappled mares to
> your chariots'

The metrical option *áyugdhuam /áyugdhvam* functions here to
maintain a substantial parallelism across the prosodic diver-
gence.

The same situation can come about because the caesura in
these meters can follow either the fourth or the fifth syllable.
For example, in 4.35.5 we have the two *Triṣṭubh* lines

> śáciā'karta / pitárā yúvānā (5+6)
>
> śácyā'karta / camasáṃ devapā́nam (4+7)
>
> 'you have skilfully made your parents young
> you have skilfully made a cup for the gods to
> drink from'

where the first colon is used twice but with different metrical
value. Such examples give the impression of being not deviations from the norm but part of it. Instead of arbitrarily
labeling them as exceptions to a preconceived form of Sievers'
Law, we should investigate the linguistic and metrical conditions that make their use in the poetry possible.

In fact, a closer look at the supposed "exceptions" shows
that the situation is linguistically much more systematic than
Edgerton supposed. We have just seen an example of the
option -*dhvam*/-*dhuam* in a case where the semivowel is
after a heavy syllable. The option for this suffix, as well as
for many others, such as -*bhyas*, -*bhyām*, in fact exists only
in this environment. After a light syllable these suffixes are
regularly scanned with nonsyllabic *y*, *v*. The second example
I cited involved an option after a light syllable: *śáciā/śácyā*.

The suffix in question, stem-forming $\bar{\imath}$ before instr. sg. $-\bar{a}$, allows this option *only* after light syllables. After heavy syllables it is regularly scanned as a syllabic segment, for instance in $\bar{u}ti\bar{a}$. Furthermore, with the exception of morphophonemically stressed semivowels, such as thematic $/\acute{\imath}/$, $/\acute{u}/$, as in $nad\acute{\imath}$ 'river,' which are always scanned syllabically in prevocalic position (e.g. instr. $nady\bar{a}$ = $nad\acute{\imath}\bar{a}$) and which I will disregard for the moment, *every suffixal semivowel falls into one of these two categories*. In other words, Sievers' Law is valid, in every suffix in which the conditions for its application are met, either after heavy or after light syllables, but every suffix also shows a sizable proportion of "exceptions" to Sievers' Law in one of the two environments. Hence, the suffixes whose semivowels are regularly syllabic after heavy syllables (e.g., the stem-forming $-\breve{\imath}-$, $-u-$, or the gerund in $-ya$) have optional nonsyllabic scansion after light syllables, and the suffixes whose semivowels are optionally syllabic after heavy syllables (e.g., $-dhvam$, $-bhyas$) have regular y, v after light syllables. There are a few suffixes, such as gen. sg. $-sya$ in a-stems, which for morphological reasons can only occur in one of the two environments. In the reduced form in which the claim made by the proposed bipartite division of suffixes is applicable in these cases, the above-mentioned scansion possibilities remain valid. There are scattered exceptions, such as three instances of $-dhuam$ after a light syllable, but I follow Arnold (1905) in distinguishing these sporadic cases from the genuine option that exists in the cases described. There are, consequently, no suffixes in which y and v are treated in the same way after heavy and light syllables.

In sum, there are two classes of suffixes possessing semivowels, which in some or all of their occurrences are prevocalic. In the first class, which I will term i-, u-*suffixes*, in accordance with the dominant allophone of the semivowel, the prevocalic semivowel is regularly syllabic after heavy syllables and optionally syllabic after light syllables. In the second class, which I will term y-, v-*suffixes*, the prevocalic semivowel is optionally syllabic after heavy syllables and regularly nonsyllabic after light syllables.

The following is a list of the most important members of each class. For more information on each case see Arnold (1905, ch. 5), Edgerton (1934, 1943)—though the latter is not completely reliable—the relevant sections of Wackernagel-Debrunner, the metrical transcriptions in Grassmann's *Wörterbuch zum Rigveda* (not always correct either), and Whitney's and Macdonell's grammars.

The following suffixes belong to the first, or *i*-, *u*-class:

(1) Stem-forming -*i*- before the vocalic endings gen. loc. dual -*os* and instr. sg. -*ā̆*. E.g., regularly *ūtiā̆* (*ūtí* 'help'), but freely either *suṣṭutiā̆* or *suṣṭutyā̆* (*súṣṭuti* 'beautiful hymn').

(2) Stem-forming -*ī*- in the same cases. E.g., regularly *pátniā* (*pátnī* 'mistress'), but alternatively *tmániā*/*tmányā* (*tmánī*, fem. of *tmán* 'self').

(3) Stem-forming -*u*- in the same cases. E.g., regularly *bāhuós* (*bāhú* 'arm'), *ádhenuā* (*ádhenu* 'giving no milk'), but *panvā̆* (*panú* 'praise')/*hánuā* (*hánu* 'jaw').

In each of these three cases there are some interesting and very revealing additional complications. Some of these I will briefly bring up later in this paper; for others (masculine -*i*- and -*u*-stems) see Kiparsky (forthcoming). The fourth semivowel stem suffix, -*ū*-, is practically always accented and thereby syllabic, so that it is not relevant here.

(4) Present tense -*nu*- (-*u*-) before vocalic endings. Classical Sanskrit reflects Sievers' Law with complete regularity: *prāpnuvanti* 'they arrive,' *śaknuvanti* 'they are able' vs. *sunvanti* 'they press,' *prahinvanti* 'they impel.' But after a light syllable the Rigvedic meter indicates a syllabic value in a number of instances, e.g., *dhánuantu* 'let them flow,' *śṛnuántu* 'let them hear,' alongside *dhánvantu*, *sṛnvántu* (cf. Arnold, p. 96).

(5) Optative -*yā*-. The glide is regularly counted as syllabic after heavy syllables (Arnold, p. 96) and sometimes after light syllables, e.g., *aśyā́ma*/*aśiā́ma* 'may we obtain.'

(6) Gerundive -*ya*. After a heavy syllable the metrical form is regularly -*ia*, e.g., *vā́ria* 'to be chosen,' *mā́rjia* 'to be cleaned,' *śáṃsia* 'to be praised,' and *yódhia* 'to be fought.' After a weak syllable both possibilities again exist: *hávya*/*hávia* 'to be invoked,' *gúhya*/*gúhia* 'to be hidden,' *śásia* 'to be praised,' and *ayudhyā́* 'not to be fought.'

(7) Gerundive -*tva*. This formation is much rarer than the gerundive in -*ya*, and the evidence is correspondingly less certain. Still, it is likely that the suffix is to be assigned to

this category. After heavy syllables we always have -*tua*, except in the form *kartva*.[2] After weak syllables the two attested verbs that take the suffix always have -*tva* (*jánitva*, *sánitva*). The absence of -*tua* after light syllables, in spite of regular -*tua* after heavy syllables, is sufficiently explained by the fact that the forms in question, if scanned with -*tua*, would have at least three light syllables in a row. This is a fairly inconvenient sequence of syllables in the Rigveda, which has basically alternating long and short syllables. *Jánitva*, *sánitva* are therefore the natural metrical utilizations of the syllabic/nonsyllabic option.

(8) Comparative -*yas*/-*īyas*. This case differs from most of the others in two respects. In the first place, *y* alternates here not with short *i(y)* but with long *ī(y)*. Second, the syllabic form is indicated, as in the case of the present suffix -*nu*- after clusters, in the traditional text itself. The distribution is typical of this class of suffixes: after heavy syllables we always have the variant -*īyas*, e.g., *óhīyas* 'stronger,' *máṃhīyas* 'more bountiful'; after light syllables both -*īyas* and -*yas* may occur: *távyas*/*távīyas* 'stronger,' *návyas*/*návīyas* 'new,' *sáhyas*/*sáhīyas* 'stronger,' and *pányas*/*pánīyas* 'more glorious.'

It is clear why the present tense marker -*nu*- and the comparative suffix are spelled with vowels after heavy syllables in the extant recension of the Rigveda. In these cases the syllabic form persisted into classical Sanskrit. The text has been normalized at a very early date in certain superficial ways to conform to post-Vedic phonology. The syllabic form was retained in the text only where it was familiar to the editors responsible for this normalization from their own form of Sanskrit.

I suspect that this first class of suffixes has at least one other member, namely, the enormously frequent suffix -*ya*, which forms derived nouns and adjectives from nouns. This suffix to some extent shares with -*nu*- and -*yas*/-*īyas* two properties: its syllabic form (-*iya*) is indicated in the traditional text, and this form survives in classical Sanskrit in the Sievers' Law environment, a fact that confirms the connection between these two phenomena indicated in the last

---

[2]Grassmann's and Whitney's "*bhávītvā*" in 2.24.5 is wrong. The form should be *bhávītuā*, as Arnold gives it.

paragraph. I am unsure, however, how many of these denominal -*ya* suffixes one should distinguish. I think that there may be several, possibly with somewhat different phonological behaviors.

Consider now the second or *y*-, *v*-class of suffixes, in which the semivowel is optionally syllabic after a heavy syllable and regularly nonsyllabic after a light syllable. This class includes the following:

(1) Dat.abl.pl. -*bhyas*. In the case of the heavy syllable, we have *prajā́bhyas/prajā́bhias* (*prajā́* 'offspring'); after a light syllable there is no option, and the type *ŕ̥ṣibhyas* (*ŕ̥ṣi* 'seer') is obligatory. See Arnold (1905:94).

(2) Instr.dat.abl.dual -*bhyām*. The facts are completely analogous (ibid.).

(3) Present tense morpheme and passive morpheme -*ya*-. After a light syllable the nonsyllabic scansion is obligatory; after a heavy syllable the syllabic scansion is possible, if rare (impf. *ā́siat* 'he threw,' from *as*, three times; cf. Arnold, p. 95; Edgerton 1934:255).

(4) 2 pl. endings -*dhve*, -*dhvai*, -*dhvam*. (Arnold p. 94.)

(5) 2 sg. middle imperative -*sva* (ibid.).

(6) Future tense morpheme -*sya*- (Arnold, p. 95; Edgerton, 1934:254).

(7) Perfect participle -*vas* (Arnold, p. 95; Edgerton, p. 255).

(8) Gerunds -*tyā́* -*tvā́* -*tvī́* -*yă̆* (Arnold p. 95).

(9) Enclitic *tvā́* (ibid.).

(10) Derivational suffix -*va* (ibid.).

(11) Abstract noun-forming -*tva*. E.g., *rakṣastuám* 'sorcery'/*anāgāstvám* 'freedom from sin,' but regularly -*tvam* after light syllables, e.g., *amŕ̥tatvám* 'immortality' and *vasutvám* 'richness' (Arnold p. 94).

(12) Adjective-forming suffix -*vant* 'having X' (Edgerton 1934:255).

What is the explanation for this division of suffixes into two classes and for the behavior of each class? It is clear from the beginning that the reason for this division is not going to be a purely metrical problem; the answer will also involve linguistic considerations. If we can establish the linguistic basis of the differentiation and then show how this linguistic differentiation accounts for the metrical facts, we will have answered the question.

3. A Solution

The first part of the answer, I propose, is the following:

(1) *The suffixes in the first class have underlying /i/ or /u/; the suffixes in the second class have underlying /y/ or /v/.*

The terms "*i-*, *u*-suffix" and "*y-*, *v*-suffix," then, refer not only to the dominant allophone, but also to its underlying form.

If this assertion can be justified—and I will offer linguistic evidence for it—we can explain the metrical facts on the basis of the following two assumptions:

(2) *Sievers' Law operated with complete regularity in the Vedic period.*

(3) *The metrical range of the Rigveda includes a level of representation prior to the rules of glide formation and Sievers' Law.*

We then have the following four cases of prevocalic semi-vowels, taking *i* and *y* as representatives:

Morpho-phonemic form	Pronunciation (by glide formation and Sievers' Law)	Metrical value in RV
(a) /i/	[i] (after heavy syllables)	*i* (pátniā)
(b) /i/	[y] (after light syllables)	*i,y* (śaciā/śacyā)
(c) /y/	[i] (after heavy syllables)	*y,i* (áyugdhvam/áyugdhuam)
(d) /y/	[y] (after light syllables)	*y* (ájuṣadhvam)

A glance at this table shows that the metrical value must agree with either the morphophonemic value or the phonetic value. If both the morphophonemic and the phonetic forms are syllabic, the metrical value must be syllabic; if both are nonsyllabic, the metrical value must be nonsyllabic; if they differ, the poet has a choice.

Note how this explanation requires that Sievers' Law apply with high regularity inside words. If it did not apply quite regularly, case (a) in the above table could not be explained. In that case we should expect to find scansions like **pátnyā*. Their almost complete absence shows that we cannot assume

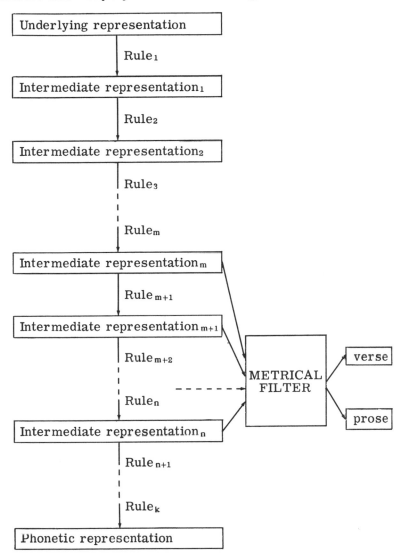

that Sievers' Law itself was optional, but that the proper explanation for the optionality within this metrical system lies in the interaction of morphophonemic, as well as phonetic, representations with the meter.

Specifically, this interaction works as follows: we can think of the meter as a kind of filter that accepts only sentences of a certain form and that a line must pass in order to be acceptable in poetry. In Rigvedic (as in Latvian and in Icelandic) the line can pass the filter not only in its phonetic shape, but also at certain earlier stages of the phonological derivation. Let us term the possibilities of scansion the *metrical range*. If the line passes the filter at any stage in the metrical range, it is acceptable. Otherwise, it is rejected and thrown into the prose bin. The accompanying diagram represents this relationship between metrics and morphophonemics.

The metrical range, then, is the set of representations that the metrical filter accepts as inputs (stages m, $m+1$, ... , n in the diagram). It will also be convenient to speak of a phonological rule as being in the metrical range if it can be disregarded in metrics, that is, if the representations constituting its input are in the metrical range. The metrical range of the Rigveda includes the phonological rules pertaining to glide formation and Sievers' Law, as well as to several contraction rules that I will refer to later.

The diagram represents the most differentiated case. The Kalevala system, in which the metrical acceptability of a line is determined at a single cutoff point in the phonological derivation, is the special case in which $m = n$. Furthermore, in the case of phonetically based meter, it is the case that $m = n = k$.

I turn now to the question of the evidence for the different underlying forms I have assigned to the two classes of suffixes. My claim is that there are almost no exceptions to Sievers' Law in Rigvedic and that apparent cases of [y] and [v] after heavy syllables are really morphophonemic scansions of /y/ and /v/, just as apparent cases of [i] and [u] after light syllables are really morphophonemic scansions of /i/ and /u/. The majority of the apparent exceptions to Sievers' Law is covered by this statement, so that /i/ and /u/ after heavy syllables are always scanned i and u, and /y/ and /v/ after light syllables are always scanned y and v, a fact that indicates the great regularity with which Sievers' Law must have operated.

What I have to show, therefore, is that the suffixes that, on *metrical* grounds, belong in the i-, u-class have, on *phono-*

logical grounds, underlying representations with /ĭ/ and /ŭ/, and that the suffixes that, on *metrical* grounds, go in the *y-*, *v*-class have, on *phonological* grounds, underlying representations with /y/ and /v/. I will consider the *i-*, *u*-suffixes first.

One type of argument for the syllabic nature of the underlying semivowel runs as follows: The stem-forming suffixes *-ī-*, *-i-*, *-ū-*, *-u-* have syllabic and nonsyllabic allomorphs. Either one of these must be basic. But the basic form cannot be the nonsyllabic one (*y*, *v*), because there would be no natural way of distinguishing *-i-* from *-ī-*, and similarly *-u-* from *-ū-*. The only way of doing so would be to invent new segments, /ȳ/ and /v̄/, which would become [ī] and [ū] before consonants, but which would otherwise merge with /y/ and /v/. These new segments would be needed nowhere else in the grammar and would plainly complicate it with no compensating advantage. If we start with the syllabic form as basic, we can simply distinguish the suffixes by the phonological feature of length, which we know is distinctive for vowels in Sanskrit, and derive the glides in the usual way.

This argument establishes the underlying syllabicity of all glides that alternate with long vowels, such as the optative and the comparative suffixes. For example, if *-yas* rather than *-īas* were taken as basic in the comparative suffix, how would we know that in the Sievers' Law environment *-yas* appears as *-īas* (→ *-īyas*) and not as **-ias* (→ **-iyas*)? An otherwise unnecessary rule would be needed to lengthen the *i* resulting from the operation of Sievers' Law in an arbitrary, phonologically uncharacterizable class of suffixes.

The fact that a glide alternates with a vowel does not, however, justify setting up an underlying vowel. There are rules in Sanskrit that convert glides into vowels in certain contexts (indeed, Sievers' Law is such a rule). Traditional treatments of Sanskrit phonology, following Pāṇini, also have an ablaut process termed *samprasāraṇa,* by which certain changes of *va* → *u* and of *ya* → *i* are derived. This process would operate in the perfect-participle suffix, which has the allomorphs *-vāṃs/-vas/-vat/-uṣ.* The fact that *-vāṃs* is metrically a *y-*, *v*-suffix would support this solution. I do not have any positive phonological evidence to back it up, however. Such evidence would have to come from a fuller study of the ablaut system than I have been able to make.

A second reason for underlying syllabic analysis is the appearance of an accent on the semivowel. We know that only syllabic segments can receive an accent. Since the gerundive suffix -*ya* is sometimes accented -*yá*, with an accent on the semivowel (phonetically realized as a *svarita* on the *a*), the semivowel must in these forms at least be syllabic at the point at which the accent-assignment rule applies. The only way it could be syllabic is by a rule making it syllabic or by starting out as syllabic in the underlying form. But there is no rule applying prior to accent assignment that makes semivowels syllabic before vowels. It follows that the cases of -*yá* with *svarita* must be derived from underlying /ia/. However, since morphemes normally have a single underlying form, all cases of gerundive -*ya*, including the root-stressed ones, go back to underlying /ia/.

A third type of reasoning that indicates underlying /ĭ/, /ŭ/ is vowel morphophonemics. The result of combining ā with a following *y* in Sanskrit is normally *āy*, as is shown for example by the gerunds; compare /upa+sthā+ya/ 'having faced' → *upasthāya*. Some suffixes beginning with *y*, however, combine with preceding ā to *e*(*y*). These are exactly the ones that belong in the *i*-, *u*-class, namely, the gerundive (e.g., *upastheya* 'to be faced'), the optative (e.g., 1 sg. *stheyám*), and the comparative (e.g., *sthéyas* 'fixed'). If the underlying form of all these suffixes begins with ĭ, the above forms can be derived by the regular Sanskrit process *a+i* → *e*, which is needed all over the phonology in any case, and by a more general form of the glide-insertion rule that we have already introduced for *ia* → *iya*, *ua* → *uva*. Note that this analysis is confirmed by the frequent disyllabic scansion of the *e* in forms like *sthéyas*, which shows that the contraction process also falls within the metrical range.

This convergence of criteria isolates a class of suffixes that I have termed the *i*-, *u*-class. The remaining suffixes, negatively defined, contain suffixes in which the semivowel is a glide, alternating at most with a short vowel, in which the semivowel is never accented, and in which the morphophonemics does not require an underlying syllabic representation. It is not unreasonable to assume that such suffixes are simply entered in the lexicon in their dominant phonetic form, with underlying /y/, /v/.

4. Consequences for Rigvedic Phonology

One of the interesting things about this metrical system is that it furnishes opportunities to peek at the abstract morphological structure of Sanskrit. For example, the question "one morpheme or two" is settled by the metrical treatment in a number of specific cases that suggest the outlines of a general set of criteria for morphological analysis. These criteria appear to be somewhat stricter than those tacitly or explicitly assumed in most current work in generative phonology. It would be pointless to try to formulate them in a very precise way, given the limited nature of the data. Some illustrations will make their general tenor clear. Consider the simple example of the three case endings instr.dat.abl.dual -*bhyām*, instr.pl. -*bhis*, dat.abl.pl. -*bhyas*. Do we treat them as single morphemes, as Pāṇini and Whitney do, or do we factor out the first part, /bhi/, and analyze /bhi+ām/, /bhi+s/, /bhi+as/, as a structural grammar might do? The metrics shows that the analysis is *not* made, since both -*bhyas* and -*bhyām* work entirely like suffixes with /y/. This result seems quite reasonable, since the segmentation under consideration would leave us some rather useless morphemes without independent motivation, n a m e l y, instr.dat.abl.dual */ām/, instr.pl. */s/, dat.abl.pl. */as/.[3]

Consider from this same point of view the gerunds -*tvā́*, -*tvī́*, -*tyā́* (e.g., *hatvī́* 'having slain'), and the gerundive -*tva* (e.g., *hántua* 'to be slain'). Taking a cue from what we suspect to be their etymology, we might analyze them as containing the noun-forming suffixes -*ti* and -*tu* plus some other elements. In the case of the gerunds, both the semantics and the phonology, if taken seriously, speak against this identification. Semantically, it would be hard to tie up the -*tv*- in *hatvā́*, *hatvī́* 'having slain' with either the -*tu*- of the infinitive *hantum* '(in order) to slay' or the -*tu*- of nouns like *vástu* 'dawn' and *dhā́tu* 'substance.' And what are we to do with -*ī́* and -*ā́*? Possibly, -*ā́* might be identified with the instrumental case ending, although the relation to the other uses of that case would not be clear. But what would the -*ī́*

---

[3]This conclusion does not deny that the partial resemblance among these three endings is of linguistic relevance. Rather, it means that morphemic segmentation is not the right way to express this relationship. Jakobson's idea of iconic relationships in morphology or perhaps Pike's notion of matrices may show the way to a solution here.

be? Also, the phonological differences between unstressed zero grade in *hatvā́*, *hatvī́* and stressed full grade in *hántum*, which are regular throughout all examples of this formation, would seem to preclude any synchronic connection. The chances of relating *-tyā*, as in *ā-ga-tyā*, to the abstract-noun suffix *-ti* are equally remote. Semantically, the relationship is probably somewhat more plausible than that between *-tvī́* and *-tu*. But what is really more important is that *-tyā* is just an allomorph of *-yă̄*, which appears always and only after a short vowel. This allomorph is generated by a relatively mechanical rule that inserts *-t-* after short root vowels in several other formations as well, for instance, in the type *soma-su-t* 'soma presser.' The *-t-* is therefore entirely predictable, in classical as well as in Vedic Sanskrit. Furthermore, we have seen above that the gerund had the underlying form /ya/, with a glide, whereas *-ti* must have an underlying vowel /i/. This fact completely blocks the possibility of a synchronic relationship between *-tyā* and *-ti*. Note furthermore that all the gerunds are predictable variants of a single morphological entity. *-tyā* and *-ya* occur in the distribution just mentioned after prefixed verbs, *-tvā* and *-tvī* after simple roots, which further deprives the relationship between *-tyā* and *-ti* of any value. The conclusion to which the metrics leads is in exact harmony with these language-internal considerations.

It is instructive to consider the gerundive *-tva*, as in *hántua* 'to be slain.' This form resembles the infinitive *hántum* in stress and ablaut behavior and shares with it its future meaning. On general semantic grounds we can analyze the infinitive as /tu+m/, where *-m* is an accusative ending, denoting the goal, so that *hantum gacchati* 'he goes to slay' is analogous to *kāśī́m gacchati* 'he goes to Benares,' just as a language like Finnish would use the same case (the illative) to render both expressions. Presumably, the *-a* of the gerundive is simply the thematic vowel, which is added to make an adjective out of *-tu*. The metrical facts again harmonize with these morphological considerations and indicate that the gerundive *-tva* has the underlying form /tua/.

I have stressed that synchronic derivation is decisive for Vedic metrics, as a rule, and not etymological origin. Usually the two are the same. That *śacyā́* contains the *ī* of *śacī́* is just as true synchronically as it is historically. The

difference becomes relevant when the etymological origin of a
suffix has become synchronically opaque because of semantic
or morphological changes. Historically, for example, the
gerunds -*tvī*, -*tvā* no doubt contain a morpheme -*tu*, which
is ultimately related to the -*tu* of *dhātu* and *hántua*. And
historically -*bhyām* and -*bhyas* surely contain the *bhi* of
-*bhis*. But such analyses were no longer productive at the
stage at which the Rigveda was composed and are therefore
irrelevant to the metrics.

There is a general moral to be drawn here for the correct
linguistic interpretation of poetry. A living poetic tradition,
especially an oral one, tends to weed out archaisms to a far
greater extent than is often realized. The Rigvedic bards
could not have memorized a traditional scansion for each
word, but rather had to grasp the general principles of the
meter. What lay outside these principles, as they were
recreated by each new generation of bards, had to go sooner
or later. If there existed pre-Vedic poetry in which the
gerund -*tvī́*, say, was disyllabic, later generations of poets
could hardly have been expected to pick up this scanning,
to them an inexplicable irregularity, in a relatively rare
suffix and to continue to treat it as disyllabic in their own
compositions just for the sake of conforming to blind tradition. Rather, each bard would have followed tradition in so
far as doing so came naturally to him in terms of his own
linguistic system. On the other hand, some forms may be
retained as conventionalized archaisms in spite of being
synchronically dead, either because of their great earlier
frequency (e.g., *thou* in 19th century English poetry; disyllabic
-*aam* for -*ām* in the genitive plural may be a Sanskrit example) or by virtue of being petrified in stock formulae. As a
result, it may well happen that the meter of a poem reflects
a historical process in some cases (the synchronically
opaque ones) but not in others (the synchronically transparent
ones).

As an example of the sort of morphological analysis that
does find support in the metrics, consider the so-called *devī*-
declension. It has the following paradigm:

	Sg.	*Dual*	*Pl.*
Nom.	devī́	devī́	devī́s
Acc.	devī́m	devī́	devī́s

	Sg.		*Dual*	*Pl.*
Instr.	devyá̄			devī́bhis
Dat.	devyaí		devíbhyām	devíbhyas
Abl.	devyás			devíbhyas
Gen.	devyás			devīnā́m
Loc.	devyā́m		devyós	devíṣu

This declension has five case forms that begin with a vowel.
They fall into two groups:

(1) Instr. sg. *devyá̄* and gen.loc.dual *devyós*. The semivowel is regularly syllabic after a heavy syllable and optionally syllabic after a light syllable.

(2) Dat. *devyái*, abl.gen. *devyás*, loc. *devyā́m*. The semivowel is optionally syllabic after a heavy syllable and never
syllabic after a light syllable.

It is the systematic contrast between (1) and (2) that is
puzzling. It looks as though the thematic suffix is an *i-*,
u-suffix in (1) and a *y-*, *v*-suffix in (2).

Compare the relevant forms of the *devī̄*-declension with
the consonant stems and the *ā̄*-stems:

Instr.sg.	devyá̄	padá̄	sénā (later sénayā)
Gen.loc.dual	devyós	padós	sénayos
Dat.sg.	devyaí	padé	sénāyai
Abl.gen.sg.	devyás	padás	sénayās
Loc.sg.	devyā́m	padí	sénāyām

The endings *-ā̄*, *-os*, *-e*, *-ās*, *-i* are transparent in the consonant stems. Obviously, they are not unrelated to the corresponding *ā̄*- and *ī̄*- stem endings. Especially since in most
other case forms the three declensions have the same inflectional endings, it is likely that the relationship here is also
analyzed out synchronically. The analysis would run as
follows:

In the instr.sg. and the gen.loc.dual, *padá̄* and *padós* are
paralleled by *devī̄+á̄* → *devyá̄* and *devī̄+ós* → *devyós*. In the
corresponding *ā̄*-stem forms we have /priyā̄+ā̄/ → *priyā̄* by
vowel contraction; the later form *priyayā̄* arises through the
generalization to *ā̄*-stems of a process *ā̄* → *ay*/___ V from the

declension of pronouns (e.g., fem. *tā+ā → tayā* 'that'). This rule also accounts for gen.loc.dual /priyā+os/ → *priyayos*.

In the genitive and dative singular we can likewise recognize the consonant-stem endings in the vowel stem. We can assume that an infix *-yā-* appears between stem and ending in these forms. We derive, by the usual rules of Sanskrit,[4]

> priyā+yā+as → priyāyās
> priyā+yā+e → priyāyai

In the locative, the ending is suppletive *-am*, but we can suppose that the same infix is present here too.

> priyā+yā+am → priyāyām

The endings of the *ī*-stems can also be stated in fullest generality if we assume the presence of the same infix in the same three case forms. Provided that there is a rule deleting the theme vowel *-ī-* before the infix, the *-ī-* and *-ā-*-stems are quite parallel, as the following derivations indicate.

> devī+yā+as → devyās
> devī+yā+e → devyai
> devī+yā+am → devyām

These are intended to be synchronic derivations. They are perfectly compatible with a number of historical hypotheses about the origin of infixed *-yā-*, including the common one that the infix originally constituted an ablaut form of *-ī-*, but was generalized to ā-stems within the prehistory of Indic. In fact, this very process of generalization presupposes that *-yā-* had ceased to be understood as an ablaut form of *-ī-* and requires that *-yā-* was an independent morphological element that could be introduced into contexts where it did not alternate with *-ī-*. In this sense, the widely held historical proposal about the origin of these forms supports the reality of the proposed analysis of the synchronic system.

Now note that according to this proposal the *y* in *devyā̇*, *devyós*, where there is no infix, represents the stem-forming affix /ī/, whereas the *y* in *devyā́s, devyaí, devyā́m*, where

---

[4]Ultimately, *e* is presumably /ai/, and *ai* is /āi/. I have disregarded this analysis for the sake of simplicity, since it does not affect the argument in any way.

there is the infix -*yā*-, represents the /y/ of that infix. But that is exactly what is required under my proposal to explain the systematic metrical difference between these two groups of case forms. Of all the arguments that can be adduced for the theory of Rigvedic meter presented in this essay, none is more striking in the way in which it explains an apparently wholly arbitrary yet consistent difference in metrical treatment between ostensibly parallel types of words.

5. Four Constraints on the Use of Language in Poetry

I will conclude this essay by turning briefly to a different question raised by such metrical systems as those of the Rigveda and the Kalevala. What are the general conditions under which nonphonetic representations may be metrically relevant? The diagram I gave on p. 185 represents only a framework for thinking about this question, not an answer to it. Any answers will have to be very conjectural at this point, because so few metrical systems have been studied from a morphophonemic point of view. But it cannot hurt to speculate, especially since progress in either line of research—the investigation of phonological structure in the light of metrics and the investigation of the general relation between metrics and phonology—immediately carries over into the other.

I will mention four general properties of the filtering system diagrammed in section 3. They appear to hold in all the cases investigated so far and are worth holding in mind as candidates for universal constraints on the use of language in poetry.

(1) *Connectedness*. In the diagram, the arrows go into the metrical filter from a connected sequence of points in the derivation. It is easy to imagine a case, however, in which the metrically relevant stages in the derivation would have to be interspersed with metrically irrelevant stages. But such systems have not yet been discovered. We can make the following conjecture: *A metrical range cannot be discontinuous.* This conjecture could also be tested by its consequences for the historical development of metrical systems. Suppose that a rule is reordered in linguistic change in such a way that the metrical range becomes discontinuous. This reordering might happen either by a metrically relevant rule moving down into

a body of rules that can be metrically disregarded or by a metrically disregarded rule moving up into the metrically relevant ones. Our connectedness hypothesis would predict that the metrical status of the rule that has been moved should change in accordance with its new place in the ordering, so that a connected range will result. What might be a real case like this is mentioned in Kiparsky (1968b:178–179).

(2) *Disjunctivity*. The Rigvedic, Latvian, and Icelandic systems require that *any one* of the representations in the metrical range pass the metrical filter in order for the line to be acceptable verse. The Kalevala gives no indication on this point because the range there consists of just one stage in the derivation. A logically possible alternative would be that *all* the representations in the metrical range pass the metrical filter. In this manner, a line is rejected unless it is metrical at every point in the metrically relevant part of its derivation. But this "conjunctive" form of scanning has not been discovered so far. Its absence leads to the "disjunctivity hypothesis": *Scanning over a metrical range must be disjunctive*. The existence of such a constraint would be readily understandable if morphophonemically based metrics originated in the way suggested in Kiparsky (1968b:176–179). Furthermore, disjunctivity may be a basic property of any metrical or linguistic constraint that involves analyzability.

(3) *Units of scansion*. In what sorts of units does the filter process a line? There are several possibilities to consider. The strongest constraint on the system would be obtained if the processing was line-by-line. In that case the same level in the phonological derivation would be required for every word in that line. That is, a certain metrical option could not be exercised differently for two words in the same line. A weaker version would be word-by-word processing, so that a given level would have to be consistently maintained within the word, whereas different words could be scanned at different levels in the derivation. The weakest form of filtering would be obtained if each segment were scanned separately over its derivation, so that even the different segments in a word could represent different stages in the derivation. In that case, the metrical representation of a word might very well be a form that appears nowhere in the derivation, but that is put together, like a mad scientist's monster, from the *disjecta membra* of its derivational history.

At this writing I do not have any clear counterexamples even to the first, and strongest, version of the filtering procedure. It may be the case that lines are metrical units in the quite new sense of having to be scanned at a single level. To illustrate the sort of argument that could be brought in to settle the question I will discuss one aspect of the interaction of Sievers' Law with another rule, that of vowel contraction.

It is easy to show that vowel contraction is within the metrical range. Such forms as *pắnti* 'they protect,' contracted from underlying *pā+anti*, are scanned both according to the underlying and the contracted form. This occurs even when the uncontracted underlying form never existed as a phonetic form, but is the result of reanalysis within the history of Sanskrit. For example, the accusative of *gaúḥ* 'cow' is *gắm*. This form is optionally scanned as disyllabic, reflecting its underlying representation, which must be *gāv+am* or the like. However, the form *gắm* historically reflects a form that was already monosyllabic in proto-Indo-European, thousands of years before the Rigveda was composed (IE *$g^w\bar{o}m$*, cf. Av. *gąm*, Gk. *bõn*). Its disyllabic status in the underlying form of Sanskrit reflects the reanalysis of the accusative singular endings in that language from original /m/ to /am/.

The contraction rule, producing as it does long vowels, creates an environment in which Sievers' Law can apply. A situation in which Sievers' Law can operate after a heavy syllable produced by contraction arises in compounds of the type /jīra#aśva/ 'having quick steeds.' The relevant portion of the phonological derivation works as follows:

input	jīra#aśva
vowel contraction	jīrāśva
Sievers' Law	jīrāśua

Since we know that the metrical range extends from a point preceding the application of vowel contraction (because of the disyllabic scansion of contracted vowels, as in *pānti*) to a point after the operation of Sievers' Law (because of the syllabic scansion of underlying glides after heavy syllables, as in *prajắbhyas*), the word-by-word filtering process would give three metrically acceptable forms for words of this type.

In fact, for the compounds with *aśva* the figures work out as follows:

-a-aśva	5 occurrences
-āśva	5 occurrences
-āśua	23 occurrences

However, the segment-by-segment filtering process allows for a fourth kind of form, in which Sievers' Law has operated, but the contraction rule, which enables Sievers' Law to apply, has not operated. Such monster forms, for instance, **jīra-aśua*, are in fact not metrically attested. This gap is predicted by the word-by-word filtering process and a fortiori by the line-by-line filtering process, but not by the segment-by-segment filtering process. This conclusion is at least somewhat encouraging for one of the two stronger filtering processes.[5]

(4) *Phonological properties of the metrical range.* It is striking that the rules whose application can be systematically disregarded in Rigvedic metrics are all purely phonologically conditioned rules. Morphologically conditioned rules, such as ablaut, are always metrically relevant, that is, they precede the metrical range. For example, *bhāga* 'gift' would always be scanned as having a long first syllable, even though it is derived from the root *bhaj*, with short *a*, by a lengthening rule. The lengthening is morphological in the sense that it is contingent on a certain class of suffixes and not on a phonologically characterizable environment and, hence, cannot be disregarded metrically. A similar observation can be made about the Ingermanland Kalevala. All the rules in this system that are not counted for purposes of the meter are processes that are phonologically conditioned. The reverse is not true, however, since there are phonologically conditioned rules that do get counted for meter. The following hypothesis might therefore be considered: *Only purely phonetically conditioned rules can be disregarded in scansion.*

An interesting prediction follows from this hypothesis: the morphologization, through some process of linguistic change, of a rule that can be metrically disregarded should lead to a metrical change in which the rule becomes metri-

---

[5]This argument is somewhat weakened by the fact that the missing fourth form is also awkward metrically, which in a pinch could also explain its absence.

cally relevant. The morphologization here causes the filter to violate the constraint that we are contemplating. As a consequence, the metrical system has to be readjusted in order to accommodate the new linguistic system.

I think it is possible that Sievers' Law is a real example of the type I have just pictured. In classical Sanskrit, Sievers' Law became morphologized. It ceased to apply generally, so that according to the rules of classical Sanskrit /ūti+ā/, for example, would be pronounced [ūtyā], in spite of the long vowel in the first syllable, and even such forms as [śvaśrvā], from underlying /śvaśrū+ā/, were possible. The rule was retained in partial operation for a certain class of suffixes, such as the present tense marker -*nu*- and the denominal adjective suffix -*iya*-/-*ya*-. In the former case, furthermore, the rule applied only when the heavy cluster was formed by two consonants rather than by a long vowel.

Also, in classical Sanskrit poetry the possibility of scanning phonetic glides as syllabic and phonetic vowels as nonsyllabic, on the basis of their morphophonemic derivation, disappeared completely, and a phonetic basis for the meter was established. Phonological changes, such as changes in underlying forms, cannot account for this development. Although certain forms may have been reanalyzed in classical Sanskrit, it still appears necessary to distinguish between underlying syllabic and nonsyllabic semivowels and to have various rules that change syllabicity under specific conditions.

Given the hypothesis that morphologized rules must be counted in the meter, however, the metrical change follows as a necessary consequence from the phonological change. Such connections between phonological and metrical structure, if established, will create new ways of investigating the history of metrical systems. In addition, they may make it possible to investigate the phonomenon of rule morphologization, one of the most baffling processes in historical linguistics, through its manifestation in metrical systems.

REFERENCES

Anderson, S. R. (1969). "West Scandinavian Vowel Systems and the Ordering of Phonological Rules." Ph.D. Dissertation, Massachusetts Institute of Technology.

Applegate, J. (1961). "Phonological Rules in a Subdialect of English." *Word* 17:186–193.

Arnold, E. V. (1905). *Vedic Metre*. Cambridge: University Press.

Chomsky, N., and M. Halle (1968). *The Sound Pattern of English*. New York: Harper and Row.

Edgerton, F. (1934). "Sievers' Law and IE Weak-Grade Vocalism." *Language* 10:235–265.

—— (1943), "The Indo-European Semivowels." *Language* 19:83–124.

Halle, M. (1962). "Phonology in Generative Grammar," *Word* 18:54–72.

Hyman, L. (1970a). "How Concrete is Phonology?" *Language* 46:58–76.

—— (1970b). "The Role of Borrowing in the Justification of Phonological Grammars." *Studies in African Linguistics* 1:1–48.

Jakobson, R. (1942). *Aphasie, Kindersprache, und allgemeine Lautgesetze*. Reprinted in *Selected Writings*, vol. I. The Hague: Mouton.

—— (1963). "On the so-called Vowel Alliteration in Germanic Verse." *Zeitschrift für Phonetik, Sprachwissenschaft und Kommunikationsforschung* 16:85–92.

Kiparsky, P. (1968a). "Linguistic Universals and Linguistic Change." In *Universals in Linguistic Theory*, edited by E. Bach and R. Harms. New York: Holt, Rinehart, and Winston.

—— (1968b). "Metrics and Morphophonemics in the Kalevala." In *Studies Presented to Roman Jakobson by His Students*, edited by C. Gribble. Page references are to the reprint in *Linguistics and Literary Style* (1970), edited by D. C. Freeman. New York: Holt, Rinehart, and Winston.

—— (forthcoming). "Sievers' Law."

Postal, P. (1968). *Aspects of Phonological Theory*. New York: Harper and Row.

Sadeniemi, M. (1951). Die Metrik des Kalevala-Verses. *Folklore Fellows Communications*, no. 139.

Sapir, E. (1933). "The Psychological Reality of Phonemes." Reprinted in *Selected Writings of Edward Sapir*, edited by D. G. Mandelbaum. Berkeley: University of California Press.

Savin, H. B., and T. G. Bever (1970). "The Nonperceptual Reality of the Phoneme." *Journal of Verbal Learning and Verbal Behavior* 9:295–302.

Sievers, E. (1878). "Zur Akzent- und Lautlehre der germanischen Sprachen." *Beiträge zur Geschichte der deutschen Sprache und Literatur* 5:63–163.

Stampe, E. (1969). "The Acquisition of Phonetic Representations." In *Proceedings of the Fifth Chicago Linguistic Circle Conference*, edited by R. I. Binnick. Chicago: University of Chicago (Dept. of Linguistics).

Sturtevant, E. (1924). "The Doctrine of the Caesura, a Philological Ghost." *American Journal of Philology* 45:329–350.

Voorhoeve, J. (1959). "An Orthography for Saramaccan." *Word* 15:436–445.

—— (1961). "Le ton et la grammaire dans le Saramaccan." *Word* 17:140–163.

Weigl, E. and M. Bierwisch (1970). "Neurophysiology and Linguistics: Topics of Common Research." *Foundations of Language* 6:1–18.

Zeps, V. (1963). "The Meter of the so-called Trochaic Latvian Folksongs." *International Journal of Slavic Linguistics and Poetics* 7:123–128.

Zimmer, K. (1969). "Psychological Correlates of Some Turkish Morpheme Structure Conditions." *Language* 45:309–321.

On Derivative Properties
of Phonological Rules

CHARLES W. KISSEBERTH
University of Illinois

I

The nature of the information that must be included in the statement of phonological rules is not something that is given by any a priori considerations, but must be determined on empirical grounds. If certain information can be shown to make some false claim about the language being described, including such information must somehow be avoided. From the very inception of generative phonology, its practitioners have consistently sought to eliminate certain kinds of information from the statement of phonological rules and have even rejected entire "rules" on the grounds that the information or rules involved were in one way or another *derivative*. To say that some piece of information is derivative means simply that it is not an isolated fact, but rather follows from some other fact. Generative phonologists have argued that to include derivative information in the rules is to miss the connection between this information and the other facts about the grammar that this information reflects. In order to avoid incorporating derivative properties of rules in the rules, generative phonologists have introduced into the theory of grammar various descriptive devices that permit these properties to be eliminated.

The preceding remarks have been highly abstract. In sections II–IV below, I will briefly discuss three examples of this effort to eliminate derivative properties in phonological rules. In my judgment, these efforts have met with only partial success; the purpose of the present paper is not, however, either to offer a critique of these attempts to deal with the problem or to try to improve upon their ability to account for the kinds of data that motivated them in the first place. Instead, I will attempt to demonstrate the existence of a class of rules whose environments, given present generative theory, would require information that is clearly derivative. To my knowledge, this class of rules has not been explicitly discussed within generative phonology, and none of the descriptive devices sketched in II–IV appear relevant to these cases. I am thus led to propose a new descriptive device—output conditions on phonological rules. This device will, it is hoped, exclude the redundant information from the rules under consideration as well as from similar rules. Because of the lack of sufficient data at the present time, certain general questions concerning the nature and role of output conditions are raised but necessarily left unanswered.

II

Rule ordering provides perhaps the best example of how information can be excluded from rules by adding a particular descriptive device to phonological theory. Generative phonologists have argued that phonological rules do not apply simultaneously to convert underlying representations into phonetic representations. Instead, phonological rules must be permitted to operate upon structures created by other phonological rules—that is, some rules apply before other rules. There are many questions about the notion of rule ordering that require extended investigation,[1] but the argument that some rules must operate upon structures resulting from the application of other rules seems incontrovertible. The essential argument in support of this position must show that, were the rules to apply simultaneously, one would have to repeat information about one rule as part of the statement of another rule.[2] An extremely simple example of this argument can be given, based on data from the Yawelmani dialect of Yokuts, a Californian Indian language.[3]

---

[1]See, in particular, Kenstowicz and Kisseberth (1970) and Kisseberth (to appear *c*).

[2]For fairly detailed discussion, see Postal (1968).

[3]Kuroda (1967) provides a generative treatment of Yawelmani phonology, based on data provided by Newman (1944). For some revisions of Kuroda's analysis and discussion of theoretical issues in light of Yawelmani phonology, see Kisseberth (1969a, 1969b, 1970).

There is a general rule of vowel harmony in Yawelmani that rounds (and backs) any number of high vowels preceded by a round high vowel or any number of nonhigh vowels preceded by a round nonhigh vowel. For example, the aorist suffix appears as *-hin* in *maxhin* 'procures,' *xilhin* 'tangles,' and *gophin* 'takes care of an infant,' but as *-hun* in *hudhun* 'recognizes.' On the other hand, the dubitative suffix appears as *-al* in *maxal* 'might procure,' *xilal* 'might tangle,' and *hudal* 'might recognize,' but as *-ol* in *gopol* 'might take care of an infant.' This rule might be formulated as in (1):[4]

$$(1) \quad \begin{bmatrix} V \\ \alpha\text{high} \end{bmatrix} \rightarrow \begin{bmatrix} +\text{round} \\ +\text{back} \end{bmatrix} \Big/ \begin{bmatrix} V \\ +\text{round} \\ \alpha\text{high} \end{bmatrix} \left(C_0 \begin{bmatrix} V \\ \alpha\text{high} \end{bmatrix} \right)_0 C_0 \underline{\quad}$$

There is also a rule in Yawelmani that inserts a vowel to break up triliteral clusters resulting from suffixation (morphemes never contain more than two adjacent consonants in underlying form). The epenthetic vowel is typically *i*. For example, the verb 'sing' has the shape *ʔilk-* when followed by a vowel-initial suffix (cf. *ʔilkal* 'might sing'), but the shape *ʔilik-* when followed by a consonant-initial suffix (cf. *ʔilikhin* 'sings'). Similarly, we find *paʔtal* 'might fight,' but *paʔiṭhin* 'fights.' These examples can be accounted for by assuming that the underlying shapes of the verb bases are /ʔilk/ and /paʔt/ and by assuming the existence of a rule stated informally as (2):

$$(2) \quad \emptyset \rightarrow i/C\underline{\quad}CC$$

A difficulty arises, however, when we consider a verb base with a high round vowel, such as /ʔuty/ 'fall.' This verb base appears unaltered in *ʔutyal* 'might fall,' but with an epenthetic *u* in *ʔutuyhun* 'falls.'

If rules were required to apply simultaneously to underlying representations (rather than to structures created by other phonological rules as well as to underlying representations), it would be necessary to amend (2), so that in cases

---

[4]The formulation of this rule could be simplified if the rule were to apply iteratively to its own output, but I give the formulation provided by Kuroda (1967), with the feature system postulated in Chomsky and Halle (1968). Incidentally, rules are formulated in terms of features in this paper only when required for the sake of clarity.

like *ʔutuyhun*, *u* rather than *i* is inserted. A rule roughly like (2ʹ) would be necessary:[5]

(2ʹ) $\emptyset \rightarrow \begin{cases} \text{u} / \text{uC} \underline{\quad} \text{CC} & \text{(a)} \\ \text{i} / \text{C} \underline{\quad} \text{CC} & \text{(b)} \end{cases}$

This revised version of the vowel-epenthesis rule contains part of the rule of vowel harmony—namely, it repeats the information that a high vowel occurring after *u* is pronounced as *u*, not as *i*. (2ʹ) treats the appearance of *u* rather than *i* in *ʔutuyhun* as an idiosyncratic fact about vowel epenthesis, whereas it is quite clear that it is the principle stated in (1) that is responsible for the *u*-quality of the epenthetic vowel. To put the point in another way, (2ʹ) claims that a *u* would be inserted in *ʔutuyhun* even if there was no rule of vowel harmony in Yawelmani.

Subpart (a) of (2ʹ) is a clear instance of derivative information. It simply repeats as part of the vowel-epenthesis rule a fact about Yawelmani pronunciation that is also expressed by the rule of vowel harmony. If we permit rules to apply to the output of other rules, then there is no need to state subpart (a) at all. All that would be required is that rule (1) apply to structures to which rule (2) has had an opportunity to apply. For example, (2) would apply to /ʔuty+hin/ to yield /ʔutiy+hin/, and (1) would apply to this output to give *ʔutuyhun*. By permitting this interaction of the phonological rules, there is no need to incorporate in the epenthesis rule any reference to the fact that the ultimate pronunciation of the epenthetic vowel is *u* when a high round vowel precedes.

One additional rule of Yawelmani might profitably be discussed at this point. When a long vowel is followed by two consonants, it is shortened. Thus we find such alternations as *doːsol* 'might report,' but *doshin* 'reports'; *ṣaːpal* 'might burn,' but *ṣaphin* 'burns.' The rule that accounts for these alternations can be formulated informally as in (3):

(3)   V → [-long] / ___ CC

---

[5]Rule (2ʹ) could, obviously, be "collapsed" to a certain extent; but such simplifications as are possible would not change the fact that the rule partly restates vowel harmony.

There are, however, verb bases in Yawelmani that have the underlying shape CV:CC, even though the sequence V:CC is not permitted phonetically (with one exception that need not concern us here). Such bases never appear unaltered. If a consonant-initial suffix follows, they have the shape CV:Ci/uC; if a vowel-initial suffix follows, the underlying vowel is shortened. The following examples illustrate these remarks: *ʔamlal* 'might help,' but *ʔa:milhin* 'helps'; *hoṭnol* 'might take the scent,' but *ho:ṭinhin* 'takes the scent.'

Consider how the above-cited facts would have to be accounted for if rules applied simultaneously to underlying forms. The underlying shape of *ʔa:milhin* is /ʔa:ml+hin/. If (3) were left unrevised, it would apply to this representation and shorten the underlying long vowel. Since a long vowel appears in the phonetic output, (3) must somehow be revised so that it does not apply to /ʔa:ml+hin/. This revision could be accomplished by writing the vowel-shortening rule as in (3'):

(3') $V \rightarrow$ [-long] / ___ CCV

(3') claims that vowels are shortened only if followed by two consonants, not if followed by three. This formulation guarantees that we will be able to derive *ʔa:milhin*.

It should be obvious that mentioning a V in the environment of (3') is required simply to ensure that vowel shortening not apply in the context ___ CCC. Vowel shortening does not apply in this context because another rule, epenthesis, operates on these structures. If epenthesis is permitted to apply before vowel shortening, then the failure of shortening to apply in the derivation of *ʔa:milhin* would be accounted for by the unmodified version of (3).

Appeal to rule ordering in the above example claims that the failure of vowel shortening to affect certain underlying sequences of the shape V:CC is derivative of the operation of another rule in the language. To formulate vowel shortening as in (3') is to claim that shortening would not occur in the environment ___ CCC even if this sequence was not broken up by epenthesis. The rule-ordering analysis claims, on the other hand, that vowel shortening would apply to /ʔa:ml+hin/ if epenthesis did not apply. The rule-ordering analysis thus regards the V in the environment of (3') as a purely derivative restriction on the operation of shortening, not as part of shortening itself but rather as part of epenthesis.

The appeal to ordered rules is clearly motivated by the need to eliminate those aspects of simultaneously applied rules which reflect information that does not seem to be part of the processes themselves, but which derive from the existence of other rules in the grammar.

III

Considerable attention has been devoted by generative phonologists to the notion of "phonological redundancy"—that is, phonological properties of the underlying form of morphemes that are predictable from other (phonological and grammatical) properties. The introduction of markedness into generative phonological theory has altered the picture somewhat, but I shall limit myself in this section to the premarkedness treatment of phonological redundancy.

Dictionary representations of morphemes in the premarkedness framework were viewed as containing plus or minus specifications for those features of pronunciation which were not predictable in terms of general constraints on the structure of morphemes. The predictable feature values were left blank, to be filled in by morpheme structure rules expressing the constraints on the phonological shape of morphemes that were operative in the language. The morpheme structure rules were distinguished from regular phonological rules by the fact that they did not apply to structures with morpheme boundaries internal to them, but just to structures between morpheme boundaries. The morpheme structure rules expressed regularities about the structure of morphemes, not about the combination of morphemes into words and phrases.

Involved in this distinction between morpheme structure rules and phonological rules proper is the assumption that the underlying representations of morphemes are constrained in ways that phonetic representations of words and phrases are not and that phonetically possible segments and sequences might not be possible in underlying forms. This basic assumption is true to a certain extent. Nevertheless, it was also recognized that the rules converting morphophonemic sequences into phonetic representations echo the constraints on the shapes of individual morphemes. For example, languages in which the members of an obstruent cluster assimilate in voicing to the final obstruent in the cluster usually contain no underlying representations of morphemes with obstruent clusters having dissimilar voicing. Similarly, many languages that contain a morphophonemic process whereby a morpheme-final nasal assimilates the point of articulation of a following obstruent also have no underlying representations of morphemes containing nonhomorganic nasal-obstruent clusters.

Generative phonologists adopted the position that to state a separate morpheme structure rule as well as a phonological rule specifying the same constraint fails to capture the fact that a single constraint is at work in such cases; such an analysis treats the phonological rule as something not only distinct from the morpheme structure rule but indeed unrelated to it.[6] Since it is quite obvious that there is a connection between some morpheme structure rules and some phonological rules, generative phonologists looked for an analysis from which this connection received a *formal* representation. The analysis that was proposed runs roughly as follows: instead of specifying *all* phonological redundancies by means of morpheme structure rules ordered before the phonological rules, some redundant information could be specified by the phonological rules themselves. This approach requires that phonological rules operate on representations that are not fully specified for all features. For example, in a language of the sort mentioned above, which requires that obstruent clusters have the same voicing as the underlying voicing of the final member of the cluster, all nonfinal members of obstruent clusters within a morpheme would be unspecified for voicing in the lexicon. These obstruents would not acquire a specification for voicing until the phonological rule of voicing assimilation applies, specifying simultaneously the voicing of nonfinal members of obstruent clusters within morphemes as well as changing the

---

[6]Underlying this position is the assumption that, in order for phonological constraints to be the *same* constraint, they must be reduced to a single statement in the grammar. For an argument that some instances of rule sameness cannot be reduced to a single formal statement, see Kisseberth (1970).

voicing of a morpheme-final obstruent to agree with the voicing of a following obstruent. A single phonological rule, according to the above approach, would perform the function of the morpheme structure rule at the same time that it performed its function as a phonological rule. The morpheme structure rule was reduced to being just one aspect of the phonological rule.

The above discussion dealt with a constraint on *sequences* within a morpheme, but there are also cases where a constraint on segments (regardless of context) in underlying representations reappears as a constraint on pronunciation of segments resulting from morphophonemic processes.

Recall the rule of vowel harmony in Yawelmani that was discussed briefly in section II—rule (1). In the formulation that I gave to this rule, I mentioned that the harmonizing vowel became both round and back. Both of these specifications appear to be required, since we must shift *i* to *u*, not to *ü*. Explicit mention of the feature [back] is dubious, however, when we consider that in Yawelmani phonological representations all round vowels are back. Vowel harmony clearly involves the assimilation of rounding. The shift of *i*, when it is rounded, to *u* seems to be a simple reflection of the more general constraint that round vowels are always back in Yawelmani. As stated in (1), the shift of *i* to a back vowel appears to be of the same status as the shift of *i* to a round vowel; both shifts appear to be idiosyncratic properties of vowel harmony. In fact, however, the rounding of *i* is the only change specific to the harmony process; the backing of the resulting round vowel is an instance of a general constraint.

Mention of the feature [back] in (1) thus constitutes an example where derivative information has been included in the statement of a rule, and generative phonologists (quite properly) sought some means of omitting such feature changes from rules. The solution suggested was, once again, to permit some underlying representations to enter the phonological rules only partially specified. In the Yawelmani example, round vowels would be unspecified in the lexicon for backness. No morpheme structure rule would apply to alter this situation. Instead, there would be a rule included in the phonology of Yawelmani, ordered after (1), that made all round vowels back. This rule would not only assign the feature [+back] to all underlying round vowels but also to all round vowels resulting from vowel harmony. Given this analysis, *i* would become *ü* by (1)—where now the only feature in the structural change would be [+round]—and then *u* by the rule backing all round vowels.

IV

In this section I turn to my last example of the attempted elimination of derivative information from phonological rules. Chomsky and Halle noted in *The Sound Pattern of English* (hereafter cited as SPE) that in many instances the morpheme structure rules of languages are largely identical.[7] For example, in most languages vowels are redundantly voiced, nonnasal, and nonpharyngealized in underlying forms. Similarly, in many languages obstruents are redundantly non-glottalized, nonlow, and nonretroflexed. Within the framework sketched in section III, there was no distinction made between "normal" phonological redundancies and "nonnormal" (e.g., labial obstruents are redundantly continuants) or impossible (e.g., all vowels are voiceless) phonological redundancies. One redundancy was on a par with any other redundancy.

The notion of markedness was introduced by Chomsky and Halle into generative phonology, partly in order to correct this deficiency in the theory. They observed that the set of normal redundant feature values was simply a subset of the set of normal feature values; that is, if we accept the notion that some feature values are *unmarked* (normal) and others *marked*, then those redundancy rules which are most common are ones that specify unmarked feature values. For example, if obstruents are voiceless in the unmarked case, the normal redundancy rule would be one that specifies that obstruents are redundantly voiceless; the unexpected case would be a language where all obstruents are redundantly voiced.

Chomsky and Halle propose that a set of universal marking conventions apply to dictionary representations that indicate only whether a given segment has the marked or unmarked

---

[7]The examples cited all involve *segmental* redundancies. But much the same point can be made about sequential redundancies. For example, in Yawelmani, morphemes do not contain three-consonant clusters nor do they contain vowel clusters: these are rather common constraints, found in many other languages—but not, of course, exceptionless.

value for a particular feature; the marking conventions "translate" these dictionary representations into representations of plus and minus feature values. In essence, a segment is automatically assigned unmarked feature values unless there is an instruction to the contrary in the lexical representation; only the specifications indicating a marked feature value increases the complexity of the grammar (i.e., marked values are viewed as deviations from the optimal situation).

From the above summary, it is clear that Chomsky and Halle's approach makes the distinction between unmarked and marked values central, rather than the distinction between redundant and nonredundant feature values. But since all normal redundancies constitute unmarked values, a good deal of overlap is involved. Chomsky and Halle suggest in SPE that only nonnormal redundancies need to be incorporated into the grammars of particular languages; normal redundancies can be dispensed with entirely in favor of universal marking conventions. This omission creates certain problems. (For example, if a language has only voiceless obstruents in underlying representation, there will be no *rule* in the grammar of that language stating this restriction; instead, the lexicon will contain no obstruents marked for voicing. Consequently, the notion "possible underlying representation" cannot be reconstructed from the rules of the grammar.)

The notion of markedness was not limited, however, to the problem of the dictionary representation of morphemes. Chomsky and Halle observed that certain aspects of phonological rules might be interpreted as instances of the same marking principles that operated to specify unmarked feature values in dictionary representations. In essence, they claimed that certain features in the structural change of phonological rules follow from the universal marking principles and are thus derivative of these principles.

One example can be discussed here: palatalization of velars before i. Typically, k shifts to $č$ rather than to the palatal stop k^y, even though in the feature system proposed in SPE the shift of k to k^y requires fewer changes than the shift of k to $č$. The normalcy of the $k/č$ alternation seems to be connected to the fact that, for palatal noncontinuants, affricates are unmarked and stops are marked—that is, $č$ is the typical underlying phoneme rather than k^y. Chomsky and Halle propose a system whereby certain unmarked feature values can be omitted from the structural change of a phonological rule; the universal marking conventions will not only operate to specify unmarked values in the lexicon but will also add feature values to the output of phonological rules. In this way, feature changes that follow from the marking conventions do not need to be stated in the rules themselves.

I will not attempt to discuss the system that Chomsky and Halle propose to accomplish the "linking" of the marking conventions to the phonological rules; the crucial point is that the system they construct is aimed at eliminating from the structural change of a phonological rule any feature that seems to be derivative of the marking principles.

V

The adequacy of the above-cited attempts to deal with derivative properties of phonological rules is by no means complete. I will not be concerned here with the question of how successful these attempts have been in getting rid of derivative information; instead, I will attempt to show that there exists at least one set of cases of derivative information that falls beyond the scope of any device in the present theory of generative phonology.

In section III I considered examples of constraints on the underlying structure of morphemes that seemed to be identical to constraints on the shape of morpheme sequences. In each of the examples cited, it was noted that a feature value assigned by a morpheme structure rule was echoed by a feature value assigned by a phonological rule. There is, however, another important way in which constraints on the shapes of morphemes interact with phonological rules; this interaction does not involve the assignment of features and thus cannot be dealt with by the method sketched in section III.

The sort of interaction I have in mind is the failure of a phonological rule to apply in contexts where its application would yield a structure not permitted by the constraints on the underlying forms of the language. Consider the following example from Tonkawa, an American Indian language formerly spoken in Texas.[8] Underlying representations of morphemes in Tonkawa contain at most two consonants in succession. In this language there is a morphophonemic process that I will refer to as "vowel elision." The environment of this rule is fairly complex, and for the purposes of this paper I will limit myself to one of the contexts in which the rule applies—namely, when a CV prefix precedes a (basically) polysyllabic stem. In numerous forms of this shape, the first vowel of the stem is deleted if short, and shortened if long. For example, the stem /netale/ 'lick' appears without its first vowel in *kentalo?* 'he licks me' (cf. *netlo?*, where the first vowel appears in the surface form). Similarly, the stem /yalapa/ 'stick in the ground' appears without its first vowel in *weilapo?* 'he sticks them in the ground' (cf. *yalpo?* 'he sticks it in the ground'; the shift of *y* to *i* in *weilapo?* is due to a general vocalization rule). When a stem has a long first vowel, however, we find vowel shortening rather than vowel deletion. Thus /ka:na/ 'throw' has a short vowel in *xakano?* 'he throws it to a distance' (cf. *ka:no?* 'he throws it'). Similarly, /pa:ca/ 'pile in a heap' has a short vowel in *wepaco?* 'he piles them in a heap' (cf. *pa:can* 'things piled in a heap').

Even though it is not clear how the unity of short-vowel deletion and long-vowel shortening in the above examples is to be best characterized, it is obvious that a single process is involved.[9] If we assume that a theory can be developed that permits both changes (deletion and shortening) to be specified by a single rule, we must take note of certain differences in the environments in which deletion and shortening operate. Short vowels fail to elide if a consonant cluster follows, whereas long vowels will shorten in this context. Thus, /xaclewa/ 'become angry' appears with its first vowel retained in *kexaclewo?* 'I am angry.' Similarly, /salke/ 'pull

---

[8]For a full discussion, see Kisseberth (to appear *a*). Hoijer (1933, 1949) provides the data upon which this discussion is based.

[9]The usual way in which linguists have attempted to capture the identity between short-vowel deletion and long-vowel shortening in the same context is by representing long vowels as a sequence of two identical short vowels. This sort of representation is suspect in Tonkawa, for in general long vowels do not share any properties with short-vowel sequences. For detailed discussion of the general problem of the representation of long vowels, see Kenstowicz (1970) and Pyle (1970).

sinew from meat' retains its first vowel in *wesalko?* 'he pulls sinews from meat.' In contrast, however, /ċa:pxe/ 'put up a bed' shortens its first vowel in *wecapxo?* 'he puts up several beds' (cf. *ċa:pxo?* 'he puts up a bed'). Also, /se:xca/ 'be full, satiated' has a short vowel in *kesecxo?* 'I am satiated' (cf. *se:cxo?* 'he is satiated').

The question that arises is whether the rule of vowel elision should be constructed so that it specifically excludes deletion of a short vowel in the context C___CC, while permitting long vowels to shorten in this environment. (It should be pointed out that every stem must begin with a single consonant; thus the short stem vowels in the above examples that fail to delete when followed by a consonant cluster are always preceded by a consonant.) To formulate the constraint as part of vowel elision claims that the difference in behavior between short and long vowels in the forms cited is an idiosyncratic property of vowel elision, unconnected with any other fact about the language. If we recall that Tonkawa morphemes are not permitted to contain triliteral clusters (a constraint that is maintained throughout the grammar; no triliteral clusters appear phonetically), then the failure of short vowels to elide in the context C___CC, even though long vowels do shorten, makes sense. Shortening a long vowel does not yield a string that violates the constraint on underlying morpheme shapes; deleting a short vowel would.

In parallel fashion, it can be shown that Tonkawa does not permit a glottalized consonant to precede a consonant in the underlying forms of morphemes—and vowel elision does not delete a short vowel in the context Ċ___C, although long vowels do shorten in these contexts. For example, /sako/ 'scrape' retains its first vowel in *wesako?* 'he scrapes them'; also, /xene/ 'sweep' retains its first vowel in *wexeno?* 'he sweeps them.' On the other hand, /ċo:ma/ 'close one's eyes' shortens its vowel in *keċomo?* 'I close my eyes' (cf. *ċo:mo?* 'he closes his eyes'). Similarly, /xe:pa/ 'pull out' has a short vowel in *kexepo?* 'he pulls me out' (cf. *xe:po?* 'he pulls it out'). Again, the question to be asked is whether the failure of short vowels to elide in the environment Ċ___C, while long vowels shorten, is an idiosyncratic fact about vowel elision. Obviously it is not, but simply reflects the fact that morphemes may not contain ĊC clusters in their underlying form. (This constraint, like the triliteral constraint,

is maintained throughout the grammar.) To incorporate the
limitation on deletion into the vowel-elision rule not only
obscures the identity of the deletion and shortening operations, but also repeats the morpheme structure constraint
as part of the environment for vowel elision.

It is such repetition that I have been referring to throughout this paper as derivative information. If this derivative
information is to be removed from the statement of phonological rules, then we must be able to state vowel elision in
Tonkawa without reference to whether two consonants follow
the first stem vowel or whether a glottalized consonant precedes that vowel. None of the methods of eliminating derivative information outlined in sections II–IV are of help here:
rule ordering is obviously irrelevant, and both the device
of using phonological rules to express redundancies as well
as feature changes and the device of permitting marking
conventions to link with phonological rules perform a function
of *assigning* feature specifications—whereas what is required
in the Tonkawa case is *blockage* of vowel elision in certain
environments. In Tonkawa, morpheme structure constraints
define contexts in which the rule of vowel elision fails to
apply, even though the general conditions for vowel elision are
satisfied. If the Tonkawa example is not atypical, then we
have evidence that we need some new theoretical machinery
that will make it possible to eliminate restrictions on the
application of phonological rules from the rules themselves,
if these restrictions mirror constraints on underlying representations.

VI

It can easily be shown that the Tonkawa example is not
atypical. Vowel-elision processes, in particular, appear to be
restricted in many cases by the same constraints that limit
consonant clustering in underlying forms. Kisseberth (1970)
discusses an example of this sort from the Yawelmani
dialect of Yokuts. Other examples exist, having to do with
processes less common than vowel elision.

For example, from Dyen's description of Trukese (Dyen,
1965) we learn that phonetically all consonants appear doubled
(i.e., long) except the semivowels *y* and *w*. Furthermore,
Dyen cites data illustrating the necessity for postulating
doubled consonants in the underlying representations of mor-

phemes—but no morphophonemic doubled semivowels seem to be necessary. We conclude then that a morpheme structure constraint bars doubled semivowels from underlying representations in Trukese. With this knowledge, we can now consider the formation of durative verbs in Trukese, which involves reduplication. Dyen writes that "reduplication is limited to bases which begin with a consonant other than a semi-vowel. It consists of a repetition of the initial consonant and first vowel of a base after which a single initial base consonant is doubled: *mööt* 'sit,' *mömmööt* 'be sitting'; *kkeciw* 'weep,' *kekkeciw* 'be weeping.'" (p. 45) The quotation indicates that this reduplication process does not apply to a semivowel-initial base. If a base begins with *y* or *w*, then a double *k* is infixed, preceded by a vowel that is a copy of the first vowel of the base. Thus, *wïn* 'drink' has the durative form *wïkkïn* 'be drinking,' and *yisöni* 'keep it' has the durative form *yikkisöni* 'be keeping it.'

As in the Tonkawa case, we must ask whether it is completely accidental that bases beginning with a semivowel undergo infixation rather than reduplication, or whether this limitation is connected with some other fact about Trukese grammar. If it is accidental, it is to be stated as part of reduplication. But if the exclusion of bases with an initial semivowel from reduplication follows from some other principle of Trukese grammar, the limitation is not to be treated as an idiosyncratic part of reduplication. The question we are asking is, given the complete grammar of Trukese, could it be the case that bases beginning in labials fail to undergo reduplication, rather than bases beginning in a semivowel?

Recall that reduplication in Trukese involves doubling the initial consonant of the base, if it is not already doubled. Recall also that semivowels may not occur doubled, in underlying forms or phonetically, in Trukese. A clear connection emerges: reduplication fails to affect bases if, by applying reduplication, the constraint against doubled semivowels would be violated. The failure of reduplication to affect bases with an initial *y* or *w* is not totally idiosyncratic; it is connected with a general constraint operative in the language.

It would, of course, be simple to state a reduplication rule that would fail to apply to semivowel-initial bases. But what is required is a theory of phonology in which the exclusion of these bases is characterized as a *motivated* phenomenon, not as a purely arbitrary limitation. It should be obvious that what I have been referring to as "derivative" information in rules is essentially information that is motivated either by universal principles of language or by other rules in the grammar. Thus, Trukese seems to provide additional evidence that there is a type of derivative information that falls beyond the range of the devices sketched in sections II–IV.

VII

Before looking at some additional examples of a similar sort, we might consider how the Tonkawa and Trukese cases could be dealt with. What is needed is a means by which the constraints on vowel elision in Tonkawa and on reduplication in Trukese—which were shown to echo morpheme structure constraints in these languages—can be eliminated from the statement of the rules and, in some way, be made to "follow from" the morpheme structure constraints.

In the present theory of generative phonology, a rule R_1 applies to a string S_1 if that string meets the structural description of R_1 (ignoring, for present purposes, many irrelevant details). That is, the only conditions that must be satisfied are conditions stated on the input string S_1. If the input is of the correct form, R_1 applies, and the output string S_2 is derived; S_2 is then the input to R_2, or, if there is no rule R_2 that is applicable to S_2, S_2 is the phonetic representation. In order to deal with the Tonkawa and Trukese examples, we might propose that, in addition to conditions on input strings, there also be conditions on output strings: if the string S_2 resulting from the application of R_1 to S_1 violates the stated "output condition," then R_2 would apply not to S_2 but instead to S_1 (if no rule R_2 could apply after R_1, then S_1 would be the phonetic representation). The effect of such a proposal would be to block a rule if its output violated some stated condition.

Furthermore, suppose that these conditions which output strings must satisfy are (at least in part) defined by the morpheme structure constraints of the language. That is, suppose that each morpheme structure constraint of the form X → Y/W___ Z implies, by convention, a corresponding output condition on rules that would block the application of a rule producing the sequence $W \begin{bmatrix} \sim Y \\ X \end{bmatrix} Z.$[10] For example, the constraint on triliteral clusters in Tonkawa might be expressed as in (4):

(4)   [+segment] → [+syll]/*CC   (where * indicates either before or after CC)

According to the proposal being sketched, (4) would imply an output condition in Tonkawa that would block application of a rule producing a consonant cluster either preceded or followed by a segment that is nonsyllabic. Thus, given the existence of (4) in the grammar of Tonkawa and the conventions suggested above, the rule of vowel elision would not have to include information to block deletion of short vowels in the context C___CC—just the consequence that is required. Similarly, the morpheme structure constraint expressed by (5)

(5)   [-syll] → [-glottalized]/___C

will imply the existence of an output condition in Tonkawa that would block (in effect) the application of a rule producing the sequence $\begin{bmatrix} -\text{syll} \\ +\text{glottalized} \end{bmatrix} C$. This output condition would then block vowel elision from applying to a short vowel in the context Č___C; there would be no need to mention in the rule of vowel elision itself that it does not apply in that environment.

If we turn now to the Trukese example, it should be clear how the proposal under discussion would work. Trukese has a morpheme structure constraint that could be expressed as in (6):

---

[10]Certain refinements in my statement on how output conditions work are necessary. For example, a language may contain, in underlying representations, sequences across morpheme boundaries that are not permitted within morphemes. Such sequences, while they may eventually be eliminated by the phonological rules of the language, may undergo various rules *before* being eliminated. Obviously, we do not want to block such rules from applying just because the output string will contain a violation of the output condition implied by the relevant morpheme structure constraint. What we are interested in blocking are cases where a rule would create an inadmissible structure.

(6) $\begin{bmatrix} -\text{syll} \\ -\text{cons} \end{bmatrix} \rightarrow [-\text{long}]$

This morpheme structure constraint will imply, automatically, an output condition blocking rules from deriving a
segment of the shape $\begin{bmatrix} -\text{syll} \\ -\text{cons} \\ +\text{long} \end{bmatrix}$; this output condition prohibits
reduplication from affecting bases with an initial semivowel.
There will be no need to mention in the statement of reduplication that semivowel-initial bases fail to undergo the rule.

At this point I might briefly summarize my proposal. I
have suggested that a string may fail to be affected by a given
rule if either the input conditions of the rule (= structural
description) are not satisfied or an output condition is violated
by the string that results from an application of the rule.
Input conditions are idiosyncratic to a particular rule; output
conditions are not limited to a single rule.[11]

Furthermore, I have suggested that the morpheme structure constraints of a language define automatically a set of
output conditions governing the phonological rules of that
language. This suggestion permits the Tonkawa and Trukese
examples to be dealt with in an intuitively quite satisfying
way, for the failure of vowel elision in Tonkawa and reduplication in Trukese to apply in the environments discussed
follows automatically from the relevant morpheme structure
constraints in these languages.

The above proposals are, however, extraordinarily vague,
leaving very important questions untouched. I discuss some
of these questions below; definitive answers must obviously
await extensive investigation of phenomena like that cited
from Tonkawa and Trukese. I feel justified in engaging in a
certain amount of speculation only because the phenomena
under discussion have not received any explicit discussion
from generative phonologists. (A rather strong argument
can be constructed, I believe, supporting the view that something akin to output conditions were implicit in much pre-
generative American structuralism.)

---

[11]I have referred elsewhere to output conditions by the label "derivational constraints," but now believe this usage to be somewhat confusing.

VIII

Although I discussed the Tonkawa and Trukese examples in terms of constraints on the underlying shapes of morphemes controlling the outputs of phonological rules, the limitations involved also held at the level of phonetic representation. The question naturally arises as to whether this situation is accidental. That is, could phonetic regularities that are *not* also underlying regularities block rules? Could underlying regularities that are *not* phonetic regularities define output conditions?

There is evidence that a phonetic regularity that is not true of underlying forms may define an output condition. In Yawelmani, words do not end in consonant clusters phonetically.[12] However, morphophonemic representations of words may end in a consonant cluster. For example, some verb stems of the shape CVCC- may be used as nouns; the subjective case of nouns consists of simply a stem, without a suffix. The verb stem *logw-* 'pulverize' (cf. *logwol* 'might pulverize' from /logw+al/) occurs in nominal form as *logiw* 'act of pulverizing,' derived from /logw/ by a rule of *i*-epenthesis in the environment C___C#. This latter rule ensures that no morphophonemic representations with a word-final cluster survive in phonetic representation.

Thus, in Yawelmani words may not end in a consonant cluster—but this regularity is not due to an underlying constraint but rather to a rule of epenthesis. It turns out that there is a rule in Yawelmani that must be restricted so that it does not yield word-final consonant clusters. This rule stipulates that a terminal verbal suffix of the shape CV, when added to a stem, deletes its vowel—but only if the stem is vowel-final. Thus, the imperative suffix *-ka* loses its vowel when suffixed to a vowel-final stem, as in *ʔilek̓* 'fan!' but retains its vowel after a consonant-final stem, as in *xatka* 'eat!'

Without a theory of output conditions, the rule under discussion would be formulated as (7):

(7) $V \rightarrow \emptyset\,/\ V + C\_\_\_ \#]_V$

(7), however, treats the failure of deletion to apply when a

---

[12]See Kisseberth (1970) for discussion.

consonant cluster precedes as an idiosyncratic fact about this rule, unrelated to any other fact about Yawelmani, that is, as an arbitrary, unmotivated limitation. Clearly, the restriction on deletion is simply a reflection of the general fact that word-final consonant clusters are not tolerated phonetically.

In order to make use of output conditions to characterize the restriction on deletion as a motivated (derivative) restriction, it must be possible for output conditions to be stated that do not derive from constraints on underlying forms. In the Yawelmani example, the output condition appears to derive from a *phonetic* constraint. Given a theory where phonetic regularities may also imply output conditions, we would replace (7) by (8):

$$(8) \quad V \rightarrow \emptyset \ / + C \underline{\quad} \#]_V$$

All the information in (8) is truly idiosyncratic to this rule. (8) would be blocked by an output condition from affecting the vowel of a terminal CV verbal suffix after a consonant-final stem.

The above example from Yawelmani raises an interesting problem. Within the standard theory of generative phonology, phonetic regularities are not directly stated anywhere in a grammar: they derive from the underlying regularities of the language in conjunction with the phonological rules. If there is no statement of phonetic regularities in the grammar, how can we permit phonetic regularities to imply output conditions? Recall that we could permit morpheme structure constraints to imply output conditions, since these constraints appear on independent grounds in the grammar. But if phonetic regularities are not stated in the grammar, then there is no independent principle from which the output condition derives. Consequently, we are claiming that the restrictions expressed by the output condition are not really connected with any other facts about the language.

There are different moves that might be made at this point. It might be claimed that a grammar will have to contain a set of statements about phonetic regularities as well as a set of statements about underlying regularities. (If this tack is taken, the problem of distinguishing between real regularities and accidental regularities arises at the phonetic level as well as at the phonological level. That this problem should arise naturally does not refute the position that there is a set of surface structure constraints as well as morpheme structure constraints.) Given this set of statements, we could then claim that they define a set of output conditions for the language.

Alternatively, we might attempt to circumvent the incorporation of a surface structure constraint component by claiming that the structural description of a phonological rule implies an output condition, provided that the rule is one that is "true" of phonetic representations—that is, if the rule is applied to the set of phonetic representations in the language, the rule would not alter these representations. (This condition could not, literally, be imposed; the class of phonetic representations is infinite, if we are referring to the phonetic representations of *sentences*. Since I will ultimately argue against the alternative being discussed, I will forego further discussion.)

For example, it might be claimed that i-epenthesis in Yawelmani, which inserts i in the context C___C#, implies an output condition that blocks rules from deriving strings of the shape to which i-epenthesis applies. This output condition would then correctly restrict (8) from deriving strings with word-final consonant clusters. The rule of i-epenthesis is "true" of Yawelmani phonetic representations, for—as I pointed out earlier—no words end in a consonant cluster; thus i-epenthesis, if applied to phonetic representations, would not affect them.

The position outlined above attempts to avoid granting independent status to surface structure regularities, trying to get at these regularities through the rules themselves. But a serious problem arises with this proposal. It claims that a rule defines an output condition if that rule is "true" of phonetic representation; but we cannot determine what the correct forms are without knowing whether there is an output condition restricting the operation of a given rule. Thus we need to know what the phonetic representations are before we can determine the correct phonetic representations. This paradoxical situation might be resolved by not requiring that phonological rules be true of phonetic representations in order to imply output conditions. We cannot dismiss this suggestion out of hand; but it should be obvious that such a view permits a grammar to imply a far larger number of output conditions than one where only rules that are true of phonetic representations imply output conditions.

Until evidence can be adduced in favor of permitting all rules to imply output conditions, I will assume the existence of a set of surface structure constraints that are independent of the derivation of phonetic forms, except that these constraints define a set of output conditions on the phonological rules.

With the introduction of surface structure constraints, we might claim that the Trukese and Tonkawa examples are not examples of morpheme structure constraints motivating restrictions on the application of rules after all. Recall that the relevant regularities held for surface structure as well as for underlying representations. If we claimed that *only* surface structure, and not underlying, constraints implied output conditions, we would thereby restrict the number of possible output conditions (since there are morpheme structure conditions that do not find reflection in surface regularities). Personally, I do not find it likely that such a position can be maintained, but I do not yet have a clear counterexample. Naturally, if there are no examples of morpheme structure constraints blocking the application of a phonological rule, where the morpheme structure constraint is not also true of phonetic forms, it would be preferable to maintain that the only possible output conditions are those defined by surface structure constraints.

IX

I have shown in the preceding sections how derivative information may be eliminated from various rules by permitting morpheme structure constraints or surface structure constraints to define output conditions that limit the application of phonological rules. But I have not been very explicit, up to this point, about precisely what is meant by saying that a given constraint *implies* or *defines* an output condition.

In particular, does the existence of a given constraint necessarily imply an output condition restricting the operation of phonological rules in the language? If one rule is restricted by an output condition, must all rules be?

It is quite obvious that morpheme structure constraints do not imply output conditions that always restrict the operation of phonological rules in the language. Otherwise, it would be impossible for phonological rules to produce strings violating the morpheme structure constraints. It is a well-known fact, however, that surface forms are generally less constrained than underlying forms. For example, a language may permit nasalized vowels in surface representations without permitting them in underlying forms. Also, even when a morpheme structure constraint also obtains phonetically, intermediate forms may violate the constraint. Thus, a vowel-dropping rule may derive a sequence of obstruents with dissimilar voicing in a language that did not permit such sequences in the underlying representation; the resulting cluster may then undergo a voicing-assimilation rule, thus giving a surface form that is in accordance with the morpheme structure constraint.

Similarly, it is easy to show that there are surface structure constraints that do not always restrict the application of phonological rules. It is well known that rules often "feed" other rules—that is, create outputs that are subject to other rules. For example, in Yawelmani there are no long vowels, phonetically, in the environment____C#. This phonetic gap can be accounted for by a rule that shortens vowels in that environment. As we saw earlier, there is also a rule that drops the vowel of a terminal verbal suffix, if that suffix has a CV structure. This rule applies regardless of the length of the preceding vowel. Thus, when a verb stem ending in a long vowel, such as /pana:/ 'bring' (cf. *pana:hin*, nonfuture), is followed by the imperative suffix /k̓a/, the final vowel is still dropped: /pana:+k̓a/ is converted to /pana:+k̓/. The vowel-shortening rule applies to this intermediate form to give *panak̓*. Obviously, the above derivation would not be possible if the surface structure constraint barring V:C# were to block application of the vowel-dropping rule. Numerous parallel examples could be cited.

It seems quite clear that neither underlying nor surface constraints necessarily stop rules from applying, although there are cases where they may block application. It could be the case that, if a constraint blocks one rule from creating a certain output, it necessarily blocks every rule in that grammar from creating that output. There is evidence, however, that, while one rule may create an inadmissible output, another rule may be blocked from doing so.

In Tunica, an American Indian language once spoken in

Louisiana, adjacent stressed syllables never occur phonetically in the word or in the phrase.[13] Adjacent stresses do
occur in the morphophonemic representation of words as a
result of the juxtaposition of morphological elements possessing intrinsic stress. Such adjacent stresses do not occur
phonetically, for a destressing rule applies to eliminate the
rightmost stress. There is a rule in Tunica that drops
unstressed vowels at the end of a morpheme if the next
morpheme in the word begins with a glottal stop. Unstressed
vowels are deleted in this environment even if preceded and
followed by stressed vowels. Thus, the verb *hára* 'sing'
combines with the auxiliary verb *ʔáki*, 3 fem. sg. form of
'be,' as *hár ʔaki*. (It is assumed that *ʔáki* is intrinsically
stressed and loses its stress in *hár ʔaki*, as opposed to
never having been assigned stress in the derivation of
hár ʔaki; for discussion of this point, see the paper referred
to in note 13.) The input to the rule dropping morpheme-final
unstressed vowels before a glottal stop (which I will refer to
henceforth as the syncope rule) is /hára+ʔáki/; the output
is /hár+ʔáki/. The rule mentioned earlier that destresses
the rightmost of two adjacent stressed syllables then yields
the correct phonetic shape. Clearly, this derivation is
possible only if the phonetic constraint against adjacent
stressed syllables does not block application of syncope.
There is, however, another significant fact. Syncope of
morpheme-final unstressed vowels also applies at the end
of a word when the following word begins with a glottal stop.
We find phrases like *túwak ʔúwakóni* 'the owl hooted,' where
túwak is underlyingly /túwa+ku/, -*ku* being the 3 masc. sg.
noun suffix. In this example, the word-final vowel is followed
by a stressed vowel but preceded by an unstressed vowel.
Thus, syncope yields no adjacent stresses. In addition, we
find syncope across words in the phrase *kâk ʔihpóʔuhki*
'someone has seen me,' which is underlyingly /ká+ku##
ʔihk+pó+ʔúhki/, *ʔihk*- being an intrinsically unstressed 1 sg.
pronominal prefix. In this example, the word-final unstressed
vowel is preceded by a stressed vowel but followed by an
unstressed vowel. Again, syncope across word boundary in
this environment does not yield adjacent stresses. There are

---

[13]See Kisseberth (to appear *b*) for discussion. Haas (1940, 1953)
provides the data upon which this paper is based.

also cases where a word-final unstressed vowel followed by a glottal stop-initial word is both preceded and followed by a stressed vowel—but in these cases the vowel is not syncopied (although in analogous situations *within* words syncope does take place). We find, therefore, phrases like *sáhku ʔúhkiškan* 'although there is one,' *yúru ʔámarʔɛhɛ* 'not long enough,' and so forth, where the final vowel is retained. In other words, syncope across word boundaries blocks if it would create adjacent stressed syllables (recall that in Tunica there are no adjacent stresses within the *phrase*), even though syncope within words is not so constrained.

If phonological theory does not contain output conditions, external syncope in Tunica would have to be formulated as in (9):

$$(9) \quad \begin{bmatrix} V \\ -\text{stress} \end{bmatrix} \rightarrow \emptyset \Big/ \begin{bmatrix} V \\ \alpha\,\text{stress} \end{bmatrix} C_0 \underline{\quad\quad} \#\#\,? \begin{bmatrix} V \\ \beta\,\text{stress} \end{bmatrix}$$

condition: α, β may not both be +

whereas syncope within words would be formulated as in (10):

$$(10) \quad \begin{bmatrix} V \\ -\text{stress} \end{bmatrix} \rightarrow \emptyset \Big/ \underline{\quad\quad} + ?$$

Clearly, the information that is included in (9) but not in (10) constitutes what I have been calling derivative information: it represents a motivated, not an arbitrary, restriction. To state the restriction as an idiosyncratic part of (9) is to completely miss the connection between the limitation on external syncope and the more general fact that Tunica does not permit adjacent stresses within the phrase. It is exactly this connection which the notion of an output condition on rules was designed to handle. I believe, therefore, it is correct to say that an output condition blocks external syncope from deriving adjacent stresses, and that, as a consequence, external syncope will have the same general form as internal syncope. The only difference is that internal syncope is not subject to the output condition, whereas external syncope is.

If the above argument is sound, we have evidence that output conditions are required that control the output of some, but not necessarily all, rules in the grammar. In other words, some rules are subject to the output conditions, but others are exempt. One might think that to accept this conclusion is to make the notion of output conditions vacuous,

since, if the Tunica example is valid, there are no general
principles that could determine when an output condition will
block a rule and when it will not. Careful consideration of
previous attempts to deal with derivative information leads,
I believe, to the conclusion that the proposed use of output
conditions is no more vacuous than any of the other attempts
to eliminate derivative information.

Chomsky and Halle proposed that marking principles
supply automatically some feature changes to phonological
rules—but they permit these changes to be blocked, if necessary. That is, the output of phonological rules is not always
in conformity with what the marking principles predict.
Given presently available evidence, there seems to be no
general way to predict when a phonological rule will yield
the expected output. This situation does not make Chomsky
and Halle's proposals thereby vacuous. Their proposals do
make a distinction between expected feature changes (i.e.,
those predicted by the marking principles) and unexpected
ones. This distinction must receive an explicit characteriza-
tion in the theory of grammar; Chomsky and Halle's suggestions are quite insufficient, but they are not vacuous.

Similarly, in the premarkedness theory of generative
phonology, it was claimed that morpheme structure constraints were to be stated *after* some phonological rules,
so that the output of these rules would be subject to the same
constraints as the underlying forms. But it was never
claimed that the output of every rule is subject to every
morpheme structure constraint. There was no general way
to predict which rules yielded outputs subject to a given
constraint and which did not. But that is no different from
saying that there is no general way of telling which rules
will be subject to an output condition. I believe that the premarkedness theory did, in part, capture certain generalizations about the interaction of morpheme structure constraints
and phonological rules. I believe likewise that output conditions capture some additional generalizations.

In conclusion, the Tunica example suggests that it is
largely unpredictable whether the output condition implied
by a given constraint will actually block the application of a
given rule. Presumably, a system is required for coding
this information in a grammar. Developing a detailed system
of coding the applicability of an output condition to a rule

must await more extensive investigation of data from a wide variety of languages. The crucial point that I hope I have made in this paper is that a notion like output conditions on the application of phonological rules makes it possible to eliminate instances of derivative information that cannot be eliminated by devices already existing in grammatical theory.

REFERENCES

Chomsky, N., and M. Halle (1968). *The Sound Pattern of English.* New York: Harper and Row.
Dyen, I. (1965). *A Sketch of Trukese Grammar. American Oriental Series*, 4.
Haas, M. (1940). *Tunica.* Handbook of American Indian Languages, vol. 4. New York: Smithsonian Institution, Bureau of American Ethnography.
—— (1953). *Tunica Dictionary.* University of California Publications in Linguistics, vol. 6, no. 2, pp. 175–352. Berkeley and Los Angeles: University of California Press.
Hoijer, H. (1933). *Tonkawa: An Indian Language of Texas.* Handbook of American Indian Languages, vol. 3. New York: Smithsonian Institution, Bureau of American Ethnography.
—— (1949). *An Analytical Dictionary of the Tonkawa Language.* University of California Publications in Linguistics, vol. 5, no. 1, pp. 1–74. Berkeley and Los Angeles: University of California Press.
Kenstowicz, M. J. (to appear). "On the Notation of Vowel Length in Lithuanian."
——, and C. W. Kisseberth (1970). "Rule Ordering and the Asymmetry Hypothesis." Papers from the 6th Regional Meeting of the Chicago Linguistic Society, pp. 504–519.
Kisseberth, C. W. (1969a). "Theoretical Implications of Yawelmani Phonology." Ph.D. dissertation, University of Illinois.
—— (1969b). "On the Abstractness of Phonology: The Evidence from Yawelmani." *Papers in Linguistics* 1:248–282.
—— (1970). "On the Functional Unity of Phonological Rules." *Linguistic Inquiry* 1:291–306.
—— (to appear *a*). "Vowel Elision in Tonkawa and Derivational Constraints."
—— (to appear *b*). "The Tunica Stress Conspiracy."
—— (to appear *c*). "A Global Rule in Klamath Phonology."

Kuroda, S.-Y. (1967). *Yawelmani Phonology*. Cambridge: M. I. T. Press.

Newman, S. (1944). *Yokuts Language of California*. *Viking Fund Publications in Anthropology*, no. 2.

Postal, P. (1968). *Aspects of Phonological Theory*. New York: Harper and Row.

Pyle, C. (to appear). ''West Greenlandic Eskimo and the Representation of Vowel Length.''

A Reanalysis of English Word Stress
Part I

JOHN ROBERT ROSS
Massachusetts Institute of Technology and
The Language Research Foundation

0. Introduction

As suggested by its title, this work will be based on a previous analysis of English stress, namely, that contained in Noam Chomsky and Morris Halle's fundamental and awe-inspiring work, *The Sound Pattern of English* (hereafter SPE. Otherwise unidentified page references are to SPE. All references to examples and rules in chapter 3 of SPE will be cited in square brackets, to distinguish them from the parentheses I will use.). The paper will also be formulated within the framework of generative phonology that is elaborated in SPE. It should therefore be obvious that the present paper presupposes SPE in two respects: first, it will not be possible for one who is not thoroughly familiar with SPE to evaluate the reanalysis I will propose below; and second, my work, while it suggests that considerable restructuring is necessary in the system that is built up in SPE, is a direct descendant

NOTE: This work was supported in part by the National Institute of Mental Health (Grant 5-PO1-MH 13390-03) and by the National Science Foundation (Grant GS-3202). There are many, many whose comments and criticisms have dramatically improved what I say in this paper, probably too many to mention them all. Let me single out for special thanks the following friends: Mike Brame, Noam Chomsky, Francois Dell, Bruce Fraser, Vicki Fromkin, Chuck Kisseberth, Terry Langendoen, Greg Lee, Jim McCawley, Marc Schnitzer, Sandy Schane, Dave Stampe, and Arnold Zwicky. For service above and beyond the call of duty, the Award of the Golden Schwa, with Oak Leaf Cluster, to Morris Halle, Jay Keyser, Paul Kiparsky, and Ted Lightner.

of SPE. It would not have been possible to write it without
the great stimulus provided by SPE or without the many hours
of discussion and criticism that Chomsky and Halle have
generously given me, and for which I am deeply grateful to
them.

The title also suggests the main area of the revisions that
I will propose for the phonology of English stress below the
word level. The rules that stress constituents larger than
words, the Nuclear Stress Rule for phrases (pp. 89–91) and
the Compound Rule (pp. 91–94), seem to me to be basically
correct, and I will not be concerned below with the stress
contours that these rules characterize, except in §8 where
I will argue that these two rules must be somewhat extended.
Nor will I be concerned, except briefly, in §8, with the Stress
Adjustment Rule (hereafter SAR), which, in the words of SPE
(p. 94), "reserve[s] secondary stress for phrases that contain
more than one word," or with the rules that assign secondary
stress in words like *Monòngahèla* and *Wìnnipesàukee* and that
account for the contrast between words like *bàndànna* and
bànàna. (Cf. SPE, pp. 110–126.) My major concern will be the
two rules in SPE that assign primary stress: the Main Stress
Rule (cf. pp. 29–43, 69–77, 79–89, 94–110, and 126–162;
hereafter MSR) and the Alternating Stress Rule (cf. pp.
77–79; hereafter ASR). Both rules will be reviewed briefly
in §1 below. In §2, an argument will be given for the addition
of a new case to the ASR, so that it will shift primary stress
back not only in words having three or more syllables, but
also in disyllables. In §3, evidence will be given that a new
case should be added to the MSR. The consequences of the
proposed new case, which are profound, are discussed in
detail in §4. In §5, the ASR will be given a final reformulation. In §6, I will examine in detail the interrelationship of
the Stressed Syllable Rule (cases (c) and (d) of the MSR) and
the ASR, concluding that in fact they must be subcases of
one rule, the Retraction Rule. These paragraphs will conclude Part I. In an envisioned Part II, in §7, I will discuss
a number of phonological processes not treated in SPE, a
discussion that will lead to the formulation of the rules of
Destressing, Medial Laxing, Penult Tensing, and Medial
e-Elision, as well as to a new treatment of the SPE segment
/y/ and to some suggestions for a revision of the underlying
vowel system of SPE. In §8, I will argue that some cases of

stress retraction that are treated in SPE as instances of case (c) of the MSR be regarded as instances of a suitably extended version of the Compound Rule instead. In §9, I will examine several cases of "conspiracies" in English—that is, groups of rules that have the same function, but that have no formal similarities. In §10, I will summarize, listing in their final form, all the redundancy rules and phonological rules that I have proposed in earlier sections. I will investigate the extent to which these rules allow English stress to be predicted. Finally, in §11, I will examine the evidence for the existence of cyclically ordered rules below the word level in English in particular, and the question of the abstractness of the underlying phonological representations that can be justified for English, in general.

1. A Review of the System of Rules in SPE

The MSR is based upon the contrast in stress between such words as those in (1) below.[1]

(1)　(a) édit　　abándon　　(b) érǎse　dénỳ
　　　　develóp　reconnóiter　　allów　atóne

　　　(c) relént　avért
　　　　molést　divést

Making use of the notion *weak cluster* (cf. p. 29 for a preliminary, and p. 83 for a final, definition) Chomsky and Halle propose to account for the stress on the verbs in (1) with rule (2) (cf. p. 29):

(2)　V → [1 stress] / —— C_0(W)]　　case (e)

This rule I will refer to as case (e) of the MSR, for reasons that will become apparent below. By the conventions pertaining to disjunctively ordered rules (cf. pp. 30–36), it will stress the words in (1a) on the penult, since they end in weak clusters—a simple syllabic nucleus followed by no more than a single consonant. Since the words in (1b) and (1c)

---

[1] The tertiary stress on the first syllables of such words as érǎse, dénỳ, and rèconnóiter in (1) is assigned by rules discussed in SPE (cf. pp. 110–126), and need not concern us here. Unless this tertiary stress is of some immediate interest, I will omit it in the citations of forms below.

do not end in weak clusters, rule (2) will assign final stress to them.

Chomsky and Halle noted that many nouns that end in syllables containing a complex nucleus, such as those in (3), have final stress, just like the verbs in (1b).

(3)   attíre
      rávine
      affáir
      lagóon

However, for many nouns ending in weak clusters, such as those in (4), stress is on the antepenult or penult, depending on whether the penult is weak or strong, respectively.

(4)   (a) vénison   (b) horízon   (c) phlogíston
          ínteger   Octóber   Septémber
          sýllabus   Uránus   meníscus
          Connécticut   pílot   Narragánsett
          América   aróma   Aláska

These forms necessitate the establishment of a new environment in which rule (2), which is referred to in SPE as the Romance Stress Rule (hereafter RSR), can apply. This environment, which is stated in (5), and added formally to rule (2) in (6), is case (b) of the MSR.

(5) $- \begin{bmatrix} V \\ -tns \end{bmatrix} C_0 \ ]_N$ case (b)

(6) $V \rightarrow [1 \text{ stress}] / \underline{\quad} C_0 \ (W) / \underline{\quad} \begin{bmatrix} V \\ -tns \end{bmatrix} C_0 \ ]_N$

We find that the stress patterns of many adjectives can also be assigned by rule (2), in such cases as those in (7).

(7)   (a) clandéstine   (b) obscéne   (c) adépt
          hándsome   immúne   robúst
          vúlgar   urbáne   overt
          sólid   remóte   occúlt

That is, since the adjectives in (7a) end in weak clusters, they will receive penultimate stress by rule (2), while the adjectives in (7b) and (7c), which end in strong clusters, will receive final stress.

However, if we consider adjectives ending in monosyllabic

suffixes containing a lax vowel, such as those in (8), a stress
pattern parallcling that in (4) is observed.

(8) (a) *pérsonal*   (b) *collòidal*   (c) *placéntal*
         lìbelous   *desìrous*   *portèntous*
         vìgilant   *defìant*   *obsérvant*

That is, if the affixes *-al*, *-ous*, and *-ant* were to be disregarded in the adjectives in (8) and the RSR were to apply
to the remainder, the correct stress patterns would result.[2]
Thus, the MSR must be amended in such a way as to take
this generalization into account. The revised version is
stated in (9).

(9) $V \rightarrow [1 \text{ stress}] /$ —— $C_0(W) /$ —— $+C_0 \begin{bmatrix} -cns \\ -tns \end{bmatrix} C_0]_{NA}$

case (a)

—— $\begin{bmatrix} V \\ -tns \end{bmatrix} C_0]_N$

case (b)

——]   case (e)

Rule (9), if applied to such underlying representations
as those roughly indicated in (10) (I have disregarded the
fact that the MSR would have applied on an earlier cycle
to the verbs *advise* and *promise*),

(10) (a) inhibit + ɔ̄r + y   (b) advīz + ɔ̄r + y
                (c) contradict + ɔ̄r + y

would yield forms whose primary stress was incorrectly
located on the penultimate syllable. Since the word *inhìbitòry*
manifests tertiary stress on its penult, however, Chomsky
and Halle suggest that primary stress be placed on this syllable (by case (a), where the sequence +y is the affix that is
disregarded) and that primary stress be reassigned to the

---

[2]The final vowel of the noun *placenta* must be deleted, by rules that
have been inadequately studied, in forming the adjective *placental* (cf. fn.
38 below). The fact that the nouns *còllòid* and *pòrtènt* do not have primary
stress on the final syllable, as would be expected from what has been said
so far, will be explained below in connection with a revision of the ASR
that I will propose.

second syllable of the word, with automatic stress weakening of the stress on the penult, by a convention that is independently motivated. This stress-retraction rule reassigns stress in accordance with the RSR: in (10a), where the syllable preceding the original primary stress ends in a weak cluster, the stress is placed on the syllable that precedes this cluster. In (10b) and (10c), however, since the syllables that originally bore primary stress are preceded by strong clusters, the RSR will place primary stress on these clusters, deriving the intermediate forms in (11).

(11)   *adv$\overset{1}{i}$s$\overset{2}{o}$ry   *contrad$\overset{1}{i}$ct$\overset{2}{o}$ry

These forms subsequently undergo a rule that states (essentially) that medial syllables that immediately follow a syllable bearing primary stress cannot bear stress (this rule is discussed on pp. 119–125). Since these vowels are stressless, they will be subject to the rule of Vowel Reduction, and the correct forms adv$\overset{1}{i}$s$\overset{0}{o}$ry and contrad$\overset{1}{i}$ct$\overset{0}{o}$ry will be derived.

Thus, we see that the MSR must again be revised, to account for such forms as those in (10). The RSR must be able to apply to retract primary stress in certain cases, when a previous rule has placed stress on the final syllable, that is, in an environment that, following SPE, I will schematically symbolize as in (12), which represents cases (c) and (d) of the MSR.

(12)   —— $\overset{\prime}{\Sigma}$ cases (c) and (d)

There are a number of complications pertaining to contrasts like those in (13), which SPE extends case (c) to handle (cf. pp. 100–110).

(13)   m$\overset{1}{o}$nogr$\overset{3}{a}$ph – m$\overset{1}{o}$nos$\overset{3}{y}$llable – m$\overset{3}{o}$nog$\overset{1}{e}$nesis
        perm$\overset{1}{i}$t$_V$ – p$\overset{1}{e}$rm$\overset{3}{i}$t$_N$ – h$\overset{1}{e}$rm$\overset{0}{i}$t$_N$

These cases of the MSR are highly complex, and I will postpone further discussion of them until I take up the matter of the relationship between the stress retraction that is effected by these two cases and that effected by the ASR (cf. §6 below).

To sum up, then, the MSR of SPE takes the type of stress contrast exemplified in (1) and (7) to be paradigmatic. Rule (2), the RSR, which accounts for these cases in isolation (case (e)), is then extended to apply before monosyllabic affixes whose final vowel is lax (case (a)), before the last syllable of nouns whose final vowel is lax (case (b)), and before a final-stressed syllable (cases (c) and (d)). The final, albeit unabbreviated, form of the MSR that is arrived at in SPE is given in (14):

(14) $V \rightarrow [1 \text{ stress}] /$ —— $C_0 (W) /$ —— $C_0 \begin{bmatrix} -\text{cns} \\ -\text{tns} \end{bmatrix} C_0 \,]_{NA}$

case (a)

—— $\begin{bmatrix} V \\ -\text{tns} \end{bmatrix} C_0 \,]_N$

case (b)

—— $\overset{\prime}{\Sigma}$ cases (c) and (d)

—— $]$ case (e)

Rule (14) is not adequate, however, to account for all observed instances of primary stress within words. Such words as those in (15) would fall within the scope of case (e) of the MSR and would, in the absence of other rules, end up with the stress incorrectly located on the final syllable.

(15) (a) hùrricáne   gálvanìze   àsiníne
         dýnamìte   gállivànt   mànifést
         díocèse   mágnifỳ   èrudíte
         Sátterthwàite   antícipàte   mòribúnd
         àrtichòke   execùte   béllicòse
     (b) ànecdòte   exàcerbàte   sáturnìne
         mágistràte   dèvastàte   ínfantìle

To account for the stress pattern of these words, Chomsky and Halle proposed a second stress-retraction rule, the ASR, which I have stated approximately in (16). (Note that rule (16) must apply to all major categories, for all are represented in (15).)

(16) $V \rightarrow [1 \text{ stress}] /$ —— $C_0 (=) C_0 V C_0 \overset{1}{V} C_0 \#$

From the examples in (15b), it is clear that the stress is not retracted in accordance with the RSR, for if this were the case the words in (15b) would have penultimate, instead of the correct antepenultimate, stress. Thus, two stress-retraction rules are necessary—cases (c) and (d) of the MSR, which retract primary stress in accordance with the RSR, and the ASR, which retracts stress two syllables, regardless of

whether the immediately preceding syllable contains a strong
or a weak cluster.

2. An Extension of the Alternating Stress Rule

The MSR and, following it, the ASR are the two major
rules for the placement of primary stress within English
words. Let us now consider a large class of words that
cannot be accounted for by the rules given in SPE, without
postulating highly counterintuitive underlying forms.

(17) $\overset{1}{A}rg\overset{3}{y}le$ $\overset{1}{a}rch\overset{3}{i}ve$ $m\overset{1}{a}ngr\overset{3}{o}ve$
     $c\overset{1}{a}rb\overset{3}{i}ne$ $c\overset{1}{a}rb\overset{3}{o}y$ $M\overset{1}{o}sc\overset{3}{o}w$
     $qu\overset{1}{i}n\overset{3}{i}ne$ $g\overset{1}{a}rg\overset{3}{o}yle$ $\overset{1}{O}s\overset{3}{a}ge$
     $m\overset{1}{o}h\overset{3}{a}ir$ $g\overset{1}{e}nt\overset{3}{i}le$ $pr\overset{1}{o}t\overset{3}{e}in$
     $s\overset{1}{a}t\overset{3}{i}re$ $g\overset{1}{a}ngr\overset{3}{e}ne$ $t\overset{1}{i}r\overset{3}{a}de$

The only available rule in SPE that could produce the 1–3
stress patterns on the words in (17) is rule [158] of chapter
III, which I reproduce here for convenience.

$$[158] \quad \begin{bmatrix} V \\ +tns \end{bmatrix} \rightarrow [1 \text{ stress}] \, / + \underline{\quad\quad} C_0 \#$$

This rule, which applies before the MSR to assign primary
stress to the final syllable of *vac+ate,* will provide the environment necessary for the Stressed Syllable Rule of the
MSR to retract the stress to the first syllable. Chomsky and
Halle thus account for the stress contrast between $v\overset{3}{a}c\overset{1}{a}te$ and
$cr\overset{3}{e}\overset{1}{a}te$ by postulating that the former, but not the latter, verb
is analyzed into stem and suffix. This account is rendered
plausible by the existence of such related forms as *vacant,*
but the absence of corresponding forms related to *create.*
However, in order to explain the stress contrast between the
words in (17) and those in (18),[3]

(18) $b\overset{3}{o}ut\overset{1}{i}que$ $p\overset{3}{a}st\overset{1}{i}che$ $\overset{3}{e}st\overset{1}{e}em$
     $c\overset{3}{a}nt\overset{1}{e}en$ $tr\overset{3}{a}p\overset{1}{e}ze$ $d\overset{3}{o}m\overset{1}{a}in$
     $p\overset{3}{o}nt\overset{1}{o}on$ $c\overset{3}{a}y\overset{1}{u}se$ $c\overset{3}{o}c\overset{1}{a}ine$
     $cr\overset{3}{u}s\overset{1}{a}de$ $c\overset{3}{a}ff\overset{1}{e}ine$ $ch\overset{3}{a}mp\overset{1}{a}gne$
     $sh\overset{3}{a}mp\overset{1}{o}o$ $b\overset{3}{a}mb\overset{1}{o}o$ $l\overset{3}{a}mp\overset{1}{o}on$

Chomsky and Halle must postulate that the words in (17)

---

[3] I am grateful to Morris Halle and Jay Keyser for furnishing me with a
large number of examples like those in (18).

contain morpheme boundaries, while those in (18) do not. It is important to note that there is no independent justification for such a segmentation. Inserting morpheme boundaries into words like those in (17) is therefore exactly equivalent to marking these words with a rule feature to indicate that they will undergo rule [158].[4] But if a solution making use of ad hoc morpheme boundaries is only notationally different from a solution making use of rule features, we might ask whether it is necessary to have rule [158] in the grammar at all, or whether it would not be equally possible to mark words like those in (17) and (18) as being exceptions to some independently motivated rule.

In fact, this latter possibility seems to be feasible. Joseph Emonds (personal communication) and Paul Kiparsky (class lectures at MIT in the spring of 1968) have pointed out that if the ASR is extended to retract stress in disyllables as well as in trisyllables, the stress patterns of the words in (17) and (18) can be accounted for. The modified ASR appears in (19).

(19) $V \rightarrow [1 \text{ stress}] / \underline{\quad} C_0 (=) C_0 (VC_0) \overset{1}{V} C_0 \#$

The conventions on disjunctive ordering of rules would stipulate that the stress be moved back two syllables in trisyllables and one syllable in disyllables. If rule [158] is dispensed with, all the words in (17) and (18) would first receive primary stress on their final syllables by case (e) of the MSR. The words in (17) would be marked in the lexicon with the feature [+ASR], and those in (18) with the feature [-ASR]. As far as I can tell, it is impossible to predict whether stress retraction will take place in disyllabic nouns: words like (17) are as numerous as words like (18). The situation is slightly more complex for verbs and adjectives, which I will discuss in §6.3 below.

In support of the proposed extension of the ASR to disyllables, note that the ASR has many exceptions for trisyllabic words (which is noted in SPE, pp. 157–158). Thus, not only words like those in (18) would have to be marked [-ASR], but also the trisyllables in (20).[5]

---

[4]The notion of rule feature is discussed on pp. 172–176 and pp. 373–380.

[5]Note also that many speakers have douplets for such words as *lemonade*, *gasoline*, *magazine*, etc., which can be either initially or finally stressed.

(20) $b\overset{3}{u}ccan\overset{1}{ee}r$ $\overset{3}{a}cqui\overset{1}{e}sce$ $\overset{3}{a}rab\overset{1}{e}sque$
       $br\overset{3}{i}gad\overset{1}{oo}n$ $b\overset{3}{a}rric\overset{1}{a}de$ $\overset{3}{a}prop\overset{1}{o}s$
       $L\overset{3}{i}ster\overset{1}{i}ne$ $g\overset{3}{u}arant\overset{1}{e}e$ $d\overset{3}{e}bon\overset{1}{a}ir$
       $\overset{3}{I}llin\overset{1}{o}is$ $\overset{3}{a}scert\overset{1}{a}in$ $J\overset{3}{a}pan\overset{1}{e}se$

While the stress of words like $\overset{3}{I}llin\overset{1}{o}is$ and $L\overset{3}{i}ster\overset{1}{i}ne$ cannot be predicted apparently by any general rules (compare such words as $\overset{1}{I}roqu\overset{1}{o}is$, $c\overset{1}{o}rdur\overset{3}{o}y$, $\overset{1}{O}valt\overset{3}{i}ne$, $amph\overset{1}{e}tam\overset{3}{i}ne$), there are many suffixes, such as *-esque, -ese, -esce,* which never, or almost never, have primary stress moved back off them by the ASR. The same is true of certain phonological sequences that end monomorphemic stems. Thus, in most dialects, all trisyllables that end in graphic *-oon* have final stress. Some examples are provided in (21).

(21) $m\overset{3}{a}car\overset{1}{oo}n$ $gr\overset{3}{a}nfal\overset{1}{oo}n$
       $br\overset{3}{i}gad\overset{1}{oo}n$
       $p\overset{3}{a}ntal\overset{1}{oo}n$
       $C\overset{3}{a}mer\overset{1}{oo}n$
       $S\overset{3}{a}skat\overset{1}{oo}n$

This fact can be used to give even stronger support for the proposed extension of the ASR to disyllables. As noted by Emonds and by Kiparsky, whenever there are regularities governing words to which the trisyllabic ASR does not apply, disyllables will also have final stress. For example, paralleling trisyllabic words in *-oon,* which all have final stress, we find that all disyllabic words in *-oon* also have final stress. Some examples are given in (22).

(22) $pont\overset{1}{oo}n$ $racc\overset{1}{oo}n$ $poltr\overset{1}{oo}n$
       $lamp\overset{1}{oo}n$ $lag\overset{1}{oo}n$ $buff\overset{1}{oo}n$
       $harp\overset{1}{oo}n$ $sal\overset{1}{oo}n$ $mar\overset{1}{oo}n$
       $mons\overset{1}{oo}n$ $drag\overset{1}{oo}n$ $ball\overset{1}{oo}n$
       $coc\overset{1}{oo}n$ $doubl\overset{1}{oo}n$ $spitt\overset{1}{oo}n$

Similarly, just as trisyllabic adjectives in *-ese* retain final stress, as in the examples in (23a), so the disyllabic adjectives in *-ese* in (23b) are also finally stressed.

(23)   (a) $Japan\overset{1}{e}se$ (b) $Chin\overset{1}{e}se$
           $Portugu\overset{1}{e}se$ $Truk\overset{1}{e}se$
           $Javan\overset{1}{e}se$ $Siam\overset{1}{e}se$
           $journal\overset{1}{e}se$ $Malt\overset{1}{e}se$
           $Tyrol\overset{1}{e}se$ $Burm\overset{1}{e}se$

The fact that stress retraction in disyllables fails to occur under precisely the same conditions under which it fails for trisyllables is a generalization that should find formal expression in a descriptively adequate grammar of English. This is possible if the ASR is extended as I have suggested in (19) and if a lexical redundancy rule like the one stated informally in (24) is contained in the grammar.

(24)   All words ending in the morpheme /+ēz/ or the phonological sequence /ōn/ are [-ASR].

Interestingly, cases can also be found where the ASR *must* apply. All words that end in a lax vowel followed by a voiced stop must retract the stress from their final syllable.[6] Thus, the trisyllabic words in (25a) have undergone stress retraction, as have the disyllabic words in (25b).[7]

(25)   (a) Beélzebùb   Íchabòd   pòllywòg
             shìshkabòb   Gálahàd   scálawàg
                              kátydìd   chùgalùg

        (b) nàbòb   Nímròd   hùmbùg
             Cántàb   gònàd   shìndìg
             Áhàb   mònàd   mùskèg

This fact also supports the revision of the ASR given in (19) and necessitates adding to the grammar a redundancy rule like that informally expressed in (26).

(26)   All words ending in $/\begin{bmatrix} V \\ -tns \end{bmatrix} \begin{bmatrix} +obs \\ -cnt \\ +voi \end{bmatrix}/$ are [+ASR].

Paul Kiparsky has observed parallel facts about the phonological sequences /ɔf/ and /īn/ (class lectures at MIT). Thus, the trisyllabic nouns in /ɔf/ in (27a) must retract stress, as must the disyllables in (27b).

(27)   (a) Rómanòff   (b) Lùkòff
             Málenkòv   Lákòff
             Mólotòv   Smìrnòff
             Jáckendòff   Kárlòff

---

[6]How this final weak cluster receives primary stress will be discussed in §3 below.

[7]I know of only four words that do not conform to the pattern of (25): *Madrìd, kabòb, nawàb,* and *agòg.*

Similarly, the stress has been retracted from the final syllable of the trisyllables in graphic *-ine* in (28a) as well as in the disyllables in (28b). Actually, the redundancy noted by Kiparsky about *-ine* can be generalized: any word ending in /ĪC₀/, except for disyllabic verbs, must retract stress. Thus, the trisyllables in (28c) exhibit stress retraction, as do the disyllables in (28d). The words in (28e) are the only true exceptions to this broader generalization that I have been able to find.

(28)

(a) *Pálestìne*   *phílistìne*   *ánodỳne*   *cóncubìne*
     Túrrentìne   *íodìne*   *sáturnìne*   *pórcupìne*
     túrpentìne   *Válentìne*   *cólumbìne*   *ásinìne*

(b) *quínìne*   *súpìne*   *félìne*
     cárbìne   *túrbìne*   *cánìne*
     Álpìne   *bóvìne*   *vúlpìne*

(c) *sámurài*   *Whítsuntìde*   *máritìme*   *érudìte*
     álkalì   *ínfantìle*   *páradìse*   *éxpedìte*
     álibì   *mércantìle*   *mérchandìse*   *récondìte*
     Géminì   *cámomìle*   *énterprìse*   *sátellìte*
     díatrìbe   *crócodìle*   *ímprovìse*   *dýnamìte*
     sácrifìce   *réconcìle*   *súpervìse*   *áppetìte*
     hómicìde   *dómicìle*   *párasìte*   *légalìze*
     bármecìde   *júvenìle*   *ánthracìte*   *líonìze*
     cýanìde   *pántomìme*   *plébiscìte*

(d) *rábbì*   *cárbìde*   *núbìle*   *sátìre*
     brómìde   *óxìde*   *prófìle*   *ésquìre*
     árchìve   *túrnpìke*   *sénìle*   *éxcise*ₙ
     vámpìre   *rámpìke*   *géntìle*   *térmìte*
     úmpìre   *álsìke*   *téxtìle*   *Sémìte*
     émpìre   *fébrìle*   *éxìle*   *Híttìte*
     Árgỳle   *Cárlìsle*   *fránchìse*   *báptìze*

(e) *Jùlý*   *surpríse*ₙ   *divíde*ₙ   *divíne*
     Bahái   *devíce*   *assíze*   *sùblíme*
     attíre   *advíce*   *políte*   *èntíre*
     *disgùíse*ₙ   *delíght*ₙ   *contríte*

The fact that there is no stress retraction in such verbs as *relý, defý, applý, advíse, reclíne,* and *excíte* will be discussed in §6.2 below, in connection with rule (95).

Thus, for trisyllables as well as for disyllables, stress retraction is obligatory under the same conditions and impossible under the same conditions. This fact can be captured if the ASR is extended to apply to both types of words, as in (19). This extension allows us to dispense with rule [158] entirely[8] and makes the stress differences between (17) and (18) a purely unpredictable lexical fact, except where there exist such lexical redundancy rules as I have just discussed. From now on, therefore, when I refer to the ASR, I will mean the extended version of (19).

3. A New Case for the Main Stress Rule

3.1. Let us now consider such words as the nouns in (29).

(29) *Ámazòn   ócelòt   kátydìd   Íchabòd*
     díadèm   Béelzebùb   bólshevìk   Mámaronèck
     dáffodìl   tómahàwk   Márrakèch   álbatròss

I assume that these nouns have no internal structure, so that their stress cannot be assigned by case (a) of the MSR. Since

---

[8]To the extent that the generalization is valid—that it is only to the disyllabic verbs in *ate* (for which a morphemic analysis can be independently justified, e.g., *vacate, locate, rotate, migrate, gyrate*) that stress retraction applies—a lexical redundancy rule can be formulated to express this fact as a condition upon the applicability of the extended ASR. It is my impression, however, that except for verbs in *-ate*, the generalizations that can be found are not worth setting up a rule like [158] for. For instance, many, though not all, of the disyllabic adjectives in *-ose* retain final stress, despite the fact that they are bimorphemic. Compare *verbóse, jocóse* (cf. *jocular*), *bulbóse, morbóse* (cf. *morbid*), etc., which retain final stress, with *spínose, fílose* (cf. *filament*), etc., in which stress retraction has occurred. The retraction, therefore, does not seem to coincide with analyzability. Also, it would seem that such words as *maríne, sáltine, cáffeine* (perhaps), *extréme, téchnique, úrbane, mótif,* etc., should all have morphemic analyses, and yet stress is not retracted, as it would be if [158] were in the grammar. Furthermore, even in the class of words in *-ate*, there are some exceptions: *iráte* (cf. *ire*), *órnate* (cf. *adorn, ornament*), and *sedáte* (cf. *sedentary*). It seems that stress retraction is essentially random, and that whether or not a form is morphemically complex has few consequences for predicting its stress, so I will not pursue the matter further here.

all end in syllables containing a lax vowel, and since all
have weak clusters in their penults, case (b) will assign
primary stress to the antepenult, producing such unacceptable
intermediate forms as (30a), which will result in the phonetic
sequence shown in (30b). (The symbol "V̆" designates the
lax vowel archiphoneme, and the symbol "V" any vowel.
Unless specifically marked long with a macron, e.g., ǣ, ū,
etc., particular vowels should be understood to be lax.)

(30) (a) æ̀mV̆zɔn   (b) *[æ̀məzn̩]

The final syllable of the words in (29) must somehow receive
stress, so that the rule of Vowel Reduction will not convert
the final vowels to [ə].

    Observe first that the stress difference between words like
Ȧmazȍn and *Napȯleȍn* cannot reside in some difference in the
feature composition of the final vowel: the underlying form
of the former must be /æmV̆zɔn/, and the underlying form
of the latter must be /nV̆pɔliɔn/, because of the related
adjective *Napoleȯnic*, where the underlying quality of the final
vowel appears under stress.

    The stress difference must be due, therefore, to a differ-
ence in the rules applying to the parallel underlying forms.
Two possible analyses suggest themselves. First, one might
postulate the existence of a lexically governed rule like (31),
which would place secondary stress on the final syllable of
certain idiosyncratically marked lexical items.

(31)   V → [2 stress] / V́C_0VC_0—— C_0 #

The Stress Adjustment Rule would then lower the [2 stress] to
the phonetically observed [3 stress]. *Amazon* and the other
words in (29) would be marked to undergo (31), while *Napoleon*
and the words in (4) would not.

    A second possible analysis would be to postulate a new
case of the MSR that placed final stress on certain nouns.
The ASR, following this new case, could then be applied to
move the stress back from the final syllable, with automatic
lowering of the final stress. Thus, the derivation of the 1–3
stress contour of *Ȧmazȍn* would exactly parallel that of the
1–3 stress contour of *hùrricȁne* and of other words like those
in (15). Also, since the ASR must be extended so that it
moves the stress back in disyllables as well as in trisylla-

bles, as I argued in §2 above, the derivation of the 1–3 stress contour of words like those in (32) and (25b)

(32) péòn   atöll   Óshkòsh   Igòr
      chàòs   Aztèc   fùrlòng   Òmàr
      Móhàwk   bùrláp   iàmb   màyhèm

would be derived by first assigning final stress by this new case of the MSR, which I have stated in (33),

(33) $V \rightarrow [1 \text{ stress}] / \underline{\quad} C_0]_N$ case (f)

and by then applying the disyllabic case of the ASR. Thus, Àmazòn would parallel hùrricàne, and péòn would parallel Àrgỳle. Of course, it would be necessary to mark *Amazon* and *Napoleon* differently with respect to Rule (31), as well as to mark whether a noun is to undergo case (b) of the MSR (like *Napoleon*), or (33), case (f) (like *Amazon*).[9]

---

[9]One further, rather ingenious, way to account for the stress of Àmazòn might suggest itself: provide this word and the others in (29) with geminate final consonants and a final *e* in their underlying representations. The derivations would then proceed as follows:

Underlying form:	/æmV̆zɔnne/	MSR, case (b)
	æmV̆zɔ́ne	Cluster Simplification
	æmV̆zɔ́n	*e*-Elision
	æ̀mV̆zɔ́n	ASR
	[æ̀məzǽn]	Other Rules.

Such derivations would require the two rules of Cluster Simplification and *e*-Elision to be placed before the ASR in the rule ordering, but this ordering would not cause any problems, as far as I know.

There is only one argument that I know of against such an analysis, and it is rather weak. In order for the final vowel of such words as àzòth and Kùràth to have received final stress by case (b), underlying representations like /æzɔθθe/ and /kuræθθe/ would have to be postulated. But it seems that elsewhere in English, a general restriction exists that prohibits the sequence /θθ/. For example, although we can infer the existence of underlying /tt/, /ss/, /ll/, /dd/, and even /zz/ clusters from the penultimate primary stress on such trisyllabic nouns as spaghètti, Odèssa, vanílla, Aláddin, muèzzin, there are, to the best of my knowledge, no forms like *spaghèthi, *odètha, *vanítha, *alàthin, *muèthin, etc., which would constitute one justification for postulating an underlying /θθ/ sequence. (The words Hìawátha and Àbernáthy, which must receive penultimate stress by case (b), can be derived from forms containing a tense /ǣ/, which will regularly be shortened in this position

3.2. There are two strong arguments I know of for pre-ferring the second analysis to the first, that is, for assuming that (33) is a rule of English, but that (31) is not. Note, first of all, that there is a large class of nouns with final stress, but with a lax vowel in their final syllable. Some examples are given in (34).

(34)
Berlín	pecán	cadét	saróng
Madríd	corrál	cornét	shebáng
Suéz	shellác	batón	Péking
Quebéc	abýss	chiffón	meríngue
Brazíl	Chinóok	catárrh	gestált
Tibét	gazélle	guitár	foulárd
Ceylón	crevásse	cigár	Lucérne

Such forms must be marked so that case (b) will not apply nor, except for the last column in (34), case (e), for if either of these cases applied, the nouns in (34) would incorrectly receive initial stress. Thus, some rule like (33) must be postulated for these forms.

The second argument for case (f) concerns such words as *Hòttentòt*. Since this word has a lax vowel in its final syl-lable, but a strong cluster in its penult, case (b) would incor-rectly produce **Hottèntòt*. While the first-proposed analysis, which contains rule (31), could not avoid this incorrect result, the second analysis could. If *Hottentot* were to receive final stress by case (f), the ASR, which retracts stress regardless of the phonological composition of the penult, would correctly assign primary stress to the first syllable, the stress on the

─────────

[note the impossibility of *[hãyəwèyθə], *[ǽbərnèyθiy]] after the MSR has applied.)

Another indication that /θθ/ sequences should be excluded by a mor-pheme structure rule is that the phonetic sequences [ʌθ] and [ʌð] are almost unknown in English (the only exceptions I know of are *Rútherford* [in one pronunciation], and *southern*). Since underlying sequences of the form /... uθV .../ will all be converted to [... yūwθV ...] or [... yūwðV ...] by the rules of SPE (cf. such words as *ēuthanasia*, *Lútheran*, etc.), we could explain the absence of phonetic [ʌθ] and [ʌð] by excluding the sequence /θθ/ from underlying representations.

If these arguments are correct, the tertiary stress on the final syllables of *ázòth* and *Kúràth* cannot be due to an underlying final sequence /θθe/. Thus, another explanation for its stress must be sought. The fact that the final vowel of *Óregòn* must be tensed in *Óregōnian* (cf. the discussion of this form in §3.3 below) provides further evidence against assuming an underlying /nne/ for this form.

final syllable being automatically weakened. The derivation
would proceed as follows.

(35)   Underlying form: $[\text{hɔtV̌ntɔt}]_N$
       $[\text{-case (b)}]$
       $[\text{-case (e)}]$

MSR case (f)		1
ASR	1	2
SAR	1	3

       Other rules $[\overset{1}{\text{hă}} \text{tn} \overset{3}{\underset{\cdot}{\text{tă}}} \text{t}]$

There is a fairly large class of words like *Hòttentŏt*—
trisyllabic nouns with a 1–3 stress contour—whose final
vowels are lax and whose penults contain strong clusters. I
have given a selection of these in (36).

(36)   *Ălgernŏn*   *Sămarkănd*
       cŭmmerbŭnd   *hăversăck*
       ămpersănd   *Bròbdingnăg*
       Măckintŏsh   *Ărbuthnŏt*
       Căvendĭsh   *ăbelmŏsk*
       Vănderbĭlt   *gŭbbertŭsh*
       bălderdăsh   *gălempŭng*
       pălimpsĕst   *bătterfăng*
       păroxỹsm   *kĭzilbăsh*
       Hăckensăck   *bŭrkundăz*[10]

[10]At this point, one might object that many of the words in the right
column of (36) are so infrequent as to impeach any argument based on
them. I do not find this objection valid. It is a perfectly valid research
strategy to submit nonsense forms to native speakers and to use their
phonetic intuitions about such forms as an indication of what phonological
processes operate in their language. Indeed, it is precisely this type of
intuition that morpheme structure rules (or conditions) are designed to
capture. I take it that the forms in the right column are sufficiently
rare as to effectively constitute nonsense forms for most speakers.
However, these forms will be given 1–3 stress contours by English
speakers just as readily as the more familiar forms in the left column,
a phenomenon I take to be as significant as the fact that English speakers
can distinguish between possible nonsense forms like [blik] and impossible ones like *[bnik]. Thus, it seems irrelevant that some of the words
I cite as examples are more uncommon than others, unless it can be
shown that the phonological processes I infer on the basis of these examples are in conflict with those which can be inferred from more everyday
forms. To the best of my knowledge, this conflict does not exist in the
case here, or elsewhere in the paper.

On the basis of the above words and of nouns with final stress on lax vowels, like those in (34), I conclude that Rule (33), case (f), must be added to the MSR. Note that any noun that is not stressed by case (b) must receive final stress by case (f). Thus, if a noun is marked [-case (b)], as the nouns in (34) must be, we must also mark it [-case (e)], so that case (e) cannot assign penultimate stress. But instead of marking all [-case (b)] forms [-case (e)] in addition, I will restrict case (e) in (37), the revised version of the MSR, to verbs and adjectives. Nouns will only be stressed by case (b) or case (f).

$$(37) \quad V \to [1 \text{ stress}] / \left\{ \begin{array}{ll} \underline{\quad} C_0(W) / \left\{ \begin{array}{ll} \underline{\quad} +C_0 \begin{bmatrix} -\text{cns} \\ -\text{tns} \end{bmatrix} C_0]_{NA} & (a) \\ \underline{\quad} \begin{bmatrix} V \\ -\text{tns} \end{bmatrix} C_0]_N & (b) \\ \underline{\quad} \acute{\Sigma} & (c),(d) \\ \underline{\quad}]_{VA} & (e) \end{array} \right. \\ \underline{\quad} C_0]_N & (f) \end{array} \right.$$

3.3. The question that now arises is the following: given that both case (b) and case (f) can be used to stress a noun whose final syllable contains a lax vowel, is there any general way of predicting, from the phonological shape of a noun, which case will apply? Above, I showed that, while *Napoleon* must be stressed by case (b), *Amazon* must be stressed by case (f). To be sure, these words must end in the underlying sequence /ɔn/, so that the choice of which case to apply cannot depend on the final syllable alone. One might believe that one of the many other properties that differentiate these two words, or the words in (4) from those in (29), might be criterional. The following example, however, should convince anyone that this choice is not always predictable, for it is a perfect minimal pair.

Consider the word *Oregon*. In my dialect, it has a 1–3 stress contour and would therefore have to be stressed by case (f). There are dialects, however, in which it is produced with a 1–0 stress contour—[ɔ́rəgṇ̀] phonetically— and thus it must have been stressed by case (b) in these dialects. However, it is not possible that there is any phonetic distinction in the underlying forms postulated for this word in the two dialects, for they both have the adjective *Oregonian*, which indicates that the underlying representation in each dialect must be /ɔrV̌gɔn/. Thus, here is a case where stress must be assumed to be unpredictable and distinctive.

However, when we ask where else stress must be lexically marked, we find that the final consonant cluster of a noun plays a decisive role in determining stress. In general, any noun ending in more than one consonant must be stressed by case (f). Examples of this regularity can be seen in the words in (38), all of which have 1–3 stress contours.

(38) parallax   kiosk   dithyramb   transept
      anthrax   arimasp   iamb   saraband
      aphelops   boomerang   Heffalump   eland
      Cyclops   mustang   mugwump   catapult
      cataclysm Kennebunk   cataract   cobalt
      orgasm   Podunk   insect   Ozark
      asterisk   avalanche   nympholept[11]

As far as I know, the only final clusters that do not require final stress in nouns are those given in (39):[12]

(39) *nt, st, ts, ns, rt, rd, rn*

For nouns ending in the above clusters, stress cannot be predicted. Whether such a noun will be stressed by case (b) or by case (f) must be lexically indicated. In (40a), I have cited nouns that must receive final stress, and in (40b) and

---

[11]It is immaterial that this word and several others in (38) contain more than one morpheme. All nouns that end in a consonant cluster (with the exceptions to be discussed immediately below) must receive final stress, no matter how many morphemes they contain. Thus, any analysis of *nympholept* is beside the point for the purposes of assigning stress by the MSR.

[12]There are a number of apparent exceptions to this generalization, such as *lozenge, Lenox, monarch, mollusk*, etc., which do not appear to have been stressed by case (f). I will argue in § 3.4 below, however, that they have in fact been finally stressed, that stress has been retracted by the ASR, and that a *Destressing Rule* has subsequently removed the tertiary stress on the final syllable. There are several real exceptions to the generalization—*Egypt*, for instance.

The cluster /nd/ raises special problems, which I will discuss in § 7.1.

(40c) I have cited parallel forms that are assigned antepenultimate or penultimate stress by case (b).

(40)

(a)	(b)	(c)
s[1]ycoph[3]ant	[1]eleph[0]ant	opp[1]onent[13]
c[1]oryb[3]ant	c[1]ormor[0]ant	lieut[1]en[1]ant
l[1]ophod[3]ont	c[1]oven[0]ant	g[1]i[0]ant
ev[1]ent	[1]elem[0]ent	m[1]om[0]ent
affr[1]ont	d[1]ocum[0]ent	s[1]erp[0]ent
p[1]eder[3]ast	[1]Ever[0]est	
P[1]entec[3]ost	c[1]atal[0]yst[14]	
p[1]alimps[3]est		
b[1]omb[3]ast		
Kibb[1]utz	H[1]orow[0]itz	Massach[1]usetts
		Manisch[1]evitz
		M[1]oritz[15]
rom[1]ance	inh[1]er[1]it[0]ance	res[1]ist[0]ance
d[1]avenp[3]ort		c[1]omf[0]ort
M[1]oz[3]art		c[1]ul'v[0]ert
B[1]og[3]art		[1]exp[0]ert
ret[1]ort		G[1]ilb[0]ert
[1]Abel[3]ard		[1]orch[0]ard
B[1]og[3]arde		c[1]ow[0]ard
foul[1]ard		b[1]ast[0]ard
		[1]Edw[0]ard (cf. *Edwardian*)

[13]It is irrelevant here that this word is susceptible of analysis into stem and affix, so that it could also be stressed by case (a). In §4.1 below, I will attempt to show that when case (b) is reformulated correctly, it is possible to collapse it with case (a), for it is apparently not the case that words with lax affixes are stressed differently than words without affixes.

[14]Most words in /st/ are stressed by case (f). The only two words that I have been able to find in which stress is on the antepenult are given in (40b), and I know of no trisyllabic words in /st/ that have penultimate stress. Possibly, therefore, the two words in (40b) should be regarded as exceptions, although they can be accounted for with exceedingly minor modifications in the otherwise necessary apparatus.

[15]There are almost no nonplural English words that end in /ts/, except for names in *-itz*. Perhaps the few remaining words should merely be treated as exceptions to the generalization that words ending in final consonant clusters other than /nt/ are stressed by case (f).

$$\overset{1}{u}nic\overset{3}{o}rn \qquad\qquad l\overset{1}{a}nt\overset{0}{e}rn$$
$$\overset{1}{a}c\overset{3}{o}rn \qquad\qquad\quad l\overset{1}{e}ct\overset{3}{e}rn$$
$$\qquad\qquad\qquad\qquad c\overset{1}{i}st\overset{0}{e}rn$$

The marginality of contrasts for words ending in the last five clusters cannot be overemphasized. The paucity of longer words ending in these clusters makes it impossible to ascertain whether there is a genuine contrast here between cases (b) and (f). It is only when reasonably large numbers of contrasts of the type exhibited in (4), which constituted the original motivation for case (b), can be found, that one can be sure that a given final consonant cluster can be disregarded by case (b). What evidence I was able to find suggests that probably the only consonant cluster meeting this condition is /nt/. However, although there are few words having three or more syllables and ending in one of the clusters /rt/, /rd/, and /rn/, there are a fair number of stress contrasts like $B\overset{1}{o}g\overset{3}{a}rt$–$G\overset{1}{i}lb\overset{0}{e}rt$, $\overset{1}{a}c\overset{3}{o}rn$–$l\overset{1}{a}nt\overset{0}{e}rn$; I know of no better way of handling them than by postulating that the first member of each pair is stressed by case (f) and the second by case (b). I will therefore reformulate the MSR below in such a way that case (b) can apply to nouns ending in all six of the clusters given in (39), but this decision is obviously provisional.

The above considerations suggest that the original formulation of the environment for case (b) given in (5) is too strong. The words in (38) show that, in general, any noun ending in more than one consonant will receive final stress. The exceptions to this generalization are the six clusters of (39). Thus, C_0 in (5) should be restricted so that it can designate, except for these six clusters, at most one consonant. Thus (5) must be replaced by (41):

(41)

$$-\begin{bmatrix} V \\ -tns \end{bmatrix} \left\{\begin{matrix} C_0^1 \\[4pt] \begin{Bmatrix} n \\ r \\ s \end{Bmatrix} t \\[4pt] r \begin{Bmatrix} d \\ n \end{Bmatrix} \\[4pt] \begin{Bmatrix} t \\ n \end{Bmatrix} s \end{matrix}\right\}_N$$

However, (41) is not restrictive enough yet, for it turns out that not all final consonants can be disregarded by case (b)—only dentals and sonorants can. That is, if a word ends in a nondental obstruent—one of the sounds {p, b, f, v, š, ž, č, k, g}[16]—it must be stressed finally by the MSR, which can be seen from the examples in (42) and (43). In (42a), (42b), and (42c), I give examples of nouns ending in sonorants or dentals that receive final stress (by case (f)), penultimate stress (by case (bii)), and antepenultimate stress (by case (bi)), respectively.

(42)	(a)	(b)	(c)
	$\overset{1}{A}$brah$\overset{3}{a}$m	amá$\overset{1}{l}$g$\overset{0}{a}$m	m$\overset{1}{o}$dic$\overset{0}{u}$m
	di$\overset{1}{a}$d$\overset{3}{e}$m	dec$\overset{1}{o}$r$\overset{0}{u}$m	m$\overset{1}{a}$rjor$\overset{0}{a}$m
	c$\overset{1}{a}$rdam$\overset{3}{o}$m	c$\overset{3}{a}$rbor$\overset{1}{u}$nd$\overset{0}{u}$m	$\overset{1}{o}$pi$\overset{0}{u}$m
	m$\overset{1}{a}$yh$\overset{3}{e}$m	b$\overset{1}{a}$ls$\overset{0}{a}$m	al$\overset{1}{u}$min$\overset{0}{u}$m
	S$\overset{31}{i}$am	j$\overset{1}{e}$ts$\overset{0}{a}$m	str$\overset{1}{a}$teg$\overset{0}{e}$m
	w$\overset{1}{i}$gw$\overset{3}{a}$m	h$\overset{1}{a}$r$\overset{0}{e}$m	$\overset{1}{i}$di$\overset{0}{o}$m
	c$\overset{1}{a}$rav$\overset{3}{a}$n	Po$\overset{1}{s}$eid$\overset{0}{o}$n	$\overset{1}{a}$li$\overset{0}{e}$n
	m$\overset{1}{a}$rath$\overset{3}{o}$n	W$\overset{3}{a}$uke$\overset{1}{g}$a$\overset{0}{n}$	S$\overset{1}{a}$rac$\overset{0}{e}$n
	p$\overset{1}{a}$rag$\overset{3}{o}$n	W$\overset{1}{i}$sc$\overset{3}{o}$ns$\overset{0}{i}$n	c$\overset{1}{i}$nnam$\overset{0}{o}$n
	s$\overset{1}{a}$mp$\overset{3}{a}$n	B$\overset{1}{y}$r$\overset{3}{o}$n	d$\overset{1}{e}$niz$\overset{0}{e}$n
	$\overset{1}{i}$k$\overset{3}{o}$n	s$\overset{1}{e}$rm$\overset{0}{o}$n	p$\overset{1}{e}$mmic$\overset{0}{a}$n
	Verd$\overset{1}{u}$n	$\overset{1}{E}$d$\overset{0}{e}$n	g$\overset{1}{a}$rris$\overset{0}{o}$n
	s$\overset{1}{a}$mov$\overset{3}{a}$r	$\overset{3}{O}$ct$\overset{1}{o}$b$\overset{0}{e}$r	$\overset{1}{i}$nteg$\overset{0}{e}$r
	m$\overset{1}{e}$taph$\overset{3}{o}$r	att$\overset{1}{a}$ind$\overset{0}{e}$r	c$\overset{1}{a}$lip$\overset{0}{e}$r
	m$\overset{1}{e}$te$\overset{3}{o}$r	sem$\overset{1}{e}$st$\overset{0}{e}$r	$\overset{1}{O}$liv$\overset{0}{e}$r
	$\overset{1}{I}$g$\overset{3}{o}$r	c$\overset{1}{i}$ph$\overset{0}{e}$r	v$\overset{1}{i}$neg$\overset{0}{a}$r
	$\overset{1}{A}$g$\overset{3}{a}$r	m$\overset{1}{a}$n$\overset{0}{o}$r	b$\overset{1}{a}$chel$\overset{0}{o}$r
	guit$\overset{1}{a}$r	sph$\overset{1}{i}$nct$\overset{0}{e}$r	$\overset{1}{i}$dolat$\overset{0}{e}$r
	$\overset{1}{a}$lcoh$\overset{3}{o}$l	ut$\overset{1}{e}$ns$\overset{0}{i}$l	c$\overset{1}{a}$pit$\overset{0}{o}$l
	p$\overset{1}{a}$rall$\overset{3}{e}$l[17]	en$\overset{1}{a}$m$\overset{0}{e}$l	$\overset{1}{a}$rsen$\overset{0}{a}$l
	d$\overset{1}{a}$ffod$\overset{3}{i}$l	app$\overset{1}{a}$r$\overset{0}{e}$l	c$\overset{1}{o}$dic$\overset{0}{i}$l
	gaz$\overset{1}{e}$lle	br$\overset{1}{o}$th$\overset{0}{e}$l	f$\overset{1}{u}$ner$\overset{0}{a}$l

---

[16]Words ending in [ǰ] will be discussed separately below.

[17]The question of whether this word is basically a noun or is deadjectival as a noun is of no importance here. Note that *parallel* has a 1–3 stress whether it is an adjective or a noun. Below, I will show that case (f) must be extended to apply to all major categories, so the fact that *parallel* has the same stress no matter how it is used will be accounted for.

atoll $^{3\,0}$	*mongrel* $^{1\,0}$	*cannibal* $^{1\,0}$
decal $^{1\,3}$	*symbol* $^{1\,0}$	*hospital* $^{1\,0}$
Endicott $^{1\,3}$	*Narragansett* $^{3\,1\,0}$	*Connecticut* $^{1\,0}$
scuttlebutt $^{1\,3}$	*Nantasket* $^{3\,1\,0}$	*idiot* $^{1\,0}$
baccarat $^{1\,3}$	*Pawtucket* $^{3\,1\,0}$	*Lilliput* $^{1\,0}$
savssat $^{1\,3}$	*pilot* $^{1\,0}$	*Titicut* $^{1\,0}$
boycott $^{1\,3}$	*carpet* $^{1\,0}$	*chariot* $^{1\,0}$
duet $^{3\,1}$	*poet* $^{1\,0}$	*cheviot* $^{1\,0}$
Ichabod $^{1\,3}$	*Mohammed* $^{1\,0}$	*Iliad* $^{1\,0}$
katydid $^{1\,3}$	*bicuspid* $^{1\,0}$	*myriad* $^{1\,3\,0}$
Galahad $^{1\,3}$		*pyramid* $^{1\,0}$
gonad $^{1\,3}$	*druid* $^{1\,0}$	*period* $^{1\,0}$
Nimrod $^{1\,3}$	*David* $^{1\,0}$	*invalid* $^{1\,0}$
nomad $^{1\,3}$	*fluid* $^{1\,0}$	*tabanid* $^{1\,0}$ [18]
sassafrass $^{1\,3}$	*meniscus* $^{1\,0}$	*syllabus* $^{1\,0}$
albatross $^{1\,3}$	*Charybdis* $^{1\,0}$	*rhinoceros* $^{3\,1\,0}$
blunderbuss $^{1\,3}$	*papyrus* $^{1\,0}$	*Priapus* $^{1\,0}$
chaos $^{1\,3}$	*Silas* $^{1\,0}$	*abacus* $^{1\,0}$
abyss ^{1}	*surface* $^{1\,0}$	*genesis* $^{1\,0}$
morass ^{1}	*porpoise* $^{1\,0}$	*animus* $^{1\,0}$
Alcatraz $^{1\,3}$	*Fernandez* $^{1\,0}$	
alveloz $^{1\,3}$	*Ramirez* $^{1\,0}$ [19]	
burkundaz $^{1\,3}$		
topaz $^{1\,3}$		
Suez $^{3\,1}$		
Natchez $^{1\,3}$		
opsimath $^{1\,3}$	*goliath* $^{1\,0}$	*azimuth* $^{1\,0}$
sabbaoth $^{1\,3}$	*behemoth* $^{1\,0}$	*shibboleth* $^{1\,0}$
naprapath $^{1\,3}$		*Elizabeth* $^{1\,0}$
Kurath $^{1\,3}$	*Edith* $^{1\,0}$	
azoth $^{1\,3}$	*bismuth* $^{1\,0}$	
Derleth $^{1\,3}$	*zenith* $^{1\,0}$	

[18]Contrasts with words ending in /d/ are exceedingly rare: most words get final stress. The eleven words I have cited here are the only ones I know of that appear to be stressed by case (b).

[19]I have not been able to find any words ending in /z/ with antepenultimate stress, or any except Spanish names like those cited here which have penultimate stress. Thus, the contrast between cases (b) and (f) seems to be very marginal for voiced dental obstruents.

The contrast in stress between the words in the first column and those in the second two shows that case (b) must be able to disregard final sonorants and dental obstruents. In (43), however, there are no columns that would correspond to (42b) and (42c): all words that end in a nondental obstruent must receive final stress.[20]

(43)

¹handic³ap	¹Bandersn³atch	Mam¹aron³eck
¹lollyp³op	¹tsarev³itch	¹tomah³awk
¹wicki³up		¹Bolshev³ik
¹Carn³ap	¹eldr³itch	¹shamr³ock
¹satr³ap	¹sandw³ich	¹kay³ak
¹beb³op	¹nuth³atch	¹kop³eck
¹Beelzeb³ub		¹pollyw³og
¹shishkab³ob		¹scalaw³ag
¹baob³ab		¹demag³og
¹nab³ob		¹musk³eg
¹Cant³ab		¹shind³ig
¹Ah³ab		¹humb³ug
¹fistic³uff	¹succot³ash	
¹shandyg³aff	¹mackint³osh	
¹Jackend³off	¹balderd³ash	
¹Lak³off	¹Oshk³osh	
¹pont³iff	¹Wab³ash	
¹pilaf	¹goul³ash	
¹Yugosl³av	¹camoufl³age	
¹cytofl³av	³sabot¹age	
¹rotan³ev	¹persifl³age	
¹Neg³ev	gar¹age	
¹Az³ov	³mont¹age	
	³Arp¹ege	

The only remaining consonant-final segment is [ʃ]. There are several puzzling problems connected with this segment.

---

[20]There are a large number of apparent exceptions to this generalization, e.g., ¹Ar⁰ab, ¹cher⁰ub, ¹syr⁰up, ¹hamm⁰ock, ¹hav⁰oc, etc. These words will be treated the same way as the apparent exceptions in fn. 12. Cf. §3.4 below.

₃There are also a number of true exceptions, such as Pass¹a⁰ic, ³Willim¹antic, Pot¹om⁰ac, etc. I will list all exceptions to my final formulation of case (b) in §3.4 below.

First of all, no polysyllabic word ending in $\begin{bmatrix} V \\ -tns \end{bmatrix}$ ǰ] ever has stress on the final syllable—that is, final [ǰ] is always preceded by [ə]. Second, there are alternations between [ǰ] and [ž], which also appear to involve the length of the preceding vowel. Compare the words in (44a) with their alternants in (44b).

(44)　(a) *mùcilàge* [myûwslàž] (b) *mùsilàge*　[myûwsləǰ]
　　　　prèstìge [prestīyž]　　*prèstìgious* [prèstíǰəs]²¹

Finally, there are no final sequences of the form *[...əž], which strongly suggests that, in final position at least, [ž] and [ǰ] are realizations of the same underlying segment. But which of the two is basic and under what conditions the more basic segment is converted to the less basic²² are problems that I have not solved and can only indicate here. Thus, the revision of the environment for case (b) that I will propose below will not account for stress contrasts like those between *pìlgrimàge* and *advántàge*, although on the face of it, it would seem that this contrast is a paradigm example of case (b) at work.

To sum up, then, the contrast in stress between (38) and (40) indicates that, with the exception of words ending in the six clusters in (39), any noun ending in a consonant cluster must receive final stress by case (f) of the MSR. Furthermore, all words that end in nondental obstruents must also be stressed by case (f), as the contrast in stress between (42) and (43) shows. That is, stress in nouns is only un-

²¹I am grateful to James D. McCawley for calling this example to my attention. Note that though the quality of the stressed syllable of *prèstìgious* would suggest an underlying form /prestīž/, this form would produce the incorrect [prèstáyž] if the vowel shift were allowed to apply to this word. As far as I know, there are no words in English containing the phonetic subsequences *[... āy$\begin{Bmatrix} ž \\ š \end{Bmatrix}$ ...] or *[... āw$\begin{Bmatrix} ž \\ š \end{Bmatrix}$ ...], which suggests that the Vowel Shift Rule must be prevented from applying before palatal continuants for some totally mysterious reason.

²²More precisely, the fact that [ž] appears when *mucilage* has tertiary stress on the final vowel, whereas [ǰ] appears when the final vowel bears no stress, is related to the stress differences between these two variant pronunciations; however, it is not clear what accounts for the stress alternations. For some tentative suggestions, cf. the discussion of *adjective* in §7.1.

predictable when the noun ends in the sounds informally characterized in (45).

$$(45) \quad \left\{ \begin{array}{l} \left[\begin{array}{l} \left[\left\{ \begin{array}{l} [\text{-obs}] \end{array} \right\} \right]^1 \\ \left\{ \begin{array}{l} \left[\begin{array}{l} +\text{cor} \\ +\text{ant} \end{array} \right] \end{array} \right\} \end{array} \right]_1 \\ \left\{ \begin{array}{l} s \\ r \\ n \end{array} \right\} t \\ \quad r \left\{ \begin{array}{l} d \\ n \end{array} \right\} \\ \left\{ \begin{array}{l} n \\ t \end{array} \right\} s \end{array} \right\}$$

In the following, for ease of exposition, I will refer to this unnatural and cumbersome class with the symbol "C_b." It designates that word-final class of sounds to which case (b) can apply to assign nonfinal stress in nouns. For nouns ending in anything but C_b, final stress is mandatory. Therefore, the unpredictability of stress that I called attention to above in the case of *Oregon* can be limited to those nouns which end in C_b, as *Oregon* does. For these nouns, stress must be marked lexically, but for all others it is predictably final. Thus, we must reformulate (41) as (46).

$$(46) \quad - \left[\begin{array}{l} V \\ -\text{tns} \end{array} \right] (C_b) \;]_N$$

C_b must be parenthesized in (46) in order to account for the stress on words like *América*, *Aláska*, *Arizòna*, which end in a lax vowel. Interestingly, no word ending in a lax vowel is ever stressed by case (f), a fact presumably to be accounted for by a redundancy rule. I will return to the topic of redundancy rules in §10.

3.4. Let us now return to the problem of how stress is to be assigned to the large class of words like those in (47).

(47)   wallòp   spinàch   hammòck
       dollòp   buttòck
       Philìp   stomàch
       tròllòp   dèrrick
       stìrrup   hillòck
       sỳrup   Dèrek

sc$\overset{1}{a}$ll$\overset{0}{o}$p		$\overset{1}{E}$r$\overset{0}{i}$k
b$\overset{1}{i}$sh$\overset{0}{o}$p		h$\overset{1}{a}$dd$\overset{0}{o}$ck
h$\overset{1}{y}$ss$\overset{0}{o}$p		c$\overset{1}{a}$ss$\overset{0}{o}$ck
$\overset{1}{A}$r$\overset{0}{a}$b		cr$\overset{1}{a}$nn$\overset{0}{o}$g
ch$\overset{1}{e}$r$\overset{0}{u}$b		
sc$\overset{1}{a}$r$\overset{0}{a}$b		
sh$\overset{1}{e}$r$\overset{0}{i}$ff	r$\overset{1}{a}$d$\overset{0}{i}$sh	
t$\overset{1}{a}$r$\overset{0}{i}$ff	r$\overset{1}{e}$l$\overset{0}{i}$sh	
s$\overset{1}{e}$r$\overset{0}{i}$f	n$\overset{1}{e}$bb$\overset{0}{i}$sh	
$\overset{1}{o}$l$\overset{0}{i}$ve		
c$\overset{1}{o}$l$\overset{0}{u}$mn	m$\overset{1}{o}$n$\overset{0}{a}$rch	ch$\overset{1}{a}$ll$\overset{0}{e}$nge
m$\overset{1}{o}$ll$\overset{0}{u}$sk	$\overset{1}{o}$r$\overset{0}{a}$nge	$\overset{1}{o}$n$\overset{0}{y}$x
d$\overset{1}{a}$m$\overset{0}{a}$sk	l$\overset{1}{o}$z$\overset{0}{e}$nge	L$\overset{1}{e}$n$\overset{0}{o}$x

Note that all these words, since they do not end in C_b, would necessarily receive final stress by case (f). If the ASR were to apply, and then the SAR, the words would all end up incorrectly with 1–3 stress contours, as can be seen from the derivation in (48).

(48)   Underlying form: /æræb/

$$
\begin{array}{ll}
1 & \text{case (f)} \\
1 \ 2 & \text{ASR} \\
1 \ 3 & \text{SAR} \\
*[\overset{1}{æ}r\overset{3}{æ}b] &
\end{array}
$$

In general, such phonetic sequences as [$\overset{1}{æ}$r$\overset{3}{æ}$b] are impossible in English, so I propose to complete the derivation of the correct [$\overset{1}{æ}$r$\overset{0}{ə}$b] by adding a rule of Destressing, which will remove all traces of the original final stress in such words as those in (47), so that their final vowels will reduce. This rule is stated in (49).

(49)   DESTRESSING

$$
\begin{bmatrix} -\text{cns} \\ -\text{tns} \\ \beta \text{ stress} \end{bmatrix} \rightarrow [-\text{stress}] \ / \ \begin{bmatrix} -\text{cns} \\ -\text{tns} \\ \alpha \text{ stress} \end{bmatrix} C_0^1 \text{---}
$$

    where $\alpha > \beta$

This rule can explain the difference in stress contour between M$\overset{1}{i}$ddles$\overset{0}{e}$x and $\overset{0}{E}$ss$\overset{0}{e}$x. Since [ks] is not in C_b, the final syllable, /seks/, of each of these words will receive primary stress. The ASR will then retract this primary stress in both words. At this point, rule (49) will apply to remove the secondary stress on the final syllable of *Éssèx*, since a stressed weak cluster immediately precedes it, but the secondary (ultimately tertiary) stress on the final syllable of *Míddlesèx* will remain.

I have stated rule (49) in such a way that it will not only destress final syllables but also syllables earlier in a word. That this destressing is necessary was pointed out by Paul Kiparsky,[23] who noted that the rule should be made general enough to account for such alternations as those in (50), which were cited in SPE, page 161.

(50) *prèsèntàtion* [prĭyzéntĕyšņ] — *prèsèntàtion* [prĕzņtĕyšņ]
èmèndàtion [ĭyméndĕyšņ] — *èmèndàtion* [ĕmņdĕyšņ]

Assuming that the alternate forms of *present, emend, relax, progress,* and so on, with tense or lax initial vowels, have been accounted for, either by rule or by entering these words with different allomorphs of their prefixes in the lexicon, the contrasts in (50) could be accounted for by rule (49). If the prefix contained a lax vowel at the time rule (49) applied, rule (49) would destress the second vowels of the forms in (50), and the right-hand-column forms would result.

James L. Fidelholtz, in his compendious and important paper "Vowel Reduction in English," was the first to notice the contrasts between such words as those in (51), which provided the original impetus for rule (49).

(51) *Aràb* [ǽrəb]
èyràb [ĕyrǽb]
Càntàb [kǽntǽb]

Working within the framework of SPE, Fidelholtz assumed the version of case (b) stated in (5). Thus, for him, it was not the stress pattern of words like *Aràb* that constituted a problem, but rather that the last syllables of words like *Càntàb* and *èyràb* and those in (25b) were unreduced. Noting that all words with unexplained tertiary stress had strong initial clusters, Fidelholtz proposed a rule that performed the

---

[23]In lectures at MIT in the spring of 1968.

inverse operation of rule (49): it assigned tertiary stress to the final syllable of words whose first syllable was strong.

There are two reasons why I have chosen rule (49) in preference to the solution proposed by Fidelholtz. The first has to do with the definition of C_b. As I argued above, all words that end in a nondental obstruent must receive final stress by case (f). Since *Arab* meets this condition, it should be finally stressed. To modify the definition of C_b so that the sequence /æb/ could be disregarded by the MSR in applying case (b) to such words as *Arab*, but not when applying it to such words as *baobab* and *Cantab*, would produce a highly complicated and unnatural MSR. A second, more important, reason for preferring rule (49) to Fidelholtz's solution is that only the former can account for the 1–0 stress contours of such verbs and adjectives as those in (52):

(52)　(a)　hággàrd
　　　　　hónèst
　　　　　mòdèst
　　　　　mòdèrn
　　　　　sòlèmn
　　　　　stùbbòrn

　　　(b)　chállènge
　　　　　scávènge
　　　　　gòvèrn
　　　　　wàrrànt
　　　　　bàlànce

Since these forms end in strong clusters, case (e) would incorrectly assign final stress, as Chomsky and Halle note on page 162 of SPE. But if the grammar contains rule (49) and an ASR that can shift stress back in disyllables, the 1–3 stress contour that will be produced by the application of the ASR and the SAR to such forms as *solèmn* will be converted to the correct 1–0 contour by rule (49). That is, the derivation of *sòlèmn* would proceed as follows:

(53)　Underlying form:　　/sɔlemn/

1	MSR (eii)
1 2	ASR
1 3	SAR
1 0	Destressing
[sắləm]	Other rules

I thus conclude that rule (49) is to be preferred to the secondary stressing rule proposed by Fidelholtz. Rule (49) is a very general process, but it does, as do almost all rules of English,[24] have a number of exceptions. An exhaustive list of all those I know is given in (54).

(54)　ádult　　　　Chémex　　　húbbub
　　　próduct　　　Krávif　　　sýrinx
　　　prócess　　　azóth　　　larýnx
　　　ánnex　　　Wábash　　　pharýnx
　　　Athól　　　hiccóugh　　cómment
　　　autópsy　　　áffix

3.5. To give some idea of how successful the set of rules, including the modified version of case (b) stated in (46), case (f), and Destressing, is in accounting for the facts of primary-stress placement, I have given in (55) an exhaustive list of all nouns that these three rules assign incorrect stress contours to. Any noun that does not end in C_b but that has an unstressed final syllable not preceded by a weak cluster is an exception.

(55)　Róderick　　Jácob　　Égypt　　wórship
　　　máverick　　Ísaac　　báiliff　　túrnip
　　　límerick　　Cáleb　　pláintiff　Dúnlop
　　　Potómac　　Jóseph　tulip　　Nórthrop
　　　phóenix　　Énoch　　júlep　　Wínthrop
　　　Nátick　　eúnuch　cátsup　　Nórfolk
　　　fórceps

To be sure, this number of exceptions is not negligible, but the number of nouns whose stress contours are correctly accounted for by restricting C_b to sonorants and dentals is many times this list, so I will provisionally assume that the definition of C_b given in (45) is a linguistically significant one, and I will incorporate it into the reformulation of the MSR that I will propose in §10.

4. Consequences of Case (f)

4.1. The addition of case (f) to the MSR occasions a number of other changes in the MSR. First of all, let us re-

[24]Exceedingly important for the theory of grammar is the fact that some phonological rules, such as the rule that tenses vowels prevocalically and the related rule of glide insertion, have *no* exceptions. I will explore some consequences of this constraint in a forthcoming paper, "English Vowel Non-sequences."

examine a possible simplification that was considered but rejected in SPE. It concerns the possibility of collapsing cases (a) and (b). On page 81 of SPE, Chomsky and Halle say (I have used square brackets for my own parenthetical comments),

The similarity of these examples [adjectives with suffixes like those given in (8) above—JRR] to those of (18) [verbs like (1) above—JRR] (24) [nouns like (4) above—JRR] and (42) [adjectives like (7) above— JRR] is evident, and we therefore would naturally expect that the Main Stress Rule (25) [like my rule (6)—JRR] would account for [these examples] with at most minor modifications. Notice, in fact, that rule (25) would account for these examples directly if we were to extend condition (b) of (25) [= case (b)] to adjectives as well as nouns. We cannot simply do this, however, for consider the effect on the examples of (42), in particular those of column III. [These are the words *absurd, corrupt, immense, abstract, robust, overt, august, succinct, occult, direct.*] If these are assigned stress by the noun rule (25b), stress will fall on the first syllable.[29] [Footnote 29 deals with adjectives like *honest, modern,* and *haggard,* and proposes to label them as exceptions to the MSR, since they end up with initial stress, despite the fact that they end in a strong cluster. But, as I argued above, if my rule (49) is in the grammar, such adjectives become regular. —JRR] Similarly, the examples of column IV of (42) [consisting of the words *manifest, resolute, derelict, difficult, moribund, comatose, saturnine, retrograde, lach- rymose, erudite*] with final double consonant require the verb rule (25e) [= case (e)], rather than the noun rule (25b), to account for the tertiary stress on the final syllable.

We conclude, then, that the adjectives of (43) [adjectives with suffixes, like those in (8) above] are subject to the noun rule, while those of (42) are not. The basis for the distinction of these two classes is evident: the examples of (42) are primary adjectives, unanalyzable into stem plus adjectival suffix, while those of (43) are secondary adjectives, formed by adding a suffix to a stem. Thus primary adjectives are assigned stress by the verb rule (25e), while secondary adjectives are assigned stress by the noun rule (25b).

Thus, Chomsky and Halle reject the possibility of allowing the environment of case (b) to be stated so that it will apply to adjectives as well as to nouns, as in (56),

$$(56) \quad - \begin{bmatrix} V \\ -tns \end{bmatrix} C_0 \ ]_{NA}$$

because this formulation would allow the derivation of such

incorrect forms as $*s\overset{1}{u}cc\overset{0}{i}nct$, $*\overset{1}{o}cc\overset{0}{u}lt$, $*d\overset{1}{e}rel\overset{0}{i}ct$, $*m\overset{1}{o}rib\overset{0}{u}nd$. But, as I argued in §3.3 above, the C_0 in (56) must be replaced by C_b, as defined in (45); otherwise such incorrectly stressed nouns as $*pr\overset{1}{e}c\overset{0}{i}nct$, $*c\overset{1}{o}b\overset{0}{a}lt$, $*c\overset{1}{a}tar\overset{0}{a}ct$, $*cumm\overset{1}{e}rb\overset{0}{u}nd$ would also result. That is, case (b) of SPE could not be extended to apply to adjectives because the formulation of this case as given in SPE is too inclusive, even for nouns. If C_0 in (56) is replaced by C_b, the true parallel between the stress contours of the adjectives in (57a) and the nouns in (57b) becomes apparent.

(57) (a) $abs\overset{1}{u}rd$ (b) $pet\overset{1}{a}rd$
         $corr\overset{1}{u}pt$ $tr\overset{1}{a}ns\overset{3}{e}pt$
         $imm\overset{1}{e}nse$ $rom\overset{1}{a}nce$
         $abstr\overset{1}{a}ct$ $\overset{1}{i}ns\overset{3}{e}ct$
         $rob\overset{1}{u}st$ $g\overset{1}{y}mn\overset{3}{a}st$
         $ov\overset{1}{e}rt$ $dess\overset{1}{e}rt$
         $aug\overset{1}{u}st$ $rep\overset{1}{a}st$
         $succ\overset{1}{i}nct$ $pr\overset{1}{e}c\overset{3}{i}nct$
         $occ\overset{1}{u}lt$ $res\overset{1}{u}lt$
         $dir\overset{1}{e}ct$ $pr\overset{1}{e}f\overset{3}{e}ct$
         $m\overset{1}{a}nif\overset{3}{e}st$ $\overset{1}{a}nap\overset{3}{e}st$
         $d\overset{1}{e}rel\overset{3}{i}ct$ $\overset{1}{a}nal\overset{3}{e}ct$
         $d\overset{1}{i}ffic\overset{3}{u}lt$ $V\overset{1}{a}nderb\overset{3}{i}lt$
         $m\overset{1}{o}rib\overset{3}{u}nd$ $c\overset{1}{u}mmerb\overset{3}{u}nd$

There is one systematic difference between the adjectives of (57a) and the nouns of (57b): disyllabic adjectives typically do not retract stress by the ASR (cf. §6.6 below for some discussion of this fact), whereas the applicability of the ASR to a disyllabic noun is not generally predictable. Otherwise, however, the generalization for nouns and adjectives is clear: if a noun or an adjective does not end in C_b, final stress is mandatory.

Thus, it would appear that the argument given in the passage quoted above is invalid and that case (b), amended so as to specify C_b in its environment, can be used to account for the stress of adjectives ending in a suffix, such as those in (8).

Moreover, extending case (b) to all adjectives has an added advantage, for under case (a) there are many adjectives whose stress can only be accounted for by postulating the existence of otherwise unmotivated morpheme boundaries. An example is ádequàte, which must be analyzed /ædV̌kʷ+V̌t/, if case (a) is to apply. And case (a) would have to be the case of the MSR that is operating here, for, if case (e) were to apply, the incorrect *adèquàte would be produced. Thus, the stress contrast between ádequàte and decrèpìt is only accountable for, under the analysis proposed in SPE, by the device of assuming a morphological analysis for the former, but not for the latter, word. This proposal again amounts to marking stress with the symbol "+," a device I consider no more justifiable for the pair àdequàte–decrèpìt than for the stress difference between the nouns in (17) and those in (18). Moreover, I believe that in both cases it is possible to give a more satisfactory analysis of the stress difference than the one proposed in SPE.[25] I will, however, defer this reanalysis until I have taken up the matter of how verbs are to be stressed, which will be the topic of §4.3 below.

Notice also that the device of assuming an otherwise unmotivated morpheme boundary, as in *adequate*, must be resorted to in a large number of cases. Some examples are given in (58).

(58)   (a) *accurate, profligate, intricate, adequate, obstinate*

     (b) *impudent, indigent, succulent, patient, salient, feculent, esculent, diligent, exigent, cogent, ancient, opulent, sapient, l a m b e n t, imminent, immanent, decent, recent, strident, lenient, prurient, esurient, silent, truculent, latent, patent, renitent, frequent*

     (c) *stagnant, pregnant, m e n d i c a n t, extravagant, arrogant, insouciant, brilliant, flamboyant, poi-*

---

[25]Aside from the fact that the analysis in SPE must rely on ad hoc morpheme boundaries to assign stress correctly to such words as *adequate*, there are two fairly clear cases where what seem to be well-motivated morpheme boundaries must be disregarded, in order to prevent case (a) from incorrectly assigning antepenultimate stress: the words illícit (cf. *license*) and explícit (cf. *explicate*). It cannot be maintained that stress can never be placed on the prefixes *in-* and *ex-* as a result of some special following boundary, because of such words as impòtent and èxquisìte, where stress does appear on these prefixes. In §4.3, I will suggest reasons for positing /in+lı̄k+ite/ as the underlying form for *illicit*, where the final /e/ will cause the tense underlying /ı̄/ in the stem to lax before dropping.

gnant, exuberant, flagrant, fragrant, reluctant, truant

(d) *obstreperous, papaverous, nidorous, ubiquitous, furfurous, sedulous, orgulous, invidious, insidious, punctilious, egregious, fastidious, pernicious, precarious, nefarious, copious, impetuous, deciduous, arduous, indigenous, serious, hideous, vicarious, deleterious, s p u r i o u s, surreptitious, p r e v i o u s, lascivious, meticulous, boisterous, exiguous*

(e) *gordian, quotidian, ogygian, permian, alburnian, riparian, milesian, lacertian, cerulean*

It seems to me to be totally gratuitous to assume that English speakers must analyze the words in (58) into stem + affix in order to determine their stress. Rather, the correct generalization about stress on adjectives appears to be that stated in (59).

(59)   All adjectives ending in $\begin{bmatrix} V \\ \text{-tns} \end{bmatrix} \begin{Bmatrix} [\text{-obs}] \\ s \\ (n)t \end{Bmatrix}$ are stressed

by case (b). All others receive final stress.

4.2. Thus, (59) suggests that case (b) should be formulated to apply to both nouns and adjectives, although in slightly different ways. For nouns whose final vowel is lax, those which end in a sonorant or *any* dental (and the clusters specified in (45)) can be non-finally stressed. For adjectives whose final vowel is lax, only a subset of the dentals, namely, /s/ and /t/ and the single cluster /nt/, can be disregarded in assigning nonfinal stress by case (b). Furthermore, while stress is not predictable for nouns ending in $\begin{bmatrix} V \\ \text{-tns} \end{bmatrix}$ (C$_b$), if an adjective ends in a permitted group, stress is never final: the adjective *must* be stressed by case (b).[26]

---

[26]I know of only seven real exceptions to (59) (but cf. (62) below): the adjectives *bizarre, remiss, parallel, intent, content, nonchalant,* and *wayward.* The stress on the first three words will presumably have to be lexically marked. The analysis of *parallel* into [pæræ[lel]$_S$]$_A$, which is proposed on p. 101, is not independently justifiable, as far as I know. Thus, the stress contour on this word must be regarded as irregular.

There are three large classes of adjectives that constitute apparent

To see that the only consonant cluster that can be disregarded in adjectives by case (b) is /nt/, as in the forms in (58b) and (58c), compare the nouns in (40b) and (40c), which have nonfinal stress, with the adjectives in (60), which all must have been stressed by case (f).

(60) $\overset{1}{\text{m}}\text{a}\text{ni}\overset{3}{\text{fe}}\text{st}$, $\overset{3}{\text{r}}\text{o}\overset{1}{\text{bu}}\text{st}$, $\overset{3}{\text{a}}\text{u}\overset{1}{\text{gu}}\text{st}$, $\text{agh}\overset{1}{\text{a}}\text{st}$
   $\text{in}\overset{1}{\text{e}}\text{rt}$, $\text{al}\overset{1}{\text{e}}\text{rt}$, $\overset{1}{\text{m}}\text{ala}\overset{3}{\text{pe}}\text{rt}^{27}$
   $\overset{1}{\text{t}}\text{aci}\overset{3}{\text{tu}}\text{rn}$,^{27} $\overset{3}{\text{f}}\text{or}\overset{1}{\text{lo}}\text{rn}$
   $\text{abs}\overset{1}{\text{u}}\text{rd}$

As was pointed out in §3.4 above, the words in (61) constitute only apparent counterexamples to (59), for rule (49), Destressing, would remove all stress on the final syllable, if case (f) and the ASR had applied.

(61) $\overset{1}{\text{m}}\text{o}\overset{0}{\text{de}}\text{st}$, $\text{h}\overset{1}{\text{o}}\text{n}\overset{0}{\text{e}}\text{st}$
   $\overset{1}{\text{m}}\text{o}\overset{0}{\text{de}}\text{rn}$, $\overset{1}{\text{a}}\text{z}\overset{0}{\text{u}}\text{rn}$, $\text{st}\overset{1}{\text{u}}\text{b}\overset{0}{\text{bo}}\text{rn}$, $\overset{1}{\text{a}}\text{u}\overset{0}{\text{bu}}\text{rn}$
   $\overset{1}{\text{h}}\text{a}\overset{0}{\text{gga}}\text{rd}$
   $\overset{1}{\text{l}}\text{a}\overset{0}{\text{vi}}\text{sh}$

The five words in (62) are also not accounted for by (59) and rule (49),

(62) (a) $\overset{1}{\text{f}}\text{o}\text{rw}\overset{0}{\text{a}}\text{rd}$, $\overset{1}{\text{a}}\text{wkw}\overset{0}{\text{a}}\text{rd}$, $\text{st}\overset{1}{\text{a}}\text{lw}\overset{0}{\text{a}}\text{rt}$
   (b) $\overset{1}{\text{e}}\text{arn}\overset{0}{\text{e}}\text{st}$, $\text{p}\overset{1}{\text{e}}\text{rf}\overset{0}{\text{e}}\text{ct}$

but it may be possible to amend rule (49), so that vowels will be destressed if an optional glide follows the C_0^1 specified in the rule, and to order rule (49) after the rule that converts the sequence /crC/ to the sequence [ɝC]. If the first possibility can be realized, the words in (62a) will cease to be exceptional, and if the suggested rule ordering can be maintained, the words in (62b) will no longer be exceptional. However, I have not studied the wider implications of these revisions enough to know whether they will cause complica-

---

counterexamples to (59)—adjectives in *-ic*, *-id*, and *-ive*. I would concur with Chomsky and Halle in deriving the suffix *-ic* from an underlying /ik+æl/ (cf. p. 88). Below, in §4.3, I will attempt to justify deriving *-id* from a disyllabic underlying representation. In §7.1 I will take up the difficult matter of how adjectives in *-ive* are to be stressed, in connection with the discussion of case (c).

[27]I assume that the final syllables of the words *malapert* and *taciturn* must have some stress, because the consonants preceding them are aspirated, which only happens pretonically.

tions elsewhere. In any case, the number of exceptions to (59) is very small.

If I have been correct in arguing that (59) is the correct generalization for stress in adjectives, then cases (a) and (b) of the MSR need not be distinguished, except insofar as the classes of final consonants that can be disregarded in assigning nonfinal stress to the two categories are not the same. The fact that C_b for adjectives—that is, the class of sounds specified in (59)—is a subset of C_b for nouns (I will designate these classes as $C_b(A)$ and $C_b(N)$, respectively) is specifiable with the help of the angled bracket notation. I will defer a formal statement of this regularity until §4.4 below. The fact that SPE specifies that affixes beginning with a consonant can be disregarded in applying case (a) (to produce $est\overset{1}{a}blishm\overset{0}{e}nt$, etc.) will be discussed in §8. This apparent difference between cases (a) and (b) can thus be sidestepped, and the two cases collapsed.

But what of the stress on nouns ending in affixes, such as those in (63)?

(63) (a) $inh\overset{1}{e}rit\overset{0}{a}nce$ (b) $contr\overset{1}{i}v\overset{0}{a}nce$ (c) $indep\overset{1}{e}nd\overset{0}{e}nce$
     $b\overset{1}{u}ri\overset{0}{a}l$ $betr\overset{1}{a}yal$ $transf\overset{1}{e}rr\overset{0}{a}l$[28]
     $oppr\overset{1}{o}bri\overset{0}{u}m$ $dec\overset{1}{o}rum$ $add\overset{1}{e}nd\overset{0}{u}m$
     $gr\overset{1}{a}di\overset{0}{e}nt$ $opp\overset{1}{o}n\overset{0}{e}nt$ $corresp\overset{1}{o}nd\overset{0}{e}nt$
     $l\overset{1}{u}bric\overset{0}{a}nt$ $ass\overset{1}{a}il\overset{0}{a}nt$ $def\overset{1}{e}nd\overset{0}{a}nt$
     $reb\overset{1}{e}lli\overset{0}{o}n$
     $serv\overset{1}{i}lit\overset{0}{y}$

All the words in (63) end in $C_b(N)$, and all must be assigned stress by case (b). Apparently, stress is never final, although

---

[28]The noun-forming affix *-al* raises some problems of considerable theoretical interest. Apparently it can only occur after the *phonetic* sequence $\begin{bmatrix} \begin{bmatrix} +voc \\ +stress \end{bmatrix} \left(\begin{bmatrix} -voc \\ -cns \end{bmatrix} \right) [+cns]_0^1 \end{bmatrix}$ (that is, there are words like $betr\overset{1}{o}th\overset{0}{a}l$, $ref\overset{1}{u}s\overset{0}{a}l$, $betr\overset{1}{a}y\overset{0}{a}l$, $disav\overset{1}{o}w\overset{0}{a}l$, $acqu\overset{1}{i}tt\overset{0}{a}l$, $dism\overset{1}{i}ss\overset{0}{a}l$, $reb\overset{1}{u}tt\overset{0}{a}l$, $ref\overset{1}{e}rr\overset{0}{a}l$, etc., but none like $*acc\overset{1}{e}pt\overset{0}{a}l$, $*res\overset{1}{i}stal$, $*conv\overset{1}{i}nceal$, $*f\overset{1}{i}dget\overset{0}{a}l$, $*pr\overset{1}{o}miss\overset{0}{a}l$, $*ab\overset{1}{a}ndonal$, $*dev\overset{1}{e}lopal$, etc. The only exceptions to this generalization that I have in my dialect are the words *rental*, *reversal*, *dispersal*, and *rehearsal*). This situation suggests either that the affix must be added to a word after stress has been assigned (in fact, if *dismiss* and *rebut* can be argued to end in geminate obstruents, it cannot be added before the rule of Cluster Simplification), or that there must be phonetic output conditions on the well-formedness of words. I will return to this interesting topic in §9.

it is not in general predictable whether a noun that ends in $C_b(N)$ will be stressed finally or nonfinally (witness the contrasts in (40)), if the noun ends in an affix containing a lax vowel.[29] Since this generalization can be captured in a redundancy rule, I propose to dispense with case (a) altogether. Thus, in Part II, where the MSR will be given its final formulation, I will make no mention of affixes. The redundancy rule will also be stated in Part II.

4.3. Let us now reconsider the problem of how verbs are to be assigned primary stress. Chomsky and Halle have proposed that the MSR should assign either penultimate or final stress to all verbs, and have formulated in case (e) (cf. (2) above) a rule that will have this effect. They thus claim that, although nouns may have stress assigned on any one of the last three syllables, verbs may not be stressed on the antepenultimate syllable.

There are two fairly clear counterexamples to this claim—the verbs *j$\overset{1}{e}$ttis$\overset{0}{o}$n* and *m$\overset{1}{o}$nit$\overset{0}{o}$r*. Even if it can be maintained that the last verb is denominal, a possibility for which there seems to be no independent evidence, no such possibility exists for *j$\overset{1}{e}$ttis$\overset{0}{o}$n*. These examples suggest that case (b) should be extended to stress all major categories. That is, just as the nouns in (64b) and (64c), by virtue of the strong syllables in their penults, receive penultimate, instead of antepenultimate, stress, so the verbs in (65b) and (65c) receive penultimate stress.

(64) (a) *v$\overset{1}{e}$nis$\overset{0}{o}$n*   (b) *hor$\overset{1}{i}$z$\overset{0}{o}$n*   (c) *phlog$\overset{1}{i}$st$\overset{0}{o}$n*
      $\overset{1}{i}$nteg$\overset{0}{e}$r   *Oct$\overset{1}{o}$b$\overset{0}{e}$r*   *Sept$\overset{3}{e}$mb$\overset{0}{e}$r*
      $\overset{1}{a}$rsen$\overset{0}{a}$l   *adr$\overset{1}{e}$n$\overset{0}{a}$l*   *ut$\overset{1}{e}$ns$\overset{0}{i}$l*
      m$\overset{1}{o}$dic$\overset{0}{u}$m   *dec$\overset{1}{o}$r$\overset{0}{u}$m*   *memor$\overset{1}{a}$nd$\overset{0}{u}$m*

(65) (a) *j$\overset{1}{e}$ttis$\overset{0}{o}$n*   (b) *embl$\overset{1}{a}$z$\overset{0}{o}$n*   (c) *ab$\overset{1}{a}$nd$\overset{0}{o}$n*
                                                        det$\overset{1}{e}$rm$\overset{0}{i}$ne

          m$\overset{1}{o}$nit$\overset{0}{o}$r   *man$\overset{1}{e}$uv$\overset{0}{e}$r*   *rem$\overset{1}{e}$mb$\overset{0}{e}$r*
                                  reconn$\overset{1}{o}$it$\overset{0}{e}$r

                                  inv$\overset{1}{e}$igl$\overset{0}{e}$
                                  bamb$\overset{1}{o}$ozl$\overset{0}{e}$

[29]There are very few exceptions to this claim. The word *pr$\overset{1}{o}$test$\overset{0}{a}$nt*, which probably is one, will be discussed in §7.1. Furthermore, there are certain affixes, such as *-on*, which sometimes bear stress (cf. *phen$\overset{1}{o}$men$\overset{3}{o}$n*, *el$\overset{1}{e}$ctr$\overset{3}{o}$n* [the derivation of the stress contour on this word will be discussed in §7.1]).

The above examples suggest that case (b) is applicable to verbs (immediately below I will argue that there are many more verbs with the antepenultimate stress than one would expect if this case of the MSR applied to verbs), and, since adjectives can be stressed by case (b) (*indigent*, *familiar*, etc.) or by case (f) (*bizàrre*, *agòg*), one might also expect to find verbs that receive their stress by case (f). In fact, many such verbs exist. A sample is given in (66).

(66)

(a)

equíp	*abèt*	*amàss*	*àmbùsh*	*attàck*
kìdnàp	*abùt*	*carèss*		*rànsàck*
hòbnòb	*rebùt*	*haràss*		*hìghjàck*
demòb	*regrèt*	*possèss*		*bùshwhàck*
	forgèt	*embòss*		*renège*
	acquìt	*nonplùs*		*pèttyfòg*
	omìt	*redrèss*		*lòllygàg*
	combàt	*surpàss*		
	revèt	*dehìsce*		
	besèt			
	bòycòtt			
	maràud			

(b)

succùmb	*begìn*	*rebèl*	*avèr*
		excèl	*demùr*
		appàl	*intèr*
		càterwàul	*detèr*

Unless these verbs were to be derived from underlying forms containing a geminate final cluster, an analysis for which no independent evidence exists (except possibly for *rebut*—cf. fn. 28), case (e) would incorrectly assign penultimate stress to them. However, if case (f) is extended to apply to verbs, as well as to nouns and adjectives, primary stress can be correctly placed on the final syllable. The ASR will then regularly retract the stress on the three verbs *càterwàul*, *lòllygàg*, and *pèttyfòg*, and will apply exceptionally to a small set of disyllabic verbs like *ambush* and *bushwhack* to retract their stress as well. These verbs will have to be lexically marked, for, as is the case with disyllabic adjectives, stress is normally not retracted in disyllabic verbs (cf. (95) below).[30]

---

[30] I propose that the two pronunciations of the verb *harass*, i.e., [hə̀ǽs] and [hǽrə̀s], be accounted for, not by assuming an underlying final geminate for the first, although not for the second pronunciation

We have seen, then, that the verbs in (66) can be stressed by case (f) and those in (65) by case (b). Why must there be a case (e) at all? Verbs that end in strong clusters, like *cajóle* and *lamént*, can be stressed by case (f), instead of by case (e), and it could be argued that disyllabic verbs with 1–0 stress contours, like those in (67),

(67) góssip   crédit   prómise   vánish   frólic
      wállop   édit   ménace   fínish   róllick
      gállop   fídget   préface   rélish
               cóvet   sólace   mánage
               plúmmet   prémise
               vísit
               pívot
               mérit
               vómit
               prófit
               límit

should be derived not by case (e), but by the sequence case (f)–ASR–Destressing.

There is, however, a class of words that seems to require the retention of case (e): verbs with more than two syllables whose penult, though containing a weak cluster, bears main stress. Examples of this type of verb appear in (68).

(68)

(a) develóp   inhábit   embárrass   admónish
    envelóp   cohábit   dimínish
               inhíbit   embéllish
               exhíbit   estáblish
               prohíbit   abólish
               inhérit   demólish
               solícit   replénish
               elícit   dispárage
               depósit

(this is the analysis proposed by Chomsky and Halle on p. 46), but rather by assuming that the ASR may optionally retract the stress on this verb. Case (f) will assign final stress, and, if the ASR does not apply, the first pronunciation results. If, however, the ASR does apply, the intermediate form [hǽrǽs] will result. But rule (49), Destressing, will now apply, and the secondary stress on the second vowel will be removed, eventually causing it to reduce to [ə].

John Robert Ross

(b)   imȧgine
                 exȧmine

                 endeavȯr
                 considėr

If the verbs in (68) were to be stressed by case (b),
as formulated in SPE, such incorrect forms as *dèvelòp,
*èxhibìt, and *àbolìsh would result. Alternatively, if case (f)
were to apply, the ASR would retract the stress to the antepenult, not to the penult, and such incorrect forms as
*dèvelòp, *èxhibìt, and *àbolìsh would result. To be sure,
if stress could somehow be blocked from retracting to the
antepenult and could be retracted instead to the penult, Destressing would cause the final vowels to reduce, but there
appears to be no general way to make the ASR perform in
this way.[31] Thus, the words in (68) seem to justify case (e)
of the MSR.

However, there are other facts that invalidate this conclusion. Since I have proposed to allow verbs to be stressed
either by case (b) or by case (f), and since I have shown that
the choice of case to be used in stressing nouns and adjectives
is phonologically determined—that is, only a noun or an
adjective ending in $C_b(N)$ or $C_b(A)$ can be stressed by
case (b)—it is natural to enquire whether there is not also
phonological conditioning in the choice of which of these cases
to apply in stressing verbs. The verbs in (65), which show
most clearly that case (b) can apply to verbs, all end in
sonorants. By and large, every verb that ends in a lax vowel
followed by a single sonorant must receive nonfinal stress
by the MSR. There are ten counterexamples cited in (66b),
which constitute an exhaustive list, to the best of my knowledge. In contrast, there are hundreds of verbs like *gambol,
chatter, blossom,* and *cotton (to)* that conform to this generalization and show it to be an important one. Thus, $C_b(V)$
seems to include the class of sonorants, as do $C_b(N)$ and $C_b(A)$.

However, there are apparently no final clusters in $C_b(V)$.
For convenience, I have relisted in (69) the clusters in $C_b(N)$.

(69)   *st, rt, nt, rd, rn, ns, ts*

[31]Words like *Achilles* and *neosynephrine,* in which such a retraction
must take place, appear to be real exceptions to the ASR. They will be
discussed in connection with this rule, in § 5.3 below.

As the examples in (70) show, any verb ending in one of these clusters must receive final stress by the MSR.[32]

(70)

mol$\overset{1}{e}$st	des$\overset{1}{e}$rt	lam$\overset{1}{e}$nt	rew$\overset{1}{a}$rd	ad$\overset{1}{o}$rn	inc$\overset{1}{e}$nse
acc$\overset{1}{o}$st	cav$\overset{1}{o}$rt	rep$\overset{1}{e}$nt	aff$\overset{1}{o}$rd	adj$\overset{1}{o}$urn	cond$\overset{1}{e}$nse
fl$\overset{1}{a}$bberg$\overset{3}{a}$st	res$\overset{1}{o}$rt	rec$\overset{1}{a}$nt	acc$\overset{1}{o}$rd	ret$\overset{1}{u}$rn	disp$\overset{1}{e}$nse
arr$\overset{1}{e}$st	ex$\overset{1}{e}$rt	rel$\overset{1}{e}$nt	aw$\overset{1}{a}$rd		r$\overset{1}{e}$comp$\overset{3}{e}$nse
	ret$\overset{1}{o}$rt	affr$\overset{1}{o}$nt	reg$\overset{1}{a}$rd		enh$\overset{1}{a}$nce
	disp$\overset{1}{o}$rt	torm$\overset{1}{e}$nt	ret$\overset{1}{a}$rd		fin$\overset{1}{a}$nce
	esc$\overset{1}{o}$rt	fragm$\overset{1}{e}$nt	rec$\overset{1}{o}$rd		adv$\overset{1}{a}$nce
	ass$\overset{1}{e}$rt	segm$\overset{1}{e}$nt	bomb$\overset{1}{a}$rd		comm$\overset{1}{e}$nce
	dep$\overset{1}{a}$rt	g$\overset{1}{a}$lliv$\overset{3}{a}$nt			ev$\overset{1}{i}$nce
					conv$\overset{1}{i}$nce
					ensc$\overset{1}{o}\overset{0}{n}$ce

Thus, not even the single cluster that can be disregarded when assigning nonfinal stress to adjectives, the cluster /nt/, can be disregarded when stressing verbs. I also think it can be argued that not even the two obstruents /s/ and /t/, which are the only two in $C_b(A)$, can be disregarded if they occur at the end of a verb. That is, I believe the correct generalization about stress in verbs to be that stated in (71).

(71) Polysyllabic verbs ending in a lax vowel followed by at most a single sonorant are nonfinally stressed; all others receive final stress.

What are the exceptions to this claim, aside from the ten verbs of (66b)? On the one hand, the verbs in (68a), and on the other, those in (72), which cannot be accounted for by the sequence of rules case (f)–ASR–Destressing, because their first syllables contain strong clusters, and Destressing would not be able to apply.

(72)

w$\overset{1}{o}$rsh$\overset{0}{i}$p[33]	qu$\overset{1}{i}$$\overset{0}{e}$t	pr$\overset{1}{a}$ct$\overset{0}{i}$ce	f$\overset{1}{u}$rn$\overset{0}{i}$sh[33]	g$\overset{1}{a}$rn$\overset{0}{i}$sh
	f$\overset{1}{o}$rf$\overset{0}{e}$it	tr$\overset{1}{e}$sp$\overset{0}{a}$ss	b$\overset{1}{u}$rn$\overset{0}{i}$sh[33]	l$\overset{1}{a}$ngu$\overset{0}{i}$sh
		p$\overset{1}{u}$rch$\overset{0}{a}$se[33]	v$\overset{1}{a}$rn$\overset{0}{i}$sh	v$\overset{1}{a}$nqu$\overset{0}{i}$sh
		s$\overset{1}{u}$rf$\overset{0}{a}$ce[33]	br$\overset{1}{a}$nd$\overset{0}{i}$sh	
		s$\overset{1}{e}$rv$\overset{0}{i}$ce[33]	bl$\overset{1}{a}$nd$\overset{0}{i}$sh	
		c$\overset{1}{a}$nv$\overset{0}{a}$ss		

---

[32] I know of only one real exception to this claim—the verb c$\overset{1}{o}$unten$\overset{0}{a}$nce. The verbs of (52b) will be handled by Destressing, as has been indicated above.

[33] As I pointed out in §3.3 above, in connection with adjectives like

There is, however, a further fact about verbs that suggests a way of preserving generalization (71) in the face of these apparent counterexamples: all verbs that end in an obstruent and that have penultimate stress have lax vowels in their penults. That is, there are no verbs like *develop* [dəvíyləp], *solícit* [səlásət], *embárrass* [embéyrəs], *góssip* [gówsəp], *fídget* [fáyjət], and *ménace* [míynəs].[34] Since there are nouns that do not conform to this regularity, such as those in (73),

(73)   *pílot, Tóphet, tóilet, sécret, égret, affidávit, clímate,
       Púget, pírate
       Mídas, Sílas, Vénus, mínus, ónus, Úranus, pénis,
       ánus, bónus, génus, fóetus, fócus, crócus, frácas
       zénith, Édith, behémoth
       Dávid*

it would appear that some rules must be formulated to explain this phonological difference between nouns and verbs.

What I propose is that the verbs in (68a) and (72) be given underlying representations ending in a lax /e/. That is, I assume that *develop* and *menace* are to be derived from /dVvelVpe/ and /menVse/, respectively. Stress will be assigned to the antepenult by case (b), and the independently motivated rule of *e*-Elision (cf. SPE, pp. 45–46) will delete the final vowel.[35] The final /e/ can be used to explain the

---

earnest and *perfect,* these words might not constitute genuine counterexamples to Destressing.

[34]There are only two exceptions to this claim, as far as I know—the verbs *nótice* and *pílot.* If it is correct to analyze the former verb as containing the morpheme *note,* then the long vowel in *notice* is because this morpheme never laxes or reduces (cf. *denotation*). Such verbs as *quíet* and *intúit,* which have long penults, can be analyzed as having short vowels in their underlying representations, with these vowels later being tensed in the environment of a following vowel.

[35]There is an interesting gap in the distribution of final lax vowels in verbs. There are verbs in /i/ (cf. *bury, hurry, harry, marry,* etc.), verbs in /e/ (cf. *allege–allegation, produce–production,* etc.), and verbs in /o/ (cf. *follow, shadow* [note that here, the /d/ is realized as the flap [D], which shows that no stress has been assigned to the final vowel], *borrow, wallow,* etc.). There are no verbs in /u/, but I suspect that there are no nouns in /u/ either, and that examples like *hindu* should come from /hindō/, by case (f) and the ASR, thus assigning a 1–3 stress

absence of long vowels in (68a), for the Trisyllabic Laxing Rule (cf. pp. 180–181) would shorten any underlying long vowel in this position. In fact, there are a few rather marginal cases that suggest that it is this final /e/ which I am proposing that accounts for some lax vowels in verbs that show up in apparently related forms as tense vowels. For example, consider *credit*. Presumably, the underlying morpheme is /krēd/ (cf. *crēdence*, *crēdo*), so somehow this vowel must be shortened in the verb. If an underlying representation like /krēd+ite/ is assumed, the position of stress and the shortening of the vowel are accounted for. Similarly, if *estăblish* is to be related to *stăble*, or *fĭnish* to *fīnal* and *fĭnite*, or *dimĭnish* to *mĭnus* and *mĭnor*, or *pŏsit* to *pōse* and *compŏsite* to *compōse*, all of which seem reasonable, a final /e/ can be used to account for the vowel alternations. The fact that this final vowel does not cause the final /t/ to become [s] in words like *credit*, *inherit*, and *licit* can be accounted for by marking each stem (or possibly just the morpheme (?) /ite/) [-spirantization], or by postulating that the deleted vowel is low, along the lines suggested in footnote 35. I have not come to any decision on this matter.

The above remarks apply in a limited way to adjectives: any penultimately stressed adjective that ends in /V̆d/ or /V̆t/ has a lax vowel in its penult.[36] Thus, adjectives like *decrĕpit*

-----

contour, which to my ear is correct, instead of the 1–0 contour assigned by SPE. I will take up this matter again in §7.6. What is more important is that there are no verbs ending in phonetic [ə], except some clearly denominal verbs like *to samba*, *to rhumba*, *to conga*, and *to subpoena*. I know of no verb ending in [ə] that has no related noun. This gap could be explained by assuming that the rule of *e*-Elision deletes any final nonhigh nonround vowel for verbs (and adjectives, as will be seen shortly, for the facts noted in this footnote hold also for adjectives), while being restricted to deleting only /e/ for nouns. That is, the rule would be stated as the following:

$$\begin{bmatrix} +\text{voc} \\ -\text{tns} \\ -\text{back} \\ -\text{high} \end{bmatrix} \rightarrow \emptyset \bigg/ \left[\underline{\hspace{1.5cm}} \langle -\text{low} \rangle \right] \langle \text{N} \rangle$$

[36]Note that adjectives ending in /s/, the only other obstruent that can be disregarded in applying case (b) to adjectives, do not manifest this property. That is, although there are no verbs (except *notice*) that

[dᵊkrīypᵊt], *tắcit [tḗysᵊt], and *lĭ̄cit [lắysᵊt] do not exist.[37]
All adjectives in *-id* are preceded by a lax vowel, which
Chomsky and Halle note on page 181, footnote 16, of SPE;
I would propose to account for this fact by representing *-id*
as /ide/ in underlying representations. Thus, in my analysis,
the stress difference between *ádequáte* and *decrĕ́pĭt* is not
accounted for by assuming a morphological analysis for the
former, but not for the latter. Rather, I assume the latter to
be derived from the underlying form /dV̆krepV̆te/. My solution seems to be slightly preferable, since it correctly excludes such forms as **decrĕ̱́pĭt*, but not much is at stake
here. Similarly, I propose to account for the contrast in
stress between verbs like *fídgĕt* and *abét* by postulating a
final /e/ for the former verb but not for the latter, and by
restricting $C_b(V)$ to sonorants only. Thus, any verb ending in
an obstruent (like those in (66a)) will be stressed by case (f),
while all others will be stressed by case (b).

   I concede that to analyze only certain verbs as ending in
/e/, which will ensure that case (b) will apply, but others
as ending in obstruents, which can only be stressed by
case (f), is little better than the solution proposed in SPE—
that *fidget* and *abet* be entered as /fiǰV̆t/ and /V̆bett/, respectively—but my solution at least has the slight additional virtue
of accounting for the absence of penultimate long stressed
vowels in verbs ending in obstruents, so I will very tentatively
adopt it below.

---

end in [. . . V̄C₀ᵊs], there are a number of adjectives that do. A sample
follows:

decŏ́róus	*hḗinóus*
sonŏ́róus	*pŏ́rous*
desĭ́róus	*fám̆óus*
	vēnóus
	vínóus
	fíbróus
	nītróus
	mŭ́cóus
	bŏ́gus

[37]If the two words *lĭ̆cit* and *līcense* are to be related, as was suggested
in fn. 25, deriving the former from /līs+ite/ will allow the shortening
of the stem vowel to be accounted for by the Tri-syllabic Laxing Rule,
as was the case for verbs like *credit, finish,* etc.

4.4. To recapitulate, I am proposing that cases (a) and (b) of the MSR be merged and that case (e) be dispensed with altogether in favor of an analysis involving the deletion of a final /e/ (or possibly /æ/). All major categories can then be stressed either by case (b) or by case (f), subject to slightly differing conditions as to the phonetic properties of what consonant(s) can be disregarded in applying case (b). For verbs, only sonorants can be disregarded; for adjectives, sonorants and $s, (n)t$; and for nouns, sonorants, dentals, and the clusters specified in (45). Thus, we see that $C_b(V)$ is a subset of $C_b(A)$, which in turn is a subset of $C_b(N)$. This subset relationship can be captured notationally by the device of angle brackets, as I have done in (74), which formally expresses the arguments presented in §3 and §§4.1–4.3 above.

(74)

$$V \rightarrow [1 \text{ stress}] / \underline{\quad} C_0 \left((W) \begin{bmatrix} V \\ -tns \end{bmatrix} \left(\left\langle \left\langle \begin{bmatrix} -obs \end{bmatrix} \\ s \\ (n)t \\ \begin{bmatrix} +cor \\ +ant \end{bmatrix} \\ \begin{Bmatrix} s \\ r \end{Bmatrix} t \\ r \begin{Bmatrix} d \\ n \end{Bmatrix} \\ \begin{Bmatrix} n \\ t \end{Bmatrix} s \right\rangle_a \right\rangle_b^a \right) \right) \left\langle \left\langle N \right\rangle_{b\,a\,a}^{} A \right\rangle_b$$

5. Further Extensions of the Alternating Stress Rule

5.1. In this section, I will take up the problem of completing the modifications of the ASR that were begun in §2 above, where I argued that the ASR must be allowed to apply to disyllables. Consider, for example, the word *piccalĭlli*.

How can the 1–3 stress contour of this word be obtained? If it is entered in the lexicon in its conventional orthographic form, the incorrect **piccalĭlli* will be produced by case (b) and by the rule that assigns secondary stress to words like *Monongahela*, rule [120] in chapter 3 of SPE. If entered as /pV̆kælV̆li/, the incorrect form **[pəkǽləlīy] will result. If entered as /pikælily/, the incorrect *[pìkə̀lə̀lĩy] will result. The only solution possible within the framework of SPE, as far as I can see, is the representation /pikVlill+y/. Case (a) will disregard the /+y/ "affix," assigning [1 stress] to /lill/, and case (d) will then retract the stress. Once again, as was the case with the contrast between (17) and (18), where Chomsky and Halle posit a morphemic analysis for words like *carbine,* but not for *boutique,* so that rule [158] would apply to cause stress retraction only for the former words; or as was the case with the contrast between *adequate* and *decrepit,* the set of rules given in SPE can account for the stress contrast between *pìccalìlli* and *vèrmicèlli* only by assuming a morphemic analysis for the former word, but not for the latter. Other words that would be assumed to be morphologically complex are those in (75a), while those in (75b) and (75c) would have to be analyzed as single morphemes.

(75)   (a) *càssowàry, Tìpperàry, McGìllicùddy, tèstimòny, Àlbuquèrque, àllegòry,*[38] *càtegòry,*[38] *càpillàry,*[39] *Pìccadìlly,*[40] *Mòosilàuke, apòthecàry, tèrritòry, pìckanìnny, mèlanchòly, Àlleghèny, mìscellàny, mèrcenàry, pàrsimòny, cèremòny, àlimòny, Mùngojèrry, jànizàry, àcrimòny*

[38] It might seem plausible to argue that *allegory* must be represented as /ælV̆gɔr+y/, on the basis of the word *allegorical,* which, it could be claimed, must contain the morpheme /ælV̆gɔr/, followed by the affix sequence /ik+æl/. I do not think, however, that this analysis is tenable. Rather, it seems to me that *allegorical* should be derived as follows:

Base form:	/ælV̆gɔri+ik+æl/
Vowel Drop	∅
MSR (b)	1
Rule [120]	2 1
SAR	3 1
Vowel Reduction, etc.	[æ̀ləgɔ̀rəkl̩]

The rule of *Vowel Drop* that I propose would be stated roughly as follows:

$V \rightarrow \phi/VC_0\text{——}+V$

This rule is independently motivated. For example, it can be used to account for alternations like the following:

propaganda-propagandize (from *propagandⱥ+ize*)
cello–cellist (from *cellⱥ+ist* [but why *solo̲ist, oboo̲ist?*])

(b) *Gàrìbáldi, màcaròni, fèttucìni, Àlberghètti, tùttifrùtti, cò/ gnoscènti, Màseràti, Gìacomètti, pèperòni*

(c) *Tàllahàssee, Mìssissìppi, Àssinìppi, Chàttahòotchee, àbalòne, kàmikàze, Cìncinnàti, mùlligatàwny, Tàtamagòuchi, Wìnnipesàukee, Ýpsilànti, sàlmagùndi, Hìndustàni,*[41] *gàllimàufry, Pùnxutàwney*

---

allege –allegation (from /æl₊legǿ+ǣt+iV̆n/)
Africa –African (from /æfrV̆Kǽ+æn/; compare *suburb –suburban*)
Mexico –Mexican (from *Mexicǿ+an*)

There are various complicated restrictions on the operation of this rule—thus, high vowels do not delete before low vowels (cf. *remedy+al* ✶→ *✶remedal; gregory+an* ✶→ *✶gregoran; virtue+al* ✶→ *✶virtal*, etc.), but /i/ does delete before affixes beginning with /i/ (cf. *analogý+ize, analogý+ic, germaný+ism*), though other vowels often do not (cf. *Shintoism, euphuism, Yankeeism*). The whole rule needs much more study, but it seems clear that one or more processes of vowel deletion must be assumed to exist in English. Thus, I see no reason to assume a morphological analysis of words like *allegory*. Precisely the same remarks apply with respect to the word *category*.

[39]As with *allegorical*, I would suggest deriving *capillarity* from /kæpV̆lǣri+iti/, with the rule of Vowel Deletion operating to delete the last vowel of the stem. In other words, I see no reason to assume, merely because of *capillarity*, that *capillary* has any analysis.

[40]I pronounce this word with a 1–3 stress contour, although most dialects have a 3–1 contour. Similarly, some speakers, according to Kenyon and Knott, pronounce *Moosilauke* with a 3–1 stress contour. I will argue immediately below in favor of extending the ASR so that it will retract the stress of words like those in (75a) but not of those in (75b) or (75c). As in other cases involving the ASR, whether this rule applies to a form must be marked lexically. Thus, I would expect to find words like *Piccadilly* or *Moosilauke* being given 1–3 contours by some speakers, but 3–1 contours by others, just as words like *lemonade* and *magazine* can have either contour. Just as I would find it dubious to assert that speakers who say *màgazíne* impose an internal analysis on this word, while speakers who say *màgazìne* do not, I would also find it dubious to make the corresponding claim about the two possible pronunciations of *Moosilauke*. In the case of *magazine*, Chomsky and Halle propose to account for the differing pronunciations by means of a rule feature indicating whether the ASR applies.

(But cf. the alternative proposal involving =, on p. 157.) Why should such a dissimilar device be adopted in the case of words like those in (75)?

[41]Note that this word, although it must obviously be analyzed as being at least trimorphemic (i.e., Hindu+stan+i), cannot be assumed to end in /+y/ within the framework of SPE, because the sequence of rules

The arbitrariness of this proposed way of accounting for the contrast between *piccalilli* and *vermicelli* should be apparent. As was the case with the *carbine–boutique* contrast, and with the *adequate–decrepit* contrast, no facts other than those of stress retraction are accounted for by postulating final $/+y/$ affixes for the words in (75a) but not for those in (75b) and (75c). I therefore propose that the stress contrast of (75) be accounted for by a rule feature, exactly as I proposed for the *carbine–boutique* contrast. As a matter of fact, I propose to use a feature on the same rule, the Alternating Stress Rule. That is, I propose that rule (20) above be reformulated as in (76):

(76) $V \rightarrow [1 \text{ stress}] / \underline{\quad\quad} C_0(=) \; C_0(VC_0) \; \overset{1}{V} \; C_0(i) \; \#$

This rule will not only retract stress in words whose final vowel bears main stress, but also in words that are stressed on the penult when these words end in $/i/$.[42] The forms in (75a) will be marked so that they will undergo rule (76), but those in (75b) and (75c) so that they will not undergo this rule.[43] Note that the traditional orthography uses the nonphonetic distinction between *i* and *y* in a way that roughly corresponds to this rule feature. Thus, words ending in graphic *i* are by and large [-ASR], while words ending in graphic *y* are generally [+ASR].

It is necessary to restrict the final vowel in (76) to $/i/$, for with words ending in other vowels, like $/o/$ and $/æ/$ (graphic *o* and *a*, respectively), no contrasts paralleling those in (75) can be found. That is, all words in *o*, like those in

---

case (a)–case (c) would assign an incorrect 1–3 contour. Rather, it must be assumed to end in $/+i/$. However, such an ad hoc representation must cast further doubt on the claim that stress is retracted in such words as those in (75) only if they are morphologically complex. The same obtains for the obviously trimorphemic word *vigilante*. It must be assumed that this word also ends in $/ti/$, for, if it ended in $/+y/$, an incorrect 1–3 contour would be assigned by case (c).

[42]I have not adopted the device used in SPE of deriving some final $[\text{iy}]$ sequences from an underlying glide $/y/$. The matter is a complex one, however, and I will defer discussion of it until § 7.5.

[43]It will be noted that all the words in (75b) have an Italian "feel" to them. If a morphemic feature [+Italian] could be justified elsewhere in the grammar, which seems not implausible, it would be advantageous to state the following redundancy rule:

[+Italian] → [-ASR]

(77a), and in *a*, like those in (77b), keep main stress on their penults.[44]

(77)　(a)　*Mŏnticèllo, ărmadíllo, pĕccadíllo, Ãmaríllo, ãllegrètto, pĭzzicàto, cĭgaríllo, Amŏntillàdo, mŭmbojùmbo, dĕsperàdo, Ãlamagòrdo*

　　(b)　*Tŭscalòosa, lŏllapalòoza, Cŏnestòga, Ticŏnderòga, Mĭnnesòta, sãrsparílla, Tĕxarkàna, jãcarànda*

Just as rule (20) had to be stated with parentheses in its environment, so that stress would be retracted in disyllables as well as in trisyllables, the revision of this rule, (76), must retain these parentheses, so that the stress contour of such words as *industry* can be derived. Chomsky and Halle propose the underlying representation /industr+y/, with the derivation shown in (78) (cf. p. 134):

(78)　Underlying form　　　　$[\text{industr+y}]_N$

MSR (aii)	1
MSR (cii)	1 2
[118d]	1 0
Other rules	$[\text{ìndə̀striy}]$

Thus, stress retraction by case (c) is only possible because of the morphological analysis assumed for *industry*. Stress retraction in words like *malàrkey* is prevented by assigning them an underlying representation like /mV̌lǽrkĭ/. Other words like *industry*, for which a morphemic analysis would be assumed in order to account for stress retraction, are given in (79a). The words in (79b) and (79c) would, like *malarkey*, be given no analysis.

(79)　(a)　*tràvĕsty, bùrgŭndy, òrgăndy, frùmĕnly, ànchŏvy,[45] chàmpĕrty, Gràmĕrcy (Park), tàpĕstry,*

[44]The inevitable counterexample, in this case, is the word *rutabaga*, which some speakers pronounce with a 1–3 stress contour. Amazingly, I know of no counterexamples to the claim that words in *-o* never exhibit stress retraction.

[45]This word, when pronounced with an unreduced penult, must, like the words *aùtŏpsy* and *bìŏpsy*, be marked as an exception to [118d].

líturgy,[46] állergy,[46] cálumny, Cóventry, Dóugh-erty, Ráfferty, Tímilty, léthargy, Fláherty, Píc-cardy, Hággerty

(b) spúmóni, spághètti, Pírèlli, Lómbàrdi, zúcchini, salámi, bólógna, Róssini, chiánti, Cámpàri, Fèr-rári, pàstràmi, cônfètti, màrtìni

(c) Bílóxi, Zámbèzi, Kéntúcky, Mílwáukee, safári, cúràre, èpóxy, Pèrquáckey, Sewíckley, attórney, górblìmey, jàlópy, Sándúsky, Maràthi, adóbe, tamàle, Salòme, effèndi, cóyòte, Mahóney

If the feature [+Italian] can be justified, the rule suggested in footnote 43 could be used to predict that stress will not be retracted in words like those in (79b), another fact that suggests that the rule retracting stress two syllables and the rule retracting it only one must be the same rule.

Again, it seems to me that the formal device of replacing rule features by arbitrarily inserted morpheme boundaries should not be countenanced on theoretical grounds. In the earliest generative treatment of English stress,[47] Chomsky, Halle, and Lukoff noted that absurd "simplifications" of the phonemic inventory would result if there were no constraints imposed on the location of word boundaries in underlying representations.[48] The constraint they suggested as neces-sary was that all junctures be syntactically justified. I view this constraint as the earliest attempt at formulating "nat-uralness conditions" on underlying representations, in the sense proposed by Postal. Although this constraint is proba-bly too strong as it stands,[49] I think it is basically correct and should only be deviated from in extraordinary circumstances.

---

[46]As I argued above, in fn. 38, I see no reason why such forms as *allergic* and *liturgical* should constitute evidence for the existence of morphemes like /ælV̆rg/ and /litV̆rg/.

[47]Cf. Chomsky, Halle, and Lukoff (1956).

[48]The example they presented was from German, where there is a rule devoicing obstruents before word boundaries. Given this independently necessary rule, if word boundaries can be inserted freely in underlying representations, the contrast in voicing between *Bein* [bayn] 'leg' and *Pein* [payn] 'pain' could be accounted for by deriving the latter form from /b#ayn/.

[49]The well-worn example of *cranberry* is a case in point. Although I know of no syntactic evidence for it, the 1–3, instead of 1–0, stress con-

Incidentally, it must not be thought that the Chomsky-Halle-Lukoff constraint can be restricted to higher-level junctures like word boundaries and that lesser junctures, such as morpheme boundaries, can be inserted with impunity. Imagine a hypothetical language in which proper nouns are stressed unpredictably on one of the last three syllables. That is, suppose the language exhibited such forms as those in (80):

(80) (a) míwori   (b) fakráyseks   (c) pipapó
          stápenšap   yuhúha   wɔnhɔŋló
          húpdidu   pisóvas   yihɔŋgúy

The following rule would "predict" the stress on these forms,

$$(81) \quad V \rightarrow [1 \text{ stress}] / \left[\overline{+\text{Proper}} \right] C_0(+VC_0(+VC_0)) \ ]_N$$

assuming that the forms in (80c) were given no internal analysis, that the forms in (80b) were derived from /fakrays+eks/, /yuhu+ha/, and /pisɔv+as/, and that those in (80a) were all "trimorphemic"—that is, that they derived from /miw+or+i/, /stap+enš+ap/, and /hupd+id+u/. I take this "solution" to be as absurd as /b#ayn/, and I therefore cannot see any general way of exempting morpheme boundaries from the Chomsky-Halle-Lukoff constraint, although in particular cases it may be possible to argue for nonsyntactic morpheme boundaries. I also do not wish to convey the impression that I think this extraordinarily difficult question is closed—it is merely that to discuss it in the detail it deserves would go far beyond the bounds of the present study, so I will not pursue it here.[50] Since SPE accounts for the stress differences between (75a) and (75b,c) and between (79a) and (79b,c) by making use of ad hoc morpheme boundaries, I have rejected this analysis

---

tours of words ending in -*berry* (*raspberry, loganberry, huckleberry,* etc.) and the fact that there is no nasal assimilation in *cranberry* (Kenyon and Knott give [krænberi]) suggest that this form should be represented in the lexicon as /kræn#beri/, with a nonsyntactic interior word boundary.

[50]Morris Halle and I will take up this matter again, in a paper that is now in limbo.

in favor of one expanding the ASR, as in (76), and making use of rule features on this rule.[51]

It may be necessary to revise rule (76) again to account for the stress of the words in (82) and (83).

(82)　(a) íntervàl (cf. ìntervállic)

　　　(b) Áristòtle (cf. Àristotélian)
　　　　pùmperníckel

(83)　(a) mínistèr (cf. mìnistérial)
　　　　cálendàr (cf. càlendárian)

　　　(b) cáuliflòwer[52]
　　　　lámmergèyer[53]
　　　　cáterpìllar

Paul Kiparsky has called to my attention that there is no way for SPE to derive the stress on the noun *filibúster*. If entered /filV̆bustṛ/, case (b) will produce *[fílə̀bə̀stɚ]. If entered /filV̆bustV̆r/, case (b) and rule [120] will produce *[fíləbʌ́stɚ]. Only if C_0 is replaced by C_b can stress be properly assigned.[54] Given the first of the two underlying

---

[51]Noam Chomsky has pointed out to me that, although my contention may be true that it is not *only* words that have a morphemic analysis in which penultimate stress is retracted, it is the case that stress retraction does occur in (almost) all words that *are* morphologically complex. That is, words like *mónàrchy, *órthodòxy, *próərty, and *lóyàlty are impossible. Though I believe Chomsky's claim to be by and large a correct one (but cf. fn. 41), I propose to account for it by stating a redundancy rule on the rule feature [± ASR], making the ASR obligatory for words ending in /+i/ or /+ti/. It seems to me that this solution is theoretically preferable to one involving the insertion of ad hoc morpheme boundaries into the words of (75a) and (79a).

[52]This word must derive from /kɔlV̆flūV̆r/ and not from /kɔlV̆flūr/ for those dialects, like that of Kenyon and Knott, which can distinguish between *flower* ([flawɚ]) and *flour* ([flawr]), because *cauliflower* rhymes with the former word, not with the latter. Assuming that *flower* derives from /flūV̆r/, while *flour* derives simply from /flūr/, the 1–3 stress on /kɔlV̆flūV̆r/ could not be assigned by (76), the modified version of the ASR, or by any other rules in SPE, unless the word were treated as a compound, a solution having no independent support.

[53]A parallel to the discussion in fn. 52: for all dialects that pronounce *Meyer* as [mayɚ] but *mire* as [mayr], where *lammergeyer* rhymes with the former, it must presumably derive from /læmV̆rgīV̆r/.

[54]In line with my belief that the insertion of ad hoc morpheme boundaries (or ad hoc syntactic structure, for that matter) should be excluded

representations above, case (f) will assign final stress (since /str/ is not in C_b), and then the ASR, as formulated in SPE, could apply to assign initial stress. Only if there were independent motivation for assuming the second of the above underlying forms would the ASR need modification. Since I know of no such evidence in the case of *filibuster*, I have cited only the eight forms of (82) and (83), for which I believe it is possible to argue for final $/\breve{V} \left\{ {r \atop l} \right\}/$ sequences in underlying representation.

The word *càterpìllar* cannot be accounted for at all, assuming the inadmissibility of such underlying structures as $/\text{kæ} \begin{bmatrix} \text{t}\breve{V}\text{rp} \\ +D \end{bmatrix} \text{ill}+r/$, which would be assigned the correct stress by case (a) followed by case (c), or $[[\text{kætr}]_N[\text{pilr}]_N]_N$, which could be stressed by the compound rule. If entered as /kætV̆rpillV̆r/, case (b) and rule [120] would produce an incorrect 3-1 stress contour. If entered as /kæterpilr/, case (b) would yield *[kə̀tɚpɔ̀lɚ]. If entered /kætrpilr/, assuming that the first /r/ could somehow be syllabified by a non-ad hoc rule, case (b) would yield *[kæ̀tɚpɔ̀lɚ]. As far as I can see, no other reasonably natural underlying representation will work. The situation is parallel for *pùmpernìckel*.

Slightly more difficult problems arise with the word *Àristòtle*. If entered as /æristɔttel/, case (b) and [120] would produce an incorrect 3-1 contour. If entered as /æristɔtel/, case (b) will produce *[ə̀ristátl̩]. Even if it were entered in the totally unnatural form /æristɔtt+l/, which would require an ad hoc rule of *e*-insertion for the derivation of the adjective *Aristotelian*, the stress rules of SPE would not work. Case (a) would assign [1 stress] to the final vowel, but case (c) would then retract the stress only one syllable, yielding *[ə̀ristátl̩]. The syllable /rist/ could not be automatically assigned the feature [+D]—as is done with the final syllables of the words *legend* and *moment*, so that case (c) will retract

---

on theoretical grounds by the Chomsky-Halle-Lukoff naturalness condition, I would regard as inadmissible proposals for accounting for the stress of *filibuster* that made use of such underlying representations as /filV̆bust+r/, which would yield the correct stress by case (a) and then case (c), or $[\text{fil}\breve{V}[\text{bustr}]_{stem}]_N$ or $[[\text{fil}\breve{V}]_N[\text{bustr}]_N]_N$, etc.

the stress two syllables in $l\overset{1}{e}gend\overset{3}{a}ry$ and $m\overset{1}{o}ment\overset{3}{a}ry$ (cf. pp. 138–139)—because /rist/ does not end in a [-obs][+cns] sequence, as is required by the rule at the bottom of page 138. It would therefore be necessary to mark /rist/ lexically with the feature [+D]—as is done with /sign/, so that $d\overset{1}{e}sign\overset{0}{a}te_N$ can be derived (cf. p. 138, fn. 95)—as well as to create an ad hoc rule of e-insertion, in order for $A\overset{1}{r}ist\overset{3}{o}tle$ to be derived from /æristɔtt+l/.

Admittedly, the forms in (82) and (83) are marginal, but they are easily accounted for if the ASR is modified one further time, so that it allows stress to retract when a final vowel is stressed, or when main stress is on a penult that is followed by the vowel /i/ or by any lax vowel and a liquid. This modification has been carried out in (84).

$$(84) \quad V \rightarrow [1 \text{ stress}] / \underline{\quad} C_0(=)C_0(VC_0)\overset{1}{V}C_0\left(\left\{\begin{matrix} i \\ \overset{\smile}{V} \begin{Bmatrix} r \\ l \end{Bmatrix} \end{matrix}\right\}\right) \#$$

With this modification, the forms $c\overset{1}{a}l\overset{0}{e}nd\overset{0}{a}r$ and $A\overset{1}{r}ist\overset{3}{o}tle$ can be derived from the natural underlying forms /kælendær/[55] and /æristɔttel/, respectively:

(85) Underlying representation: /kælendær/ /æristɔttel/

MSR—case (b)	1	1
ASR	1 2	1 2
SAR	1 3	1 3
[118]	1 0	
Vowel Reduction, etc.	[kǽləndɚ]	[ǽrɘstãtl̩]

The other forms in (82) and (83) will be derived in a similar fashion. Of course, just as the forms in (18) and (20), as well as those in (75b,c) and in (79b,c), must be marked in such a way that the ASR will not apply to them, so the forms in (86b) must be marked [-ASR], in contrast with the [+ASR] forms in (86a).

(86) (a) $b\overset{1}{a}nn\overset{0}{i}ster$ $h\overset{1}{a}berd\overset{3}{a}sher$ $m\overset{1}{o}llyc\overset{3}{o}ddle$
$b\overset{1}{a}rr\overset{0}{i}ster$ $h\overset{1}{e}lic\overset{3}{o}pter$ $p\overset{1}{a}rad\overset{3}{i}ddle$

[55]Note that though *calendar* must be considered to derive from an underlying trisyllabic form, so that *calendarian* can be derived, the form *calendrical* indicates the need for a rule that will drop the final vowel of this morpheme under certain conditions. This matter will be taken up again in § 7.4.

    c¹árp⁰enter   n¹ecrom³ancer t¹arad³iddle
    h¹arb⁰inger   g¹errym³ander
    m¹ess⁰enger   ¹allig³ator
    p¹ass⁰enger   t¹amosh³anter
    c¹ol⁰ander   ¹alab³aster
    c¹yl⁰inder   s¹alam³ander
    d¹err⁰inger   p¹oet³aster
    s¹in⁰ister   kn¹ickerb³ocker

  (b) s⁰em¹ester   ³Eben¹ezer   ⁰ap¹ostle (cf. *apostolic*)
      s⁰equ¹ester   ³Alex¹ander   ⁰ep¹istle (cf. *epistolary*)
      ph⁰il¹ander   ³ol¹eander   sk³ed¹addle
      m³erg¹anser   ³antimac¹assar ⁰ev¹angel
      d⁰is¹aster   f³and¹angle
      p⁰om¹ander   c⁰ath¹edral
      ³Oct¹ober (D⁰ec¹ember, etc.)
      r⁰em¹ember
      c⁰ad¹aver
      p⁰al¹aver
      d⁰ec¹anter
      tr³och¹anter
      p⁰il¹aster
      ch³¹iaster

In addition, it will be necessary to restrict the ASR so that it never retracts stress before the adjectival affix -al: forms like *¹anecd³otal, *d¹ial³ectal, *m¹at⁰ernal, and *³orch⁰estral must be prevented. This restriction can be accomplished by adding a branch containing [-next rule] to (84). I will defer this until the final statement of the ASR, in (88). A better solution will emerge in §7.1.

5.2. Now consider the stress contrast between *dec¹amer³on* and *c¹atamar³an*. Given the underlying representations /dVkæmVrɔn/ and /kætVmVræn/, assigning of original final stress can be ensured by marking each [-case (b)]. Rule (84) will then correctly retract the stress on the first word, but if it is applied to the second, where stress has to be retracted three syllables, it will produce the incorrect *cat¹amar³an*. Note, however, that, while this particular word cannot be pronounced with this contour, such a pronunciation does not sound un-English in the least. Nor does the pronunciation *d⁰ecamer³on*. Thus, I conclude that the ASR must be extended one final time, to allow stress to be retracted three syllables for words like *catamaran*. In the unmarked case, the ASR will only retract the stress two syllables, in a quadrisyllabic word, but it will be possible to mark certain lexical items, like *catamaran* and the other words in (87), in such a way that the ASR will retract their stress three syllables.

(87)   (a) $r\overset{1}{a}zz(a)mat\overset{3}{a}zz$ $r\overset{1}{i}gamar\overset{3}{o}le$
              $th\overset{1}{i}ng(a)mab\overset{3}{o}b$ $f\overset{1}{o}thering\overset{3}{a}y$
              $g\overset{1}{o}bbledyg\overset{3}{o}ok$ $t\overset{1}{o}read\overset{3}{o}r$
              $t\overset{1}{a}camah\overset{3}{a}c$
              $h\overset{1}{o}bbledeh\overset{3}{o}y$

      (b) $\overset{1}{i}diol\overset{3}{e}ct$ ($\overset{1}{i}deogr\overset{3}{a}m$, $\overset{1}{i}deogr\overset{3}{a}ph$, etc.)
              $h\overset{1}{e}liotr\overset{3}{o}pe$ ($h\overset{1}{e}liosc\overset{3}{o}pe$, $h\overset{1}{e}liogr\overset{3}{a}ph$, etc.)
              $h\overset{1}{e}terocl\overset{3}{i}te$ ($h\overset{1}{e}teron\overset{3}{y}m$, $h\overset{1}{e}terod\overset{3}{o}x$, etc.)
              $h\overset{1}{e}licosc\overset{3}{o}pe$ ($h\overset{1}{e}licogr\overset{3}{a}ph$, etc.)
              $m\overset{1}{e}teor\overset{3}{i}te$ ($m\overset{1}{e}teor\overset{3}{o}id$, etc.)

      (c) $\overset{1}{a}lien\overset{3}{a}te$ (d) $det\overset{1}{e}rior\overset{3}{a}te$ (e) $v\overset{1}{e}terin\overset{3}{a}ry$
           $\overset{1}{o}rient\overset{3}{a}te$ $am\overset{1}{e}lior\overset{3}{a}te$ $h\overset{1}{e}terod\overset{3}{o}xy$
           $p\overset{1}{e}regrin\overset{3}{a}te$ $d\overset{1}{i}sciplin\overset{3}{a}ry$

These words illustrate a number of points:

a. Because of the two words in (87d), it is not possible to argue that the stress on the other words in (87) is assigned by a rule that, after case (f), merely assigns initial stress. Rather, the rule in question must be one that retracts stress three syllables.

b. Because of the words in (87a) and the verb $p\overset{1}{e}regrin\overset{3}{a}te$, the solution proposed in SPE for the words in (87c) and (87d)—which involves the assumption that when the retraction applies, the [i] in the antepenultimate is still a glide (cf. SPE, p. 277, fn. 56)—will not work.

c. If stress is to be retracted three syllables, the syllable immediately following the one that comes to bear main stress must end in a weak cluster. That is, words like $*c\overset{1}{a}t\overset{0}{a}sp\overset{0}{a}r\overset{3}{a}n$ do not seem to occur.[56]

d. The words in (87e) exhibit this stress retraction when the tertiary-stressed (phonetic) penult is followed by [īy], as was the case with the words in (75a). Thus,

---

[56]In §6.9 below, this fact will be shown to have an important consequence.

if rule (84) is extended to account for the words in (87a–d), the words in (87e) will also be automatically accounted for. Since rule (84) also allows a final $/V\left\{{r \atop 1}\right\}/$ to be disregarded, we should expect to find such examples as $\overset{1}{a}rimost\overset{3}{o}tle$ and $f\overset{1}{i}liab\overset{3}{u}ster$, which would also correctly receive stress by an expanded rule (84). While I know of no actual cases with this stress contour (except for $wh\overset{1}{a}tsamaj\overset{3}{i}gger$, which can be handled a number of ways), they sound like possible English words, which again suggests that it is the ASR at work here.

In keeping with the above, I propose rule (88) as the final revision of the ASR.

(88)   THE ALTERNATING STRESS RULE

$$V \rightarrow \begin{cases} [\text{-next rule}] \; / \; \underline{\quad} C_0 \text{+æl} \; \# \\ [1 \text{ stress}] \end{cases}$$

$$/ \underline{\quad} C_0(=)C_0((\begin{bmatrix} V \\ \text{-tns} \end{bmatrix} C_0^1(\{{r \atop w}\}))VC_0)\begin{bmatrix} V \\ 1 \text{ stress} \end{bmatrix} C_0(\begin{bmatrix} i \\ \text{-tns} \\ \text{-cns} \\ \text{-tns} \end{bmatrix}\begin{bmatrix} +\text{cns} \\ +\text{voc} \end{bmatrix})\#$$

I am aware that the words in (87b) and (87e) have an internal structure that is such that one might argue that they should be assigned their stress contours by case (c). I will go into this point in §6.4 below.

5.3. Consider now such words as the quadrisyllables in (89a) and the trisyllables in (89b).

(89)   (a) $\overset{3}{A}dir\overset{1}{o}nd\overset{3}{a}ck$ (b) $al\overset{1}{o}h\overset{3}{a}$ $W\overset{3}{y}\overset{1}{o}m\overset{3}{i}ng$
        $\overset{3}{E}niw\overset{1}{e}t\overset{3}{o}k$ $Ach\overset{1}{i}ll\overset{3}{e}s$ $Mon\overset{1}{a}dn\overset{3}{o}ck$
        $M\overset{3}{a}ssap\overset{1}{e}qu\overset{3}{o}d$ $L\overset{3}{a}\overset{1}{e}rt\overset{3}{e}s$ $Pen\overset{1}{o}bsc\overset{3}{o}t$
        $c\overset{3}{a}co\overset{1}{e}th\overset{3}{e}s$ $Or\overset{1}{e}st\overset{3}{e}s$ $H\overset{3}{o}p\overset{1}{a}tc\overset{3}{o}ng$
        $\overset{3}{A}gam\overset{1}{e}mn\overset{3}{o}n$ $Ul\overset{1}{y}ss\overset{3}{e}s$ $(neo)syn\overset{1}{e}phr\overset{3}{i}ne$
                                                $del\overset{1}{i}ct\overset{3}{i}$

By the rules given thus far, we would expect an underlying form like /ædirɔndæk/ to yield, by case (f) and the ASR, either $Ad\overset{1}{i}rond\overset{3}{a}ck$ or, if the trisyllabic retraction discussed in §5.2 were called for by some lexical mark, $\overset{3}{A}dirond\overset{1}{a}ck$. While neither of these pronunciations sounds hopeless, neither accords with the standard pronunciation of this word. How then can the desired stress contour be derived?

I have noted above, in §2 and §5.1, that the ASR has many lexical exceptions. In its final form, (88), the rule applies in three main environments, which I have listed in (90).

(90)   Case (3): $— C_0WVC_0\overset{1}{V}C_0(\left\{\begin{matrix} i \\ \breve{v} \left\{\begin{matrix} r \\ 1 \end{matrix}\right\} \end{matrix}\right\})$ #

Case (2): $— C_0VC_0\overset{1}{V}C_0(\left\{\begin{matrix} i \\ \breve{v} \left\{\begin{matrix} r \\ 1 \end{matrix}\right\} \end{matrix}\right\})$ #

Case (1): $— C_0\overset{1}{V}C_0(\left\{\begin{matrix} i \\ \breve{v} \left\{\begin{matrix} r \\ 1 \end{matrix}\right\} \end{matrix}\right\})$ #

In other words, the ASR retracts stress three syllables, two syllables, or one syllable. Assuming that all words to which case (3) applies will have to be marked, due to the rarity of such words as those in (87), we see that it would be possible to account for the stress contour on *Adirondack* merely by marking it [-case (2)] in the lexicon. We have already seen that the theory of grammar must provide some mechanism for blocking the application of subrules of a rule schema, for if *Oregon*, with a 1–3 stress contour, is to be generated, it must be marked [-case (b)] in the lexicon. I therefore see no theoretical reason for excluding the feature [-case (2)] from the lexical representations of the words in (89). Since all words will be marked [-case (3)] by a general redundancy rule, to which the words in (87) constitute exceptions, the word *Adirondack*, having received final stress by case (f), will not be able to undergo either case (3) or case (2) of the ASR, but will be able to undergo case (1). The derivation will proceed as follows:

(91)   Lexical representation: /ædVrɔndæk/
                                    [-case (2)]

Redundancy rule   [-case (3)]

                   /ædVrɔndæk/

MSR—f		1
ASR—case (1)		1 2
Rule [120][57]	2	1 2
SAR	3	1 3

The stress contours on the other words in (89) would be derived in a similar fashion.

6. A Comparison of the Stressed Syllable Rule and the Alternating Stress Rule

6.1. As I have tried to show above, the addition of case (f) to the MSR leads to a number of changes in the other branches of this rule. Investigation of the question of when to stress a noun by case (b) and when by case (f) leads to replacing C_0 in the SPE version of case (b) with C_b (cf. §3). Establishment of C_b leads in turn to the realization that adjectives and nouns are stressed in basically the same way, which allows cases (a) and (b) to be collapsed (cf. §§4.1–4.2). Note that case (f) duplicates one of the functions of case (e)—that of assigning final stress. This fact, coupled with the observation that some verbs, like *jettison*, must be stressed by case (b), suggests that the other function of case (e), assigning stress to the penult, might be assumed by an existing rule. In §4.3, I have argued that in all cases where verbs that end in an obstruent have penultimate stress, an underlying final vowel must be postulated to account for the laxness of the stressed surface penult. This analysis thereby eliminates case (e) entirely: one half is subsumed by case (f), the other by case (b). The basic regularity concerning the initial assignment of primary stress in English is, therefore, I would argue, the one stated informally in (91):

(91) English words are stressed finally or nonfinally. With certain final consonant sequences, final stress is mandatory, but for other final consonant sequences, the choice of final vs. nonfinal stress is unpredictable. If stress is nonfinal, the stress is

---

[57]I cannot hear any difference in stress level between the first and the last syllables of *Adirondack*, so I have followed the convention suggested by Chomsky and Halle on pp. 118–119, whereby assigning [2 Stress] by rule [120] does not cause other lower stresses in a word to weaken. I will return to this convention in § 8.

assigned to the penult if it contains a heavy cluster, otherwise, to the antepenult.

In other words, primary stress is initially assigned either by case (b) or by case (f).

After the initial assignment of primary stress, however, primary stress can be retracted in one of two ways. Excluding the problem of assigning stress to such words as m$\overset{1}{o}$nos$\overset{3}{y}$llable, to which I will return in §8, SPE asserts that stress assigned in the same cycle by case (eii) (= case (f)) is retracted two syllables by the ASR in words of three or more syllables, regardless of the phonological composition of the preceding syllable. In words stressed on a previous cycle by case (a), or by case (eii), or by rule [158], however, final stress is retracted one or two syllables, in accordance with the Romance Stress Rule. This second type of retraction is effected by the Stressed Syllable Rule, which I will refer to below merely as case (c).

In §2 above, I argued that the ASR must be reformulated so that it retracts stress one or two syllables (or even three, in exceptional cases—cf. §5.2). And in §5.1, I argued that the ASR must, in certain cases, be able to retract primary stress that had been initially assigned to the penult. Thus, the changes effected by case (c) and by the extended ASR are identical. What remains to be investigated is whether the rules must be ordered differently, that is, whether they apply in disjoint environments.

SPE makes use of case (c) for the following types of words:

(92)   (a) c$\overset{1}{a}$rb$\overset{3}{i}$ne–m$\overset{3}{o}$ns$\overset{1}{o}$on
       (b) piccal$\overset{1}{i}$lli–v$\overset{3}{e}$rmic$\overset{1}{e}$lli, ind$\overset{1}{u}$stry–sp$\overset{3}{u}$m$\overset{1}{o}$ni
       (c) perm$\overset{1}{i}$t$_V$–p$\overset{1}{e}$rm$\overset{3}{i}$t$_N$, interc$\overset{3}{e}$pt$_V$–$\overset{1}{i}$nterc$\overset{1}{e}$pt$_N$
       (d) b$\overset{1}{i}$pl$\overset{3}{a}$ne–m$\overset{1}{o}$nopl$\overset{3}{a}$ne, $\overset{1}{e}$ngr$\overset{3}{a}$m–t$\overset{1}{e}$legr$\overset{3}{a}$m
       (e) st$\overset{1}{e}$reosc$\overset{3}{o}$pe–kal$\overset{1}{e}$idosc$\overset{3}{o}$pe
       (f) d$\overset{1}{e}$leg$\overset{3}{a}$te$_V$–d$\overset{1}{e}$leg$\overset{0}{a}$te$_N$
       (g) d$\overset{1}{o}$cum$\overset{3}{e}$nt$_V$–d$\overset{1}{o}$cum$\overset{0}{e}$nt$_N$, t$\overset{3}{o}$rm$\overset{1}{e}$nt$_V$–t$\overset{1}{o}$rm$\overset{3}{e}$nt$_N$
       (h) $\overset{1}{i}$llustr$\overset{3}{a}$te–ill$\overset{1}{u}$str$\overset{3}{a}$te, $\overset{1}{a}$ggrand$\overset{3}{i}$ze–aggr$\overset{1}{a}$nd$\overset{3}{i}$ze, in-
           fant$\overset{1}{i}$le–perc$\overset{1}{e}$ntile
       (i) adv$\overset{1}{i}$s$\overset{0}{o}$ry – pr$\overset{1}{o}$miss$\overset{0}{o}$ry, confiscat$\overset{1}{o}$ry–anticipat$\overset{3}{o}$-
           ry–classificat$\overset{3}{o}$ry, exempl$\overset{1}{a}$ry–urin$\overset{3}{a}$ry, moll$\overset{1}{u}$s-
           c$\overset{3}{o}$id–cryst$\overset{1}{a}$ll$\overset{3}{o}$id

I will take up each of these cases in turn below, arguing that only the last two provide evidence for case (c).

6.2. To start with, as I have argued in §2, the SPE analysis of the stress contrast in (92a)—which depends on adding rule [158] to the grammar and introducing morpheme boundaries into *carbine* and other words like those in (17), but not into *monsoon* or other words like those in (18)—has a number of defects. First, there are morphologically complex forms that do not undergo rule [158] and subsequent stress retraction by case (c) (e.g., ȯrnáte, vėrbȯse, sůprème, spittóon, etc.). Second, this analysis must state as separate the fact that disyllables in /[-cns -tns] [+obs +voi -cont]/, /ɔf/, /īCₒ/, and so on, must retract stress (by rule [158] and case (c)), as well as trisyllables ending in the same phonological sequences (by the ASR). Similarly, the fact that retraction is impossible under the same conditions for disyllables and trisyllables (e.g., for all forms ending in /ōn/, /ēk/, /ēr/, /ēz/, etc.) must be stated twice. Third, this analysis requires an extra rule in the grammar, rule [158]. Worse yet, this rule duplicates exactly the function of an already existing rule, case (f) (equivalently, case (cii)), in that both assign final stress. Fourth, and most serious of all, in my estimation, the analysis violates the Chomsky-Halle-Lukoff naturalness condition on the use of junctures in phonology. All these difficulties can be avoided, however, if the ASR is extended to handle contrasts like those in (92a), which is the course I have followed.

The rules in SPE would account for the stress contrasts in (92b) by deriving these forms from the underlying representations /pĭkV̆lĭll+y/, /vermV̆čelli/, /industr+y/, and /spumōni/. The postulation of /+y/ affixes in *piccalilli* and *industry* and in the other words in (75a) and (79a) also constitutes a violation of the Chomsky-Halle-Lukoff condition, which is a serious enough defect. However, as I argued in §5.1 above, there are other facts that seem to indicate that the ASR must be stated in such a way that stress may be retracted from stressed final syllables, or from stressed penults, when these are followed by /i/ or /[-cons -tns] [+cons +voc]/. Without this extension, the stress contours on such words as *Aristotle*, *calendar*, and *cauliflower* cannot be accounted for unless bizarre underlying forms like [[ærV̆][stɔttel]], /kælen+dær/, and the like are resorted to. For these reasons, I have chosen to extend the ASR to account for the forms in (92b) also.

6.3. Forms like those in (92c)–(92g) are of particularly great theoretical interest because they have been advanced as evidence not only for case (c), but also for the necessity of allowing the transformational cycle to apply below the level of word boundaries. I will defer until §11 a discussion of all the evidence for the latter claim and restrict myself at present to a demonstration that the SPE account of the stress difference in (92c)–(92g) is not the only one possible.

For contrasts like those in (92c), Chomsky and Halle propose the following derivations:

(93) (a) Base form $[\text{per=mit}]_V$
           MSR (eii)   1
           Other rules $[\text{p\v{e}r mit}]$

      (b) Base form $[[\text{per=mit}]_V]_N$
           MSR (eii)   1
           MSR (cii)   1   2
           SAR   1   3
           Other rules $[\text{p\v{e}r mit}]$

(94) (a) Base form $[\text{inter=kept}]_V$
           MSR (eii)   1
           ASR   DNA
           Rule [120]   2   1
           SAR   3   1
           Other rules $[\text{int\v{e}r s\v{e}pt}]$

      (b) Base form $[[\text{inter=kept}]_V]_N$
           MSR (eii)   1
           ASR   DNA
           MSR (ci)   1   2
           SAR   1   3
           Other rules $[\text{int\v{e}r s\v{e}pt}]$

The ASR does not apply to retract stress for words like *intercept* because of the = boundary before the final syllable, as discussed by Chomsky and Halle in SPE, on pages 95–96. However, exactly the same effect can be achieved by adding a redundancy rule that states that stress does not retract in verbs and adjectives ending in $=C_0VC_0\#$.

The immediate objection to such a redundancy rule is that it is ad hoc and that to use such a redundancy rule is to give up an explanation of the stress contrast in (92c) that can be attained by an analysis making use of case (c) and the transformational cycle. This objection can be countered, however. First of all, the redundancy rule blocking the ASR for verbs and adjectives ending in $=C_0VC_0\#$ can be made a branch of a redundancy rule that prevents stress retraction in disyllabic verbs and adjectives. This rule is stated in (95).

$$(95) \quad \begin{bmatrix} +\text{voc} \\ \left\{ \begin{matrix} +V \\ +A \end{matrix} \right\} \end{bmatrix} \rightarrow [-\text{ASR}] \; / \; \left\{ \begin{matrix} \#C_0V \\ = \end{matrix} \right\} \; C_0 \underline{\quad\quad} C_0 \# \quad \begin{matrix} (a) \\ (b) \end{matrix}$$

Rule (95a) must be in the grammar in any event in order to account for the fact that the following constitutes an exhaustive list of disyllabic verbs and adjectives that undergo stress retraction.[58]

(96)   (a) All adjectives in (61) and (62) and *prólìx*

         (b) All verbs in (52b) and *bóycòtt, ámbùsh, híghjàck, búshwhàck, cómmènt, tríùmph, wígwàg, éavesdròp, clímàx, délùge, úmpìre, híccòugh, séesàw, vácùum, xéròx, vétò,*[59] *kídnàp, hóbnòb*

The enormous lists of disyllabic verbs and adjectives that do not exhibit stress retraction, of which the examples in (57a) and (66) and those in SPE on page 69 (cf. [18 II, III]) and page 80 (cf. [42 II, III]) constitute only a small fraction, testify amply, I think, to the fact that (95a) expresses a significant

---

[58]I have not included in (96) many morphologically complex words. Other rules apply to these forms, which include the adjectives in *-ive*. I will argue (in §7.1) that all these have originally been finally stressed and have subsequently undergone stress retraction and a special rule of Destressing. Nor have I included verbs and adjectives in *-ate*, because for many of these the redundancy pointed out by Chomsky and Halle on p. 155 obtains. Nor have I included adjectives in *-oid*, such as *rhómbòid*, which all undergo case (c), or verbs in *-ize*, such as *báptìze*, whose stress retraction will be discussed in §8. Adjectives in *-ine*, such as *félìne, cánìne*, etc., have also been excluded, since their stress retraction follows from the fact that all words in /iC_0/ undergo the ASR, as was pointed out above, in connection with the words in (28).

[59]Following a suggestion made to me by Paul Kiparsky, I propose to account for the *vétò–mòttò* contrast (cf. pp. 190–191) by entering *veto* as /vētɔ/ and *motto* as /mɔtto/. Case (f) will assign final stress to *veto*, +ASR and the ASR will retract the stress. This proposal allows rule [45] on p. 191 of SPE to be dispensed with.

generalization and should be included in the grammar. Clearly, adding (95b) to (95a) to account for the nonretraction of
stress in words like *intercept*$_V$ and *comprehend* (and, incidentally, in such words as *permit*$_V$, *import*$_V$, etc., which do
not undergo stress retraction because they are disyllabic
and because they contain the boundary =) complicates the
grammar in only a minor way. I will show below, however,
in §6.5, that even this minor complication can be avoided
when (95b) is made part of rule (107).

The other objection to (95b), namely, that it misses an
explanation of the contrasts in (92c), an explanation that the
analysis in SPE can provide, is wrong in a deeper way. That
is, I cannot see that the rules in SPE have explained the
following observation, which is due to Paul Kiparsky,[60] and
which I take to be a very deep fact about English:

(97)   If verbs or adjectives that are homophonous with
        nouns differ from the noun in the location of primary
        stress, this stress is never to the right of the
        primary stress of the noun.[61]

Thus, (97) rules out as impossible such noun-verb pairs as
*$import_N$–$impȯrt_V$, *$police_N$–$polĭce_V$, and so on, or such noun-
adjective pairs as *$extrĕme_N$–$extrȇme_A$, *$divĭne_N$–$divȋne_A$,
and so on.

How could the rules of SPE exclude the first of these
pairs? Observe that if the base forms shown in (98a) are
possible base forms, the derivations shown in (98b) will produce the unacceptable result that (97) excludes.

(98)   (a) $[im{=}port]_N$ $[[im{=}port]_N]_V$
       (b) MSR (eii)   1   1
           MSR (cii)   ————————
                                                   1   2
           SAR   1   3
                          $[impȯrt]$ *$[impȯrt]$

---

[60]Personal communication.

[61]The only counterexample I know of, although I am not sure any such
dialect exists, would be a dialect that exhibited only *defēnse*$_N$ and *defȇnse*$_V$
(as in football). I am not sure, but I think that in my speech the noun can
be pronounced with or without stress retraction, while the verb is more
natural with stress retraction, though it does not seem impossible without
retraction.

The only way I can see to avoid (98), within the framework of SPE, would be to state ad hoc that (98a) contains inadmissible base forms, in particular, that $[[X]_N]_V$ and $[[X]_N]_A$ are inadmissible surface structures. But such a claim seems to me to be far too strong, at least insofar as the bracketing $[[X]_V]_N$ is to represent the intuition that such nouns as those in (99) are deverbal and deadjectival, that is, that the homophonous verb or adjective "feels," in some at present totally mysterious way, more basic than the homophonous noun.

(99) (a) *transfer, sneeze, spring, construct, walk, sleep, snore, wait, move, repair,* etc.

(b) *extreme, divine, remote, modern, particular, partial, harmonic, elective,* etc.

Note that, in order to prevent the derivation of 1–3 stress contours on any nouns in (99b), lexical items like *extreme, divine,* and *remote* could be marked [-case (c)] in the lexicon.

However, just as some nouns "feel" deverbal, some verbs "feel" denominal. A selection is given in (100).

(100) *to police, to snag, to stone, to pattern, to voice, to machine, to shellac, to fool, to boot, to package, to balloon,* etc.

The question that now arises is the following: if a base form like $[[kɔn\text{=}strukt]_V]_N$ is allowable as a formal representation of the fact that *a construct* is felt to be less basic than *to construct*, why is the base form $[[pɔlēs]_N]_V$ not admissible as a representation of the fact that *to police* is felt to be less basic than the noun *police*?[62] And if it is allowable, what stops the derivation in (101)?

(101) $[[pɔlēs]_N]_V$

MSR (eii)	1
MSR (dii)	$\overline{1\ 2}$
SAR	1 3
Other rules	*[pŏwli̊ys]

To be sure, it would be possible to mark *police* as [-case

---

[62]I am not interested at present in whether the noun or the verb of a given pair is felt to be more basic. As far as I know, all speakers have some feeling about whether certain words belong in (99) or (100), and the point I am concerned with here does not depend on the particular examples I have used.

(c)], as is necessary with *extreme* and *remote*, but to do this is to miss the real generalization expressed in (97). (97) states that *no* words (but cf. fn. 61) will be of the form *$police_N$–$pólice_V$. Clearly, to mark *police*, *shellac*, and *machine* as being [-case (c)] is not to provide an explanation for (97). Nor, in fact, would (97) be explained, even if some redundancy rule could be formulated that automatically assigned [-case (c)] to structures of the form $[[X]_N]_V$.[63] The question would merely be pushed back to the question of why such a redundancy rule should exist.

If rule (95a) is in the grammar, a formal explanation of (97) can be achieved, a fact that constitutes evidence of the strongest kind for the correctness of rule (95). I will defer, until §6.7, where I discuss the contrast between $tórmént_V$ and $tòrmént_N$, a presentation of my proposed explanation. Here I would merely like to point out that (97) must, in any adequate theory of grammar, be related to the fact that C_b for nouns is a superset of C_b for adjectives and C_b for verbs. Thus, there are more *types* of nouns that can have penultimate or antepenultimate stress than there are types of adjectives or verbs that can be stressed in this way. The larger regularity, which includes both this fact about the assignment of primary stress by the MSR and Kiparsky's observation about stress retraction, is that nouns tend to exhibit primary stress on earlier syllables of a word than adjectives or verbs. The theoretical consequences of this broader fact will be discussed in some detail in §9.[64]

6.4. Let us turn now to the contrasts in (92d), which Chomsky and Halle propose to account for as in (102).

(102)

(a) Base form	$[bĭ[plǽn]_S]_N$			$[mɔnɔ[plǽn]_S]_N$		
(b) MSR (eii)		1		MSR (eii)		1
MSR (cii)	1	2		MSR (ci)	1	2
SAR	1	3		SAR	1	3
Other rules	$[bǎyplĕyn]$			Other rules	$[mǎnəplĕyn]$	

[63]Such a redundancy rule would be too strong in any case, as the noun $détour_N$ and the denominal verb $[[détòur]_N]_V$ show. The point is not that denominal verbs (or adjectives) cannot retract stress, but that stress can only be retracted in the verb (or adjective) *if it also is in the noun*. This fact cannot be accounted for in the SPE analysis.

[64]Cf. also Ross (1971).

We see that these forms can also be handled without case (c) and without having to assume two passes through cyclical rules. If *biplane* and *monoplane* are entered as /bi+plæn/ and /mɔnɔ+plæn/, respectively, case (f) will assign final stress, and the ASR and SAR will produce the desired 1–3 stress contours. The same is true for *engram* and *telegram*. If these are entered as /en+græm/ and /tele+græm/, respectively, the same sequence of rules can be used to derive the desired stress contours. Thus, neither pair provides evidence for case (c) or for the cycle. The kind of word that would provide conclusive proof that case (c) is necessary for the contrasts in (92d) would be a word like *belówpláne* or *insèctpláne*, where the stress would only be retracted one syllable, to the strong penult. However, such words do not exist. All words that end in such stems as *-phone*, *-graph*, *-photo*, *-plasm*, *-chrome*, *-tome*, and so forth can only be preceded by prefixes that end in a weak cluster, such as *bio-*, *tele-*, *phono-*, *photo-*, *endo-*, and *zygo-*; and stress can be retracted to the initial syllable of such prefixes equally well by case (3) of the ASR or by case (ci). I will discuss the status of such trisyllabic prefixes as *stereo-*, *audio-*, and *hetero-* in §6.5 below.

Note that it is only case (f) that makes it possible to derive the stress for such words as *engram* and *telegram* without having recourse to case (c), for the rules of SPE could only stress such underlying forms as /en+græm/ and /tele+græm/ by case (b), which would produce the incorrect results *[éngrɔm] and *[tèlɔgrɔm]. But an MSR that includes case (f) can produce the correct 1–3 contours by lexically marking the morpheme *gram* [-case (b)], just as the morpheme *Siam* will be marked.

However, there is a point being overlooked here that is captured in the analysis of SPE. No word composed of a prefix followed by a monosyllabic stem can be stressed by case (b),[65] even if the stem ends in C_b. This statement is true both of Greek stems like *-gram*, *-crat*, and so on, and also of Latin stems like *-mit* and *-cuss*. That is, such pronunciations as *démocràt, *ìsobár, *pèrmìt, and *discúss are

---

[65]The restriction to monosyllables is necessary because of such words as *tèlephóto* and *tètrahédron*.

impossible.[66] Chomsky and Halle account for this fact by postulating such surface structures as the one shown in (103) (cf. SPE, p. 100, paragraph 2),

(103)

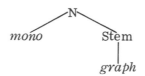

and by mentioning the category S(=Stem) in the statement of the MSR, thus ensuring that [1 stress] will be assigned to *graph* on the first cycle. However, there is no *syntactic* justification for such a phrase structure category as Stem. Since no transformational rule refers to this category, this solution cannot be considered adequate.

I do not dispute the fact that the morphemes in the lexicon must be segregated into a large number of combinatorial classes, since only certain sequences of such morpheme classes are possible words. That is, although *autocyclophonistic* is a possible English word, the same sequence of morphemes in reverse order, or pairwise permuted, is not. Such facts should be accounted for by including in the lexicon a set of *word-formation rules.* This idea is by no means novel, although the problem of accounting for the set of possible morpheme sequences has been largely ignored in previous work on generative grammar.[67] I would imagine that the class of stems—e.g., such words as *-graph, -hedron, -cycle, -mit, -ceive, -cuss,* and so forth, which play no role in the syntax of English, to the best of my knowledge—will play an important part in the eventual set of word-formation rules for English. Let us assume, for the sake of discussion, that the word-formation rules will refer, among other things, to word-formation features like [+Stem]. These features will be listed in the lexicon proper in the entries of such morphemes as *-graph* and *-hedron.* I would propose that the fact that there

[66]Jay Keyser has pointed out to me that there are exceptions to this generalization, especially in British English. Thus, the pronunciations *prógràm, díagràm, Péntagòn,* etc., are not uncommon, even though 1–3 contours are also possible. I propose that such forms be lexically marked as exceptions to redundancy rule (107). This point is developed below.

[67]Halle and I will present some preliminary speculations about such word-formation rules in the paper mentioned in fn. 50 above.

are no such words as $*d\overset{1}{e}mocr\overset{0}{a}t$ (but cf. fn. 66) be captured not by writing rules that will necessitate ad hoc surface structures like (103), but rather by assuming the existence of a redundancy rule like (104).

(104) $\begin{bmatrix} V \\ +\text{Stem} \end{bmatrix} \rightarrow \begin{bmatrix} -\text{case (b)} \\ +\text{ASR}^{68} \end{bmatrix} / +C_0 \underline{\quad} C_0 \#$

This rule only affects monosyllabic stems, for stems like *-photo* and *-hedron* must be stressed by case (b). Note also that it is necessary to specify that all words consisting of prefix and stem not only undergo case (f) but also exhibit stress retraction, for such words as $*b\overset{3}{i}pl\overset{1}{a}ne$ and $*K\overset{3}{o}da$-$chr\overset{1}{o}me$ are impossible. This fact about retraction would have to be stated in the SPE analysis as well, since it must be possible to mark lexical entries [-case (c)], as the discussion in §6.7 below, dealing with the stress of the word *lament*, shows. Some way must be found to ensure that prefix-stem words like *monoplane* can never be marked [-case (c)]; otherwise the undesired $*m\overset{3}{o}nopl\overset{1}{a}ne$ would result. Thus, something corresponding to rule (104) would have to appear in the set of redundancy rules for SPE also.

Recall that in §6.3 above, I proposed that a branch be added to rule (95a) to block the ASR from retracting stress in such verbs as $perm\overset{1}{i}t_V$ and $interc\overset{1}{e}pt_V$. The device used followed closely the analysis suggested in SPE, pages 95–96, which depended on whether the ASR could retract stress from a syllable preceded by the boundary =. However, the resulting rule, (95b), resembles rule (104), in that both specify conditions under which words that end in stems undergo stress retraction.

This similarity can easily be exploited. Obviously, any adequate set of word-formation rules for English will have to separate stems and prefixes into at least two classes, as shown in (105) and (106).

(105)　(a) *ab-, ad-, con-, contra-, de-, in-, inter-, per-,*
　　　　　　pro-, re-, sub-, trans-, omni-, equi-, ambi-,
　　　　　　etc.

---

[68]The exact interpretation of the feature [+ASR], when on the right side of the arrow of a redundancy rule, will be discussed in §10. Roughly, it can be thought of as a formal device that ensures the application of the ASR if its environment is met.

(b) *-cuss, -ceive, -cide, -cede, -tain, -pose, -mit,*
     -gress, -pend, -spect, -late, -fer, -rode, -here,
     etc.

(106)   (a) *bio-, psycho-, mono-, iso-, hexa-, cata-, para-,*
            physio-, tele-, syn-, proto-, etc.

(b) *-phone, -graph, -gram, -gon, -spore, -tome,*
     -log, -phage, -hedron, -plasm, etc.

Roughly, any prefix in (105a) can be followed by any stem in (105b), or any prefix in (106a) by any stem in (106b), and a possible English word will result. However, no words can be formed if one part is from (105) and the other from (106). To account for this fact, some feature will be necessary. Let us therefore, in accordance with etymology, assign to the morphemes in (106) the ad hoc feature [+Greek].

Reconsidering the words that rules (95b) and (104) must account for, we see that in [+Greek] prefix-stem words, stress is always retracted, in both nouns and verbs. Some examples are $\overset{1}{tele}\overset{3}{phone}_{NV}$, $\overset{1}{tele}\overset{3}{scope}_{NV}$, $\overset{1}{cata}\overset{3}{log}_{NV}$, and $\overset{1}{para}$-$\overset{3}{phrase}_{NV}$. However, in [−Greek] words, stress is only retracted in nouns.[69] These facts can be accounted for by reformulating (104) as (107):

$$(107) \quad \begin{bmatrix} V \\ +Stem \end{bmatrix} \rightarrow \begin{bmatrix} -\text{case (b)} \\ \langle +ASR \rangle \end{bmatrix} / +C_0 \begin{bmatrix} \langle | \{ \overline{\begin{smallmatrix} +N \\ +Greek \end{smallmatrix}} \} | \rangle \end{bmatrix} C_0 \#$$

[69]This statement is not quite accurate, in a way that I do not see at present how to remedy. Consider, for instance, the word *abstract*. With a 3–1 (or 0–1) contour it can be an adjective meaning "not concrete," or a verb meaning "to remove, or steal, from." With a 1–3 contour, it can be a noun with the meaning "précis, condensation, summary," or *it can be a verb*, with the meaning "to construct an abstract for or of" (as in *This journal sure did a rotten job in abstracting my paper.*). Other examples are *to $\overset{1}{inter}\overset{3}{cept}_V$* ("give the intercepts of"), *to $\overset{1}{permit}_V$* ("provide with a permit"), *to $\overset{1}{re}\overset{3}{ject}_V$* ("mark as a reject"), etc. These examples, which all "feel" strongly denominal, seem to suggest that rather than notations like $[[\ \ ]_N]_V$ and $[[\ \ ]_V]_N$, what may be necessary is a notation $[\ \ ]_{\{N,V\}}$, where the node subscripts form an unordered set, and where some rule or convention will stipulate that the symbol N predominates. If a subscript set contains N, the word with such a subscript set will undergo rules referring to nouns, *even though it may be functioning syntactically as a verb*. I realize, of course, that it is far too early to propose this or any other formal solution with any confidence, so the above should be regarded as speculation.

This rule looks terribly ad hoc until it is compared with the theoretical machinery that SPE uses to achieve the same effect. First, instead of the ad hoc word-formation feature [+Stem], SPE makes use of ad hoc surface structures like (103) and of the boundary =. (I will argue in §7.2, in connection with the rule of *Medial Laxing*, that this boundary is not only unnecessary, but that it also actually makes it impossible to derive the stress contours of such words as *prèsident* and thus must be dispensed with in favor of the feature configuration [+Stem -Greek] or possibly [+Stem +Latin].)

Second, while it is indeed ad hoc to mention the feature [+N] in the environment of (107), there is no non–ad hoc way for derivations such as that in (101) to be blocked within the framework of SPE. That is, within the SPE framework, allowing nouns to be derived from verbs by an additional pass through the cycle, but not allowing verbs to be derived from nouns in a parallel fashion, is an ad hoc restriction on underlying forms that corresponds exactly to my mentioning [+N] in the environment of (107).

Finally, mentioning the feature [+Greek] in (107) is ad hoc, but no more so than postulating the structures shown in (108) in place of any of those shown in (109).

(108)   [tele [fɔn]$_S$]$_{NV}$ [inter=kept]$_V$
                                            [[inter=kept]$_V$]$_N$

(109) (a) [tele [fɔn]$_S$]$_{NV}$ [inter [kept]$_S$]$_{NV}$

       (b) [tele=fɔn]$_N$ [inter=kept]$_V$
            [[tele=fɔn]$_N$]$_V$ [[inter=kept]$_V$]$_N$

       (c) [tele=fɔn]$_N$ [inter[kept]$_S$]$_{NV}$
            [[tele=fɔn]$_N$]$_V$

The underlying representations in (109a) will yield 1–3 contours on both the nouns and the verbs. The representations in (109b) will yield 3–1 contours on the noun *telephone*$_N$ and on the verb *intercept*$_V$, and 1–3 contours on the verb *telephone*$_V$ and the noun *intercept*$_N$. The representations in (109c) will yield a 1–3 contour on both variants of *intercept* and on the verb *telephone*$_V$, but a 3–1 contour on the noun *telephone*$_N$. Obviously, it would be easy to increase the number of underlying representations in (109), which will yield even more unattested types of alternation. Of course, I do not dispute that the representations given in (108) will yield the desired output, given the rules in SPE. My point is merely that there is no independent motivation, from the syntax or from any other part of the grammar, for choosing any one of these representations over any other. After all, if there can be a stress cycle on *-phone*, why can there not be one on *-cept*? Thus, the choice of the representations in (108), instead of any of those in (109), is ad hoc—just as the use of the feature [+Greek] in the environment of (107) is.

In fact, it seems that although the stress contours of prefix-stem words are completely predictable, given the knowledge of whether or not the word is [+Greek] and of what its syntactic category is, the particular *content* of the stress contour (that is, whether the final syllable is stressed and whether retraction applies) is completely random and unrelated to other facts about English stress contours. The predictability of stress in prefix-stem words is a particular fact and is not related to other, more general, rules of stress.[70] Therefore, I can see no reason to prefer the SPE analysis, which makes use of ad hoc representations like those in (103) and (108), over my rule (107), which connects the MSR and the ASR in an ad hoc way to the features [+Stem], [+Greek], and [+N].[71]

There is one difference, however, between rule (107) and the analysis in SPE that seems, despite the ad hocness of both, to clearly motivate choosing the former over the latter. If the noun $intercépt_N$ is to be derived from the verb by an extra pass through the cycle, what is to prevent the verb $telephóne_V$ from being derived in a parallel fashion from the noun $telephóne_N$? If this is allowed, such incorrect derivations as that in (110) will result.

(110)   Base form: $[[tele[fɔ̃n]_S]_N]_V$

MSR (eii)		1
MSR (ci)	1	2
MSR (ci)	1	3
SAR	1	4
Other rules	*[tèlɔfə̀n]	

[70]This claim is somewhat too strong. That the environment of rule (107) contains the feature [+N] is related to a more general phenomenon, which will be discussed in §9.

[71]One disturbing feature of rule (107) does require comment, namely, the fact that its environment essentially repeats the environment of case (f). I have not been able to find a way to remedy this obvious defect.

The reason that the vowel of the last syllable of the derived member of the noun-verb pair *telephone* will undergo Vowel Reduction is discussed by Chomsky and Halle on page 107, in connection with the noun $\overset{1}{dele}\overset{0}{gate}_N$. (Obviously, the incorrect derivation in (110) would not be affected if the noun *telephone* were assumed to be deverbal.) I will discuss the SPE analysis of this word in detail in §6.6. Here, suffice it to say that, unless the underlying representation in (110) is ruled out on some ad hoc basis, the analysis in SPE will produce an incorrect 1–0 contour on the derived member of the noun-verb pair for *telephone*. Again, let me emphasize that this difficulty cannot be satisfactorily sidestepped by disallowing underlying representations of the form $[[X]_N]_V$, which would, however, have the correct results, in that it would prevent (98), (101), and (110). The question would still have to be faced as to why $[[X]_V]_N$ representations *are* admissible, if $[[X]_N]_V$ representations are not. Until that question had been given a satisfactory answer, it could not be claimed that the stress contrast between $\overset{3}{intercept}_V$ and $\overset{1}{intercept}_N$ had been *explained*—since the proposed account would depend on the ad hoc prohibition of one of two kinds of underlying representation, each of which seems equally well motivated, syntactically or intuitively.

Note that if cyclical rules are prohibited from applying below the level of word boundaries, the difficulty occasioned by the incorrectness of the form $*\overset{0}{telephone}_V$ vanishes. Both the noun and the verb forms of *telephone* can be derived as in (111).

(111)   Base form: /tele+fɔn/
$$\begin{bmatrix} +\text{Greek} \\ +\text{Stem} \end{bmatrix}$$

Rule (107)	$\begin{bmatrix} -\text{case (b)} \\ +\text{ASR} \end{bmatrix}$	
MSR (f)		1
ASR	1	2
SAR	1	3
Other rules	$[\overset{1}{tel}\text{ə}\overset{3}{fown}]$	

I conclude, therefore, not only that the stress contrasts in (92d) cannot be taken to provide evidence for case (c) and for the cycle, but also that the impossibility of excluding $*\overset{1}{tele}\overset{0}{phone}_V$, on a principled basis, actually argues against allowing cyclically ordered rules to apply below the level at which word boundaries are reached in English.

6.5. Let us turn now to the contrast shown in (92e), $st\overset{1}{e}reosc\overset{3}{o}pe-kale\overset{1}{i}dosc\overset{3}{o}pe$, which SPE accounts for as in (112), using case (c) and the transformational cycle.

(112)

(a) Base form $[stere+\mathfrak{o}[sk\mathfrak{z}p]_S]_N$ (b) $[kVl\bar{i}d+\mathfrak{o}[sk\mathfrak{z}p]_S]_N$

MSR (eii)		1			1
MSR (ci)	1	2	MSR (cii)	1	2
SAR	1	3		1	3

Other rules $[st\overset{1}{e}r\bar{i}y\mathfrak{o}sk\overset{3}{o}wp]$ $[k\mathfrak{o}l\overset{1}{a}yd\mathfrak{o}sk\bar{o}wp]$

Recall that there is a rule, the ASR, which has the function of retracting stress one, two, or three syllables, that we could make use of to derive the stress on $st\overset{1}{e}reosc\overset{3}{o}pe$. However, whereas the ASR does not normally retract stress three syllables, trisyllabic retraction is mandatory for all words consisting of a prefix plus a stem when the prefix is any one of those in (113).

(113)   *stereo-, idio-, helio-, entero-, hetero-, helico-, hagio-, sidero-, biblio-, physio-, cinema-, cardio-, radio-, u t e r o-, dolicho-, polio-, (en)cephalo-, audio-,* etc.[72]

On the other hand, disyllabic retraction is mandatory for the prefixes in (114), as such words as $tons\overset{1}{i}llosc\overset{3}{o}pe$ and $dagu\overset{1}{e}rrot\overset{3}{y}pe$ indicate.

(114)   *galvano-, oscillo-, p o l a r i-, tonsillo-, pupillo-, spinthari-, praxino-, daguerro-, chromato-,* etc.

Note that both these sets of words have penultimate sylla-bles that end (phonetically) in weak clusters, unless the relevant syllable precedes a vowel, in which case the Tensing

[72]It is perhaps worth noting that almost all these prefixes end in the subsequence $\breve{V}[-obs]\,\breve{V}$, and that most of the words in (87) also have subsequences of this form following primary stress. This is possibly of significance, since $\breve{V}[-obs]^1_0\,\breve{V}$ is exactly the type of two-vowel subse-quence that can be used to fill a W position in Chaucer's iambic meter, as has been pointed out by Halle and Keyser (1967). And, as Chomsky and Halle observe (p. 78), "[The ASR] produces alternations of stressed and unstressed vowels. It is thus one of the factors contributing to the frequently observed predominance of iambic rhythms in English."

Rule applies (as in *stereo-*, *radio-*, etc.). Therefore, it is not clear how it can be claimed that stress retraction is governed by the principle of the RSR. Chomsky and Halle consider these forms on page 104, in footnote 56, where they again suggest inserting an ad hoc morpheme boundary in the forms of (113), but not in those of (114). They formulate case (c) in such a way that the "morpheme" /+ɔ+/ can be disregarded along with the final stressed syllable, when stress is retracted by this case. As I have argued above, I can see no difference between such a solution and the one for the *Bein–Pein* contrast, which Chomsky, Halle, and Lukoff rejected, and I think correctly so, in 1956. Both solutions are equally suspect, and a theory that excludes on a principled basis representations like /bayn/ versus /b#ayn/ must also exclude ones like /stere+ɔ+skɔp/ versus /tɔnsilɔ+skɔp/. The last of these representations is especially suspect, in light of the existence of the word *tonsil*, which clearly indicates that there must be a morpheme /+ɔ+/ in *tonsı̆llosco̊pe*. Nor is a second analysis, mentioned in footnote 56 by Chomsky and Halle, possible, namely, the device of entering the prefixes in (114) in the lexicon with geminate consonants. While such an ad hoc representation can be made to work for a representation like /tɔnsill/, that is, for an MSR whose environment for case (b) ends in C_0, it cannot be made to work if C_0 is replaced by C_b, as I have argued is necessary. /ll/ is not in C_b, and the underlying representation /tɔnsill/ could only be stressed by case (f), yielding, eventually, *tŏnsı̆l or *tőnsı̆l, instead of the desired tŏnsı̆l, depending on whether stress retraction occurs. Nor is the third possibility entertained by Chomsky and Halle, in footnote 95 on page 138, viable. There they suggest marking the final vowel of the words in (113), though not of those in (114), with the feature [+D], which case (c) is formulated to disregard. This solution, however, will entail postulating two otherwise identical "morphemes," which differ only in the marking on the feature [+D]. In words like

hĕlicosco̊pe, the morpheme $\left/ \begin{array}{c} +ɔ+ \\ +D \end{array} \right/$ would appear (cf. *helix*),

whereas in *tonsı̆llosco̊pe* the plain morpheme /+ɔ+/ would appear. This solution also seems intolerable to me.

I see no reason to register the fact that stress retraction onto such prefixes as those in (113) and (114) is unpredictable elsewhere than on the retraction rule itself. All the facts will be accounted for if the prefixes in (113) are marked minus for the general redundancy rule, (115), which specifies that all words are [-case (3)] of the ASR.

(115)　[　　　] → [-case (3)]

Stress will be retracted three syllables when the ASR applies to words beginning with one of these prefixes, or when it applies to the monomorphemic words in (87a), which are also [-115] (since case (3) of this rule becomes applicable first, being the longest of the set of three disjunctively ordered rules). That is, the derivation of *stèreoscȯpe* would proceed as shown in (116).

(116)　Base form　　/steriV̌+skɔ́p/
　　　　　　　　　　[-115]

Rule (115)	DNA	
MSR (f)		1
ASR	1	2
SAR	1	3
Other rules	[stèrīyəskȯwp]	

Note that in this analysis, it is not possible for stress to be wrongly retracted three syllables, that is, onto the first syllable of such words as those in (117).

(117)　*kaleido-, laryngo-, ophthalmo-, galacto-, phena-kisto-, dipleido-, phonendo-, urethro-,* etc.

To see this, recall that (90a) shows that the syllable immediately to the right of the one to which case (3) of the ASR retracts stress must end in a weak cluster. Because of the non-existence of such monomorphemic words as **càtàspàrȧn*, even if we were to mark a prefix like *kaleido-* or *laryngo-* with the feature [-115], the ASR could only retract stress two syllables, because of the way case (3) of the ASR must be stated. Thus, the derivation of *kaleȉdoscȯpe* could only proceed as follows:

(118)　Base form　　/kV̌līdV+skɔ́p/
　　　　　　　　　　[-115]

Rule (115)	DNA	
MSR (f)		1
ASR case (3)	DNA	
ASR case (2)	1	2

SAR   1   3
Other rules   [kəláydəskówp]

I conclude that contrasts like those in (92e) cannot be used in support of derivations like those in (116), which involve case (c) and the cycle. On the one hand, contrasts like those between the stress-retraction phenomena exhibited by the prefixes in (113) as opposed to those in (114) cannot be accounted for in such an analysis without violating the Chomsky-Halle-Lukoff naturalness condition; on the other hand, the fact that such prefixes as those in (117) never retract stress three syllables is a natural consequence of the way case (3) of the ASR must, on independent grounds, be formulated. Therefore, it seems perfectly natural to account for the contrasts in retraction shown in (92e) by means of the ASR.

6.6. Let us now turn to such pairs as those in (92f), $\overset{1}{delegate}_V$–$\overset{1}{delegate}_N$, which Chomsky and Halle derive as in (119) (cf. p. 107).

(119)	Base forms	$[del\check{V}gæt]_V$		$[[del\check{V}gæt]_V]_N$	
	MSR (eii)		1		1
	ASR	1	2	1	2
	MSR (di)			1	3
	ASR			DNA	
	SAR	1	3	1	4
	Other rules	$[d\overset{1}{e}ləg\overset{3}{e}yt]$		$[d\overset{1}{e}ləg\overset{0}{ə}t]$	

That is, Chomsky and Halle predicate the reduction of the final vowel of $\overset{1}{delegate}_N$ upon the deverbal "feel" of this noun, requiring it, therefore, to go through the cycle of stress rules one more time than the more primary verb. The rules, in particular case (c), are formulated in such a way that this second pass through the cycle will weaken the stress on the final syllables of this noun by one degree, which will eventually cause it to reduce.

I find this explanation inadequate on three grounds. First, if a homophonous trisyllabic noun-verb pair ending in *-ate* could be found, where the noun was "felt" to be primary, we would expect the noun to have a 1–3 contour, but the verb, by hypothesis derived by means of an extra pass through the cycle, would have a 1–0 stress contour. I know of one such noun-(denominal)verb pair that is trisyllabic and one that is disyllabic. The trisyllabic example is *candidate,* which *Webster's Third New International Dictionary* lists also as a possible verb, giving it a 1–3 stress pattern. The disyllabic case is the verb *pròbāte.* Both these verbs "feel" clearly denominal to me; thus, by the rules in SPE, they should have 1–0 contours. Such a stress contour would be derived for *probate*$_V$:

(120)	Base form	$[[pr\text{ɔ}b+\text{æt}]_N]_V$
	Rule [158]	1
	MSR (cii)	1 2
	MSR (cii)	1 3
	SAR	1 4
	Other rules	*[prȯwbȧt]

Again, it is not important that all speakers share my intuition that the verbs *cándidàte* and *pròbàte* are denominal. The more important claim that I am making is that no homophonous pair of the following form *could* exist: $[1X3]_N-[1X0]_V$. This fact seems to be related somehow to Kiparsky's observation, (97), but, at present, it is not clear exactly how. Note that the problem of excluding *pròbàte*$_V$ can be reduced to the problem of excluding the base form in (120). If there were a principled way of excluding this and, similarly, of excluding (98a) and the base forms in (101) and (110), (97) would be explained, as well as the impossibility of *cándidàte*$_V$ and *pròbàte*$_V$. But at present, no way of excluding such forms exists.

The second objection I have to Chomsky and Halle's analysis is that it is far too strong. It predicts that whenever there is a homophonous verb-noun pair, regardless of which member is basic, if the basic member exhibits a 1–3 contour, the derived member will exhibit a 1–0 contour, since it will undergo a second cycle through the rules. Actually, however, it is only if the words end in *-ate* that any reduction can ever be observed.[73] To take a word that constitutes a near minimal pair with *dèlegàte*$_V$–*dèlegàte*$_N$, consider *dỳnamìte*$_V$–*dỳnamìte*$_N$, both of which I a s s u m e to derive from an underlying /dīnæmo+īt/,[74] and both of which exhibit a 1–3 stress contour.

[73] I will take up such contrasts as *dòcument*$_V$–*dòcument*$_N$ in §6.7 below.

[74] Here I make the further assumption, on which nothing depends, that the final *o* of *dynamo* will be deleted by the rule of Vowel Drop (cf. fn. 38 above).

In fact, in verb-noun or adjective-noun pairs ending in /Vt/ (for all other vowels for which I have been able to find examples), if one member has a 1–3 stress, so does the other. Some examples are *prȯstitu̇te*$_{NV}$, *párachu̇te*$_{NV}$, *créosȯte*$_{NV}$, *bȯycȯtt*$_{NV}$, *úmlȧut*$_{NV}$, *thȧrmostȧt*$_{NV}$, *álphabȧt*$_{NV}$, and *cȯunterfȧit*$_{NVA}$.

Another near minimal contrast is the noun-verb pair *rȧnegȧde*$_N$–*rȧnegȧde*$_V$, both of which presumably derive from the underlying form /renig+æd/ (cf. *renege*). In fact, regardless of the final vowel and the final consonant, I have found no examples, aside from words in *-ate*, in which one member of a homophonous pair can exhibit a 1–3 contour and the other a 1–0 contour. Some examples of the lack of this contrast are *sácrifȧce*$_{NV}$, *cȯmpromȧse*$_{NV}$, *hándicȧp*$_{NV}$, *su̇icide*$_{NV}$, *tȯmahȧwk*$_{NV}$, *cátalȯg*$_{NV}$, *pȧntomȧme*$_{NV}$, *guȧllotȧne*$_{NV}$, *mȧnicu̇re*$_{NV}$, and *rȧdicu̇le*$_{NV}$. Nor do words ending in more than one consonant, except for *-ment* (cf. §6.7 below), ever exhibit reduction in one member of a homographous pair, as is indicated by such examples as *bȯomerȧng*$_{NV}$, *sȯmersȧult*$_{NV}$, *mȧnifȧst*$_{NV}$, *áquatȧnt*$_{NV}$, *cȯunterpȯint*$_{NV}$, and *ávalȧnche*$_{NV}$. Despite all these pairs, the rules in SPE would produce a reduced vowel in the final syllable of the derived member, whichever member of the pair this was chosen to be.

In one other respect the SPE analysis of the contrast in (92f) is too strong. Consider the verb-noun *dictate*. Assuming the verb to be basic, in line with my intuition (but note that nothing would be changed with the reverse assumption), and given the rules in SPE, we would expect the following derivations:

(121)	(a) Base form	[dikt+æt]$_V$		[[dikt+æt]$_V$]$_N$	
	(b) Rule [158]	1		1	
	MSR (cii)	1	2	1	2
	MSR (cii)			1	3
	SAR	1	3	1	4
	Other rules	[diktȩyt]		*[diktȧt]	

The rules in SPE predict that the stress reduction manifested in derived trisyllabic forms like *dȧlegȧte*$_N$ should also turn up in derived disyllabic forms. In fact, however, reduction is limited to words of at least three syllables, as the following examples, all of which have 1–3 contours in both members of the pair, clearly show.

(122)   *pròstràte*$_{VA}$, *fìltràte*$_{VN}$, *trùncàte*$_{VA}$, *gỳràte*$_{VA}$, *màn-dàte*$_{NV}$, *càstràte*$_{VNA}$, *rèbàte*$_{NV}$

I know of no disyllabic pairs in *-ate* whose final vowel exhibits an [ēy]~[ə] alternation.

Summing up, it seems that the stress contrast in (92f) cannot be attributed to the operation of rules or processes of wide generality. First of all, as the pair *càndidàte*$_{NV}$ shows, denominal verbs never exhibit 1–0 contours: as far as I know, the reduction is limited to nouns and adjectives. Second, pairs like *dỳnamìte*$_{NV}$, *rènegàde*$_{NV}$, and *àquatìnt*$_{NV}$ show that the reduction only affects pairs ending in /æt/. Finally, words like those in (122) show that the process must be restricted to words with three or more syllables. All these facts find expression in rule (123).

(123)
$$
\begin{bmatrix} +\text{voc} \\ -\text{back} \\ +\text{low} \\ +\text{tns} \\ 3\ \text{Stress} \end{bmatrix} \rightarrow \begin{bmatrix} -\text{tns} \\ -\text{stress} \end{bmatrix} \Big/ \overset{1}{V} C_0 V C_0 \underline{\quad\quad} t\#\ \Bigg]_{NA}
$$

There is a class of nouns ending in the morpheme *-ate*, which is preceded by a noun denoting a role or a position, such as *sùltanàte*, *èpiscopàte*, *prìncipàte*, *pàtriàrchàte*, and *càliphàte*, many of which do not undergo rule (123) (but cf. the alternative pronunciations *sùltanàte* and the words *cònsulàte* and *protèctoràte*, which must undergo rule (123)). In general, this morpheme *-ate* would be marked [–123]. Furthermore, there is a chemical and biological affix *-ate*, as in *sìlicàte*, *vànadàte*, *cỳanàte*, *pèctinàte*, *fìbrillàte*,[75] and *pètiolàte*, that would also be marked [–123]. Except for these cases, the rule appears to be fairly general. The only real exceptions I know of are the nouns *bìllingsgàte*, *sùrrogàte*, *càndidàte*, and *màgistràte*, although the last two can optionally undergo the rule and be assigned 1–0 contours. (See SPE, p. 107, fn. 62, for further discussion.)

Thus, the stress contrasts in (92f), like those in (92c)–(92e), provide evidence neither for case (c) nor for the cycle. Unless such underlying forms as those in (120) and (121) can

---

[75]This word can be pronounced with a 1–0 contour. It would therefore have to be marked as being able to optionally undergo rule (116).

be ruled out on a principled basis, the existence of such pairs as *dynamite*NV, *renegade*NV, *compromise*NV, and of the words in (122) constitutes strong counterevidence against formulating case (c) so that a final syllable with [2 Stress] will allow for stress to be retracted, as is proposed in SPE, pages 107–108. I suggest, therefore, that case (c) be restricted so that it retracts stress only when [1 Stress] has been placed upon the final syllable, and that alternations like those in (92f) be handled by rule (123).[76] We will see in §7.1 that this rule forms part of a larger process.

6.7. Let us now examine the stress contrasts in (92g). Chomsky and Halle propose the derivations shown in (124a) for the verbs and those in (124b) for the related nouns.

---

[76]There is one piece of evidence, unfortunately ambiguous, that would support the SPE analysis of *delegate*. It concerns the verb *confiscate* and its related adjective, which *Webster's Third New International Dictionary* cites either as having a 1–3 contour, or as being pronounced [kɔnfĭskət]. The rules in SPE could not account for the former pronunciation, whereas this would be possible in my analysis, by marking this word [−123]. However, it is the latter pronunciation that is of more interest here. I can see no natural way of accounting for this form within my analysis, but it is exactly what would be predicted from the rules of SPE. The derivation would proceed as follows.

Base form	$[[\text{kɔn=fiskæt}]_V]_A$		
MSR (eii)	1		
ASR	1		2
MSR (dii)	2	1	3
SAR	3	1	4
Rule [118]	0	1	4
Other rules	[kənfiskət]		

The important fact to note about this derivation is that it is part (ii) of case (c) that retracts the stress on the second cycle. The medial syllable does not end in $V[+\text{son}][+\text{cns}]$, as specified on p. 138, so it cannot be assigned the feature [+D], which would allow case (ci) to apply. Thus, stress is retracted only one syllable, which is what is desired here.

Although this pronunciation of the adjective *confiscate* clearly supports the SPE analysis, instead of one based on rule (123), it is the only word I know of that does so; and since I see no way for the SPE analysis to avoid such forms as **candidate*V, **renegade*V, **compromise*, **dictate*, etc., I have chosen to keep rule (123) in the grammar, even though I am unable to derive *confiscate*A and *confiscate*V from the same underlying form. Note, however, that rule (123) can account for *designate*N, which has no natural analysis within SPE.

(124)

(a)

	$[\text{dɔkument}]_V$		$[\text{tɔrment}]_V$	
Base form				
MSR (eii)	1		1	
ASR	1	2	DNA	
Rule [120]			2	1
SAR	1	3	3	1
Other rules	[dắkyəmȅnt]		[tɔ̀rmȅnt]	

(b)

	$[[\text{dɔkument}]_V]_N$			$[[\text{tɔrment}]_V]_N$	
Base form					
MSR (eii)	1			1	
ASR	1	2		DNA	
MSR (di)	1	3	MSR (dii)	1	2
SAR	1	4		1	3
Other rules	[dắkyə̀mə̀nt]			[tɔ̀rmȅnt]	

I find this derivation of the noun *dòcumȅnt* unconvincing. First of all, the noun, not the verb, "feels" basic. If there is disagreement about this example, surely there can be none about the noun-verb pair *règimȅnt*$_N$–*rȅgimȅnt*$_V$, where the same contrast can be observed, but where the noun is clearly basic. Suppose, then, we were to postulate for these pairs derivations like those in (125), rather than like those in (124).

(125)

	$[\text{dɔkument}]_N$		$[[\text{dɔkument}]_N]_V$	
Base form				
MSR (bi)	1		1	
MSR (eii)			2	1
ASR			1	2
SAR			1	3
Other rules	[dắkyə̀mə̀nt]		[dắkyəmȅnt]	

This derivation produces exactly the same results, and yet it makes no use of case (c). Note also that the use of the cycle is unnecessary. The verb *dòcumȅnt* can be derived as in (126).

(126)

	$[\text{dɔkument}]_V$		
Base form			
MSR (eii) (or (f))		1	
ASR	1	2	
SAR	1	3	
Other rules	[dắkyəmȅnt]		

I see no reason to prefer the derivation of *document* in (124) to that in (126), and I conclude that such words cannot be used in support of either case (c) or the cycle.

Let us now turn to the more complex case of $\overset{3}{\text{torm}}\overset{1}{\text{ent}}_V$–$\overset{1}{\text{torm}}\overset{3}{\text{ent}}_N$. I have no quarrel with the derivation of the verb presented in (124a). But there is no necessity to assume the cyclical derivation of the noun shown in (124b). Assume that *torment* has assigned to it the feature [-case (b)] in the lexicon. As was pointed out in §3.2 above, such features are necessary in order to distinguish dialects that assign a 1–3 contour to *Oregon* from those that have a 1–0 contour.[77] That words ending in /nt/ must also be able to be stressed by case (b) or by case (f) can be seen from such minimal pairs as $\overset{1}{\text{sec}}\overset{3}{\text{ant}}$–$\overset{1}{\text{sec}}\overset{0}{\text{ant}}$ (both pronunciations are given in Kenyon and Knott) or $\overset{1}{\text{form}}\overset{3}{\text{ant}}$–$\overset{1}{\text{form}}\overset{0}{\text{ant}}$. If, therefore, we enter *torment* in the lexicon with the feature [-case (b)], the derivation of the pair $\overset{3}{\text{torm}}\overset{1}{\text{ent}}_V$–$\overset{1}{\text{torm}}\overset{3}{\text{ent}}_N$ will proceed as in (127).

(127)

		(a)	Base form	$[\text{torment}]_V$	(b)	$[\text{torment}]_N$
				-case (b)		-case (b)
				+ASR		+ASR
			Rule (95a)	-ASR[78]		DNA
			MSR (f)	1		1
			ASR	DNA		1 2
			Rule [120]	2 1		DNA
			SAR	3 1		1 3
			Other rules	$[\overset{3}{\text{t}}\text{orm}\overset{1}{\text{ent}}]$		$[\overset{1}{\text{t}}\text{orm}\overset{3}{\text{ent}}]$

Chomsky and Halle do not discuss this fact in any detail, but for verbs which end in /nt/ there are four other possible combinations of stress contours in noun-verb pairs. All five possibilities are shown in (128).

(128) (a) $\overset{3}{\text{torm}}\overset{1}{\text{ent}}_V$–$\overset{1}{\text{torm}}\overset{3}{\text{ent}}_N$. Cf. also $\overset{3}{\text{augm}}\overset{1}{\text{ent}}_V$–$\overset{1}{\text{aug}}$-$\overset{3}{\text{ment}}_N$, $\overset{3}{\text{all}}\overset{1}{\text{y}}_V$–$\overset{1}{\text{all}}\overset{3}{\text{y}}_N$, $\overset{3}{\text{alloy}}_V$–$\overset{1}{\text{alloy}}_N$, $\overset{3}{\text{surv}}\overset{1}{\text{ey}}_V$–$\overset{1}{\text{surv}}\overset{3}{\text{ey}}_N$, etc.

---

[77]The interesting discussion on pp. 175–176 concerning the tenseness of the vowels of *child* and *children* indicates the necessity of postulating rule features that refer to particular branches of rule schemata, although Chomsky and Halle, to the best of my knowledge, never discuss any cases of exceptions to a branch of the MSR.

[78]As will be discussed in greater detail in §10, I will assume that redundancy rules like (95a) can change the specifications of idiosyncratically assigned rule features. Thus, the lexical feature [+ASR] that appears in the entry for *torment* will become [-ASR], by rule (95a), when this form appears as a verb.

(b) $\overset{1}{c}\overset{3}{omm}\overset{}{ent}_V$–$\overset{1}{c}\overset{3}{omm}ent_N$. Cf. also $\overset{1}{a}mb\overset{3}{u}sh_{VN}$, $\overset{1}{b}oy\text{-}$ $\overset{3}{c}ott_{VN}$, $d\overset{1}{e}l\overset{3}{u}ge_{VN}$, $c\overset{1}{l}im\overset{3}{a}x_{VN}$, $r\overset{1}{e}b\overset{3}{a}te_{VN}$, $\overset{1}{u}mp\overset{3}{i}re_{VN}$, $tr\overset{13}{iu}mph_{VN}$, etc.

(c) $w\overset{1}{a}rr\overset{0}{a}nt_V$–$w\overset{1}{a}rr\overset{0}{a}nt_N$. Cf. also $ch\overset{1}{a}ll\overset{0}{e}nge_{VN}$

(d) $l\overset{0}{a}m\overset{1}{e}nt_V$–$l\overset{0}{a}m\overset{1}{e}nt_N$. Cf. also $\overset{0}{a}tt\overset{1}{a}ck_{VN}$, $\overset{0}{a}rr\overset{1}{e}st_{V\overset{(3)}{N}}$, $pol\overset{1}{i}ce_{VN}$, $r\overset{(3)}{e}pr\overset{1}{i}eve_{VN}$, $d\overset{(3)}{e}c\overset{1}{a}y_{VN}$, $cons\overset{1}{e}nt_{VN}$, $de\text{-}$ $m\overset{1}{a}nd_{VN}$, $deb\overset{1}{a}te_{VN}$, $def\overset{3}{e}\overset{1}{a}t_{VN}$, $c\overset{3}{o}qu\overset{1}{e}tte_{NV}$, etc.

(e) $s\overset{3}{e}gm\overset{1}{e}nt_V$–$s\overset{3}{e}gm\overset{1}{e}nt_N$. Cf. also $fr\overset{3}{a}gm\overset{1}{e}nt_V$–$fr\overset{3}{a}g\text{-}$ $m\overset{1}{e}nt_N$, $pres\overset{1}{e}nt_V$–$pr\overset{3}{e}s\overset{1}{e}nt_N$, etc.

First, let us consider how the rules I have proposed above could generate this set of related stress configurations. I have already shown in (127) how I would propose to generate the pairs in (128a), which Chomsky and Halle consider to be the normal case. In (129) appears the derivation for the noun-verb pair *lament*.

(129)	(a) Base form	[læment]$_V$	(b) [læment]$_N$
		-case (b)	-case (b)
		-ASR	-ASR
	MSR (f)	1	1
	ASR	DNA	DNA
	Rule [120]	DNA	DNA
	Other rules	[l$\overset{0}{\partial}$m$\overset{1}{e}$nt]	[l$\overset{0}{\partial}$m$\overset{1}{e}$nt]

The analysis of this type of verb-noun pair within the framework of SPE differs only trivially: where the words of (128d) are marked [-ASR] in my analysis, they would be marked [-case (c)] in the analysis of SPE.

For the words in (128e), I would propose the following derivations.

(130)	(a) Base form	[segment]$_V$	(b)		[segment]$_N$
	Rule (95a)	-ASR			DNA
	MSR (f)	1	MSR (b)	1	
	ASR	DNA			DNA
	Rule [120]	2 1			DNA
	SAR	3 1			DNA
	Other rules	[s$\overset{3}{e}$gm$\overset{1}{e}$nt]			[s$\overset{1}{e}$gm$\overset{0}{\partial}$nt]

Words like the above could be derived in a number of ways by the rules in SPE. Probably the most natural would be to assume the noun to be basic, which "feels" correct to me, and to assume an extra cycle in the derivation of the verb. Thus, the derivation of the noun *ségmènt*$_N$ would be exactly the same as that shown in (130b), while the verb would be derived as shown in (131):

(131) Base form $[[\text{segment}]_N]_V$

MSR (b)	1	
MSR (e)	2 1	
Rule [120]	2 1	(applies vacuously)
SAR	3 1	
Other rules	[sègmènt]	

The only way in which SPE can derive such words as those in (128b), however, is shown in (132). (This problem is discussed on p. 140 of SPE.)

(132) (a) Base form $[[\text{kɔment}]_S]_V$ (b) $[[\text{kɔment}]_S]_N$

MSR (e)	1	1
MSR (c)	1 2	1 2
SAR	1 3	1 3
Other rules	[kàmènt]	[kàmènt]

In other words, the fact that noun and verb are homophonous is accounted for by deriving both in exactly the same way, from an underlying stem. There is, however, no syntactic justification for postulating, in surface structure, a node Stem above *comment*, but not above *torment*, *lament*, or *segment*. Thus, this derivation constitutes another violation of the Chomsky-Halle-Lukoff naturalness condition, if this condition is strengthened appropriately, so that it not only forbids the ad hoc use of junctures but of any other syntactic information as well.

I propose, instead of the above derivations, which Chomsky and Halle admit are artificial, the following analysis:

(133) (a) Base form $[\text{kɔment}]_V$ (b) $[\text{kɔment}]_N$

	-case (b)	-case (b)
	+ASR	+ASR
	[-95a]	[-95a]
Rule (95a)	DNA	DNA
MSR (f)	1	1
ASR	1 2	1 2
SAR	1 3	1 3
Other rules	[kàmènt]	[kàmènt]

The important feature of this account is the assumption that lexical items can be marked so that they do not undergo a general redundancy rule. This assumption seems abundantly justified, independently of how words like those in (128b) are to be accounted for. Thus, for instance, such words as *hoax, traipse, Yoicks,* etc., must be marked [-Rule [8]], the rule that specifies that only dental clusters can be preceded by tense vowels (cf. SPE, p. 172 ff.). Furthermore, the words in (87a) and the prefixes in (113) are exceptions to the general rule (115), which specifies that words do not normally retract stress three syllables. Therefore, in their lexical representations these forms will be marked [-115]. They will, exceptionally, retract stress three syllables.

Likewise with *comment*: while most verbs do not retract stress, as rule (95a) stipulates, verbs like those in (96b) do, so that they will have to be marked [-95a] in addition to being marked [+ASR].[79] The derivation of the noun $c\overset{1}{o}mm\overset{3}{e}nt_N$ will not require reference to the former feature, as rule (95a) affects only verbs and adjectives, so that this derivation will exactly parallel that of the noun $t\overset{1}{o}rm\overset{3}{e}nt_N$. However, for the verb *comment*$_V$, the feature [-95a] will prevent rule (95a) from applying, as it did in the derivation of the verb $t\overset{3}{o}rm\overset{1}{e}nt_V$, which will change the feature [+ASR] to [-ASR]. Thus, the derivation for $c\overset{1}{o}mm\overset{3}{e}nt$ as a verb will exactly parallel that of $c\overset{1}{o}mm\overset{3}{e}nt$ as a noun: the ASR will apply in both derivations.

Finally, I would assume that the derivation of such forms as $w\overset{1}{a}rr\overset{0}{a}nt_{VN}$ is exactly parallel to the derivation of $c\overset{1}{o}m$-$m\overset{3}{e}nt_{VN}$, except that whereas rule (49), Destressing, idiosyncratically does not work for *comment,* it does work for *warrant.* This fact would have to be reflected either in the presence of a feature [-49] in the lexical representation of *comment* or in its segmental makeup, possibly by deriving it from a form with a geminate nasal, or even from the representation /KɔN=ment/ that is suggested on page 141 of SPE. (I disregard here the problem of =; see §7.1.)

---

[79] I have not come to any conclusion as to whether it is more normal for disyllabic nouns to retract stress by the ASR than not to retract it. Hence, I have been marking lexical items both [+ASR] (e.g., *comment* and *torment*) and [-ASR] (e.g., *lament, police*). Eventually, of course, only one of these marks will be necessary. However, since I cannot see how any points I will discuss would be affected by either choice, I have left it open for the present.

As far as I can see, there is no possible solution within the framework of SPE to the problem of assigning a 1–0 contour to the verb *warrant* that does not involve postulating the existence of a rule like (49). Thus, the forms in (128c) constitute evidence of the strongest kind for the existence of this rule.

To summarize this discussion of the stress possibilities of disyllabic verbs in /nt/, it appears that three of the five possible stress alternations—namely, those in (128a), (128d), and (128e)—can be handled equally well within the analysis of SPE or within my reanalysis. However, the derivations provided by SPE of verbs like those in (128b) and (128c) are clearly artificial, in comparison to those within the reanalysis.

There is stronger evidence for reanalyzing: within the framework of the reanalysis it is possible to provide a formal explanation for one fact that is a consequence of (97):[80] the lack of noun-verb pairs like *police*$_N$–*police*$_V$. Recall that there is no non–ad hoc way for SPE to exclude such underlying representations as the one shown in (101), which will produce the impossible stress alternation.

How can *police*$_N$–*police*$_V$ be excluded within my reanalysis? It is excluded simply because there can be no underlying representation provided for such a pair. If either member of a verb-noun pair exhibits retraction, the form must be marked [+ASR] in the lexicon. Since the verb we are trying to find a representation for—*to police*—has, by assumption, a 1–3 contour, the form *police* would have to be marked [+ASR], like *torment* and *comment*. In addition, since it is the verb in which retraction occurs, *police* would have to be marked [-95a]. Note that the first of the features we have had to postulate to derive the 1–3 contour on *police*$_V$, namely,

---

[80]As I said, I consider (97) to be a very deep observation about English stress, and there are other stress alternations it allows for which I have been able to find no explanation. Note, for instance, such pairs as *attribute*$_N$–*attribute*$_V$; *arithmetic*$_N$–*arithmetic*$_A$. These forms are discussed in SPE, on p. 159, and on p. 88, fn. 41, respectively, but no explanation is provided for why the noun's primary stress is further to the left than that of the verb or adjective. Thus, note that nothing prevents SPE from postulating a [[ ]$_N$]$_V$ structure for *attribute*, instead of the [[ ]$_V$]$_N$ structure shown on p. 159, but such a structure would yield precisely the wrong results.

the feature [+ASR], already precludes the possibility of deriving a noun in which stress retraction does not take place from the same underlying form: *any* form marked [+ASR] in the lexicon will undergo stress retraction unless it can undergo rule (95a), which can change [+ASR] to [-ASR]. But only verbs and adjectives are affected by rule (95a): thus, if the lexical entry for *police* has the feature [+ASR], the associated noun must have a 1–3 contour.

Expressed differently, there are only four logically possible combinations of the plus and minus values for the features [ASR] and (95a). These are shown in (134), and following each logical possibility is a verb that has this feature configuration.

(134) (a) $\begin{bmatrix} +\text{ASR} \\ +95a \end{bmatrix}$ $\overset{3}{t}\overset{1}{o}rment_V - \overset{1}{t}\overset{3}{o}rment_N$

  (b) $\begin{bmatrix} +\text{ASR} \\ -95a \end{bmatrix}$ $c\overset{1}{o}mm\overset{3}{e}nt_V - c\overset{1}{o}mm\overset{3}{e}nt_N$

  (c) $\begin{bmatrix} -\text{ASR} \\ +95a \end{bmatrix}$ $l\overset{0}{a}m\overset{1}{e}nt_V - l\overset{0}{a}m\overset{1}{e}nt_N$

  (d) $\begin{bmatrix} -\text{ASR} \\ -95a \end{bmatrix}$ $l\overset{0}{a}m\overset{1}{e}nt_V - l\overset{0}{a}m\overset{1}{e}nt_N$

The important thing to notice is that the distinct feature bundles in (134c) and (134d) characterize exactly the same classes of items: if a form is already marked [-ASR] in the lexicon, it makes no difference whether it undergoes rule (95a), which will vacuously reassign the feature [-ASR] to it. Thus, these two features allow for only three main classes of pairs: pairs like (128a) (*torment*); pairs like (128b) and (128c) (*comment* and *warrant,* respectively), which only differ from one another in the applicability of Destressing to the output of the ASR; and pairs like (128d) (*lament*). The existence of the type of stress contrast shown in (128e) (*segment*) is limited to verbs in /nt/; this limitation allows the possibility of case (b) assigning stress for the noun and case (f) for the verb, which is not germane to the present discussion and is a minor phenomenon in any case. There is no combination of the two features [±ASR] and [±95a] that could produce a pair like *$pol\overset{1}{i}ce_N - p\overset{1}{o}l\overset{3}{i}ce_V$. The fact that such pairs appear not to exist (but cf. fn. 61) is thus explained in my reanalysis.

  Therefore, since the contrast between $d\overset{1}{o}cum\overset{3}{e}nt_V$ and $d\overset{1}{o}cum\overset{0}{e}nt_N$ can be handled naturally without making use of

case (c) and the cycle, and since the SPE analysis of
$torment_V$–$torment_N$ not only leads to unacceptably artificial
derivations for verb-noun pairs like $comment_V$–$comment_N$,
but also can provide no explanation for the nonexistence of
such pairs as $*police_N$–$police_V$, I conclude that the forms
in (92g) cannot be construed as providing evidence either for
case (c) or for the cycle. In fact, the nonexistence of such
pairs as the latter must be taken as constituting counterevidence to the claim that cyclically ordered rules can apply
below the level of word boundaries.

6.8. Let us now briefly consider the claim that case (c)
is involved in the derivation of the words in (92h). Chomsky
and Halle discuss such contrasts as $illustrate$–$illustrate$ on
page 155 of SPE, suggesting there that the two forms be
derived as shown in (135).

(135)

	(a) Base form	/ilustræt/		(b)		/ilustr+ǣt/
	Rule [158]	DNA		Rule [158]		1
	MSR (eii)	1		MSR (cii)	1	2
	ASR	1	2			
	SAR	1	3	SAR	1	3
	Other rules	[íləstrèyt]		Other rules	[əlʌstrèyt]	

Rule [158], it will be recalled, only assigns stress to final
tense affixes; by postulating that *illustrate*, with a 1–0–3
contour, contains no affix, Chomsky and Halle can block the
application of rule [158] and assign final stress by case (e),
after which the ASR will retract stress to the initial syllable.
In order to assign a 0–1–3 contour, as in (135b), it is only
necessary to consider -*ate* to be an affix, thus triggering the
sequence of rules [158] and case (c).

It should be obvious that this account is somewhat artificial. First, it depends upon the existence of rule [158], whose
only other function is to make it unnecessary to refer to a
rule feature [±ASR] in accounting for contrasts like that
between (17) and (18). Second, however *illustrate* is to be
stressed, its relationship to the words *luster* and *lustrous*
would have to be shown. This relationship suggests that the
only possible underlying representation is /iN=lustr+ǣt/.[81]

---

[81]In §7.1, I will argue that the = boundary in /æd=umbr+ǣt/ and
/æd=grænd+īz/ be replaced by +.

Similarly, the word *adumbrate*—which can be pronounced either [ǽdəmbrḗyt] or [ə̀də́mbrḗyt], since this word presumably contains the morpheme /umbr/ (cf. *umbrella, penumbra, umbriferous*)—can only be represented by /æd=umbr+ǽt/. Whether *aggrandize* is pronounced [ǽgrəndā̀yz] or [əgrǽndā̀yz], if it is to be related to *grand,* both of its pronunciations must derive from the same form: /æd=grænd+īz/. It does not seem plausible to assume that the different pronunciations of these forms are directly traceable to independently motivated structural differences in their underlying forms. Rather, such words must differ somehow in the features that determine which rule of stress retraction will apply to them.

I agree with Chomsky and Halle that it is case (c) that is responsible for the stress retraction in examples like (92h). The clearest indication that this is the case is the nonexistence of such words as **titíllā̀te, *átòmìze, *jùvènìle,* etc., in which stress has been retracted to a penult that ends in a weak cluster. Also, there appears to be some regularity linking the applicability of case (c) with the presence of a stressed affix. The relationship, however, is not as direct as is claimed in SPE. In particular, I feel that when *aggrandize* is pronounced with a 1–0–3 contour, this pronunciation occurs *in spite of* the fact that it is trimorphemic, according to which one would expect it to exhibit a 0–1–3 contour on the basis of the indirect regularity linking stressed affixes to case (c). Therefore, when pronounced with a 1–0–3 contour, *aggrandize* will have to be marked with a rule feature. I will defer, however, until §6.9 below a precise statement of how case (c) is to be avoided formally in such cases.

6.9. Chomsky and Halle account for the contrasts exemplified in (92i) as shown in (136).

(136)

Base form	$[[æd=vīz]_V ɔr+y]_A$				$[[prɔmis]_V ɔr+y]_A$		
MSR (eii)	1			MSR (ei)	1	
MSR (ai)	2	1		MSR (ai)	2	1
MSR (cii)	1	2		MSR (cii)	1	2
[118]	1	0		[118]	DNA	
SAR	DNA			SAR	1	
Other rules	[ə̀dvā̀yzɔ̀īy]			Other rules	[prǽmə̀sɔ̀rìy]	

This analysis I find essentially correct, except that I see no need to assume the existence of two passes through cyclically ordered rules in these derivations. That is, I would propose that the stress contours on the forms in (92i) be derived by one pass through the rules, as indicated in (137).

(137)

Base form /æd+vīz+ɔr+i/[82]			/prɔmise+ɔr+i/[83]		
			Vowel Drop[84]	Ø	
MSR (bi)		1	MSR (bi)		1
MSR (cii)	1	2	MSR (ci)	1	2
[118]	1	0	SAR	1	3
Other rules [ə̆dvā̆yzɚ̃ī̆y]			Other rules [pră̆mə̆sɔ̆rī̆y]		

As Chomsky and Halle point out, the contrast between *confiscatòry* and *anticipatòry* exactly parallels the contrast in (137), so that case (c) must be formulated in such a way as to disregard a preceding *-at-*. Note that it is not possible here to make the claim that case (3) of the ASR is retracting stress for *anticipatòry*, for if one were to mark *anticip(ate)* as [-115], the incorrect **ánticipàte* would be derived in isolation. An even stronger indication that the ASR is not responsible for the stress retraction in the examples of (92i) is the word *clàssificatòry*, in which stress must be retracted *four* syllables, an operation the ASR never performs. For these reasons Chomsky and Halle formulate case (c) so that it disregards not only a preceding *-at-*, but also a preceding *-ficat-*. It is clear, therefore, that there must in fact be two processes of stress retraction in English, even though their effects often overlap.

But how do these two types of retraction differ? When is stress retracted by the ASR, and when by case (c)? If the arguments I have given in §§6.1–6.7 above are correct, many words whose stress retraction Chomsky and Halle account for by case (c) must instead undergo stress retraction by the ASR. It seems to me that arguments showing conclusively that case (c) is at work can only be constructed for words like

---

[82]I have replaced = by + in these examples. This change will be discussed in §7.1. Moreover, I assume, instead of the glide suffix /+y/ of SPE, that the final morpheme in *-ory* is a true vowel. This assumption will be justified in §7.5.

[83]The final /e/ in the underlying representation of *promise* will be deleted by the rule of *e*-Elision when this verb appears in isolation, as was discussed in §4.3 above.

[84]This rule is discussed in fn. 38 above.

those in (92h) and (92i). What differentiates these cases from the other examples cited in (92) is the biconditional stated in (138).

(138)   (a) Case (c) only retracts stress from affixes.

(b) Every affix from which stress is retracted has stress retracted from it by case (c).

Of these two generalizations, the one in (138a) seems to have the fewest exceptions. Exceptions to (138a) are words for which stress has only been retracted one syllable, but for which there is no motivation for postulating an affix. The only exceptions to this generalization that I have found are listed in (139).

(139)   *defálcàte, humèctàte, amòrtìze*

It might be argued that words like *Àdiròndàck* and the other words in (89) are also counterexamples to (138a). However, since these words seem to be monomorphemic, and since three of them (*Achìllès, Ulỳssès, (neo)synèphrìne*) have had stress retracted to a weak penult,[85] I would prefer to analyze these forms as exceptions to case (2) of the ASR, as I proposed in §5.3 above. The fact that (138a) has so few exceptions appears to me to constitute a significant enough generalization to formulate case (c) so that it will only be able to apply to a word that ends in an affix. The words in (139) will then have to be added to the small number of words in (89) that are marked [-case (2)]. Thus, when the ASR applies to the words in (139), it will not assign them the expected 1–0–3 contour, but rather a marked 0–1–3 contour.

---

[85]Of course, to claim that the penults of these words end in /ll/, /ss/, and /ffr/ (or possibly /frr/ or /ffrr/), respectively, is to reduce to near vacuity the claim that it is case (c) that is responsible for stress retraction in (89). There is no evidence, aside from stress retraction, that would support the postulation of underlying geminates. I say "near vacuity," because there is at least one segment, /θ/, that seems never to occur geminated (cf. fn. 9 above). Therefore, one who proposes that case (c) is at work in (89) is making the testable claim that such words as *Achìthès* [əkíθìyz] should be impossible. I have found no such examples, to be sure, but such a word does not sound ill-formed to me. Unfortunately, words with three or more syllables, whose last two syllables have a 1–3 contour, are rare in any event; thus, it seems impossible at present to demonstrate conclusively that an analysis depending on geminates must be ruled out.

What of (138b), the other half of the biconditional? Observe that the analysis in SPE asserts in effect both of the implications in (138), as is indicated by the discussion on pages 152–155 of SPE. To assert that rule [158] is in the grammar is to assert that stress can be retracted one syllable in a word by case (c) only if[86] the word ends in a tense affix. Ad hoc morpheme boundaries must then be inserted into the words of (139); in addition it must be claimed that such words as *íllustràte, ádumbràte, cóncentràte, cónfiscàte,* and *órchestràte* have no morpheme boundary before *-ate,* and therefore do not contain the morphemes /lustr/, /umbr/, /kentr/, /fisk/ (cf. *fiscal*), and /ɔrkestræ/, respectively. I see no reason to make this additional claim, which I find counterintuitive in both respects. Rather, it seems that a more accurate description can be attained by building (138a) into the statement of case (c)—that is, by allowing case (c) to retract stress only from affixes—and then by marking such forms as *cóncentràte* with the feature [-case (c)].

One question remains: how are the affixes from which case (c) will eventually retract stress to receive stress? Chomsky and Halle point out (pp. 34–43 and pp. 98–100) that given the principles of disjunctive ordering, since case (e) is a subenvironment of case (c), case (e) must follow case (c) with which it will be disjunctively ordered. Obviously, therefore, since case (c) must retract stress that case (a) assigns, the ordering case (a)–case (c)–case (e) is fixed. Case (a) and case (c) will be conjunctively ordered, with the other orderings being disjunctive.

Making the minor change necessary to convert this ordering into the system of the present analysis is equivalent to claiming that the ordering of the three cases is case (b)–case (c)–case (f). That is, assuming that these three cases are to be formulated as indicated schematically in (140a), (140b), and (140c), respectively, Chomsky and Halle are proposing essentially the rule stated in (141).

(140) (a) $V \rightarrow [1 \text{ Stress}] / \underline{\quad} C_0(W) \, \check{V} \, (C_b)]$

(b) $V \rightarrow [1 \text{ Stress}] / \underline{\quad} C_0(W) + \acute{\Sigma}]$

(c) $V \rightarrow [1 \text{ Stress}] / \underline{\quad} C_0]$

[86]Excluding, of course, cases where final stress has arisen through case (a) or through case (e) of an earlier cycle.

(141) $\quad$ V $\rightarrow$ [1 Stress] $/$ —— C_0 $\left(\text{(W)} \left\{\begin{matrix} \check{V}(C_b) \\ +\Sigma \end{matrix}\right\}\right)\Big]$

There is, however, a major disadvantage to rule (141): if case (c) precedes case (f), it will be necessary, by some rule other than case (f), to assign the stress to such affixes as *-oid*, from which stress is always retracted by case (c), or to *-ate*, which case (c) sometimes retracts stress from. Chomsky and Halle are therefore forced to stress these affixes before the MSR by their rule [158], which, as was pointed out above, has the defect of being, in essence, a duplication of case (f). Moreover, there are many similarities between case (c) and the ASR: both retract stress from a final syllable (which may be followed by a lax $/i/$).

I propose, therefore, to reorder the rules of (140): rules (140a) and (140c), cases (b) and (f) of the MSR, will form one natural rule, a rule that assigns primary stress to one of the last three syllables of a word. The MSR can thus retain the formulation given in (74) above, a formulation that appears complicated only because of the details of C_b.

The MSR will be followed by a Retraction Rule, which will have two cases: the first, which retracts stress in accordance with the Romance Stress Rule, will retract stress only from final affixes; the second, which retracts stress blindly, except for the choice between Case 2 and Case 3 of the ASR, will apply in all other instances.

As shown in (90) above, these two cases differ only in the optional inclusion of W in the latter, a fact that allows the ASR to be notationally collapsed with Case (c). The resulting rule appears in (142).

(142) $\quad$ RETRACTION RULE

$$V \rightarrow \Big[1 \text{ stress}\Big]/ \text{——} C_0 \left(\text{(w)} \left\{ \begin{matrix} (+C_0 V C_{0+}^1)_0 \\ V C_0 \end{matrix} \right\} \right) \left\{ \overset{1}{V} C_0 \left(\left\{ \begin{matrix} \begin{bmatrix} i \\ -\text{tns} \end{bmatrix} \\ \begin{bmatrix} -\text{cns} \\ -\text{tns} \end{bmatrix}\begin{bmatrix} +\text{cns} \\ +\text{voc} \end{bmatrix} \end{matrix} \right\} \right) \right\} \, \#$$

The term $(+C_0 V C_{0+}^1)_0$ in the top line of (142) allows for the stress to be retracted, by the case (c) branch, over any number of affixes ($+æt+$ in *antícipatòry*, $+fik+æt+$ in *clàssifìcatòry*, $+in+$ in *dìsciplinàry*, etc. None end in more than one C.).

There is one further point that must be noted in connection with rule (142). It specifies that the basic choice of type of stress retraction in English depends upon whether or not stress is being retracted from an affix. As the examples in (143) show, this claim is basically right.

(143)   phenȯ¹menȯ³n–elȇ¹ctrȯ³n
            cȳ¹anīde–perȯ³xīde
            ȧ¹nthracī³te–smarȧ¹gdī³te
            crȳ¹stallōi³d–mollȗ¹scȯi³d
            ȧ¹sinī³ne–elephȧ¹ntī³ne
            Gȇ¹minī³–alȗ¹mnī²

However, the most productive affix in all of English, *-ate*, seems generally to have stress retracted off of it by the ASR, instead of by the expected case (c): cf. *còncentrȧte, íllustrȧte, òrchestrȧte*, etc. What is necessary, then, is a redundancy rule like (144).

(144)   +*ate* → [-case (c) branch of (142)]

This concludes, then, my basic reanalysis of stress assignment and retraction. Primary stress will be assigned by the MSR (essentially as in (74)) and retracted as specified by (144) and (142).

REFERENCES

Chomsky, N., and M. Halle (1968). *The Sound Pattern of English.* New York: Harper and Row.

Chomsky, N., M. Halle, and F. Lukoff (1966). "On Accent and Juncture in English." In *For Roman Jakobson.* The Hague: Mouton.

Fidelholtz, J. L. (1966). "Vowel Reduction in English." Unpublished manuscript.

Halle, M., and S. J. Keyser (1967). "Chaucer and the Study of Prosody." *College English* 28:187–219.

Kenyon, J. S., and T. A. Knott (1944). *A Pronouncing Dictionary of American English.* Springfield, Mass., Merriam.

Postal, P. M. (1968). *Aspects of Phonological Theory.* New York, Harper and Row.

Ross, J. R. (1971). "Leftward Ho!" *Quarterly Progress Report of the Language Research Foundation,* Cambridge, Mass., number 3, pp. 12–28.

Ross, J. R. (in preparation). "English Vowel Non-Sequences."

LANGUAGE INDEX

SUBJECT INDEX